John Keble

Studia sacra: Commentaries on the introductory verses of St. John's Gospel

John Keble

Studia sacra: Commentaries on the introductory verses of St. John's Gospel

ISBN/EAN: 9783742860224

Manufactured in Europe, USA, Canada, Australia, Japa

Cover: Foto ©Lupo / pixelio.de

Manufactured and distributed by brebook publishing software (www.brebook.com)

John Keble

Studia sacra: Commentaries on the introductory verses of St. John's Gospel

Studia Sacra.

COMMENTARIES

ON THE INTRODUCTORY VERSES OF

ST. JOHN'S GOSPEL,

AND ON A PORTION OF

ST. PAUL'S EPISTLE TO THE ROMANS;

WITH OTHER THEOLOGICAL PAPERS

BY THE

REV. JOHN KEBLE, M.A.

Oxford and London:
JAMES PARKER AND CO.
1877.

PREFACE.

WE are indebted for the design and publication of this volume to the same Editor whose loving devotion to Mr. Keble's memory gave us the "Occasional Papers" a year ago.

The first and most valuable of its five parts, the fragment on St. John's Gospel, was in fact printed for that earlier collection, but was reserved when it was found that there was enough matter of like kind to form a separate volume.

In the Postscript to the Preface to the "Occasional Papers," Dr. Pusey, it will be remembered, thus refers to it:—

"It was not until past the 'threescore years and ten,' that with diffidence John Keble began what I had ventured to press upon him many years before, a Commentary on St. John's Gospel. He seems to have undertaken it, in order to do something towards the fulfilment of a long-cherished hope; yet knowing that he could never finish it. It was much in his thoughts; but his Manuscript ends in an unfinished sentence on the fifteenth verse. But this single pearl gives a thought what the golden string might have been, could he have brought himself to undertake it earlier."

This fragment may, therefore, be dated 1863.

The Manuscript of the unfinished Commentary on the Epistle to the Romans was found by the Vicar of Bisley, among his Uncle's papers, and with it there were some letters which determine its date.

In August, 1833, Mr. Hale (afterwards Archdeacon of Middlesex) wrote to Mr. Keble, asking him to be a contributor to the Commentary on the Bible which he and Mr. Lonsdale (afterwards Bishop of Lichfield) were preparing for the Christian Knowledge Society. In reply, Mr. Keble sent a small portion of this manuscript Commentary on the Epistle to the Romans by way of specimen, and on the margin of it there is the conclusion of his accompanying letter:—

"So now you have fair warning what you are to expect from me as a Commentator. I am sorry to say it is quite impossible for me to do anything in St. Matthew at present. It would be only hurrying myself and annoying you, if I were to pretend to it.—Ever, my dear Hale, yours most truly, J. KEBLE, jr."

On Sept. 17 Mr. Hale returned the specimen, entreating Mr. Keble to go on with the Epistle to the Romans, and begging that it might be ready for the press by Christmas, 1834.

This Commentary on Rom. i.—vii. was therefore then in progress; and must be dated 1833 and 1834, while he was living with his father at Fairford, and engaged on the Edition of Hooker. So far as appears, it was never completed[a].

Of later date, evidently, is the Paper on the

---

[a] The Commentary of which it was to have formed a part did not appear until 1849, and did not extend beyond the Four Gospels. It was published in quarto by Messrs. Rivington.

Doctrine of the Procession of the Holy Spirit. Mr. Keble, of Bisley, has sent me the following extracts from three letters, written by his Uncle in 1851 to a Clergyman who appears to have sought his counsel on the subject; and there seems to be a high probability that the Monograph printed at p. 149 of this volume is "the paper" referred to in the second of these extracts :—

Jan. 31, 1851. ". . . With regard to this particular point, first, are you not mistaken in treating it, as you seem to do, as a distinct Article of the Creed? I always thought it was only a difference in the wording of the Eighth article; and that, as such, it might fairly admit of various interpretations within a certain latitude; just as 'He descended into Hell,' being part of the Fifth article, or 'the Communion of Saints,' being part of the Ninth, have been and are variously interpreted, without prejudice to the orthodoxy or honesty of the different parties. Then, as to the Texts by which the wording in our copies is defended, I own that Bishop Pearson's argument from the term, 'the Spirit of His Son,' appears to me very conclusive. It is not simply saying that the One has a property in the Other, but that it is such a property as implies a relation more or less like that of a man to his own spirit or breath; see St. John xx. 22. Then your objection to the passages cited from St. John xiv., &c., that they are 'in the future tense,' will equally hold against the phraseology of the Greek Fathers, who, as I see in Pearson, argue from the phrase, ἐκ τοῦ ἐμοῦ λήψεται, as if it implied an eternal relation.

"The more I think on the passages which I have seen (few indeed), the more I seem convinced that the difference is merely verbal. I grant that this makes greatly against Rome, in forming an opinion as to which of the parties was really most blameable for the separation. But surely it ought also to take away the difficulty of joining in either formula which happened to be imposed on one by authority otherwise competent. Surely one is not called on in such a case to inquire into the history of the Editions of the Creed, with a view to reject that one of the two, which was most discreditable to its upholders in the manner of propagating it. All that individuals have to consider is, Is the doctrine sound, according to Scripture and Antiquity? Just as in the administration of the Sacraments, I may have a strong opinion as to the presumptuousness of making certain changes, which yet, having been made, I am bound as an individual to acquiesce in, provided they are consistent with the substance itself of the Sacrament.

"It is a sad, sad thought, to be sure, for one to associate with the words of a sacred formulary, however capable of a good meaning in themselves, that they should have been the occasion of anything so bad as the breach between the East and the West. But is it so in this case? They came in as a pretext, and cause a great aggravation, I allow. But surely the real matter was the Supremacy; which, from the time of the Fourth Council, if not before, had caused exceeding jealousy between Rome and Constantinople. I quite agree (as far as I know) with what you say of the disingenuity of Rome in the matter: at the same time, I cannot say that the Eastern proceedings appear to me very satisfactory. In short, I have long ago seemed to perceive that it will never do to think of settling such questions by the moral behaviour of those concerned in them. When all is said and done, we must come to the Law and to the Testimony, i.e. to Scripture and Antiquity, and where we providentially are, there we must stay; unless it is made overwhelmingly clear to us that we are being made to contradict that rule in essentials. . . ."

Dec. 1, 1851. ". . . My delay in writing again was partly owing to my having set myself the task of examining the great question a little for myself; first, in Scripture; then, in some of the Fathers: and I wanted to have something to say to you of the result of that process before I wrote.

I was on the point of writing this very day, but I will reserve the paper which I was going to send; only saying thus much, that the more I inquire, the more I seem to perceive that the two portions of the Church will probably be found to divide the blame,—the Greeks wrong in charging the Latins with false theology, the Latins wrong in adding to the Creed without sufficient authority. . . ."

Jan. 1852. " . . . May not 'Filioque' be taken as meaning, 'So proceeding from the Father as neither to damage, on the one hand, the Father's Prerogative as the sole fountain of Godhead = ἀγέννητος Θεός; nor, on the other hand, the Son's Prerogative as having, so to speak, the Holy Spirit for His own Spirit (which is = Breath) as truly and entirely as It is the Father's. So that the Holy Spirit shall be truly and properly the *Third* Person, by as true a subordination as the Son is the *Second* Person."

In editing this Monograph, apology ought perhaps to be made for taking up so much space (23 pages) with matter not included in the original Manuscript. But it was thought that readers to whom the ancient Fathers are not easily accessible, would be glad to have before them the extracts referred to by Mr. Keble. These notes, Scriptural and Patristic, read in connexion with the above extracts, will be welcomed by many who have interested themselves in the recent Conferences between the Eastern and Western Churches.

Of the three parts of the Volume now mentioned, two, the Commentaries on St. John and on the Epistle to the Romans, were carried through the Press by the Editor of the "Occasional Papers." The editing of the Paper on the Procession, and of the rest of the Volume, was entrusted to the writer of this Preface.

My connexion with the work, and especially with the latter part of it, may be very briefly told.

I had chanced to be useful in verifying some references in the Commentary on St. John's Gospel, and in looking over the Proof sheets. And while we were engaged on this, there arrived from our kind friend at Bisley a Greek Testament, interleaved in quarto, and annotated by Mr. Keble, in some places very fully, in some partially, down to the end of the Epistle to Philemon. The Greek Testament was a Clarendon Press Edition of 1813, but the manuscript annotations had no date whatever. The character of the handwriting seemed to indicate that it was all *early* work; it was begun apparently after the date of Mr. Miller's Bampton Lectures, 1817 (for there is a reference to them near the beginning), and seems to have been continually growing under his hand, over a space of ten or fifteen years. That the main part, if not the whole of it, was done before the correspondence with Archdeacon Hale (referred to above), seems probable; for there is internal evidence that the Commentary on Romans i. — vii., referred to therein, was based on this annotated Greek Testament,—large portions being word for word identical.

This precious monument of Mr. Keble's early studies was placed in my hands, and I was asked to give my opinion as to the desirableness of publishing it.

Remembering what Bentley said of Pearson, and applying it to Mr. Keble, my first impression was that it ought to be published. It seemed to me that the *personal* value of the Book more than compensated for its immaturity. What greater privilege to a student than to be admitted into the study —into the oratory and study—of one whom many would so fain call Master? And the Book is emphatically a student's Book: we seem to see him, fresh from his Ordination, spreading his folios— Hammond's *Paraphrase*, Lightfoot's *Horæ Hebraicæ*, Grotius, Wetstein, and his Savilian Chrysostom —before him; and working steadily through much of the Gospels, Acts, and Epistles. The value of the annotations is all the greater, from their being so unlike popular commentaries of our day;— the results of downright conscientious labour, condensed into the briefest possible expression; every now and then pregnant suggestions, which it would take days to unfold; and the manner of it so humble and devout,—reminding one of Albert Dürer's wood-cut of St. Jerome lifting his eyes from his page to his crucifix! Nor is the tone of his notes less wholesome in the way of example, being entirely devoid of controversy or foregone conclusion, as if he remembered what Lord Bacon says on this very subject, that the juice is ever the sweetest which the grape yields without pressure.

For these and other reasons, swayed, perhaps, too much by my affection for the dear old book, as a veritable fragment of a past life that we all venerate, I thought it might properly be published.

It might be considered out of date by those who were preparing themselves for examinations.

But I thought that many of those readers whom Bishop Butler most coveted for his Sermons,—such as seek well-digested premisses rather than ready-made conclusions,—would value it in their quiet parsonages.

With Dr. Pusey's kind approval I was asked to edit a portion at any rate, to enable us to judge the better as to the rest. When eleven chapters of St. Matthew's Gospel had been printed, we became aware that the work would occupy much more space than we anticipated,—that it must form, in short, an integral and rather costly volume of some 400 or 500 pages. This suggested further consideration :—would not the advertisement of such a work (an Annotated Greek Testament by Mr. Keble) raise great expectations? and might not many be disappointed to find that it was a comparatively youthful note-book, containing not much that was original? Misgivings of this kind grew upon us; and it was resolved that the pages already printed should be submitted to the Bishop of Salisbury, and that his judgment in the matter should be final.

The Bishop of Salisbury's advice was that its publication as an integral work should be abandoned; and that a portion only, viz. the eleven chapters of St. Matthew which were already in type, should be appended to this volume, for the sake of their personal interest, as illustrating Mr. Keble's early studies.

On further perusal of the Manuscript, I found that the latter half of the book contained a complete *analysis*, by way of abbreviated paraphrase, of St. Paul's Epistles, from Romans to Philemon; and that this was, perhaps, the most original part of the work, and might be easily disentangled from the rest.

This Analysis, therefore, with the approval of the Bishop of Salisbury and Dr. Pusey, is included in this volume.

Such is the volume;—fragmentary, containing much that Mr. Keble might have wished to revise before publication [b], and therefore to be received with such reservation as this implies.

Some who read this Preface may think, that whatever reasons lead us to withhold a portion, should prevail against the publication of any of these posthumous papers; for none appear with *his* sanction.

It is true we have not his leave. It may be true that some portions of what is here given are quite unequal to his later writings. It is probable that, had he been asked to publish them before he left us, he would have declined.

But does this close the question?

They have a value *now* and a sacredness which they had not *then*.

> "Where thou hast touched, O wondrous death!
>   Where thou hast come between,
> Lo! there for ever perisheth
>   The common and the mean."

---

[b] It should be mentioned that the Commentaries on St. John's Gospel and the Epistle to the Romans were written out in fair copy, as if for the Press.

Some things here published may be immature. They may be but his "stepping-stones" to higher things. But it is precisely this that gives them their great *personal* and *biographical* value. Surely it is well for a younger generation of students to be permitted to see how an elder Saint built himself up in the Faith, by unresting prayerful labour,—"by toil of hands and knees" winning his way up the long ascent to light!

We have not his leave, it is true. And yet the very same humility that made him, while here, put aside these earlier manuscripts as too imperfect for publication, might gently reprove us now, if in our care for his fair fame we withheld from others what might to them be useful.

If from within the Veil he could *now* speak to us, I almost hear him saying they were the sweetest hours he spent, those hours over God's Word—"inter Paradisi fluenta;" and if these pages were likely to serve in ever so small a measure to whet the thirst of others for those same fountains, he would leave it to the Holy Spirit so to use them, that their streams might still "make glad" the *Civitas Dei* he loved so well!

J. P. N.

THE ABBEY HOUSE, BRISTOL,
  October, 1877.

CONTENTS.

	PAGE
COMMENTARY ON PART OF THE FIRST CHAPTER OF ST. JOHN	1
COMMENTARY ON CHAPTERS I.—VI. OF THE EPISTLE TO THE ROMANS:—	
The Date and Scope of the Epistle	45
§ I. St. Paul's Salutation to the Church of Rome; with some account of the Grounds on which he expected them to receive him	47
§ II. Assurances of the Interest he took in the Roman Church	53
§ III. On Justification by Faith only. 1. The Subject proposed	59
§ III. 2. The Christian Doctrine of Pardon founded on the Misery of Man; and first of the Gentiles	62
§ III. 3. The Misery and Danger of the Gentile World brought home to each Individual	69
§ III. 4. Impartiality of Divine Retribution towards Jew and Gentile alike	74
§ III. 5. Futility of Jewish Privileges, supposing their Practice not answerable	79
§ III. 6. Digression to obviate an Objection which might arise on the Statement just made with regard to Jewish Privileges	86
§ III. 7. Summary and Confirmation of the Doctrine of Human Depravity out of the Scriptures	94
§ III. 8. The true Method of Justification stated	99
§ III. 9. Three Arguments in Support of the Christian Doctrine of Justification	104
§ III. 10. Justification by Faith exemplified in Abraham, and witnessed by David	109
§ III. 11. Justification by Faith not Invalidated, but Confirmed, by the Abrahamic Covenant of Circumcision	115
§ III. 12. Statement of Christian Privileges consequent on Justification	125

	PAGE
§ III. 13. Correspondence between the Manner of our Fall in Adam, and that of our Recovery by Jesus Christ	132
§ IV. Of Sanctification by the Holy Spirit, the next intended Result of Justification	141

PROCESSIO SPIRITUS SANCTI 149
    Appendix added by Editor 154

ANALYSIS OF ST. PAUL'S EPISTLES:—
    The Epistle to the Romans 177
    The First Epistle to the Corinthians . . . 186
    The Second Epistle to the Corinthians . . 200
    The Epistle to the Galatians 210
    The Epistle to the Ephesians 218
    The Epistle to the Philippians . . . 223
    The Epistle to the Colossians . . . 227
    The First Epistle to the Thessalonians . . 231
    The Second Epistle to the Thessalonians . . 234
    The First Epistle to Timothy 236
    The Second Epistle to Timothy . . . 242
    The Epistle to Titus 245
    The Epistle to Philemon 247

NOTES ON THE GREEK TESTAMENT . . 249

COMMENTARY ON PART OF THE FIRST CHAPTER OF ST. JOHN.

(VERSE 1.) *In the Beginning.* Not without many depths of meaning, we may be sure, did the Holy Ghost chuse for the beloved Disciple the very form of words which He had chosen for His servant Moses wherewith to open the Old Testament. It is an intimation given from the very first, that the later dispensation was not in any thing to be contrary to the former, but the confirmation and infinite extension of it.

The infinite extension :—no less. For this " Beginning " is far indeed, very far beyond and before that which had been spoken of in the first chapter of Genesis. *That* was the first point, so to speak, of Space—the first moment of Time :—the point or moment from which it pleased the Almighty that other beings besides Himself should begin to exist. But *This* Beginning is the mysterious Eternity which we feel in ourselves that we are to look back upon, as having (so men speak) gone by, or ever He saw fit to create anything at all. It is that of which the Holy Spirit had before spoken in the Name of Wisdom : "The Lord possessed Me [in] the beginning of His way, before His works of old. I was set up from everlasting, from the beginning, or ever the earth was*." Here we have a Beginning before the beginning—Infinite

* Prov. viii. 22, 23.

duration in the God of all, before He began to work anything (as it were) out of Himself. "Beginning of a beginning there cannot be, according to the exact and true force of the term; our discourse of it will but wander on as along a thread which cannot be spun out or overtaken: and since there is no limit to this its constant escape backwards, and retracing of all the ages in their turn, we must infer that the Son came not into being in Time, but must rather be said to exist everlastingly with the Father. For he was 'in the Beginning[b].'"

It is good surely that from time to time we should go back in our hearts, and contemplate the endless ages of that aweful solitude: (for such to our poor frail imaginations it may seem, though the Revelation of the Blessed Trinity intimate to us that it was far otherwise) ere the Great God of all began to be a Creator. Holy Scripture invites us more than once to such contemplation, instructing us to unite the two thoughts of His unchangeable Eternity and our own mere nothingness as long as we are out of Him. The one truth is set against the other, to make us at once humble and trustful. "Before the mountains were brought forth, or ever the earth and the world were made: Thou art God from everlasting, and world without end[c]." But as for us, "The days of our age are threescore years and ten; and though men be so strong that they come to fourscore years: yet is their strength then but labour and sorrow; so soon passeth it away, and we are gone[d]." The Church reminds us of it when we stand by the grave; and

---

[b] St. Cyr. Alex. iv. 11.   [c] Psalm xc. 2, P.-B.V.   [d] Ibid. 10.

again, by the bedside of a sick penitent :—" He brought down my strength in my journey: and shortened my days. But I said, O my God, take me not away in the midst of mine age: as for Thy years, they endure throughout all generations. Thou, Lord, in the beginning, hast laid the foundation of the earth; and the heavens are the work of Thy hands. They shall perish, but Thou shalt endure: they all shall wax old as doth a garment; and as a vesture shalt Thou change them, and they shall be changed: but Thou art the same, and Thy years shall not fail[e]." So far it would be simply aweful, but the next verse sings joyfully: "The children of Thy servants shall continue; and their seed shall stand fast in Thy sight." God's past eternity before we had any being is marvellously made a pledge of an eternity to come for the holy and the spiritual children of Abraham, even for us, if we do not abuse the being which He has given us Alas! what an *if* is that! too often how sadly realized! even among those who, from their Baptism upward, are constantly reminded of the great things prepared for them, and nowhere more effectually than in this Gospel of love. "Open thy mouth wide, and I shall fill it: but My people would not hear My Voice[f]." O Lord, save us from that worst of ruin, before it is too late to pray!

Was the WORD. In this *beginning* (so God's ancient people had been obscurely but really taught), that is, all along throughout that Infinity of Duration, we are to conceive of the Eternal Father as having within Himself (for as yet there was nothing ex-

---

[e] Psalm cii. 23—27. (So in the MS.; the allusion is not clear, as the Psalm in the Visitation Office is Ps. lxxi.—ED.)   [f] Ibid. lxxxi. 11, 12.

ternal to Him) a Personal Being, the Same Who declared Himself by Solomon, under the name of Wisdom, by such tokens as these: He was possessed and owned of the Father, "set up" and "brought forth" by Him, (therefore He is not the Father): but He was not made by Him, for He was "before His works of old." He was "by" the Father, especially in the Creation of the Heavens and the Earth, "as one brought up with Him," His nursling, His well-beloved, "daily His delight, rejoicing always before Him;" and finally, taking a special interest in this lower world, and in man: "rejoicing in the habitable part of His earth; and His delights were with the sons of men [g]."

This revelation had been made a thousand years before Christ, in that portion of the Old Testament which was sure (humanly speaking) to attract most regard in the Eastern world, from the name and renown of its Author. In his life-time "his fame was in all nations round about," and "there came of all people to hear the wisdom of Solomon, from all kings of the earth, which had heard of his wisdom [h]." He "exceeded all the kings of the earth for riches and for wisdom; and all the earth sought to Solomon, to hear his wisdom, which God had put in his heart [i]." And so it continues even unto this day, as not only the records of the East, but still more the popular traditions, bear witness. For the time especially between the two Testaments, how far his authority reached as a teacher of truth, we may judge by the Apocryphal books; the Son of Sirach addressing him as one whose soul

---

[g] See Prov. viii. 22—31.   [h] 1 Kings iv. 31, 34.
[i] 1 Kings x. 23, 24.

"covered the whole earth, and filled it with dark parables;" whose "name went far unto the islands" .... at whom "the countries marvelled for his songs and proverbs and parables and interpretations [k],"—while the Book of Wisdom, by its very title and by the whole framework of it, implies an exceeding deference certain to be felt by all readers towards its assumed Author and subject. These two writings, so unlike in style and in tone of thought, and originally, it would seem, in language,—the one mainly Oriental, the other Hellenistical,—take up as it were between them the whole world of civilized readers at that time. Judging by them, we must perceive that Solomon's works especially were drawing attention far beyond the limits of Palestine; that the inspired words concerning Wisdom were being taken up by Hellenistical writers of various schools; and thereby, as well as by the Chaldee Paraphrasts, one of whom was also connected with Alexandria, and by such language as Philo's (to say nothing of Plato before him), men's minds were being unconsciously prepared for the sublime announcement of St. John: Christ's way being thus made ready in Theology properly so called, as in the Œconomy by the Jewish ritual, the institution of Sacrifice and the Theocracy. Thus, in respect of the subtle inquiring mind, as well as of the frail anxious heart—in Articles of Faith as well as in Rules of life,—He who makes known and prepares the end from the beginning, never laid more on man than He had first made him able to bear—gradually, perhaps, and unconsciously, but really, educating him for what was to come.

[k] Ecclus. xlvii. 15—17.

In the beginning WAS *the Word.* Observe this word WAS : not "began to be ;" not "took place ;" not "came into being ;" but simply WAS : the words in the original which mark this difference [ἦν, ἐγένετο] are so plain, and of such constant undeniable use, that there can be no gainsaying them. In the old eternity, the Beginning before the Beginning, there was no point, no moment, in which it might be said, The Word is not yet. The saying " He was" declares absolute, necessary, continued existence ; such as is denoted by similar inflections of the verb substantive in such instances as, " the only-begotten Son, Which is in the bosom (ὁ ὢν εἰς τὸν κόλπον) of the Father¹," and " the Son of Man which is in heaven" (ὁ ὢν ἐν τῷ οὐρανῷ)ᵐ ; and " He which is of God (ὁ ὢν παρὰ τοῦ Θεοῦ), He hath seen the Fatherⁿ ;" and "Verily, verily, I say unto you, Before Abraham was, I am (ἐγώ εἰμι)º ;" "Thou sayest that I am a King" (ὅτι βασιλεύς εἰμι ἐγώ)ᵖ ; and " of whom as concerning the flesh Christ came, Who is over all (ὁ ὢν ἐπὶ πάντων), God blessed for everᵍ ;" and " The God and Father of our Lord Jesus Christ, Which is blessed for evermore" (ὁ ὢν εὐλογητὸς εἰς τοὺς αἰῶνας)ʳ ;" and " Ye did service unto them which by nature are no Gods" (τοῖς μὴ φύσει οὖσι θεοῖς)ˢ ; " Being the brightness of His glory" (ὃς ὢν ἀπαύγασμα)ᵗ ; " Though He were a Son" (καίπερ ὢν υἱός)ᵘ ; and " Which is, and Which was, and Which is to come" (ὁ ὢν καὶ ὁ ἦν καὶ ὁ ἐρχόμενος) ˣ.

Now what is This Uncreated Being, Who never *came* into being, absolutely, necessarily continuing

---

¹ Ch. i. 18.   ᵐ Ch. iii. 13.   ⁿ Ch. vi. 46.   º Ch. viii. 58.
ᵖ Ch. xviii. 37.   ᵍ Rom. ix. 5.   ʳ 2 Cor. xi. 31.   ˢ Gal. iv. 8.
ᵗ Heb. i. 3.   ᵘ Ibid. v. 8.   ˣ Rev. i. 4.

in existence? and by what name are we to call and know Him? "The Word"—that is His chosen title in this place; not the abstract "Wisdom," but "The Word;" as though to signify a continual going forth or proceeding;—an action *ad extra*. "He rather calls Him Word than Son, because the latter term has respect to the Father only, the former implies not only a speaker but a sound also, a meaning and a hearer; and so it becomes a merciful intimation of God's relation to His creatures by and through His Son[y]." But in one respect the original, ὁ Λόγος, seems to answer a little more exactly to our English "Discourse," which, as we know, stands both for the faculty by which we think and reason, and for the connected words in which we express the exercise of that faculty. "Discourse," however, is of far too confined application to express the full meaning of the Greek Λόγος, which therefore must be described rather than translated. It would be rightly described, perhaps, as a term that has two meanings, the one, Reason, or Reasoning; the other, Speech, or Speaking: in any case, then, it is a relative term, for Reason implies a Reasoner, and Speech a Speaker. Now the Reasoner and Speaker, in this highest use of the terms, was "in the beginning;" that is, before anything had been made. Therefore "The Word," in this place, signifies That Something in the Eternal Uncreated One, which answers best, in the way of analogy, to Reason and Speech in us mortals. I say, in the way of analogy; because, as far as we can judge from the condescension of the Holy Spirit in the Bible, so only can human ideas, however imperfectly, correspond

[y] Ludolphus Saxo, *De Vita Christi*.

to Divine Truths, and the things of Heaven be expressed by the words of Earth.

The knowledge indeed of these things is too wonderful for us; we cannot attain unto it. Only of one thing we are quite sure,—and God grant that it be never out of our minds!—that He, in Whom we are to be restored to God's Image, in vouchsafing to call Himself the Word and Wisdom of the Father, plainly teaches that to be negligent in ordering and guarding our own thought and speech is in a special manner pouring contempt upon that Divine Image and His offer to save us by it.

But it ought to be well understood that these sayings, "God's Reason, God's Word, God's Wisdom," and the like, do by no means denote a mere quality or attribute of the Most High, as the same form of speech might, if applied to a man or to an angel. That Something in God Almighty, which is so described, "The Word of the LORD," is a Person, distinct from the Father of all, yet of the same Substance or Nature with Him. So the phrase would be understood by those to whom St. John was immediately addressing himself—by such as were used to read the Old Scriptures in the interpretation of the Chaldee Paraphrasts. For with them it was quite a customary thing to put "the Word of the Lord," for the Lord Himself, often in places where only personal speech or action could be intended. Two instances will explain what is meant as well as a thousand. Jacob's saying in Genesis xxviii. 20, 21 : "If God will be with me ... then shall the Lord be my God;" stands in the Chaldee thus : "If the Word of the Lord will be with me, ... then shall the Word of the Lord be my God." And in Exodus xix. 17 : " Moses brought forth the people out of the camp to meet with God;" Chald. " to meet the Word of the Lord." The Word of the Lord was the God of Jacob, the God who brought Israel out of Egypt: and readers of the Old Testament, thus instructed concerning Him, would be prepared to gather from the saying, " The Word was with God," the confirmation of His distinct Personality as a Gospel Doctrine.

From all Eternity, then, *The Word* WAS—existed as a Person—*with God;*—with the Father, Whose Word He is. But what is "*with God?*"

The preposition translated " with " (πρός), prefixed to an accusative case, ordinarily answers to the English " to;" but it is often found to express not motion but position, and then is rather to be rendered by " at," or " with," according as it governs the name of a place or of a person. Thus, " the axe is lying *at* (πρός) the root of the trees," St. Matt. iii. 10; " I was daily *with* you in the Temple," St. Matt. xxvi. 55 ; " The parts *towards* or *by* the door," St. Mark ii. 2. " The multitude was *towards* or *by* the sea," St. Mark iv. 1 ; " Whom I was minded to keep *with* myself," Philemon 13. The only place besides this in St. John's writings, where the same construction is adopted, occurs in his first Epistle, i. 1, 2 ; and the two passages stand (as will be seen) in marvellous agreement with each other;—" THAT which was from the beginning"—equivalent to THAT of which it was written, " In the beginning was the Word." And again, " We declare unto you That Eternal Life which was *with* the Father"— this is equivalent to " The Word was *with* God."

Perhaps some of the places cited may suggest,

as part of their meaning, something like the French *chez*; as if one should say, "He was *at home* with God." The following seem to be instances: "His sisters, are they not all *with* us[a]?" "I celebrate the Passover (πρός σε) *at thy house*[a];" "I shall remain—tarry—*with* you[b];" "I abode *with* Peter[c];" "when we were *with* you[d];" "I was minded to retain Onesimus *with* myself[e]." In different but kindred phrase we read, "The disciples went away again (πρὸς αὑτούς) *to their own homes*[f]."

If such an allusion were intended in the saying, "The Word was *with* God," it would seem to be in keeping with the mysterious condescension which in the holy Book of Proverbs had borrowed a sort of "household words" to express the same Divine Truth. "The Lord *possessed* Me," (so we read); "*I was daily His* Delight;" literally, "the Object of His caresses," "I was as *one brought up with Him*," a nursling, "rejoicing *always before Him*[g]."

Thus Wisdom, i.e. the Word, makes Itself known as other indeed than God the Father, yet inseparable from Him. Wherever God Almighty was, there was the Word. The phrase declares His Immensity and Incomprehensibility, as the former portion of the verse had declared His Eternity. The next following sums up all, mentioning no more Attributes, but passing at once to the Substance.

And the Word *was* God. In such sense God, as not to be the Father, but to be with Him, Very God of Very God; and *therefore* (since God is One) of One Substance with the Father.

---

[a] St. Matt. xiii. 56. [a] Ibid. xxvi. 18. [b] 1 Cor. xvi. 7. [c] Gal. i. 18.
[d] 1 Thess. iii. 4. [e] Philemon 13. [f] St. John xx. 10. [g] Prov. viii. 22, 30.

With those four short words, *The Word was God*, it pleased the Holy Ghost not only to crown, complete, and establish for ever in men's sight, the doctrine obscurely intimated in the Old Scriptures,—the traditions and instinctive auguries of those who had known Christ after the flesh,—but His will was also to seal as it were anew, and verify in a way which could not be gainsaid, His own revelations poured into the hearts of His holy Apostles and Prophets on the first Whitsunday, and repeated constantly now for seventy years in their Sermons and Catechisms, their Hymns and Confessions of Faith;—often affirmed, implied throughout, in the Books of the New Testament, of which this was providentially intended to be the last.

Let any one suppose himself then living at Ephesus, or within sound of the teaching there, and more or less bewildered by what might reach him of the dreams and theories, the wild and self-sufficient talk, even among professing Christians, of which the air was beginning to be full: such an one may imagine also the relief, when, according to the tradition of St. Jerome[h], this fourth and last Gospel was given to the Church at the request of the Bishops of Asia. In answer to their earnest prayer with fasting, the Apostle was prompted by the Holy Ghost to rise up against the Cerinthians and other heretics, and chiefly, just then, against the doctrine of the Ebionites, "who affirm" (says Jerome) "that Christ had no existence before Mary[i]." "He cut them short by his Apostolical authority, and from that time forward fixed the Rule of Faith in the Church[k]."

[h] Com. in Matt. Prolog. [i] De Viris Illust. c. ix. [k] The quotation appears to be from Iren. c. Hær. iii. xi. 1.—[ED.]

In sum, S. John, we know, was one of the two who were divinely named Sons of Thunder. And surely this first verse of his gospel is like three distinct thunders uttering their voices. Or if we may borrow an illustration from what, in the abundance of the revelations, he has told us elsewhere, we may say that the Eternity of the Word having first been proclaimed from on high (for the first voice which the Evangelist heard as of a trumpet talking with him said, *In the beginning was the Word;*) the next revelation, as a second Voice, saying, *The Word was WITH God*, declared that there was between Him and the Eternal Father that separation in the mode of existence which the Church expresses by the terms First and Second Person, and such as she implies in teaching us to say, God *of* God, Light *of* Light, Very God *of* Very God; not a mere emanation, or aspect, or attribute of the Father, but a living, conscious, willing agent; for to such the word Person is applied in our ordinary language, and from that use it was adopted into Theology.

But once more: lest any hearing of First and Second—the Word with God—should imagine a division of Nature and Substance, Two Gods, equal or unequal to each other, the Voice comes graciously the third time, and says, with no uncertain sound, but positively and absolutely, *The Word was God;* completing thus, and authoritatively sealing afresh, the great Doctrine of His proper Divinity, and then, as an Eagle that has soared out of sight, returning to contemplate Him in His Dispensations and in His Works.

(VER. 2.) *The Same was in the Beginning with God.* This is the first instance of a sort of repetition not unusual in the narrative of this Evangelist, as may be seen in the places noted below[1]; all but one of which (it is observable) occur in the discourses of our Divine Master Himself. Is the repetition simply rhetorical? or can a special significance be assigned to it in each case? Of those which occur hereafter, each one in its turn will appear perhaps easy to be accounted for: it will be no presumption, then, to attempt an explanation here, although it rest but upon conjecture. May not the repetition be emphatical, to indicate the commencement of an intended contrast between the Divine WORD Himself and the chief of His human prophetic witnesses? and that expressed partly after the manner of Hebrew Parallelism? as thus :—

In the Beginning was the Word, and the Word was with God, and the Word was God.	There was a Man sent from God, whose name was John.
The Same was in the Beginning with God.	The same came for a witness, to bear witness of the Light, that all men through Him might believe.
All things were made by Him, and without Him was not anything made that was made.	
In Him was Life, and the Life was the Light of men.	He was not that Light, but was sent to bear witness of that Light.
And the Light shineth in darkness, and the darkness comprehended (overtook?) it not.	That was the true Light, which lighteth every man that cometh [coming] into the world.

[1] Chap. ii. 24, 25; iii. 15, 16; vi. 39, 40; viii. 24; x. 28, 29; xvi. 14, 15. Cf. 1 St. John v. 13 (?).

The term οὗτος, "The same," would thus be equivalent to "This Person," or "That Person." As if he should say, *This* Person (mark it well) *was*, in the very Beginning, with the Eternal Father: *That* person (I do not say *was*, but) ἐγένετο, came in time into being, a man sent from God, &c. Thus, whereas both the Son of God and His Servant the Baptist were truly subordinate to the Father of all, both, in several senses, instruments working His will, nevertheless there is and ever will be as much difference between the two, as between the Eternal and the Temporal, between the highest Heaven and His earth, between the Supreme God and one who is a mere man.

The repetition in the second verse is the Apostle's preparation—his foot planted as it were firmly behind him—when he is about to pass from the doctrine of the Word's Consubstantiality with the Father to that of the Father's manifestation of Himself by the Word. It seems, if one may reverently say so, natural and orderly, to recall just then to the Disciples' mind the personal distinction of the Two. As He was from the Beginning with the Father,—not Himself the Father, though one and the same God with Him,—so by Him, thus distinct yet identical, were wrought all the works of the Father. Their Working is as their Being, common to Both, but under the same condition or rule of subordination; as the Word Himself plainly teaches, "Verily, verily, I say unto you, The Son can do nothing of Himself, but what He seeth the Father do: for what things soever He doeth, these also doeth the Son likewise ᵐ."

^m Ch. v. 19.

This is, in other words, the Proclamation (VER. 3), *All things were made by Him.* The full meaning of the phrase cannot perhaps be given without attending to both applications of the verb ἐγένετο,—"came into being" and "came to pass." "All persons and all things that ever began to be had their beginning through" (or "by") "the Word;" and again, "All events that ever took place, all the issues of all causes, took place, in some sense, through Him." To Him the true confession is made,—

> "We all acknowledge both Thy Power and Love
> To be exact, transcendent, and Divine;
> Who dost so strongly and so sweetly move,
> While all things have their will, yet none but Thine.
> For either Thy command or Thy permission
> Lay hands on all; they are Thy Right and Left*."

Even that which goes wrong, through the free-will mysteriously allowed to some of the creatures, is so far wrought by Him, that without His Power, sustaining them in existence and in the use of the faculties which they so pervert, it could not take place. A fearful idea, bringing sin as it were into immediate contact with Him against WHOM it is wrought. But the thought is no less full of comfort, as connecting not only our moral but our physical condition, at all moments, with the very touch of our Incarnate, sympathizing God.

All things were made, and (in the sense above mentioned) all events were wrought, by the Word. And that there may be no mistake, nor inadequate notion, of the saying, he adds, *And without* (or apart from) *Him was not anything made that was made.* This I take to be much more than a mere

---

* Herbert, on "*Providence,*" in *The Temple.*

emphatical repetition. It is parallel, rather, to those Scriptures which assure us that Christ is our Preserver as well as our Creator. So in Colos. i. 16, 17; not only "in Him all things were created;" "all things were created by Him and for Him, and He is before all things"—but also "*and by* (or in) *Him all things consist* (or subsist)." Also in Hebrews i. 3, He is described as "*upholding* all things by the Word of His Power."

Had the saying been simply "All things were made by Him," there are a sort of half Epicureans in the world, ready enough to take it as implying that after one impulse given, the Great Artificer left His work to itself, to go according to the laws which He had once for all impressed on it, *impulsu remorum;* a notion most dismal to a loving, dutiful heart.

> "Hast Thou left all things to their course,
> And laid the reins
> Upon the horse*?"

Whereas now it is a doctrine not to be gainsaid by any Christian, that not only did the Universe begin out of nothing through the word spoken by our Lord at the first; but also that nothing is done or takes place in it—no motion or act of any of His creatures, visible or invisible,—can happen or be wrought, *without Him*—apart from His Presence and Power. "Not a sparrow falleth to the ground without your Father;" and ".Whatsoever He doeth, the same doeth the Son likewise;"—He Who has vouchsafed to be "our Brother and our Flesh," and "Whose delight is with the sons of men." In every

---

* G. Herbert, on "*Longing,*" in *The Temple*. Cf. St. Aug. Serm. lii. § 5. "Fieri non potest ut per Ipsum creaverit, et non per Ipsum gubernet," &c.

process of Nature without exception, and in every event of the world's course, the faithful man is privileged to see the direct Hand of his Redeemer, and to apply the promise, "All things work together for good to them that love God." A pregnant truth, and if seriously thought on, such as will pour an aweful or a consoling light into every corner of man's being.

The original has here a various reading founded on such high authority, and in itself so remarkable and suggestive, that it would seem wrong not to mention it. In St. Augustine's time, the Latin copies divided the 3rd verse differently; as thus, "*All things were made by Him, and without Him was not any thing made. What was made,*" or rather (regarding the difference in grammar between the Aorist and the Perfect Middle [ἐγένετο . . γέγονεν]) "*That in Him which hath been made,*" or "*hath come into being*" (which form, it should be noticed, implies *permanency* in the change spoken of,) "*was Life.*" The question of course will be asked, (may it be asked with all reverence!), "What is That, in The Word, Which hath been made,— Which hath come into Being; Which hath had a beginning and abides as It began?" The answer must be, "His Human Nature, doubtless—the Body and Soul of the Incarnate Son of God." And This was, and is, and ever will be, Life. From the Word made Flesh virtue evermore goeth out, whereby the generations before and after, as well as those immediately around Him, have Life;— not so much physical Life, as the true supernatural Life, whereby men and angels live unto God. So expounded, this reading, it will be clearly seen, leaves entire the blessed doctrine of our Lord's ever-present agency in all things, while it adds, as the source and formal condition of such agency, His purposing first, and eventually vouchsafing, to become and to continue for ever, a Member of His own Universe, a Creature among, though not such as, all other creatures.

Whichever of these two readings may approve itself most to the learned, the doctrine inculcated remains the same :—that The Word is eminently, (what the same Apostle styles Him in the beginning of his first Epistle) *The Word of Life*,—that the Second Person of the Most Holy Trinity has become, eminently, the Channel of Life to the creatures. The difference being that the common reading states this generally, that of St. Augustine adds, in special, that the Prerogative has regard to, or "depends on," our Lord's Incarnation. In either case, (VER. 4,) "*In Him was Life:*" whatever hath lived at any time hath derived that Life from the Father through the Son. "As the Father hath Life in Himself; so hath He given to the Son to have Life in Himself." Therefore His Title, no less than the Father's, is, "The Living God." "We both labour and suffer reproach, because we trust in *the Living God*, Who is *the Saviour* of all men, specially of those that believe [p]." "Living is the Word of God and powerful [q]." And to Him belongs the attestation exclusively divine, "*As I live.*" For the Apostle quotes the saying in Isaiah (xlv. 23): "I have sworn by Myself . . . that unto Me every knee shall bow:"—St. Paul quotes this as spoken by Him, before Whose Judgment-seat we are all to

[p] 1 Tim. iv. 10.   [q] Heb. iv. 12.

stand[r]. He Himself claims to be "The Resurrection and the Life;" and by His Spirit prompts His Beloved Disciple to declare of Him, "This is the true God and Eternal Life[s]."

JESUS is the Life of Angels as well as of men. This is implied in His being their Maker and Preserver: perhaps also, in His declaring that He "gives Himself to be the Life of the world." For "the world" may mean both Angels and men: as the Apostle says, "We are made a spectacle unto the world, and to angels and to men[t]." And from the Christian proverb, "Know ye not that the saints shall judge the world?" he infers, "Know ye not that we shall judge angels[u]?"

Now *in what sense* the Word, as the Son of Man, may be said to be the Life of Angels, or of other living creatures in God's many worlds, above or below man—this is nowhere at all revealed to us. Only the *fact* itself seems implied in such Scriptures as entitle our Lord "The First-born of every creature," and "The Beginning of the Creation of God;" also in that the whole Creation is in "travail," expecting for itself some kind of participation in "the glorious liberty of the children of God."

On this hypothesis, the verse we are now considering might be paraphrased as follows: "*In Him*,"—in That Which He vouchsafed to become at His Incarnation—*was Life;* the Life of all creatures that have ever lived was due, in God's secret and eternal Counsels, to that condescension of The Word. *And the Life was the Light of men:* of all *men* especially, that Life was, is, and ever will be,

---

[r] See Rom. xiv. 11.   [s] 1 St. John v. 20.   [t] 1 Cor. iv. 9.
[u] Ibid. vi. 3.

The Light. The "Breath of Life breathed" into Adam's "nostrils," whereby he "became a living soul," caused him to be in the Image of God, Who "is Light," and in Whom "is no darkness at all." "God saw all that He had made" in Adam "and behold, it was very good." The Life that He had given him was Light, heavenly Light. The two at the beginning were blended into one; so entirely were man's physical and intellectual powers pervaded and imbued with "righteousness and true holiness." It was "the Life of God in the soul of man;" and true Light, except so imparted, man never had nor could have any. What may seem to be such,—call it wisdom, knowledge, understanding, invention, counsel, energy, largeness of heart, or by what name soever it may be known,—is all a mere dream or worse, except so far as it comes from the Word Which was in the Beginning with God. For as the secret Presence of That Word, and His communication of Himself has been the principle of *Life* to all that have lived, so, whatever real *Light* the children of men have at any time enjoyed, or in any measure, it has been wholly due to this same Divine Presence:—a spark as it were of the vital fire mysteriously abiding within them, struck out by His providential working according to the counsel of His own will. The *Light* of Mankind has been, is, and ever will be, the Manifestation of the *Life* within them of the Living and Life-giving Word. "With Thee," says the Holy Ghost by the Prophet David, "is the Fountain of *Life:* in Thy *Light* shall we see Light[1]."

It is the same process which is described in the

[1] Ps. xxxvi. 9.

parallel passage already referred to, the opening of St. John's first Epistle. Only there the beloved Disciple traces it in a somewhat different order, backwards from the visible and tangible result to the Absolute, Eternal Cause. "We have heard Him, we have seen Him with our eyes, we have looked upon Him, and our hands have handled Him Who is the Word of Life;" and having been so made acquainted with Him, we tell you from Him, "this is the message which we have heard of Him and declare unto you, that God is Light, and in Him is no darkness at all[y]." Here, on the other hand, the Apostle sets out from the Fountain,—what our Lord is in Himself,—and traces creating and redeeming Love all the way down to the moment in which he (St. John himself) with others, "beheld His glory."

The particular step in this wondrous ascent and descent, on which we are now pausing, is "*The Life was manifested*"="*The Life was the Light of men.*" Just so far and so long as the Living and Powerful Word of God has vouchsafed to reveal Himself to man, hath man been partaker of the True Light—of the Wisdom, Purity, and Goodness of God. They are His own sayings: "I am the Light of the world: He that followeth Me shall not walk in darkness, but shall have the Light of Life[z]." "As long as I am in the world, I am the Light of the world[a]." And "I am come a Light into the world, that whosoever believeth on Me should not abide in darkness[b]."

(VER. 5.) *And the Light shineth in darkness:* As it

---

[y] 1 St. John i. 5.
[z] Ibid. ix. 5.
[a] St. John viii. 12.
[b] Ibid. xii. 46.

is the nature of all light to shew itself in the dark, so, be sure, that quality is inseparable from this, the very true, the original, archetypal Light. It is shining in darkness, always shining; even as the natural light, once kindled, has never died down or gone out, since the moment when first God spake the Word for it to shine out of darkness, so, and much more, will it ever be with This Holy and Glorious Light—The Word Incarnate, shining before and behind and around Him through all time and space. By the Almighty's permission there is still darkness, moral darkness, the darkness of the will determined to reject Him: such darkness as He, Who is the Light Himself, describes, "Light is come into the world, and men loved darkness rather than Light because their deeds were evil^e." There is a wild and blind struggle to prevail against the Light, but it may not be: the darkness did at no time really succeed in "comprehending," that is, overtaking, laying hold of, detaining, much less overwhelming, that Holy Light. No, not even at the fall of our first Parents, when more than at any moment, as far as we are told, that darkness seemed to have the mastery. Presently the Lord's Voice, His Word, was heard in the garden, and the prophetic announcement of His victory began to be "a Light shining in a dark place." And so It went on all along, variously, but on the whole more and more, "until the Day should dawn, and the Day-star arise in men's hearts;" that is, until the preparation for the actual appearance of the Word should be completed by the witness of His last and greatest Forerunner.

^e St. John iii. 19.

In this account of the probable meaning of the verse, the word "comprehended" (borrowed by our Translators from the Latin) has been taken in a different sense from that in which St. Augustine and the Fathers generally understood it. With them it expresses the kind of resistance which a mass (so to call it) of "darkness which might be felt" would offer to the strongest light; utterly refusing to admit a single ray—to be pervious to it in any degree. So they take it to signify the lost state of the Heathen—"having no hope, and without God in the world." But the Greek word (κατέλαβεν) of which "comprehended" is the rendering, is used by St. John [d] himself with "darkness," in the sense of "overtaking:" "Walk while ye have the Light, lest darkness *come upon* you." And St. Paul to the Thessalonians, "Ye are not in darkness, that the Day should *overtake* you as a thief [e]." And three or four times elsewhere in his Epistles it stands as the correlative of "pursue;" as "So run, that ye *may obtain* [f]." And it may seem, on the whole, more congruous with the tenor of the whole passage, that this clause should rather add a circumstance descriptive of what God continued to do for us, than merely deepen the picture of our wilful unbelief.

These five verses, so construed, may appear to contain an account strictly historical, yet drawn from the very depths of the spiritual world;—breathed (as one may say) from the Bosom of the Almighty;—an account of His dealings with His creatures, and especially with man, by His Word one day to

---
[d] Ch. xii. 35.   [e] 1 Thess. v. 4.   [f] 1 Cor. ix. 24.
Cf. Rom. ix. 30; Philip. iii. 12, 13.

become a Creature Himself, and Incarnate. It is a History commencing before creation, and extending down to the moment when the Baptist began his witness.

On comparing the terms used in this brief history with the vocabulary of the philosophizing Heretics (Gnostics they were commonly called) of those days, as it is recorded by St. Irenæus, there appears much reason to accept the tradition, that the former was given (among other ends) as a Providential antidote to the latter. "The Word," "the Life," the Only-Begotten, Light, Grace, Truth, and even John Baptist, with many more, came to be in their fantastic theologies or cosmogonies, the names of so many Æons, Beings, or Cycles of Being, or whatever else they might denote: which, being shaken together as in a kaleidoscope, formed themselves into a system or systems (as the Israelites' earrings into a calf) to us revolting and absurd, to the degree of incoherence, yet, as the event proved, not without attraction to the Oriental mind.

And if there be any thing in the notion of some learned and thoughtful persons that the strange mixture of Christianity and Pantheism, which now plays the part of philosophy in this and other portions of Christendom, is substantially a reproduction of those dreams of the first century, the warnings provided for that time may prove no less seasonable to us. The two first verses of this Gospel, for instance, expressly declare a Personal God against any Spinozist imagination of an *Anima Mundi*. The third is authoritative to put down any atomic or Darwinian theory, which would make

God's creatures the result of I know not what inherent appetencies or tendencies developing themselves for an unlimited time.

Then Life, according to verse 4, instead of being a necessary function of bodies organized in a particular way—a "wave" (so to speak) of certain material fluids—is a Gift directly communicated from the Most High, the Everliving Creator and Preserver. And so, depending on it, is Light, "the Light of men," the true spiritual Wisdom, Reason and Understanding. It comes not of course, begins not, nor continues, nor is perfected, in mere process of time, by experience, calculation, high cultivation of the intellect: but it comes supernaturally, of God's Word living and abiding in the man, and cannot be separated altogether from the Image in which man was created—"after God, in righteousness and true hóliness."

From which it follows, as in verse 5, that the difference between good and evil is not, as the world would have it, conventional, fantastic, and unreal; but has its roots in the eternal nature of things—in the character (so to call it) of God Himself; that the warfare between the two is irreconcileable; and that the final victory of the good cannot be really doubtful for a moment: the darkness cannot overtake or quench the Light.

The same train of thought may seem to be carried on in the next statement of the Divine History: which takes up the gradual victory of the Word over the Powers of Evil at the point immediately before that in which the whole centred, His Incarnation. (VER. 6.) "*There was a man sent from God, whose name was John.*" It appears that the Gnostics considered St. John Baptist also as an Æon, and the word "a Man" is supposed by some interpreters to be intended as an emphatical contradiction of this. But doubtless it implies also the distinction between the Word Incarnate and all other prophets. "John, than whom there was no greater, was just a *Man* sent from God, and no more." Such he was in nature; and as to his office,

(VER. 7.) *The same came for a witness; to bear witness of the Light;* no more; he was sent to declare the Name and Glory of Another : a witness, indeed, most high and supernatural, and of deepest moment to all, but still he was no more than one bearing witness; differing as widely from Him to Whom he was witnessing, as any mere human being differs from the Word which "was in the Beginning with God, and was God."

(VER. 8.) *He was not that Light, but was sent to bear witness of that Light.* The Holy Spirit repeats the words, as though in anxiety lest the interval between the Master and the Servant should be imagined less than infinite. It is true that in another place the Master declares that He Himself came for a Witness[s]; and He calls Himself in the Revelation, the Amen, the Faithful and True Witness. But He is witnessing not to another as greater than Himself, but to the Truth, the abstract Truth as against falsehood, and to good as against evil.

That all men through him might believe. One naturally pauses at so very large a declaration of the value of the one Testimony of St. John. His being the last of the Holy Order of Prophets of the Old Testament, and, so far, "sealing up the

---

[s] Chap. xviii. 37.

vision," is hardly sufficient to account for the saying, "through him." However, as matter of fact thus much is certain; i. That Christians generally are spoken of by our Lord as believing "through the word" of the Apostles; ii. That two, probably four, of the chiefest Apostles literally and bodily came to believe in our Lord through the Baptist, as this chapter goes on to relate; iii. That his witness is repeatedly alleged by our Master Himself[h], by St. Peter[i], and by St. Paul[k], as necessary and foreordained towards the conversion first of Jews, and then of Gentiles through the Jews. So that all sorts of believers may be truly said to believe through St. John Baptist. And the Church accordingly, among other special honours, has been used of old to name him in her great and solemn services, among those whom she most earnestly commemorates, and in whose communion she especially rejoices.

He was not That Light, but was sent to bear witness of That Light. There is in the original something to be noted here, besides the repetition characteristic of St. John's style: it lies in the omission of "this was so ordered," or as in our version "he was sent," before the phrase which describes the purpose of his mission. A similar omission may be seen in the following passages. "Neither hath this man sinned, nor his parents, but .... that the works of God might be made manifest in him[l];" and, "I know whom I have chosen, but .... that the Scripture may be fulfilled[m];" and, "But .... that the world may know that I love the Father[n];"

---

[h] Chap. v. 33. [i] Acts x. 37. [k] Ibid. xiii. 24. [l] Chap. ix. 3.
[m] Chap. xiii. 18. [n] Chap. xiv. 31.

and, " But .... that the word might be fulfilled which is written in their law °;" and, " If they had been of us, they would have continued with us; but .... that it might be made manifest that they were not all of us ᵖ."

No other writer of the New Testament has used this form. Is it fanciful to observe that St. John's devotional feelings would lead his mind always to the final cause of things, while his reverence would cause him to employ a degree of reserve in the manner of setting it forth? And the Holy Spirit, we know, did not supersede the human tendencies of those whose pens He guided, but, in an ineffable way, sanctified and sealed them to be His own.

(VER. 9.) *That was the true Light, which lighteth every man that cometh into the world;* or, as it may be translated without prejudice to the grammar, " It was the true Light, which lighteth every man, coming into the world."

The Fathers generally, I believe, adopt the former construction, and it has the high authority of the old Latin version. So taken, the verse would seem nearly to repeat the former statement, *The Life was the Light of men.* Only, as specifying the point of time when each child of Adam begins to exist, it would have to be understood, not universally of all Divine Illumination, but exclusively of the Image and Likeness of God given to Adam, so far as any thing remains of it in our fallen condition. " For there is a kind of Light—the Light of Reason—wherewith all are enlightened when they come here, deriving it from their first creation in the Image of God ᵠ."

° Chap. xv. 25.   ᵖ 1 St. John ii. 19.   ᵠ Rupertus.

But perhaps both the grammar and context of the passage may be thought to tell in favour of the other construction. The grammar, because according to St. John's almost invariable usage, the participle "coming" would have the article before it, if it were to be taken in the accusative [r]. The connection, because the Evangelist is in course of relating the special witness of the Baptist, which, as we know, is summed up in one saying, "The True Light is not, as former Prophets have said, to come hereafter: It is even now in the act of coming." Besides, "*He that cometh*," was, over and over, used by St. John Baptist, and may have been generally familiar at the time, as the designation of the Messiah. And the addition, "*into the world*" makes the phrase exactly conformable to our Lord's own twice-repeated way of describing His Incarnation:—"*Light is come into the world, and men loved darkness rather than Light*[s];" and, "*I am come a Light into the world, that whosoever believeth in Me should not abide in darkness*[t]."

And it was the TRUE Light: we must pause upon the word "True" (ἀληθινός). This is the first use of it in an idiomatic sense, in which it occurs frequently enough to be a characteristic of St. John's style. "*True*" is here opposed, not to the false, but to the shadowy and typical. A deep lesson attaches to the word in this application of it. Such phrases as "the True Light," "the True Bread," "the True Vine," in this Gospel; in St. Luke, "the True Riches;" and in the Epistle to the Hebrews,

---

[r] Cf. chap. iii. 8, 15, 16, 20; iv. 13; vi. 40, 45; viii. 34; xi. 26; xii. 46; xv. 2; xvi. 2; xviii. 4, 37; xix. 12; 1 St. John ii. 23, 29; iii. 3, 4, 6 (bis), 9, 10, 15; iv. 7; v. 1 (bis), 4, 18; 2 St. John 9. The only exception is in St. John xv. 2, *initio*.   [s] St. John iii. 19.   [t] Ibid. xii. 46.

"the True Tabernacle," and, "holy places made with hands, which are figures of the True,"—evidently imply a standing relation of things in sight to things out of sight;—of the first Heaven and the first Earth to the New; in the way of type and antitype, figure and reality. This relation is in some degree recognised by all. There are instances of it in Scripture so clear as to make *that* inevitable, if Scripture is at all believed. But few admit it, as the old Christians did, in its full extent. And too often it is not only misapprehended, but even (if one may so speak) inverted: the Shadow taken for the Substance, and the Substance for the Shadow. To mention one very sad instance: by some our Lord's death on the Cross is supposed to be called a Sacrifice merely by allusion to the customary sin-offerings, which are accounted sacrifices indeed; instead of their owning Him to be the One Great Reality, of which they were all but prophetic images [a].

But may God be thanked for permitting and encouraging sinful man, His unworthy servant, thus to employ the works of His Creation, and the ways of His Providence, even those which otherwise might seem to us most trivial and transitory, as so many true tokens from Him,—most helpful, if we will so take them, to purify the imagination and lift up the heart to the better, the eternal things!

The Voice from above goes on, telling us of the True Light; (VER. 10.) *He was in the world, and*

---

[a] The above passage recalls Bishop Butler's words:—"The doctrine of this Epistle" (to the Hebrews) "plainly is, that the legal sacrifices were allusions to the great and final atonement to be made by the blood of Christ; and not that this was an allusion to those."—*Analogy*, Part ii. Ch. v.—[ED.]

the world was made by Him, and the world knew Him not. As if He should say, "Whereas you have been told that the subject of John's witness was the True Light, just then in the very act of coming into the world; this must not be taken as if the Word of the Lord had ever ceased to be present with, or to manifest Himself to, His creatures, low as they had fallen." " He left not Himself without witness, in that He did good, and gave us rain from heaven, and fruitful seasons, filling our hearts with food and gladness[x]." " The invisible things of Him from the foundation of the world are clearly seen, being understood by the things that were made, even His Eternal power and Godhead[y]." The world was made by Him; it had been made, and was continually preserved by Him, and the world might have known this. Some did know it, and recognise Him—enough to leave the others without excuse, and to condemn themselves also, whereinsoever " knowing God, they glorified Him not as God." In the wisdom and goodness of the heathen; in the teaching of such as Socrates and Æschylus, Plato and Cicero, in all the glimpses and fragments of truth and self-denial, benevolence and natural piety, which any where and in any degree survived the Fall; and most especially in the chosen family and people, and the religious influences propagated around them far and near;—in all this, the Word, the True Light, was always, in presence and in energy: He was there, every where in the world which He had made; but that world knew Him not. It is the description of the old Pagans before our Saviour came: how sad to think that it should

[x] Acts xiv. 17.   [y] Rom. i. 20.

have continued to be a true account for the most part to those even to whom our Lord spake in person; as He Himself declares, "O righteous Father, the world hath not known Thee ᵃ." And yet again (which is still worse), long after the Holy Spirit had come, the last Apostle and Prophet has still to make the mournful confession, "The world knoweth us not;" and no wonder, for "it knew Him notᵃ." Alas! that the words should stand good and undeniable now at the end of eighteen centuries.

But there is a greater wonder than this, both of mercy on His part and of unbelief on ours; and to this also the Baptist testified, and the Evangelist repeats his witness: (VER. 11.) *"He came unto His own* (εἰς τὰ ἴδια), *and His own received Him not."* Here again we may remark an idiom used elsewhere by this Evangelist, and by St. Luke,—one of those phrases which denote the ineffable condescension of the Incarnate One. Bethlehem and Nazareth, Judea and Galilee, all the Holy Land and the haunts of His human forefathers;—nay, and all that marked out the Jewish people and realm as "dwelling apart, and not reckoned among the nations;" the Temple and its services, the Levitical rites, the Mosaic and Davidical politics, the schools of the Prophets, their visions and their miracles, and above all, perhaps, the Ark of the Covenant with its treasures;—all these together formed the chosen and favoured Home of the Divine Word, so long as it pleased Him to have any limited, local Home. "This shall be My Rest for ever; here will I dwell, for I have a delight therein ᵇ."

ᵃ Chap. xvii. 25.   ᵃ 1 St. John iii. 1.   ᵇ Ps. cxxxii. 15, P.-B.V.

But when He, the Great Owner and Householder, came bodily in His own Person,—knocked as it were at His own door, demanding admission, His own people, not only His servants, but those who were His own Flesh and Blood, *received Him not.* Their will was, if they could, to shut the door, and hold it fast against Him.

Mournfully mysterious is the very sound of those two verses, the 10th and 11th; especially considering by Whom they were really indited,—Whose complaint they indeed embody. Taken together they seem to represent to us, not for that time only but for all times, the two sad forms of misery which divide between them all mankind who as yet are not Christians. For either they know nothing of any such deliverer as the Name of Christ indicates to us, or, having the notion more or less distinctly, they will not confess it to be realized in Jesus Christ, God and Man. The first are Heathens; the second, in spirit, Jews. They may be called Mahometans or Unitarians, or by any other name: but with whom can their portion be, but with such as refuse to receive the Word offering Himself to them as to His own?

Observe that in each of these sayings, while the alienation of the world, and of the Jews, is confessed, their original interest in the Word is also confirmed. Against both Gnostics and Manichæans it is written, the world which knew Him not had been made by Him; the Jews who rejected Him were His own people. Whatever Philosophers may surmise, Nature is not contrary to Scripture; whatever unbelieving Israelites may affirm, the Old Testament is not contrary to the New.

But the two verses may have yet another and a still more alarming application. How many in the Christian world, which has been not only made but regenerated by Him, go on without caring to know Him! And how many go on knowing Him after a sort, account themselves to be His own, and pride themselves on it, yet have never really received Him, but are still making Him wait until they have done with the world and the flesh! Over such the Word of Life seems to lament by the lips of His beloved Disciple, as He had Himself lamented over Jerusalem [c].

But in His human condescension He comforts Himself, as continually in the old prophecies, with the thought of the remnant that should remain, and return, and stay upon the Lord; or as in His pleading with the Father in His Great Sacrificial Prayer: "The world hath not known Thee, but I have known Thee, and these have known that Thou hast sent Me [d]." The Jews as a nation rejected Him; but "there was a remnant by way of election of grace [e]." So here, from these definitions of Heathens and of Jews, and from the narrative of their unbelief, the Sacred Text proceeds to a true historical definition of Christian People (ver. 12). *As many as received Him, to them gave He power to become the sons of God, even to them that believe on His Name.* Power, that is, prerogative or privilege; as in other verses of St. John (chap. v. 27; x. 18; xix. 10); implying not only physical ability, but some kind of legal or settled right. The New Birth then—real transference into God's family— actually becoming Children of God, not merely being

---

[c] St. Matth. xxiii. 37. [d] St. John xvii. 25. [e] Rom. xi. 5.

so accounted and styled—this is the specific mark, the Differentia, as Logicians say, of a Christian. And to every person is given the right of being so transferred and adopted into the Lord's Household, when he comes to believe in the Lord's Name,—to *believe* with that peculiar trust and self-surrender, which we know belongs to Christian Faith. *On His Name*, on the Power and Virtue of it, such as the Father gave It Him at His Incarnation [f].

This faith does not formally make a man a child of God, but it entitles or qualifies him to be made so. If the question be asked, "What doth hinder me to be baptized?" the answer is ready :—" If thou believest with all thine heart thou mayest." But the New Birth itself, which makes alienated man God's Child, which causes wilful darkness to be again "Light in the Lord"—that is a work far above all human counsels or causes, physical or moral ;— *Which were born* (so he speaks, VER. 13) *not of Blood, nor of the will of the flesh, nor of the will of man, but of God.* Thou must not be misled by His condescending to use the word *born*, for these were *born, not of bloods*, of the conjunction of male and female; *nor of the will of the flesh*, through any carnal or natural appetency; *nor of the will of man*, through any goodness or wisdom of mortal man, seeking and continuing and helping forward so great a blessing; as when in charity one adopts another's child; but this is wholly and only God's work; as much so as when the world was created; —as much so as when the Word of God came into His own world as one of His creatures. It is God's

---

[f] Phil. ii. 9.

gift and God's doing: His Spirit given, and His Spirit working.

(VER. 14.) *And the Word was made Flesh, and dwelt among us (and we beheld His glory, the glory as of the only-begotten of the Father,) full of grace and truth.* Who can venture to write upon this verse? But if one may at all take upon him to consider how these Divine sayings follow one upon another, perhaps their connection may be thus stated. The first thirteen verses, having set forth, in the way of History passing from one fact to another, God's dealings with the Creatures, especially Man, by His Word, down to the period in which St. John was writing, that is, the setting up of the Church,—had simply said, *He came unto His own.* *Now* it seems good to the Divine Inspirer that the doctrine of the Church as to the *manner* of His coming should be re-affirmed, and all hearts set musing upon it, as the central point towards which all before had converged, and *from* which all after would diverge; —as leading also immediately to the outward witness of Him, which St. John in his work as an Evangelist was presently to detail.

Or (if we may express it in terms comparatively of later usage) that which is affirmed in ver. 13 is *subjective*, the inward and spiritual *result* of the Word's coming unto each one who receiveth Him: but that coming Itself, as set forth in ver. 14, is an *objective* and historical fact, the greatest of all, and from which all the rest flow: Creation itself, and all God's government of His creatures, having, apparently, some mysterious relation to That which the Holy Ghost has been vouchsafed to teach in blessed words which cannot be explained away.

And the Word was made Flesh; or rather, *became Flesh;* as really as the water at Cana *became wine,* or as the stone would have *become Bread* had the Tempter had his own way.

He does not say "became *Man,*" but "*Flesh,*" naming the inferior part of man, the more to declare His humiliation.

And dwelt among us. He not only became Flesh, but in Flesh He "tabernacled among us;"—sojourned, pitched and inhabited His tent; as of old (though not yet incarnate) among our Fathers in the wilderness. Perhaps the more exact word might be "encamped;"—a shade of meaning brought out (Rev. vii. 15) by the use of the verb with ἐπὶ and the accusative. It gives the notion of being elsewhere than in one's natural home (Rev. xxi. 3); so σκήνωμα (Acts vii. 46; 2 Pet. i. 13, 14). Then the reference to the Tabernacle suggests (if one may speak after the manner of men) the mention of the "*Glory,*" that is, the Shechinah. Whence we may gather that all the instances of the appearing of that Glory in the Old Testament, were typical of Its abode, first in Christ, and afterwards in His Church. *Among us;* in the midst of *us;* not of men generally, but of *us,* the Apostles and other disciples. For in that sense the holy writers of the New Testament, and St. John among them, constantly use the pronouns *us* and *we:* "That which *we* have heard and seen, declare *we* unto you[g];" "*We* have seen and bear witness that the Father sent the Son to be the Saviour of the world[b]."

And whereas it is here said not "we *saw,*" but

---

[g] 1 St. John i. 3. [b] Ibid. iv. 14.

"we *beheld* His glory," it is the same word which St. John uses in the place so often cited as parallel to this: "That which we have" not only "heard and seen with our eyes," but, "which we have *looked upon*," "have *contemplated*[1];" as the Baptist *contemplated* the Spirit descending like a Dove; as our Lord would have His servants *contemplate* the ripening fields; as the King came in to *contemplate*, to look narrowly on, his wedding guests; as the holy women not only beheld but *contemplated*—considered with all earnestness—"the sepulchre, and how His Body was laid."

"We" thus *contemplated* (St. John adds here) not simply the Incarnate Word Himself, but *His glory*. This has been commonly referred to the Transfiguration, which is mentioned in like manner, and with like mention of *glory*, by another favoured eye-witness of it, St. Peter:—"There came a voice to Him from the excellent glory, ... when we were with Him in the Holy Mount[k]." And St. Luke, "Peter and they that were with Him, saw His *glory*[l]." And for St. John in particular, we know that he was permitted to gaze on our Lord glorified on two other occasions at least; at His Ascension, and in the vision which preceded the Apocalypse. And if, as seems likely, his Gospel was the latest of his writings, we may understand him to be alluding here to that vision also.

There is moreover a remarkable coincidence between the phrase, *The glory as of the Only-Begotten from the Father*, and that of St. Peter in the place just quoted, " He received from God the Father

---

[1] 1 St. John i. 1; Chap. i. 32, 38; iv. 35; 1 St. John iv. 14; St. Matt. xxii. 2; St. Luke xxiii. 55.   [k] 2 St. Peter i. 17.   [l] St. Luke ix. 32.

honour and glory, when there came such a voice to Him from the excellent glory, This is My Beloved Son, in Whom I am well-pleased." St. John's "Only-Begotten" agrees critically with St. Peter's "beloved" (ἀγαπητός), which we know by the Gospels to have been the word which came from Heaven at the time.

In the Transfiguration itself, as well as in the mention of it by the holy writers, and indeed in this whole Proem of St. John's Gospel, may be discerned, I think, the special care of the Holy Ghost to keep before the eye of Faith as well the Personal Subordination of the Son to the Father, as their natural Equality and Consubstantiality.

Full of grace and truth. These high Revelations, and whatsoever else Holy Scripture announces to us from "the third Heaven," are here brought home to the lowliest believer, to the simplest little Christian child. As in Himself the Word is "*the Only-Begotten from the Father*," so to us He is "*full of grace and truth.*" Grace, that is, Favour and Mercy, as distinguished from strict justice; and Truth, that is, Reality and Substance, as distinguished from types and shadows. There is a tacit comparison with Moses' law, which is brought out a few verses after; and indeed it may be said to be developed in the whole of the New Testament; Grace (e.g.) in Romans and Galatians, Truth in Hebrews, in the way of doctrine: and in ways ineffable, Grace and Truth, "Righteousness and Peace," blending together in every line of the Fourfold Image which the Holy Comforter and Guide has drawn for us in the Gospels.

(VER. 15.) *John bare witness of Him.* From the

broad historical sketch of the Dispensation, the Holy Ghost passes to an account, more or less detailed, of the evidence vouchsafed to win our faith to it. John, the Forerunner, stands as the first witness,—the sample and specimen of the innumerable, ever-varying ways, whereby in the course of His outward Providence God introduces us, one by one, to the knowledge of His Incarnate Son. John first; then all we the rest—all Christians from the beginning to the end—are called and empowered, one after another, to bear each his several witness to Him. For to this end we have received inwardly of His Fulness, of the Grace and Truth whereof He is full [m].

In this transition, and perhaps not seldom elsewhere, St. John's manner and train of thought is like St. Paul's; as though what he began with reminded him of something which at first he had not intended. The saying quoted from the Baptist, the occasion of which he is about to narrate particularly, suggested the mention, contained the germ, as it were, of the coming Manifestation of the Word by the Spirit in the Communion of Saints. Carried away to the end of Time, and beyond, (if one may speak as a man), by the thought, the beloved Disciple interrupts the narrative which he had begun of the Forerunner's outward witness (which another Evangelist marks as, "The beginning of the Gospel of Jesus Christ, the Son of God [n],") to seal it

---

[m] It might be a question here, as perhaps c. iii. 31—36, whether the passage be a portion of the Baptist's witness, or a descant of the Evangelist upon it. Origen thinks the former, but St. Augustine and St. Chrysostom, with the Commentators in general, the latter; which is here assumed both in deference to their authority, and because verses 16 to 18 seem to have more of the Fulness of the Gospel than anything that could be uttered before Pentecost.   [n] St. Mark i. 1.

with his own and the whole Church's testimony, not outward, but inward and spiritual, by each one's actual partaking of Christ. Which being done, he is at leisure to return to the particular moment in the Baptist's Mission from which his own witness was to begin. This he does in ver. 19.

John bare [beareth] *witness of Him, and cried* [crieth], *saying, &c.* It may be reverently surmised (according to God's mode of using, not altogether superseding, the natural feelings and powers of His inspired agents,) that St. John was led to begin his narrative from this particular saying of the Baptist, because it had been the providential instrument of his own conversion. Certainly it was so, if he, as some in St. Chrysostom's time thought, was the other disciple, besides St. Andrew, who heard the Baptist speak, and followed Jesus to see where He dwelt Who was declared to be the Lamb of God. His concealing his name would be according to his custom in his Gospel, when any thing is related of himself. And other circumstances will have to be noted which favour the supposition that he had been an earnest disciple of the Baptist.

He *beareth* witness. So it stands—in the present tense, in the Greek, and though the next word, "he cried," is Perfect in form, that also is allowed by grammarians to be, in sense, a present verb, importing, "he cried once, and still continues to cry:" the loud and clear announcement which at the first he uttered has been continued on for our time and for all times. "John is the Word's witness, in that *he cried and yet crieth*, saying," &c.

The expression "*crieth*" answers well to that of

the Prophet:—"The voice of one *crying* in the wilderness º." It is applied in this Gospel and not elsewhere to our Lord's own utterances, and that three times (chap. vii. 28, 37, and xii. 44). In each case it describes an announcement both loud and sudden, applying not to any words that had passed, but to something in the hearer's mind, to which the omniscient Speaker vouchsafes to address Himself ᵖ.

And this is the very description (although the word "cry" is not there used) of the Baptist's mode of proclaiming Christ in St. Luke. The multitude being in expectation, and all men musing in their hearts of John, whether he were the Christ, or not; he speaks (as his Master used afterwards to speak) to their thoughts, and that suddenly, loudly, expressly. This was his "cry"—the same, in substance, as that recorded by St. John; but the latter is much more distinct as to the *degree* of our Lord's excellency.

This was He of whom I spake. He that cometh after me is preferred before me. The Apostle goes back, *not* to the Baptist's original testimony, but to the repetition of it in his own presence, and that in such a way as identified Jesus of Nazareth with the pre-existent Word. As if he should say, "It was of Him, the Word, Who is God, that John Baptist was witnessing, when in my

---

º Isaiah xl. 3; St. Matt. iii. 3.

ᵖ St. Luke applies the word ("cried") in a like way to St. Paul's saying before the Council, "Men and brethren, I am a Pharisee, the son of a Pharisee," (Acts xxiii. 6). He professed his Pharisaism aloud and suddenly, not called on to do so by anything that had been said or done, but instinctively observing the mixed character of the Council, and availing himself of it to interest the one side in his favour.

presence he pointed to the Son of Man and said, This is He."

"*He that is coming after me*, means ' He Who preacheth after me :' not ' He Who came into the world after me.' So St. Matthew (to allege nothing more) implies : ' One is coming after me :' not speaking of His Birth from Mary, but of His being with us to preach the Gospel. For if he were speaking of His Birth, he would not have said 'is coming,' but 'is come ;' for Christ was born when these things were spoken [q]."

In point of time our Lord, doubtless, came into this world after John by six months, and in all probability there was about the same interval between the commencement of their several ministrations. For, as our Lord Himself, in regard it may be to the Mosaical ordinance, waited until He had " begun to be about thirty years of age " before He entered on His work, His servant St. John cannot be supposed to have anticipated that time. At most he preceded his Master by six months : but he *did* precede Him, and more than that, Christ had now condescended to come as one among sinners, and to be baptized by him. Then it became necessary for the holy Baptist to repeat more earnestly than ever what he had all along been impressing on his hearers, as to his inferiority to Him whose Forerunner he was : but he bears his witness now with two remarkable differences. First, " He that is coming after me"—not "*is mightier than I*," but "*is preferred before me*," or literally, "*hath come to be before me :*" alluding, of course, to the visible dignity which our Lord, as Man, had acquired by the Descent

[q] St. Chrysostom, *In Joan. Hom.* xiii. 3.

of the Spirit upon Him and the Voice from Heaven. And next, a greater, an infinite wonder—the account of this ministerial exaltation of our Lord above John and all other Prophets is, "*He was before me*," had an existence of His own, before ever I came into this world, whereby He is the Son of God, and the Communicator of the Spirit of God—*He that baptizeth with the Holy Ghost.* Thus,—O marvellous mystery of Divine Friendship!—the blessed Jesus did, from the beginning, seal the Disciple whom He loved to be the especial Witness of His Godhead to all generations, attracting him, in the first instance, by the Baptist's saying, *He was before me*: and in the end causing him, by His Spirit, to recall and record that moment and that saying as the head and front of his written testimony. In the very act of his conversion he became eminently Ὁ Θεόλογος— St. John *the Divine*.

For He was before me. The phrase means more —indefinitely more—than simply "before me:" literally it may be rendered, "so much before me as no other can be;" and that, not by having become so, but by His very Being from the Beginning: He *was*—not He became—such. It is the same statement in regard of the Baptist, as our Lord Himself made in regard of Abraham, "*Before he was I AM.*" And as the Jews then took up stones to stone our Lord, not enduring what they rightly understood to be a declaration of His absolute Eternity:

[*Here the MS. breaks off.*]

COMMENTARY ON CHAPTERS I.—VI. OF THE EPISTLE TO THE ROMANS.

THE DATE AND SCOPE OF THE EPISTLE.

THE Date of the Epistle to the Romans may be made out with tolerable accuracy by comparing the three passages following:—

Rom. xv. 23, 24. *"Now having no more place in these parts, and having a great desire these many years to come unto you; whensoever I take my journey into Spain, I will come to you."*

25, 26, 27. *"But now I go unto Jerusalem to minister unto the saints. For it hath pleased them of Macedonia and Achaia to make a certain contribution for the poor saints which are at Jerusalem. It hath pleased them verily; and their debtors they are. For if the Gentiles have been made partakers of their spiritual things, their duty is also to minister unto them in carnal things."*

28. *"When therefore I have performed this, and have sealed to them this fruit, I will come by you into Spain."*

This shews, first, that the letter was written before St. Paul had ever been at Rome (see ch. i. 11—15). Therefore it must have been written some time before the conclusion of the history in the Acts.

Secondly, the verses above cited shew that St. Paul

was just on the point of setting out in charge of a collection of alms from the Christians of Greece for the Christians of Jerusalem. Now such a collection is mentioned, Acts xxiv. 17, "After certain years, I came to bring alms to my nation, and offerings." Looking back to the beginning of the journey spoken of, viz. to ch. xx. 3, we find St. Paul just setting out from Greece, that is, from Corinth, the chief city of Greece, for Syria, that is to say, for the Holy Land. And as it appears by the notes in the margin*, the Epistle was probably written from Corinth; and no doubt Acts xx. 2, 3, is the very point in the history to which we must assign it.

Now Acts xx. 3 is generally agreed on by interpreters to bear date A.D. 57, being the third year of the Roman Emperor Nero. And the Epistle was written, as it seems, towards the end of the three months during which St. Paul stayed at Corinth, in the spring of that year, a little before the Passover.

The general Scope of the Epistle may be thus stated:—To set forth, as against both Jew and Gentile, the process of salvation through Jesus Christ, including the two great doctrines of Justification by His Blood, and Sanctification by His Spirit:—then, to shew how those great doctrines may be applied to all parts of Christian morality, and especially to the solution of certain doubtful cases of conduct, then engaging men's attention, or very likely soon to do so.

* Rom. xvi. 1, 23; comp. 2 Tim. iv. 20.

§ I.

ST. PAUL'S SALUTATION TO THE CHURCH OF ROME; WITH SOME ACCOUNT OF THE GROUNDS ON WHICH HE EXPECTED THEM TO RECEIVE HIM (Ch. i. ver. 1—7).

(VER. 1.) *Paul, a servant of Jesus Christ, called to be an apostle, separated unto the gospel of God.*

A servant[b].] More properly '*a slave*,' one who is no more his own, but absolutely and entirely belongs to another. To stand in this relation to our Saviour was accounted by St. Paul the foundation of all honour; which feeling he expresses by so styling himself in the opening of this Epistle, as also of those to the Philippians and to Titus. And not St. Paul alone, but all the Apostles, of whom Epistles are remaining, employ this style. See St. James i. 1; 2 St. Pet. i. 1; Rev. i. 1. In the Old Testament the title is given to Moses[c], to Joshua[d], to David[e].

Separated unto the Gospel.] That is, unto the office of preaching the Gospel, especially among the Gentiles; to which office St. Paul, in the counsels of God, was "separated from his mother's womb[f];" and to which he, with St. Barnabas, had been solemnly "separated" in the Church of Antioch, by inspiration of the Holy Ghost and laying on of hands, about thirteen years before this was written[g].

(VER. 2.) (*Which He had promised afore by His prophets in the holy Scriptures.*)

In the holy Scriptures.] One great purpose of this Epistle being to reconcile Jewish Christians to

---

[b] (α) Gal. i. 10; (β) Acts ix. 15, Jerem. i. 5; (γ) Gal. iv. 4.
[c] Josh. i. 1. [d] Judges ii. 8. [e] Ps. cxxxii. 10.
[f] Gal. i. 15. [g] Acts xiii. 2.

the favour which the Gospel offered to the Gentiles, the Apostle loses no time in introducing this clause, by which he establishes the connection of the two Testaments, and shews how honourably all Christians were bound to think of the Law and the Prophets.

(VER. 3.) *Concerning His Son Jesus Christ our Lord, which was made of the seed of David according to the flesh.*

Our Lord.] In the original the order of this sentence, from ver. 3 to ver. 5, is different from that of the English; as thus:—"Concerning His Son, which was made of the seed of David according to the flesh, which was ordained [to be] the Son of God with power, according to the Spirit of holiness, by the Resurrection of the dead, Jesus Christ our Lord; by Whom we have received grace," &c. Which order seems to answer beautifully to the gradual march of divine knowledge concerning our Saviour. In Him, this passage gives us to understand, the whole Gospel is summed up. And again, the doctrine concerning Him is summed up in two points,—His Manhood, in that He was made, or born, of the seed of David according to the Flesh—by His natural descent through Mary;—and His Godhead, or His being the Son of God with power, declared by His Incarnation, the worker of which was the Holy Spirit, and the proof of it, His raising Himself from the dead.

In fact, the whole sentence corresponds exactly with the third article of the Apostles' Creed, "Who was conceived by the Holy Ghost, born of the Virgin Mary," only the order of the clauses being changed. For the Creed gives the history of our

Lord according to the actual succession of events; St. Paul, in this place, gives it according to the order in which those events were made known to the world.

(VER. 4.) *And declared to be the Son of God with power, according to the Spirit of holiness, by the resurrection from the dead.*

From the dead[h].] This and the former verse together come to much the same as 1 St. Peter iii. 18, "Being put to death in the flesh, but quickened by the Spirit."

(VER. 5.) *By Whom we have received grace and apostleship, for obedience to the faith among all nations, for His Name.*

Grace and apostleship.] That is, the undeserved favour of being an Apostle. He calls it by the same name, ch. xii. 3, xv. 15; Gal. ii. 9; Eph. iii. 2, 7, 8.

Among all nations.] Properly, all the Gentiles; a point which St. Paul's drift in this Epistle required him to keep continually in view. Compare Acts xxii. 21, xxvi. 17, 18.

For His Name.] To be connected with the beginning of the verse; "We have received grace and apostleship in the Name and on the behalf of Jesus Christ;" "we are ambassadors for Him."

(VER. 6.) *Among whom are ye also the called of Jesus Christ.*

Among whom are ye also.] And therefore it is no presumption in me to address you; you are within the limits of my commission.

(VER. 7.) *To all that be in Rome, beloved of God,*

---

[h] (8) Acts xiii. 33; (e) ch. xvi. 26.

called to be saints: Grace to you and peace from God our Father, and the Lord Jesus Christ.

Called to be saints,] i.e. Christians; for so this word is used constantly, both by St. Paul and St. Luke. See below, ch. xv., in which he repeatedy speaks of the collection for *the saints*, and of the *poor saints* which are at Jerusalem; and see also the addresses of the following Epistles:— 1 and 2 Cor., Ephes., Philip., Coloss. Compare Acts ix. 13, 32, 41.

Grace to you and peace, &c.] The regular Christian salutation, being an enlargement of the common salutation of the Jews and all Oriental nations, which is simply, "Peace be unto you." All the Epistles of St. Paul, except that to the Hebrews, have it: (those to Timothy and Titus adding, "mercy," "Grace, mercy, peace" unto thee). It appears also in the two Epistles of St. Peter, and in the Apocalypse. St. John's second Epistle has the same form as those to Timothy and Titus. One or other of the two forms was very commonly used by Christians, in their letters on sacred subjects, for several ages of the Church.

OBSERVATIONS ON § I.

Credentials of a Christian Teacher.

ST. PAUL is here writing to a Church which knew him not, and had never seen his face in the flesh. That, indeed, was the case also when he was writing to the Colossians; but with this difference, that Colosse was near to Ephesus, to Iconium, and many other places, in which St. Paul had been much in person, and had wrought many great miracles; whereas, hitherto, his ministry had been exercised at a very great distance from Rome. On this account perhaps it is, that he sets forth more largely than in other salutations his claim to be heard even by those who had never seen him, as one speaking with all authority on the highest and most aweful subjects. Now, on what does he rest his claim?

It is worthy of very exact observation; for, as the diligent reader will perceive, the case between St. Paul and these Romans whom he had never seen, was in substance the very same with the case between any newly-appointed Pastor and his flock, to whom he is as yet a stranger. What credentials ought the Pastor to bring, and the flock to require of him?

Reply may be made in two words. The congregation must require, and the Bishop or Priest must produce, Apostolical Doctrine, and an Apostolical Commission. The Apostles' Doctrine and Fellowship,—by these, as St. Luke intimates, men continued members of the first Church at Jerusalem, the root and pattern of the whole Catholic Church,—these, therefore, in every change of pastors, are the great points to be secured.

Accordingly, the Apostle sets out by referring the Church of Rome to two remarkable events of his life, on which he grounded his claim to their obedience. First, he had been "called to be an Apostle;" this is a very evident allusion to his first call upon his miraculous conversion, as related in the Acts of the Apostles. Then he had been "set apart to the Gospel," i.e. to the preaching of the Gospel, "of God;" this is a no less evident allusion to his being separated, with Barnabas, by special command of the Holy Ghost, to the work whereunto He had called them both, namely, to the conversion of the Gentiles. Whoever would consider these two transactions, which were both of them now made solemn and public, could have no doubt of St. Paul's being an Apostle, though not one of the first Twelve, nor of his being especially the Apostle of the Gentiles.

Having thus made his *commission* clear, he briefly sums up his *doctrine*:—That he preached Christ to be the Son of God with power, and the Son of David according to the flesh. Whatever he taught was grounded on two grand points,—the Divinity of our Lord, and His Incarnation; the Resurrection being the great evidence of both: of which Resurrection he, like the other Apostles, was ordained and qualified to be an original witness.

Now it is a great privilege of our Church, and of every branch of the Orthodox Catholic Church, that her Bishops and Presbyters are at once introduced to their people on terms which secure both these essential points. Their Apostolical *commission* is made sure by their public consecration or ordination; their Apostolical *doctrine*, by their adherence to the formularies of the Church, particularly to her three Creeds. These are surely great blessings, especially to the great mass of the people.

Consider how much edification would be lost, how much anxiety and discomfort incurred, how many ruinous errors committed, if every person had to judge for himself, as often as a new pastor was set over him, whether he might with a safe conscience receive that pastor's instructions. All which being obviated in orthodox Catholic Churches by the two precautions above mentioned, all that is needed further is affectionate simplicity and constancy, on the one part, in conveying, on the other, in receiving God's grace. Whatever personal defects may unhappily be found in the pastor, the consciences of the flock continue untouched, and free to communicate with the Church through him.

In this point of view, it would seem most unkind to weak brethren, as well as unwise and disorderly in itself, to encourage slight thoughts of the Apostolical commission, or to be forward in undervaluing creeds and formularies.

§ II.

ASSURANCES OF THE INTEREST HE TOOK IN THE ROMAN CHURCH (Ch. i. ver. 8—15).

(VER. 8.) *First, I thank my God through Jesus Christ for you all, that your faith is spoken of throughout the whole world.*

My God.] This expression is used occasionally by St. Paul: see 1 Cor. i. 4; 2 Cor. xii. 21: and often by David in the Psalms; now and then, too, by other prophets, as Ezra, Nehemiah, Isaiah, Hosea, Micah. But generally in passages of high devotional feeling, and not so as to warrant the use of like expressions by ordinary Christians in common conversation.

Through Jesus Christ.] Compare the places in the margin[1], by which it appears that Thanksgiving, as well as Prayer, should always be offered by Christians to the Almighty *in* our Saviour's Name.

Spoken of in the whole world.] A Church in Rome, the capital of the world, would of course draw general attention, rather than in any other place. According even to heathen historians, it had existed at least years before St. Paul wrote this letter. This ancient and famous Church must ever be considered the great glory of Rome; and we ought not to suffer our just abhorrence of her later errors to interfere with our admiration of her long-continued orthodoxy and deep sense of the many obligations we owe her.

(VER. 9.) *For God is my witness, Whom I serve with my spirit in the Gospel of His Son, that without ceasing I make mention of you always in my prayers.*

---

[1] Eph. v. 20; Heb. xiii. 15; 1 St. Pet. ii. 5.

God is my witness.] Here we see that St. Paul, in serious matters, and with strict truth, did not think it unchristian to invoke God as a witness, i.e. in fact, to take an oath. Compare the places in the margin [k].

With my spirit.] That is, "in the purpose of my heart;" "in spirit and in truth," as our Lord expresses it, St. John iv. 24.

Without ceasing.] That is, without leaving you out of any of my prayers of intercession. The same assurance is given to the Thessalonians, 1 Thess. I, 2; and to Timothy, 2 Tim. i. 3. Such passages warrant and encourage the charitable and Christian custom of interceding for those in whose behalf we are especially interested *by name;* which is a good sign of piety as well as of friendship, for it shews that people are in no such great hurry to have done with their prayers.

(VER. 10.) *Making request, if by any means now at length I might have a prosperous journey by the will of God to come unto you.*

If by any means now at length.] Observe how full he is of doubt, how afraid to be confident in his hope of visiting them, and how much he had it at heart. Why, we shall see presently.

(VER. 11.) *For I long to see you, that I may impart unto you some spiritual gift, to the end ye may be established.*

I long to see you.] No doubt there were many then and at all times eager to pay a visit to Rome; but how many with the devout and charitable mind of the Apostle? Those who set their hearts wildly and eagerly upon going to fresh places

---

[k] 2 Cor. i. 23, xi. 31; Gal. i. 20; Philip. i. 8.

and seeing fresh people, merely for their own pleasure and fancy, may do well, perhaps, to compare their eagerness with his.

That I may impart unto you some spiritual gift.] Here he refers to his Apostolical Commission, as being one of those through whom the Holy Spirit had pledged Himself ordinarily to impart His gifts and graces to men. In the same sense, when a man is ordained Priest, the Bishop bids him " receive the Holy Ghost for that Office and Work." The expression is no more presumptuous, than it was presumptuous in that ancient Bishop, St. Paul, to speak of himself as imparting spiritual gifts. This is remarked for the satisfaction of those who may happen to have heard the phrase in our service objected to.

To the end ye may be established.] Or "strengthened," in the faith. Compare ch. xvi. 25, where he speaks of God as of " Him who is able to *establish* you;" thus hinting that they stood in great danger of falling, living as they did in the dissolute metropolis of the world, and the very centre and spring of persecution.

(VER. 12.) *That is, that I may be comforted together with you by the mutual faith both of you and me.*

This verse is an instance of a kind of courtesy (or ought it rather to be called sweetness) very remarkable in St. Paul's character. It seems to have come into his mind that he had been taking rather a high tone with them, and that in the last verse especially, in which he had spoken of imparting to them spiritual gifts. He qualifies, therefore, what he had said, telling them that he longed so much to see them, for his own sake as well as for theirs. He wanted to taste the consolation arising from the mutual faith, i.e. the firm, unreserved confidence in one another, subsisting between himself and the Roman Church. To enter into the spirit of this, consider what a peculiar satisfaction it must be, in bad times, when the true friends of the Church are few, to go where one is sure of meeting with cordial sympathy in one's cares and wishes for her good. If even ordinary Christians feel this, how must a keen and ardent spirit, a self-devoted, single-minded Apostle, have felt it!

(VER. 13.) *Now I would not have you ignorant, brethren, that oftentimes I purposed to come unto you, (but was let hitherto,) that I might have some fruit among you also, even as among other Gentiles.*

I would not have you ignorant, brethren.] This was a form of speaking which marked St. Paul's style in particular, as the places noted in the margin shew[1].

That I might have some fruit.] The only fruit or proof St. Paul thought of, either at Rome or anywhere else, was the edifying and saving souls. "I desire that fruit," says he to the Philippians, "which aboundeth to your account:" to the Corinthians, "I seek not yours, but you." In this only respect, St. Paul was truly greedy and covetous. As some men like to have estates in a great many countries, so St. Paul could not rest till he had acquired to himself a spiritual estate, a set of souls profited by his exertions, in Rome as in other Gentile Churches.

---

[1] Ch. xi. 25; 1 Cor. x. 1; 1 Thess. iv. 13.

(VER. 14.) *I am debtor both to the Greeks, and to the Barbarians; both to the wise, and to the unwise.*

Observe that he is writing from Corinth, where doubtless every day they kept ringing in his ears the difference between Greeks and Barbarians, between the wise and the unwise, i.e. as they proudly accounted it, between themselves and other men.

I am a debtor.] i.e. I have a special duty to perform: so ch. viii. 12, " We are debtors, not to the flesh;" Gal. v. 3, " He is a debtor to do the whole Law."

Barbarians.] It is hardly needful to observe that this means all nations besides the Greeks; who employed the word not in our common meaning, but simply as the Jews used the word Gentiles.

OBSERVATIONS ON § II.

The Intercommunion of Churches.

ST. PAUL, in these verses, offers an example of that truely fraternal spirit which animated our Lord's Apostles, and after them the primitive Christians, towards the partakers of the same faith, however distant from them, and unconnected in other respects. For we must not too hastily ascribe this and other like expressions of feeling to the fervent and overflowing charity of the Apostle himself. It was in great measure characteristic of those early generations of Christians; as may appear by the accounts, in the Acts of the Apostles, of communications between different bodies of Christians; and by many epistles still preserved, which passed among distant Churches for very many centuries afterwards.

The Bishops in Africa, for example, presently knew, and keenly felt, whatever heresies arose in Gaul; and encouraged themselves in primitive usages by correspondence with their colleagues of Asia Minor. The religious

Communities of Gaul and Egypt compared notes, as it were, concerning the more or less edifying effect of the several observances in use among them. In short, a kind of sympathy pervaded the whole frame of the Christian world: any string that was touched, vibrated to the very farthest point which the Apostolic faith and discipline had reached.

That such is not the fact now must be allowed; not, indeed, altogether through any fault of the present generation of Christians. But, without entering into the causes of the change, which are many, and some of them most lamentable, one may observe and regret it, made more striking as it is by the recollection, of how difficult, in comparison, and how expensive it was then, to hold communication between remote countries.

It forms one of the many painful blanks, which meet the eye on looking at things as they are, after a survey, however cursory, of the sacred and primitive history. But if we at all enter into the mind of the Apostle here, if we are sincere in regretting the dearth of brotherly intercourse between Churches in different countries, our regret will not evaporate in empty feeling: it will enter, soberly but very seriously, into our thoughts when we pray for Christ's holy Catholic Church: it will make us, the very poorest of us all, rejoice that he has still opportunities of contributing though it be but two mites, to the welfare of that Church in other regions: it will set us more than ever on our guard against that spirit of irreverence and self-will, which has broken up the Visible Church, formerly one fair whole, into such a number of shattered fragments, loosely and obscurely, if at all, connected. In a word, the humiliation a good Christian must feel, at this and other marks of decay in the Church, will prove, by God's blessing, an effectual aid when he is tempted to heresy or schism, or any kind of presumptuous dealing with the old paths and the good way. God knows, we all stand in need of all the help we can obtain towards learning a due mistrust of ourselves, and of the arrogant principles and practices of the age we live in.

§ III.

ON JUSTIFICATION BY FAITH ONLY (From Ch. i. ver. 16 to Ch. v. ver. 21).

1. *The Subject proposed* (ver. 16, 17).

(VER. 16.) *For I am not ashamed of the Gospel of Christ: for it is the power of God unto salvation to every one that believeth; to the Jew first, and also to the Greek.*

Ashamed.] This was a word of our Saviour's own teaching; see St. Mark viii. 38, "Whosoever *shall be ashamed* of Me and My words . . . . of him shall the Son of Man *be ashamed.*" See also St. Luke ix. 26; 2 Tim. i. 8, 12, 16; Heb. ii. 11, xi. 16; by which it seems that the word means a disavowing, or a shrinking from any thing, for fear especially of ridicule or human censure.

To the Jew first, &c.] The same expression is found, ch. ii. 9, 10; and in both places denotes the perfect impartiality of the Gospel; such, however, as to allow for the preference assigned in the order of God's counsels to His first elect people.

(VER. 17.) *For therein is the righteousness of God revealed from faith to faith: as it is written, The just shall live by faith.*

The righteousness of God.] As if he had said, "A righteousness altogether supernatural, such as man, left to himself, could never have so much as imagined, much less attained unto; a righteousness, not of men, nor of angels, but of God." Comp. Rom. iii. 5, 21, 22, x. 3; Heb. xi. 7; St. James i. 20; 2 St. Pet. i. 1.

From faith to faith.] That is, by a gradual progress, from one degree of faith to another; the same divine principle unfolding itself, through an infinite variety of examples, and under several different dispensations, from the foundation of the world to the establishment of the Kingdom of Heaven. In fact, as St. Chrysostom observes, the whole of the eleventh chapter of the Epistle to the Hebrews is, as it were, an expansion of this short clause, "from faith to faith."

As it is written.] In Habak. ii. 4, which, both here and in the Epistle to the Hebrews[m], the Apostle takes, as it were, for a Text, whereon to discourse of justifying and saving Faith. By this we are quite sure that Faith, in this Epistle, means the same as in that; and the obscurer parts in the one cannot be better explained than by comparison with the other, which is in some respects plainer. Now faith, in the Epistle to the Hebrews, is explained to be "the considering things hoped for as present, and making practical trial of things unseen;" that is, behaving as if those things were real. The same, therefore, must be the meaning of the word, both here and in the Epistle to the Galatians (iii. 11). For there, too, the Text from Habakkuk is quoted, and applied to the saving Faith of a Christian.

Observations on § III. 1.

The Nature of Faith which Justifies.

TRUE Devotion, Justifying and Saving Faith, the righteousness of God revealed from Heaven in the Gospel, is not a single act, not an impulse, emotion, or feeling; but it is a fixed and regular Habit of the mind, capable, like

[m] Heb. x. 38.

other habits, of gradual improvement, and depending for that improvement on Practice. It is not a single act, but a progressive habit, for it goes on, we are told, "from Faith to Faith," from a lower Faith to a higher. And it depends on Conduct, rather than on Feeling; for it is the *practical* "*trial* of things unseen;"—*behaving* as if God's word was true.

Keep steadily, not only with your lips but in your life, to this notion of justifying Faith, and you will, by God's blessing, escape the errors and perplexities which are very apt on that point to beset unguarded or presumptuous minds. Remember that Faith is a *habit*, not a *feeling;* you will not then value yourself on impulses seemingly good, which may visit you, as it were, from time to time; nor will you be too much disheartened if you find no raptures in religion.

Remember, again, that this habit, in order to be strengthened, must be *practised,*—practised in continual acts of Devotion to your Saviour, and Resignation to His will.

Thus you will perceive that true Faith is not an object to take its turn with others, but that it naturally twines and blends itself with every part of a man's life and conduct. This will warn you against the error of those who allow that religion is all very well, *at proper times*, and *in its own province*, but do not see why they should be called on to give themselves up *wholly* to it.

And observe particularly, that it is called throughout, not *our* righteousness, but "the righteousness *of God;*" because, in truth, from beginning to end, it is His; *His*, in that He graciously accepts it *as* righteousness, for the sake of our Mediator, Jesus Christ, imperfect and blemished as it ever must be in us; *His*, in that His gracious Spirit forms the habit of Faith in our minds, and helps us to cherish it by the right use of the Sacraments, and other aids which His good Providence affords; *His*, because, without His teaching, the wisest of men could never have dreamed either of the reward to which Faith aspires, or of the process of Christian Devotion by which

God prepares men for it, much less of the mysterious Sacrifice, the sole meritorious cause of either.

From beginning to end it is the righteousness of God: how then can it be attained, except by entire surrender of one's self to God, through Him who is both God and Man?

§ III. 2.

The Christian Doctrine of Pardon founded on the Misery of Man; and first of the Gentiles (Ch. i. ver. 18—32).

(VER. 18.) *For the wrath of God is revealed from heaven against all ungodliness and unrighteousness of men, who hold the truth in unrighteousness.*

Is revealed.] That is, by the Gospel, as a part, and the first part in order, of the doctrine of "the righteousness of God." For "revealed" here is taken up as it were from "revealed" in the verse before. It follows, that no man must pretend to understand the Gospel, except he have a deep and serious sense of his own and the world's condition without it, as being a condition of misery and ruin. It follows also, that it is a great mistake to consider the Gospel as a dispensation of mercy only, and to forget the terrors of the Lord revealed in it—the terrors of the judgment-day and of eternal punishment, which are, strictly speaking, a part of the Revelation by our Saviour.

Ungodliness and unrighteousness.] The first opposed to our duty to God, the latter to our duty to our neighbour.

That hold the truth in unrighteousness.] Here St. Paul touches the very ground of God's wrath against the Gentile world: They are inexcusable, *because they knew, or might have known, better.*

A fearful sentence for any age or country, which prides itself on superior light and knowledge, except true religion and virtue thrive in proportion.

(VER. 19.) *Because that which may be known of God is manifest in them; for God hath shewed it unto them.*

In them.] Rather, *among* them.

(VER. 20.) *For the invisible things of Him from the creation of the world are clearly seen, being understood by the things that are made, even His eternal power and Godhead; so that they are without excuse.*

(VER. 21.) *Because that, when they knew God, they glorified Him not as God, neither were thankful; but became vain in their imaginations, and their foolish heart was darkened.*

When they knew God.] The Fathers not unfrequently remark on the unconscious testimony which the Heathens used to bear to the one living and true God in their familiar conversation. In their oaths and exclamations, they oftener called on "God" than on "Gods." Thus they were self-condemned for their Idolatry, as common swearers are now for their irreligion.

In their imaginations.] Rather, "in their reasonings;" they were *ingeniously* wrong and absurd. "Reason," says a devout commentator here, "must be very corrupt, since, being given to help men in *finding* God, it has served to remove them farther from Him."

Became vain.] The same phrase appears to be employed emphatically in the Old Testament, of Saul, 1 Sam. xiii. 13; and of makers of idols, Jer. li. 17.

Foolish heart.] Rather, *inconsiderate*, not taking

notice of plain truths and duties. A greater sin than is commonly thought, since it was the source of the guilt and misery of heathenism.

(VER. 22.) *Professing themselves to be wise, they became fools.*

Professing themselves to be wise.] This verse, and indeed the whole tenour of the passage, shews that St. Paul was writing with an especial eye to the so-called wise men among the Greeks. This shews us what to judge, and what to expect, of refinement, civilization, philosophy, without true religion.

(VER. 23.) *And changed the glory of the uncorruptible God into an image made like to corruptible man, and to birds, and fourfooted beasts, and creeping things.*

Changed the glory ... into the likeness, &c.] An expression borrowed from the Psalmist, cvi. 20, "They turned their glory into the similitude of a calf that eateth hay;" and Jer. ii. 11, "My people hath changed their glory for that which doth not profit."

(VER. 24.) *Wherefore God also gave them up to uncleanness through the lusts of their own hearts, to dishonour their own bodies between themselves.*

Gave them up.] So Acts vii. 42, "God turned, and *gave them up* to worship the host of heaven;" and Eph. iv. 19, "Who, being past feeling, have *given themselves over* unto lasciviousness."

(VER. 25.) *Who changed the truth of God into a lie, and worshipped and served the creature more than the Creator, who is blessed for ever. Amen.*

Into a lie.] i.e. into an Idol, which in Scripture is emphatically "a lying vanity." Compare Isa. xliv. 20, "A deceived heart hath turned him aside, that he cannot deliver his soul, nor say, Is there not *a lie* in my right hand?" and Jer. xiii. 25, "Thou hast forgotten me, and trusted in falsehood."

Worshipped and served.] These words involve in the Apostle's censure those Gentiles who, pretending to greater refinement, rejected the Idols in their hearts and opinions, but conformed to their worship and ceremonies. For "worshipped and served" relate properly to *outward* ritual honour. Of course the censure touches also all who, anywhere, on "liberal" or worldly principles, conform to superstition and falsehood, deriding it in their hearts.

Who is blessed, &c.] He adds these words to express most fully his detestation of the impieties he had mentioned, and, as it were, to ask pardon for the very naming of such things. Natural Piety has ever taught devout men to do the like on the like occasions.

(VER. 26.) *For this cause God gave them up unto vile affections: for even their women did change the natural use into that which is against nature.*

This verse takes up and continues the statement which had been begun in ver. 24, and interrupted to insert (ver. 25) a remark on the way in which God's forsaking them did, as it were, answer to their forsaking Him.

(VER. 27.) *And likewise also the men, leaving the natural use of the woman, burned in their lust one toward another; men with men working that which is unseemly, and receiving in themselves that recompence of their error which was meet.*

That recompence of their error, &c.] As righteousness is part of the reward of righteousness (see Ps. cxix. 55, 56, and xix. 11), so one sin is, in a certain sense, the "recompence" or punishment of another.

(VER. 28.) *And even as they did not like to retain God in their knowledge, God gave them over to a reprobate mind, to do those things which are not convenient.*

Did not like.] Did not think proper, did not judge it sound and right.

To a reprobate mind.] A mind, or temper, or way of thinking, altogether unsound and wrong, such as cannot stand the test, proof, or assay. So we read of "reprobate" silver in Jer. vi. 30; and compare Titus i. 16, 2 Tim. iii. 8.

Not convenient.] Not right or becoming: so Eph. v. 4; Philemon 8. The word was then used in a graver sense than it commonly is now.

(VER. 29—31.) *Being filled with all unrighteousness, fornication, wickedness, covetousness, maliciousness; full of envy, murder, debate, deceit, malignity; whisperers,*

Backbiters, haters of God, despiteful, proud, boasters, inventors of evil things, disobedient to parents,

Without understanding, covenant-breakers, without natural affection, implacable, unmerciful.

The terms, in catalogues of this sort, need not always be nicely distinguished from each other: the purpose of them being frequently, only to take in every shade and variety of the general subject, by whatever name denoted. The whole, as a description of unregenerate men, may be compared with that of apostate Christians in 2 Tim. iii. 1—5. There, as here, we have "proud, boasters, disobedient to parents, covenant-breakers, without natural affections," and some other terms which, though not the same, are equivalent to those used in the text. In general, there appears to be this difference; that the vices there mentioned as likely to prevail in the latter times are in general less *outrageous*, more consistent with external *decency*, than those here laid to the charge of the Pagan world before Christ's coming.

Malignity.] Properly, an ill-natured way of expounding questionable conduct; taking everything by the worst handle; contrary to that charity which thinketh no evil, which hopeth all things, and believeth all things.

Whisperers, backbiters.] The first concealed, the second open, defamers.

Without understanding.] Rather, *inconsiderate*, refusing to take notice of God's ways, and the Church's instruction. How many are there, especially among the young, who look on this as a trifle, and a matter of course at their age! Yet here we see it is joined, by St. Paul, with the very worst tempers of lost and condemned man.

(VER. 32.) *Who knowing the judgment of God, that they which commit such things are worthy of death, not only do the same, but have pleasure in them that do them.*

The judgment of God.] That is, the ordinance of God; the law written in their hearts, and preserved among them, heathens as they were, by loose fragments of patriarchal tradition, and faint notices of Hebrew Revelation.

This verse refers especially to the civilized nations of antiquity, and to the writings of their great moralists, as contrasted with their own conduct, and that of those whom they allowed and praised. The emphasis in the latter part of it is much to be observed. If they had only committed the crimes themselves, it might have been by surprise or sudden impulse, their mind and principles not yet being corrupted. But their having pleasure in them that do them, their consenting to other men's shameful conduct, was too plain a proof of the evil having wrought itself into the very grain. It is the same kind of temper which is touched in the Psalm, where in describing the ungodly it is said: " He speaketh good of the covetous, whom God abhorreth." And Psalm l. 18, " When thou sawest a thief, thou consentedst unto him, and hast been partaker with the adulterers." Such is the disposition which makes men idolize heroes and conquerors, and admire men splendid in their crimes; a disposition, as appears by this verse, thoroughly heathenish and unchristian.

OBSERVATIONS ON § III. 2.

How God deals with Men who divorce Morality from Religion.

THE main purpose of this fearful description, no doubt, is to prove the need of supernatural pardon and grace, by exhibiting, in true colours, the actual condition of the world left to itself: to lay the foundation of the Christian scheme in the real, habitual, universal corruption of man; which corruption is, itself, afterwards accounted for (ch. v. 12, &c.) by the original taint derived from Adam.

One very terrible circumstance is, the manner in which God's dealings with the wicked answer to their dealings with Him. *They*, knowing God, would not glorify, nor thank Him: HE permitted them to err and be darkened in their very reasonings and ingenious disputations,— the things on which they prided themselves most. *They* prided themselves in their self-sufficient *wisdom:* HE allowed them to "become fools." *They* changed His glory into vile images: HE gave them up to change the course of nature by vile affections, and lusts that cannot be named. *They* refused to retain Him in their knowledge, in the serious attention of their hearts: HE gave them over to a reprobate mind, interfered not to prevent their moral taste from becoming utterly perverted and corrupt.

And yet there are persons who think, or pretend to think, first, that Morality is all in all; and, secondly, that it may very well be without any particular religion, that is, in other words, without any fear of God. High civilization, polish of mind and manners, order, exactness, conveniency of social intercourse, the luxuries of refined life, corporeal and mental,—these are to many persons as objects, for the sake of which they are even content not to retain God in their knowledge. And this more and more, as generations go on, adding, by ever new discoveries in art and science, to the outward comforts of this present world.

What are the consequences? We see them too plainly in the ordinary vices of great and highly-polished cities, even here where all men call themselves Christians; between which and the Apostle's description, as the resemblance is undeniable, so it cannot be thought on, in the fear of God, without exciting serious reflection what the end of such things must be, how near it may be, and what must be done by each of us, that we may be able to stand when it comes.

§ III. 3.

The Misery and Danger of the Gentile World brought home to each Individual (ch. ii. ver. 1—10).

(VER. 1.) *Therefore thou art inexcusable, O man, whosoever thou art that judgest: for wherein thou judgest another, thou condemnest thyself; for thou that judgest doest the same things.*

Inexcusable.] So above, ch. i. 20, "so that they are *without excuse.*" *There*, it is applied to the world collectively, convicted by the works of the Almighty which are exhibited to it in vain; *Here*, to each particular person, who, on reading the catalogue of sins in the preceding chapter, should express or feel a natural abhorrence of them.

The Apostle speaks to what may reasonably be supposed to pass in every reader's mind. As if he had said, "You are shocked, of course, at such a picture as I have now truly set before you. By that very feeling you condemn yourself. For if you consider the sins which I have enumerated, you will find them, or some of them, a faithful counterpart of your own doings, or at least of your own tendencies." The whole passage is an appeal to the Moral sense, the testimony of God in every man's heart to the present deformity and certain end of sin.

Another.] Rather, "the other;" the other person, whoever he be, of whose transgressions at any time mention is made in your hearing.

(VER. 2.) *But we are sure that the judgment of God is according to truth against them which commit such things.*

We know.] This word St. Paul uses when a thing is evident to people's common sense; so ch. iii. 19, "We know that whatsoever things the law saith, it saith to them which are under the law;" and 1 Cor. viii. 4, "We know that an idol is nothing in the world."

According to truth.] Compare ch. iii. 7, "If *the truth* of God hath more abounded through my lie unto His glory;" and 1 Cor. xiii. 6, "Charity...

rejoiceth not in iniquity, but rejoiceth in *the Truth.*"

(VER. 3.) *And thinkest thou this, O man, that judgest them which do such things, and doest the same, that thou shalt escape the judgment of God?*

Thinkest thou?] q. d. Dost thou *calculate* or *reckon?* referring to the utter, inexpressible *absurdity* of the reasoning.

(VER. 4.) *Or despisest thou the riches of His goodness and forbearance and longsuffering; not knowing that the goodness of God leadeth thee to repentance?*

The riches.] Compare ch. ix. 23; Ephes. i. 7, 18.

Goodness, and patience, and long-suffering.] These words form a kind of gradation, rising one above another: "goodness" is "kind intention at first;" "patience, or forbearance," the same kindness continued even towards sinners; "long-suffering," unwearied perseverance in it.

The goodness of God leadeth—"is leading," or, "would lead"—*thee to repentance.*] Perhaps this is the verse quoted by St. Peter, 2 Ep. c. iii. 9, 15, "The Lord is long-suffering to usward, not willing that any should perish, but that all should come to repentance." ... "And (do ye) account that the long-suffering of our Lord is salvation: even as our beloved brother Paul also according to the wisdom given unto him hath written unto you."

(VER. 5.) *But after thy hardness and impenitent heart treasurest up unto thyself wrath against the day of wrath and revelation of the righteous judgment of God.*

Hardness.] Stiffness, stubbornness, obstinacy of heart. It is the same word in the original which is so often applied to the Jews, when the Scripture terms them "stiff-necked."

(VER. 8.) *But unto them that are contentious, and do not obey the truth, but obey unrighteousness, indignation and wrath.*

Contentious.] Literally, on the side or party of contentiousness. The whole verse strikingly represents the enemies of God in this particular point of view, namely, as a *factious* and *rebellious* set. Comp. Phil. i. 16.

Indignation and wrath.] It may be observed that St. Paul does not say "eternal death," as he had in the verse before, "eternal life," but uses the general phrase, to all such "there is indignation and wrath." The idea having been sufficiently conveyed, he shrinks from the word, and thereby makes his denunciation, taken all together, more aweful.

(VER. 9.) *Tribulation and anguish, upon every soul of man that doeth evil, of the Jew first, and also of the Gentile.*

Anguish.] The same as "straitness," which is used in the Old Testament to express particularly the last extremity of a siege: want, desolation, perplexity, and dread combined. See especially Deut. xxviii. 53, &c.; Isa. viii. 22.

Of the Jew first, &c.] Here St. Paul, having laid his foundation upon principles which must meet with universal assent, gives the first hint of the particular controversy which he meant to settle, by mentioning the distinction between the Jew and the Greek.

Observations on § III. 3.

The Self-condemnation of Christians who believe in the Impartiality of God.

THE statement in the preceding chapter was addressed more particularly to the readers of history, and to those who have leisure, and think they have skill, to take "general views" of things. It cannot, therefore, be fully appreciated without some knowledge of Pagan Antiquity.

But the argument arising from it is such as may be thoroughly comprehended and assented to, even by those who have not the means of comparing it with the testimony of books. For thus it runs. As you read of these things (the horrid immoralities of the Gentiles), you feel a natural shrinking and horror; you condemn them, as it were, by instinct, and at once. Apart from all consideration of their reality, your heart rises up in judgment against them. It needs no learning to help you to that feeling.

Now, then, consider that by such feeling you bear witness against yourself, that it is not through ignorance you transgress when you do the same things. And who has not often done them? Who can say, I have made my heart clear from impurity, covetousness, envy, deceit; my tongue from evil speaking and boasting; my conduct from faithlessness, inconsideration, ill-nature, disobedience to parents, and the like?

Therefore, whatever fair pretences you make, you must be condemned by your own behaviour, compared with what conscience whispers and revelation confirms of "the righteous judgment of God." Privileges, if abused, only serve to make the condemnation more signal and certain. And therefore it is emphatically remarked that the Jews, God's own people, must expect in some especial sense to be *first* in tribulation and anguish if they go wrong, as they may hope to be first in glory, honour, and peace, if found faithful. Jew and Greek will be impartially tried by the same great and eternal principles; only the Jew comes first, as the appointed specimen and sample of God's moral government. He *has* come first, in his temporal sufferings, as one of a nation on which God's mark is set, according to that of the Prophet Amos: "You only have I known of all the families of the earth, therefore I will punish you for all your iniquities."

Recollect how these words have been accomplished, what the Jews as a nation have endured, and judge thereby what Christian souls must expect, if they abuse their greater privileges, and force God finally to cast them away.

§ III. 4.

Impartiality of Divine Retribution towards Jew and Gentile alike (ch. ii. ver. 10—16.)

(VER. 11.) *For there is no respect of persons with God.*

Respect of persons.] Having been brought, as it were incidentally, to the great topic of the present Epistle, the Impartiality, namely, of the Gospel of Christ, as well in respect of Gentiles as Jews, St. Paul begins his discourse on it by repeating the maxim of St. Peter, "God is no respecter of persons,"—a maxim uttered on a remarkable occasion, namely, when the first Gentile was converted, and which would seem to have passed afterwards into a sort of proverb among Christians. See Gal. ii. 6; Eph. vi. 9; Col. iii. 25; 1 S. Peter i. 17.

(VER. 12.) *For as many as have sinned without law shall also perish without law: and as many as have sinned in the law shall be judged by the law.*

Without law.] That is, without any distinct revelation of God's will;—persons who are left to the misgivings of nature, and the relics of original tradition. See the same phrase, 1 Cor. ix. 21. The sum of the verse is, that whether they enjoyed, or considered themselves as enjoying, any special revealed light or not, there will be wilful transgression enough to condemn and ruin them.

(VER. 13.) *For not the hearers of the law are just before God, but the doers of the law shall be justified.*

Justified.] Or "acquitted," or "accounted righteous." So Isaiah v. 23, "which *justify* the wicked for reward." This verse is a confirmation, out of the mouth of God, of the dictate of common sense, that "he that doeth righteousness is righteous." It is opposed to the Rabbinical notion that all Jews, as such, were sure of final acceptance. See St. Matt. iii. 9.

(VERS. 14, 15.) *For when the Gentiles, which have not the law, do by nature the things contained in the law, these, having not the law, are a law unto themselves:*

Which shew the work of the law written in their hearts, their conscience also bearing witness, and their thoughts the mean while accusing or else excusing one another.

These verses come in by way of explanation, the connection with ver. 12, 13, standing as follows: "I say, 'those without law will be judged as well as the Jews.' For in fact they have, though not a distinct revelation, yet a law written in their hearts, their consciences also bearing witness, and their thoughts the mean while accusing or else excusing one another."

When.] That is, as often as; for example, in

their obedience to parents, their gratitude to benefactors, &c. The whole seems to run thus: "In those instances in which Gentiles, not having any definite law from above, do by nature those things which the Law of Moses enjoins," &c.

By nature.] See 1 Cor. xi. 14, for an appeal to the dictates of nature, even on the part of the inspired Apostle himself.

The work of the Law.] That is, what the Law would have them do. "In every such case as has now been mentioned, they shew that they are aware of their duty, though it be not written, as to the Jews it was, on tables of stone" (see 2 Cor. iii. 3), "but only in their hearts and minds." The whole verse presents a kind of picture of a court of justice, (if one may so say,) set up by God's ordinance in every man's heart; the Moral Sense being the Rule or Law, Conscience the witness, and the thoughts and discourses of the man accusers or defenders, as the case may be.

(VER. 16.) *In the day when God shall judge the secrets of men by Jesus Christ according to my Gospel.*

This verse connects with the termination of ver. 13; the two intervening verses forming a kind of parenthetical note.

According to my Gospel.] The same phrase is used, 2 Tim. ii. 8, in speaking of the Resurrection of our Lord. Its being applied here to the judgment to come, shews the error of those who would exclude the "terrors of the Lord" from their notion of "the Gospel."

OBSERVATIONS ON § III. 4.

Concerning the Goodness of Unbelievers.

THERE are two opposite extremes into which men are apt to fall, according to their tempers and course of life.

The most usual is, overvaluing mere natural religion in respect of its worth and efficacy; as though there were any such thing apart from Revelation, which can either make men truely good, or put away the terrors of God's wrath. All such pretences St. Paul at once annuls, by shewing how the very virtues of heathen men and unbelievers would reasonably lead us to judge of their whole condition.

There are some cases in which it may be said, they do the things contained in the Law. There are among them noble examples of fortitude, patience, self-denial, loyalty, filial love, and other real virtues; nay, even (as in the case of Socrates) something nearly approaching to martyrdom for the truth of God. What then? are they thereby justified? No, in no wise; except their whole conduct, both towards God and man, had been consistent with these bright spots.

But, as plain facts shew concerning the best of them, what they did rightly might serve—not indeed of itself to condemn them, God forbid!—but to shew that their wrong-doings were their own fault,—that they knew, or might have known, better.

Now it is evident that this argument turns upon the supposition that they might do, and in some cases did, "by nature the things contained" in the Law. By advancing it, therefore, St. Paul would seem to discountenance also the opposite error of charging them with total unmitigated depravity. Heathens are not left, indiscriminately, without any spark of goodness. Compare ch. vii. 15, "The good that I would, I do not; and the evil that I would not, that I do." Which passage, taken together with the text, would seem to furnish materials for judging, sadly and seriously, but without exaggeration, of the wretchedness of the very best that man can arrive at without the Gospel.

The opposite ways of thinking, thus obviated, are far from being mere speculative errors. Those, on the one hand, who think too much of mere heathen virtue, have great reason to suspect themselves, lest in their own temper and conduct *they*, too, be endeavouring to do without the Gospel. There is a spurious charity abroad in the world, which would give such persons but too much encouragement. For why? "It is enough," people think, "to be *good;*" if you are so, it does not much signify, "be it on natural, that is on heathen, or on evangelical, that is on Christian principles." But they should consider (to go no further at present) what sort of *goodness* that can be, which allows habitual, gross *ingratitude*. For, undoubtedly, it *is* gross ingratitude, if Christ's redeemed do less than surrender themselves, wholly and unreservedly, to their Redeemer.

On the other hand, the opposite temper, I mean the disposition to slight and vilify whatever the Gentiles did right "by nature," has these evil tendencies: It gives advantage to the sneering Infidel, in his constant efforts to persuade men that Faith has little to do with Morality: It perplexes and disheartens those whom our Lord would have cheered, as good beginners, "not far from the Kingdom of God:" And, worst of all, and in our time especially most perilous, it discourages in all men attention to the particulars of conduct, and encourages a kind of national shadow of religion.

Better, surely, on every account, to keep that middle way, which the Apostle not obscurely points out:—To acknowledge the virtues of heathen men and unbelievers, so far as may make us ashamed of our own sins; and to understand, by their gross blemishes and corruption, what must be the end of learning, civilization, liberality, if men think to do without Faith in Christ, and constant Communion with Him in His own appointed way.

§ III. 5.

Futility of Jewish Privileges, supposing their Practice not answerable (Ch. ii. ver. 17—29).

Having established the great principle of impartial retribution on all alike, the Apostle proceeds now to consider how the Jews stand in regard of it. First he allows their privileges (ver. 17—20); then compares their privileges with their performances, (ver. 21—24); then answers a tacit plea of theirs, which they grounded on the promises made to Circumcision (ver. 25—29).

(VER. 17.) *Behold, thou art called a Jew, and restest in the law, and makest thy boast of God.*

Restest in the law.] "*Leanest*, or *reposest* on it; puttest all thy trust in it, and art at ease."

Makest thy boast.] The proper meaning of the word is, "to congratulate one's self upon" any thing. It bears a good or a bad sense, according as the object of self-gratulation is to be really trusted or no; bad, for example, in Psalm xcvii. 7, where mention is made of "delighting one's self in vain gods;" good, in Rom. v. 2, "We rejoice," or "make our boast," "in hope of the glory of God."

(VER. 18.) *And knowest His will, and approvest the things that are more excellent, being instructed out of the law.*

Approvest.] That is, knowingly, after examination had. See ch. xiv. 22; 1 Cor. xvi. 3; and the whole phrase, Philip. i. 10. The expression is addressed to that ordinary feeling of educated persons, that "*they* know better than to be led implicitly by any one;" "*they* are able to compare and judge for themselves."

Instructed.] Literally, "catechized," "trained up as a scholar;" as Theophilus was in Christianity (St. Luke i. 3), and Apollos in the doctrine of St. John the Baptist (Acts xviii. 25).

(VER. 19.) *And art confident that thou thyself art a guide of the blind, a light of them which are in darkness.*

A guide of the blind.] Compare St. Matt. xv. 13, xxiii. 16. It should seem that this and the other titles enumerated here were studiously assumed by the Judaical teachers. For example, Moreh Nevochim, "Instructor of the simple," is the title of the most celebrated work of the most celebrated of the Rabbins, Maimonides.

(VER. 20.) *An instructor of the foolish, a teacher of babes, which hast the form of knowledge and of the truth in the law.*

Form of knowledge.] So 2 Tim. iii. 5, "Having a *form* of godliness, but denying the power thereof." Compare with this whole description the conduct of the Pharisees in the seventh, eighth, and ninth chapters of St. John's Gospel.

(VERS. 21—23.) *Thou therefore which teachest another, teachest thou not thyself? thou that preachest a man should not steal, dost thou steal?*

Thou that sayest a man should not commit adultery, dost thou commit adultery? thou that abhorrest idols, dost thou commit sacrilege?

Thou that makest thy boast of the law, through breaking the law dishonourest thou God?

Compare Ps. l. 16—21; St. Matt. xxiii.

Abhorrest idols.] The original word is one which, of all others in the Greek language, expresses the utmost detestation and loathing.

It is observable that, in this clause, the Apostle gives up the exact correspondence of the members of the sentence with each other; he does not say, as in former instances, "Thou that abhorrest idols, dost thou commit idolatry?" but changes the word to "sacrilege;" probably because idolatry, properly so called, had ceased among them ever since the captivity; on which they greatly prided themselves; not however, as St. Paul intimates, with any very good reason, unless they could be sure that as great a sin, namely sacrilege, had not taken the place of idolatry among them. For the tendency to sacrilege among the reformed Jews, see Malachi i. 6—14, iii. 7—18; St. Matt. xxi. 12, 13; St. John ii. 14—17. There seems to be a hint in this clause well worthy the attention of those Churches, States, and individuals, which think themselves farthest from superstition, and pride themselves most on the purity of their worship; namely, that covetousness, and much more sacrilege is in God's sight as bad as idolatry.

(VER. 24.) *For the Name of God is blasphemed among the Gentiles through you, as it is written.*

FOR *the Name, &c.*] Observe here once for all, that in St. Paul, as in all argumentative writers, such words as "*For,*" "*Therefore,*" "*Because,*" &c., are often used where the object is to make out, not *the thing itself which is being stated*, but *the reason why it is stated*, or *why such and such a form is used in stating it.* Thus here; it is as if he had said, "*I say*, 'Dishonourest thou God?' because God is really, in a Scripture sense, 'dishonoured;' that is, His Name is reproached, &c., through your ill-conduct."

As it is written.] Not in so many words, but in the substance of two famous prophecies: first, Isa. lii. 5, "My people is taken away for nought; they that rule over them make them to howl, saith the Lord, and My Name continually every day is blasphemed." This, however, refers rather to the reproach incurred by their state of captivity; to the punishment of their sin, than the sin itself. The other passage is more directly to the purpose, Ezek. xxxvi. 20—24, "When they entered unto the heathen, whither they went, they profaned My holy Name, when they said to them, These are the people of the Lord, and are gone forth out of His land. But I had pity for Mine holy Name, which the house of Israel had profaned among the heathen, whither they went. Therefore say unto the house of Israel, Thus saith the Lord God: I do not this for your sakes, O house of Israel, but for Mine holy Name's sake, which ye have profaned among the heathen, whither ye went. And I will sanctify My great Name, which was profaned among the heathen, which ye have profaned in the midst of them; and the heathen shall know that I am the Lord, saith the Lord God, when I shall be sanctified in you before their eyes."

Now compare with this prophecy the following statement by Josephus of the general conduct and character of his countrymen and contemporaries: "Those whom the Babylonian warred against, who took our city, and burned it, with the Temple, had not, I conceive, committed any impiety worthy to be compared with your crimes. I for one am persuaded that God has withdrawn Himself from the holy places, and taken part with those against whom now ye are combating. A good man, though he be but a man, will fly from an impure house, and loathe its inmates; and think you that the great God still abides with you in your crimes, He by Whom all hidden things are seen, and all that is buried in silence heard? Although, in fact, among you nothing is kept silent or hidden; all is made known to the very enemies. For you make an open show of your iniquities, and daily contend which of you shall be most abandoned, displaying your profligacy as if it were an excellence." And in another place he says, "To enumerate the details of their iniquity is impossible. I may say in one word, Never did any city suffer so much, nor ever was there, since the world began, a generation more fruitful of crime." And elsewhere, "I cannot refrain from expressing what deep feeling dictates to me. I verily believe, had the Romans been slack in coming upon these devoted ones, that the city would have been swallowed up by the earth opening her mouth, or overwhelmed with a flood, or would have had her portion of such thunders as fell on Sodom. For they who suffered such things fell far short in impiety of the generation which Jerusalem had now bred."

(VER. 25.) *For circumcision verily profiteth, if thou keep the law: but if thou be a breaker of the law, thy circumcision is made uncircumcision.*

Circumcision verily profiteth, &c.] In other words, the being, or not being, a partaker of God's covenant by Moses, of which circumcision was the outward sign.

(VER. 26.) *Therefore if the uncircumcision keep the righteousness of the law, shall not his uncircumcision be counted for circumcision?*

The uncircumcision.] That is, the uncircumcised person. The name was applied to Gentiles in disdain, as appears by Eph. ii. 11, "Ye being in time past Gentiles in the flesh, *who are called Uncircumcision by that which is called Circumcision in the flesh made by hands.*"

(VER. 27.) *And shall not uncircumcision which is by nature, if it fulfil the law, judge thee, who by the letter and circumcision dost transgress the law?*

Judge.] That is, condemn. The same word, among many other places, as in ch. xiv. 20, "Happy is he that *judgeth* not himself in that thing which he alloweth." Parallel places (in sentiment) are St. Matt. xii. 41, 42; the case of the centurion, St. Matt. viii. 10; and that of the Samaritan leper, St. Luke xvii. 18. The Apostle's argument does not suppose that any Gentile had, properly speaking, fulfilled the Law; but that *in those instances in which they obeyed it*, they were a silent condemnation to the Jews disobeying it.

By the letter and circumcision dost transgress the law.] "By way of literal obedience to the law of circumcision," i.e. by a way consistent with such obedience.

(VER. 28, 29.) *For he is not a Jew, which is one outwardly; neither is that circumcision, which is outward in the flesh:*

But he is a Jew, which is one inwardly; and circumcision is that of the heart, in the spirit, and not in the letter; whose praise is not of men, but of God.

Outwardly . . . inwardly.] Or, as in the Sermon on the Mount, "openly . . . in secret," St. Matt. vi. 4, 6, 18.

Spirit . . . letter.] The substance, meaning, and drift of the commandment, opposed to the mere outward thing expressed by it. Compare Rom. vii. 6; 2 Cor. iii. 6. This shews the meaning of "letter" in ver. 27.

OBSERVATIONS ON § III. 5.

The Case of the Jews brought home to Degenerate Christians.

To the Jew first, and also to the Gentile. So the Apostle had told us before it would be found, in the matter both of punishment and reward. The Jew would come first, as a kind of signal pattern or sample of what all might expect from God's sovereign justice and mercy.

The present section enforces and indicates the *fearful* half of this dispensation, the decree of Almighty God to make the *incorrigible* Jews a pattern and sample of His *justice*. Even to our human eyes, says the Apostle, such a proceeding would seem reasonable. For what can be more reasonable, than for the highest privileges, being abused, to bring on the severest punishment?

Granting, then, the very utmost which the Jews thought, and justly thought, of their privileges, what is it but aggravating their guilt and their misery, their conduct being such as it was? Their two chief privileges were, (1) their knowledge of the One God and His will; (2) their especial Covenant with Him, of which Circumcision was the symbol. What if their conduct were notoriously a virtual contradiction of their knowledge, and renunciation of their Covenant? Must they not expect to be "first," that is, most exemplary and conspicuous, in "wrath and anguish," as they had been in talents and privileges?

The application to corrupt and degenerate Christians is too clear to need explanation. Would that it were as easy to impress it on men's consciences, as to lay it before their understandings!

"Thou art called a Christian, and restest in Faith, and makest thy boast in the Redeemer. Thou knowest His good, and acceptable, and perfect will; thou art able to distinguish not only good from evil, but of several goods which is the best, being instructed out of the Gospel. Thou thinkest with reason that God, in calling thee to be a Christian, has called thee to a state of much light and liberty, has taught thee truths, in comparison of which all other knowledge is no better than blindness, darkness, folly, and childishness. Thou, therefore, which art so ready to correct another, dost not thou correct thyself? Thou that sayest, Love thy neighbours, art thou selfish? Thou that professest purity, dost thou indulge wantonness? Thou that abhorrest superstition, dost thou practise irreverence? Thou that makest thy boast in Faith, do thy actions, disowning Faith, dishonour thy Saviour. For, on account of such as you it is, that the Name of Christ is cheaply thought of among the nations which remain unconverted; as the prophets of old foretold would be the case.

"Then, again, as to privileges: thy sanctification by God's Sacraments is a real blessing to thee, if thou keep the law evangelical; otherwise thy sanctification becomes, as it were, unsanctified, and the very heretics, heathens, and infidels, in what they do right, effectually condemn thee. For (as to our acceptance before God) he is not a Christian which is one outwardly, neither is that sanctification which is outward, and of which the world can judge. But he is (in God's sight) a Christian, who is one inwardly, and sanctification is of the heart and mind and purpose, in meaning, not in form only; a kind of character, whereof the discernment, the praise, and the reward belongs to God only, and not to man."

§ III. 6.

Digression to obviate an Objection which might arise on the Statement just made with regard to Jewish Privileges (Ch. iii. 1—8).

(VER. 1.) *What advantage then hath the Jew? or what profit is there of circumcision?*

The course of the argument, in the last section,

might be taken advantage of by those who were inclined to disparage the Jewish Dispensation, or to undervalue Church privileges generally. In order to leave them without pretence, St. Paul suggests principles on which they and all such objectors may be answered. This verse contains the objection; the next, the substance of the answer.

(VER. 2.) *Much every way: chiefly, because that unto them were committed the oracles of God.*

Much every way.] That is, the condition of a Jew has much advantage over that of a Gentile. The word *much* in the original refers to "advantage," and has no particular respect to the ceremony of "circumcision."

Chiefly.] Rather, "in the first place;" as though the writer were commencing an enumeration, which the course of the objector caused him to break off suddenly, not, however, until he had said enough for his present purpose. It was (to say no more) advantage enough to the Jew, and profit enough in Circumcision, that to them were entrusted the Oracles of God. Compare ch. ix. 4, 5.

The Oracles of God.] The supernatural means of knowing God's will, written or unwritten. See Acts vii. 38; Heb. v. 12; 1 St. Peter iv. 11. The unwritten Oracles of God among the Jews were words of Angels or inspired Prophets, sent to them from time to time; signs from heaven, by fire coming down on the altar, or the like; and the revelations made occasionally to the High Priest, through what outward means not distinctly known.

(VERS. 3—8.) *For what if some did not believe? shall their unbelief make the faith of God without effect?*

God forbid: yea, let God be true, but every man a liar; as it is written, That Thou mightest be justified in Thy sayings, and mightest overcome when Thou art judged.

But if our unrighteousness commend the righteousness of God, what shall we say? Is God unrighteous who taketh vengeance? (I speak as a man)

God forbid: for then how shall God judge the world?

For if the truth of God hath more abounded through my lie unto His glory; why yet am I also judged as a sinner?

And not rather, (as we be slanderously reported, and as some affirm that we say,) Let us do evil, that good may come? whose damnation is just.

The argument here seems to proceed as follows. To the statement, in ver. 2, of the great privilege of the Jews in having God's revealed word, it might be objected, that they proved unworthy of that privilege by their sin and unbelief (ver. 3). In short, that practically the Mosaical Dispensation seemed a failure. It is answered (ver. 3, 4), that God's truth and mercy are just the same, and will end to His glory, let men behave as they will.

It is objected again (ver. 5), "Then it seems hard to punish men for what turns out so much to God's glory at last." Answer (ver. 6): "This would prove too much. For by the same rule all distinction of right and wrong will be taken away. As thus: If God cannot justly inflict judgment on the Jews because their unbelief, by His wisdom and goodness, is made to serve the ends of His glory; by the same rule, He cannot judge the world at all. For, when He comes to do so, I or any man might plead as in ver. 7. 'And then (ver. 8) it would be, indeed, as we (the Apostles) are falsely charged with teaching :—All evil might be excused on the plea of leading eventually to good. A doctrine which whosoever holds, his damnation is just." The objection, therefore, against the Christian system, from its pre-supposing a sort of practical failure in the Jewish, falls to the ground; being found to rest on a proposition which would strike equally at the root of all religion, natural as well as revealed, that is to say, at GOD'S MORAL GOVERNMENT. And thus, the Jewish privileges having been vindicated, the argument against sinful man may proceed without prejudice to God's glory.

(VER. 3.) *For what if some did not believe? shall their unbelief make the faith of God without effect?*

Did not believe.] Were not faithful, had the temper of rebels. "Some," in this place, does not mean "a few out of many," but "any, be they who they might." The whole nation, if it should so happen.

Unbelief.] Not simply "not believing," but "having a rebellious, irreligious mind, contrary to the obedience of faith; not submitting one's self to God." So 2 Tim. ii. 13, "If we believe not, yet He abideth faithful;" and compare St. Mark xvi. 16.

(VER. 4.) *God forbid: yea, let God be true, but every man a liar; as it is written, That Thou mightest be justified in Thy sayings, and mightest overcome when Thou art judged.*

Let God be true, but every man a liar.] "Let us regulate our thoughts and conduct on the supposition that God is true, though it involve the other supposition, that every man is a liar." See a like form of expression, ch. vi. 17, "God be thanked that ye were the servants of sin, but ye have obeyed," &c.; meaning, "that *although* ye were the servants of sin, yet now ye have obeyed," &c.

As it is written.] In Psalm li. 4. As if he had said, "The spirit in which we ought to regard this melancholy subject is that expressed by the Psalmist, when he so unreservedly lays the whole blame of his sins upon himself, none of it at all on his Maker." And see St. James i. 13.

In Thy saying.] "In Thy pleadings," an expression borrowed from law proceedings; as also is the following, "when Thou art judged," which is the same in the Greek, as in 1 Cor. vi. 1, "go to law."

(VER. 5.) *But if our unrighteousness commend the righteousness of God, what shall we say? Is God unrighteous who taketh vengeance? (I speak as a man).*

Commend.] Or, as in modern English, "recommend," i.e. "set forth to advantage," "bring into notice and honour." See the same word, ch. v. 8; 2 Cor. iii. 1; vi. 4.

I speak as a man.] So 1 Cor. ix. 8; Gal. iii. 15. It is a sort of apology for introducing topics or expressions which might sound at first unworthy of the subject; as here, for uttering but in a question the thought of God being unrighteous or unjust.

(VER. 7.) *For if the truth of God hath more abounded through my lie unto His glory; why yet am I also judged as a sinner?*

This verse seems to be unfolding the argument alleged in the verse before. A Jew is supposed, pleading against St. Paul's assertion, "that the Law would in general fail to reform men, yet God would somehow turn that failure to His glory. Nay, replies the Jew, then it were unjust for God to take vengeance on our nation, they doing what redounds to His glory." "That argument," rejoins the Apostle, "can never stand, for it makes it unjust for God to judge the world at all. For since, no doubt, all the sin and misery in the universe is somehow overruled to God's glory, any other sinner might say, 'Why am I also judged more than these Jews?' Which being manifestly absurd (for it destroys the difference between right and wrong, and is contrary to all moral feeling, as well as all revealed religion), the allegation of the supposed objector is proved absurd also.

(VER. 8.) *And not rather, (as we be slanderously reported, and as some affirm that we say,) Let us do evil, that good may come? whose damnation is just.*

And not rather.] The sense of the whole verse is, "On the supposition in ver. 8, why should we not even do evil, that good may come?" Of which sort of persons the damnation is most righteous, although some calumniously ascribe that very principle to us Christians.

OBSERVATIONS ON § III. 6.

On the "Failures" of the Gospel.

WHAT St. Paul owns here concerning the Law, we must with shame and sorrow confess, has in a great measure proved true, thus far, concerning the Gospel of Jesus Christ. There are fearful appearances in the world of its failure, I mean, its wanting the success one would have expected from it, considered as a mean of actually reforming mankind. We are not, of course, judges to what extent it has failed: but to say that it *has* failed more or less, is merely affirming the unquestionable truth, that the Christian world is far from what it ought to be.

Now if any person be perplexed at this, and begin to wonder how the plans of Eternal Wisdom should be seemingly so far made void, he may be answered as the Apostle here answers the like difficulty concerning the Jewish dispensation. Man's unbelief, or rebellion, cannot make void the Faith or Veracity of God. As He found a way of accomplishing His promise to Abraham, so He will find a way of performing His Covenant through Christ, however scornful and unbelieving the world may prove. Any appearances to the contrary ought no more to stagger our faith, than the like appearances in the natural world ought to make us Atheists. We doubt not, for example, that the Creator of our bodies had an eye to their health and well-being, though the gracious purpose be so often frustrated by our own intemperance or other causes. Apply the same rule of common sense to matters of Religion, and you will perceive that no amount of seeming failure in the conversion and amendment of souls ought in the least to shake your faith either in the Old or in the New Testament.

A much more ordinary result, however, of the unsatisfactory behaviour of Christians in general, is not so much to perplex one another's faith, as to lower their standard of practice. When all seem to move quietly on, in a sphere so very much below what the Gospel precepts require them to be moving in, a vague but not the less mischievous impression takes place, as though God would not take vengeance, as though He were not so strictly a Moral Governor as the Bible assuredly represents Him. Men silently persuade themselves that allowances and abatements will be made; and thereupon take liberties more and more; taking it for granted, that some examples, indeed, must be made, but that the Almighty will never endure to destroy finally the whole or the greater part of His reasonable creation. And so, if they are no worse than the generality, they somehow or other dream themselves safe.

These whisperings of unbelief should be silenced by reference to God's plain declarations, which no sophistry can argue out of the Bible, that He will judge the world by the rules there laid down. And it should be seriously considered, that to expect impunity after such clear and full warning, is no better than downright Atheism. It is denying God's moral government, which is, practically, having no God, whatever such persons may say or speculate about the order, beauty, and stability of creation.

There is another consideration, which may help such persons to receive, in their full force, those terrible passages of Scripture which they are most anxious to explain away. It is this: that they are not to fancy God's saving word "returning to Him void," though it fail, through man's depravity, to accomplish its saving purpose. We know not what other ends the Gospel Dispensation may be intended to answer, though men should refuse to be the happier for it. One purpose our Saviour has hinted, in saying that it should be preached "for a witness" unto all nations. "Whether you will hear, or whether you will forbear," that purpose is equally accomplished. Away, then, with the vain thought of unrevealed abatements to be made in God's laws, on the ground that otherwise His scheme of Mercy will fail!

This most dangerous and immoral way of thinking, is not the less immoral or dangerous for taking, as it too often does, the pretended form of high Gospel doctrine. As thus: "Our Lord having died for us sinners, His grace in saving any one of us is the more magnified, the deeper the stain of our sins. Therefore, I have the less need to be very careful of my conduct." In this form, the error takes the name of Antinomianism; and it is surely no uncommon error in substance, though, of course, none or very few ever stated it, as above distinctly, to their own minds. Indeed, it is sure by unperceived degrees to spread itself over a man's mind, if he unfortunately use himself to speak much or speculate much on the mystery of Atonement, without corresponding Practice in heart and life. Presently, if he watch, he will find himself making abatements, considering what wrong indulgence he may take, and yet obtain pardon at last; that is, doing evil that God may be glorified in forgiving him.

You see how peremptorily St. Paul denounces such wilful self-deceit: "Their damnation"—who practise it—"is just." Enough, surely, to put every man, who believes at all, on his guard against it. And the only effectual guard is, constantly and humbly endeavouring to *keep the Commandments*.

§ III. 7.

Summary and Confirmation of the Doctrine of Human Depravity out of the Scriptures (Ch. iii. ver. 9—20).

(VER. 9.) *What then? are we better than they? No, in no wise: for we have before proved both Jews and Gentiles, that they are all under sin.*

What then?] Here the argument is taken up from the second verse. "The Jews had much advantage every way;"—then comes in an objection, ver. 3, which is discussed and answered to the end of ver. 8, all which being considered as in a parenthesis, the Apostle here returns to the main argument. "The Jews had much advantage. What then? are we [Jews] better [than they, Gentiles] in the matter of Justification? Have we more right to claim God's pardon than they? No, in nowise."

We have before declared.] Of Gentiles, in ch. i. 18—32; of Jews, ch. ii. 17—29.

(VER. 10.) *As it is written, There is none righteous, no, not one.*

As it is written.] In several places of Scripture, relating to the conduct of several generations of men; which is stronger to prove universal corruption, than if the whole were taken from one passage only. According to the Prayer-book version, which, in that instance, is taken from the Greek, the following verses do occur all together, Ps. xiv. 2—7. But the Bible version of that Psalm, which is more exact from the original Hebrew, corresponds with the text of this chapter only to the end of ver. 12. Compare Psalm liii., whether in the Prayer-book or Bible.

(VER. 11.) *There is none that understandeth, there is none that seeketh after God.*

Understandeth.] Or "taketh notice." The thing complained of is man's profane inattention, as in St. Matt. xiii. 19, "When any man heareth the word of the kingdom, and understandeth it not :"—"pays no attention to it."

(VER. 12.) *They are all gone out of the way, they are together become unprofitable; there is none that doeth good, no, not one.*

They are all gone out of the way.] So Isaiah liii. 6, "All we like sheep have gone astray, we have turned every one to his own way."

Unprofitable.] The word in the original is much stronger; it means, "become rotten, or loathsome." Compare Job xv. 16, "How much more abominable and filthy is man, which drinketh iniquity like water."

(VER. 13.) *Their throat is an open sepulchre; with their tongues they have used deceit; the poison of asps is under their lips.*

The two first clauses of this verse are taken from Psalm v. 9, the last from Psalm cxl. 3.

An open sepulchre.] Deadly, and full of corruption, and so like a sepulchre: ever ready to do mischief to the incautious, and so "an *open* sepulchre." Compare St. Matt. xxiii. 27 ; St. Luke xi. 44.

(VER. 14.) *Whose mouth is full of cursing and bitterness.*

Whose mouth is full of cursing.] From Psalm x. 7. The Apostle adds, "and bitterness," by way of explanation.

(VERS. 15—17.) *Their feet are swift to shed blood: Destruction and misery are in their ways: And the way of peace have they not known.*

These verses are taken from Isaiah lix. 7, 8, and therefore are quite a distinct testimony from the former, referring to a different generation of men; the one to David's time, the other to Hezekiah's. It has been observed that from ver. 10 to 12, men are charged with the evil *root*, irreligion of heart; from ver. 13 to 14, with evil *words;* from ver. 15 to 17, with evil *actions* and habits of life; and then, ver. 18, from Psalm xxxvi. 1, sums up the whole with the want of the fear of God.

(VER. 19.) *Now we know that what things soever the law saith, it saith to them who are under the law: that every mouth may be stopped, and all the world may become guilty before God.*

The Law.] Put here for the whole Old Testament. For the quotations were from the Psalms and Prophets. So St. John x. 34; 1 Cor. xiv. 21.

All the world.] The Gentiles, by the judgment of the Jews, confirmed by the reasoning in ch. i.; the Jews themselves, by these strong passages out of their own inspired Prophets. For there is no reason at all to think that they were worse in David's time and Hezekiah's, than they were before and after.

(VER. 20.) *Therefore by the deeds of the law there shall no flesh be justified in His sight: for by the law is the knowledge of sin.*

"Wherefore by no works of any law can any mortal be accounted righteous before God; neither by the Law of Nature, which failed so deplorably with the Gentiles; nor by the Law of Moses, which failed, as we have seen, no less with the Jews. For all that any law, considered in itself, can do, is to augment people's '*knowledge* of sin,' to make them see more clearly the difference between good and evil, and their respective consequences; which knowledge, if men will not act on it, of course aggravates instead of justifying. And it is now most clear that men *have* always refused to act on it." Compare ch. vii. 7.

Observations on § III. 7.

Human Guilt.

THE Apostle has now brought his argument to this point:—that he has laid the whole world as it were prostrate before God's throne of judgment, waiting for the sentence due to their sins.

But if there be any persons who, not being in their own account guilty of gross and flagrant transgressions, feel as if they could not thoroughly consent to this portion of Scripture, nor enter into the spirit of it; they may do well to consider what use St. Paul here teaches them to make of the sins of others, which they do not deny nor question. St. Paul takes the fashionable sins of the Jews, in the decline of God's kingdom over them; their lying and evil-speaking, their cursing and bitter words, their murderous and turbulent proceedings:—these things St. Paul charges on the whole race of mankind, so far as they are symptoms of that alienation from God of which all mankind are guilty.

This may instruct us what use to make of any remarkable instance of wickedness, whether read of in books, or seen in real life; not too hastily to congratulate ourselves on having no share in that guilt, but rather to turn our thoughts inward, and recollect that, be it what it may, we, too, have the seed of the like iniquity within us. And if we have not plunged to the like depth in actual crime, no thanks surely to ourselves, but all to God's restraining and correcting grace.

Boerhaave, one of the greatest physicians and wisest men of the last century, whenever he heard of a criminal condemned to die, was accustomed to say to himself, "Who can tell if this man is not better than I? or, however, if I am better, it is not to be ascribed to myself, but to the goodness of God." This is more easily said, than thought; and yet it is no more than the dictate of plain common sense. Every man's conscience, if he would consult it, would most likely tell him of many occasions, in which, had he been left to himself, he would have fallen inevitably into great transgression. But some cause which he had nothing to do with, that is, in other words, God's unknown and wonderful Providence, put in his way this or that impediment: something happened to divert his thoughts; or he found he was not alone; or scruples arose unaccountably in his mind.

Can a man have recollections of this kind (and who has not?)—can he own them to himself, and not own, at the same time, that his nature is *very* corrupt? that he owes to the Just God, for this virtual if not actual sinning, an infinitely greater satisfaction than he can pay?

Let this be *seriously* considered, *as in the presence of Him who reads the heart:* it may prepare not only the flagrant sinner, but those too, who, by God's mercy, are or seem comparatively innocent, to open their hearts unreservedly to the gracious remedy provided for this universal disease: "THE RIGHTEOUSNESS OF GOD BY FAITH IN JESUS CHRIST," which St. Paul next proceeds to set forth.

§ III. 8.

The true Method of Justification stated (Ch. iii. ver. 21—26).

(VER. 21.) *But now the righteousness of God without the law is manifested, being witnessed by the law and the prophets.*

" But, as things are, a righteousness supernatural, the free gift of God, is manifested: a righteousness ' without law,' that is, not purchased, earned, or merited, by strict obedience to any law, either of nature or of Moses."

Witnessed by the law.] In the history of Abraham, and in the whole ritual of atoning sacrifice.

And the prophets.] Especially David, Psalm xl.; Isaiah, ch. liii.; Jeremiah, ch. xxxi.; Ezekiel, ch. xxxvi., xxxvii.; Daniel, ch. ix.; &c. Compare St. Peter's words in Acts iii. 24, x. 43.

(VER. 22.) *Even the righteousness of God which is by faith of Jesus Christ unto all and upon all them that believe: for there is no difference.*

The righteousness of God.] That is, a free pardon, proceeding from God, and entirely His own gift. " Pardon," by an easy figure of speech, is called " Righteousness," because, as far as the law is concerned, it puts a person on the same footing as if he had never transgressed.

By Faith.] It comes from God, and is His free, that is, utterly unmerited, gift; and the mean by which we lay hold on it, the condition on which we receive benefit by it, is Faith in Jesus Christ; that is, as it is explained in Heb. xi., a sincere, practical surrender of ourselves to be Christ's own in every respect:—*Behaving as if the Gospel were true.*

Unto all and upon all.] Reaching to all sorts, and abiding upon each individual, so believing; without distinction of Jew or Gentile. Compare ch. x. 12.

(VER. 23.) *For all have sinned, and come short of the glory of God.*

The glory of God.] If this translation be right, it must mean, "such conduct as is to God's glory." But the Greek phrase is the same as in St. John v. 44, "The *honour* which cometh from God only:" and St. John xii. 43, "They loved the praise" (or "good opinion") "of men, more than *the praise of God.*" Thus it would mean, "there is not a man living, but is very far short of what God approves." Where it is said, "all have sinned," perhaps it should be, "*they* all," meaning all that believe, who had been mentioned in the verse before, and whom the verse following goes on to describe as "being justified freely," &c.

(VER. 24.) *Being justified freely by His grace through the redemption that is in Christ Jesus.*

Freely by His grace.] Words could not express more strongly this plain truth, That God's pardon is His free and absolute gift, not earned, or deserved, by our works, or faith, or anything else that can be in us. *Freely*, is used as in St. Matt. x. 8, "Freely ye have received, freely give." *By His grace*, His own mere bounty or favour.

Through the redemption.] This seems to be a sacrificial word, which would be understood by the Jews, because they were used in the service of God to substitute one kind of offering for another, and call it Redemption: thus Exod. xxxiv. 20, "All the first-born of thy sons thou shalt redeem;" and

Levit. xxvii. 28, "No devoted thing shall be sold or redeemed." Compare Heb. ix. 15; Eph. i. 7; 1 Cor. i. 20.

(VER. 25.) *Whom God hath set forth to be a propitiation through faith in His blood, to declare His righteousness for the remission of sins that are past, through the forbearance of God.*

Set forth.] Or "purposed" to be.

A propitiation.] It is the same word which in Heb. ix. 5, and also in the books of Moses, repeatedly denotes the Mercy-seat, or Throne, over which the Lord of hosts, who "sitteth between the Cherubims," was accustomed to reveal Himself miraculously to His people, and from which He vouchsafed to give signs of His accepting their prayers and sacrifices; especially their sacrifices of Atonement. Hence it is applied to our Incarnate Saviour, the true Medium of communication between God and man, through Whom only sinners dare look upward for pardon. And note, that the word, being so applied, conveys a clear hint of His divine nature; since it implies, that in the Man Christ Jesus abode the very fulness of the Godhead.

To declare His righteousness for the remission of sins that are past, through the forbearance of God.] This seems to point out one final cause of the mysterious sacrifice of our Lord. "God designing, in His forbearance, to remit all the past sins of those who should believe, made that awful sacrifice the cost, as it were, of their pardon, and thus reconciled His perfect justice, and holy anger against sin, with His justifying, or pardoning the sincere believer in Jesus."

(VER. 26.) *To declare, I say, at this time His righteousness: that He might be just, and the justifier of him which believeth in Jesus.*

Him which believeth.] Literally, "the man who is of the faith of Jesus;" which turn of expression, in St. Paul, denotes a person's being of such and such a class, side, or party. Thus Gal. iii. 7, "They who are of Faith," are opposed to those who "are of the works of the Law:" so Rom. iv. 16. The full force, therefore, of the words translated "him which believeth," is, "That person who is such as Faith in Jesus requires him to be."

OBSERVATIONS ON § III. 8.

Practical Errors regarding Justification.

MUCH, indeed, were it to be wished, that Christian people might be left free to receive these comfortable assurances of Pardon and Hope in Jesus Christ, without any mention of human errors and perplexities, even by way of warning against them. But since such warnings are absolutely necessary, it may not be amiss to give the substance of them here, in as few words as possible. For there is hardly a page in holy Scripture in which the doctrine of Justification by Faith only is more expressly and strongly stated.

Let no one be startled or confounded at the fact that such errors and perplexities do exist. What else could be looked for in a fallen and corrupt world? Souls naturally alienated from God, would, of course, find themselves alienated and indisposed towards His method of bringing them to Himself. And if the evidence be too strong for them, if they dare not expressly *resist*, they will be tempted somehow to *pervert* His teaching. Perversion and resistance were to be expected beforehand; Scripture itself had warned us of them; therefore, let it be no objection to the faith when such things really occur.

Human nature *resists* the Gospel, because men cannot bear to be told that they do really deserve such things as are revealed from Heaven against them. They go talking and dreaming on, as if they might do well enough, provided they were no worse than their neighbours, only giving way to ordinary infirmity. That is, they first frame to themselves low and mean notions of the Law of God, and thèn insist on being justified *by virtue* of that Law. Each is apt to fix on that point on which he thinks himself most unblemished. This man relies on his generosity; that, on his good temper and mildness; another, on what he calls liberality and candour in his opinions; a fourth, on his industry and zeal in his calling; a fifth, it may be, on his orthodoxy and sincerity in support of true religion; and so on. This seems the *natural* tendency of us all in our view of our condition towards God:—To make our own liking our law, and then, according to our temper, either to *claim* justification by that law, or to *hope* we may be so justified. To indulge such a mind as this, is directly *resisting* the Gospel doctrine. It is the spirit either of Heathenism or Judaism: Heathenism, if men trust to their *natural* good feelings, or good works; Judaism, if they think they may claim God's pardon *in right of* their obedience to *revealed* duties.

Next, suppose a man, by early education, or by consideration afterwards, brought to give up all notion of Justification by works,—brought to perceive (what it seems wonderful that any one should fail to perceive, when his attention is once drawn that way),—That it is in vain for a sinner to think of *deserving* God's mercy. Such a person is no longer a *resister* of the truth in this matter.

But is he free from all danger of *perverting* it? Certainly not, if our Judge require practical Faith, and if it be possible for us to fail in practically believing. A man may renounce all merit but our Saviour's, and yet fall short of saving Faith, either mistaking what faith means, or indolently imagining that it means nothing which at all concerns our practice.

For instance; is it not a clear mistake if you construe

Faith to be simply *feeling* sure that Christ has done all this for you? when Scripture so expressly tells you that the Faith which justifies "worketh by love," that is, it is a practical Habit, gradually forming a man's conversation to the likeness of our Saviour Jesus Christ. In which sense St. James feared not to write, "By works a man is justified, and not by faith only." As if he had said, "That faith which the Holy Ghost, by St. Paul, requires as the only condition of God's pardoning favour, is not to be so understood, as if mere believing were enough; it is *practical* Faith, Trust, Resignation; it is submitting ourselves to the will of Christ *actually* in what we think, speak, and do." In a word, St. Paul's "*Faith*" is the principle in the heart, St. James' "works," the same principle in the life and conduct. Neither of the two is at all *meritorious;* both are equally *necessary to salvation.*

The whole doctrine is briefly contained in the eleventh Article of the Church of England: "We are accounted righteous before God, only FOR the merit of our Lord and Saviour Jesus Christ:" trust we, therefore, no more to "our own works or deservings."

Again, this our pardon or justification is to be applied, as it were, to each of us "by Faith." Therefore, we have need to practise Faith continually; to surrender and resign ourselves wholly to our divine Saviour, not only with our lips, but in our lives.

§ III. 9.

Three Arguments in Support of the Christian Doctrine of Justification (Ch. iii. ver. 27—31.)

(VERS. 27, 28.) *Where is boasting then? It is excluded. By what law? of works? Nay: but by the law of faith.*

Therefore we conclude that a man is justified by faith without the deeds of the law.

The Apostle now proceeds to suggest considerations, very briefly, for confirming and illustrating the doctrine above delivered.

The first may be stated as follows. Boasting (not so much boasting in words, as an irreverent, careless self-sufficiency of mind) is above all things to be avoided in religion : now the notion of being justified by works may offer some encouragement to that evil disposition; the Christian principle of pardon by free grace, takes away from it all excuse,—a great advantage, surely, in the practical tendency of the one doctrine above the other; and consequently a reason why we should "conclude that a man," if justified at all, "is justified by faith, without works of any law."

Boasting.] Not only what is usually called spiritual pride, but also all presumption and light ways of talking and thinking about our eternal state : see note on ch. ii. 17. The Sadducee, no less than the Pharisee, the confident man of the world as well as the hypocritical devotee, comes under the censure implied in this word.

It is excluded.] " Self-sufficiency is now entirely out of the question, since both nature's law and that of Moses, having had a full trial, are found incapable of justifying any man : that is, experience has now proved, what otherwise would not have been so readily allowed, that there is no hope of obtaining pardon in virtue of our obedience to any law."

By what law? of works?] The force of these questions seems to be somewhat as follows : " By which kind of dispensation is it natural to suppose self-sufficiency most entirely excluded ? By a dispensation which supposes men to *earn* God's favour? you will not surely say so. Evidently it must be a rule or dispensation of Faith thoroughly to exclude such irreligious presumption, by sending us to God's unmerited grace for the only fountain of pardon."

Wherefore we conclude.] "We reason, or calculate." As far as this topic, exclusion of self-sufficiency, goes, common sense of itself would lead us to expect, that man should be invited to seek pardon through grace, not through any kind of works of their own.

(VER. 29.) *Is He the God of the Jews only? is He not also of the Gentiles? Yes, of the Gentiles also.*

Is God the God of the Jews only?] One of the strongest prejudices of the Jews against the Gospel doctrine of pardon, was grounded on the indiscriminate admission of the Gentiles to the privileges which they deemed peculiar to themselves. St. Paul, intending to say more on that subject afterwards (see ch. ix.—xi.), here just points out that it was, in one very material respect, a presumption in favour of the Gospel. "The prime Article of that very Law, for the honour of which you are so zealous, is the sovereignty of One God over Jews and Gentiles alike. If He is God of both equally, what so reasonable as to suppose that He will deal with both by the same rule, so that even the very privileges of the Jews might turn out to be part of a dispensation extending to the Gentiles also?"

(VER. 30.) *Seeing it is one God, which shall justify the circumcision by faith, and uncircumcision through faith.*

There is One God.] Compare Zech. xiv. 9, where the Prophet connects in a like way the Unity of God with the future conversion of the world : " The Lord shall be King over all the earth ; in that day shall there be One Lord, and His Name One."

(VER. 31.) *Do we then make void the law through faith? God forbid: yea, we establish the law.*

A third test of truth, in the Gospel doctrine of pardon, is its establishing, or fulfilling, the Law of Moses. This is only affirmed here, by way of protest against an objection sure to arise in almost every mind. In like manner (ver. 21), having said that justification was "without law," he had added immediately the clause, "Being witnessed by the Law and the Prophets." The subject is afterwards enlarged on, ch. vi., vii., viii., and in the concluding part of the Epistle; also especially in the Epistle to the Hebrews. As far as the morality of the law goes, no one who acknowledges the Sermon on the Mount can doubt its being established by the Gospel. "Why ask," says one of the Fathers of the Church, " why ask whether the Gospel keeps entire the command against adultery, when it adds a command against adulterous desire ?"

OBSERVATIONS ON § III. 9.

Humility, Impartiality, Dutifulness, of the Christian Temper.

FAITH being that temper by which men receive God's pardoning mercy exactly as He has revealed it, a sincere believer will take notice of whatever is made known concerning that mercy, in order that he himself may learn to live and act accordingly.

For example ; it being here declared that one purpose of the dispensation of grace was to exclude all boastfulness, those who take God at His own word will above all things be anxious to keep themselves in a very *reverential* frame of mind. They will feel, that whatever else is right or wrong, all lightness, familiarity, carelessness, presumption, in our dealings with our God and Saviour, *must* be wrong, and contrary to the Gospel. If any man indulge himself in such a mind, under the notion that *he* is pardoned, that God is surely on *his* side, that *he* has Faith, and need not live in constant fear and self-denial; such a person, without knowing it, is falling back into that irreverence from which the Gospel was meant to deliver him.

Again, *impartiality*, we are here assured, is a characteristic of God's saving way. He has shewn Himself, by His Son and Spirit, to be no respecter of persons,—a God of the Gentiles no less than of the Jews. It becomes us, according to the good advice of the Church of England in her seventeenth Article, to receive all His gracious promises as they are *generally* set forth in Holy Scripture, that is, as they are set forth of such and such *sorts* of people, not of such and such *favoured individuals*. And as His offers are large and universal, yet always under certain conditions, so should our language be, and our hopes, concerning our brethren; never absolutely despairing of any, nor yet often daring to speak of individuals in a very exulting, triumphant tone; keeping our feelings a good deal to ourselves, and proportioning our judgments, (as far as we *must* judge of them,) to their steadiness and consistency in *bearing the fruits of Faith*. Thus will Christian toleration be kept up, without encouraging lightness and indifference.

Nor let it be supposed that, in cautions like these, too much stress is laid upon our works, to the disparagement of Divine mercy.

For see what, in the next place, is required in him who would receive the Gospel as it is. He must receive it so as not to make void, but on the contrary to establish, the Law. Grace, Faith, Pardon, Mercy, do in no wise annul the declaration of God's good and acceptable and perfect will, but enact it anew, and enforce it with better, and higher, and more endearing sanctions. In a word, the spirit of the Gospel is a *dutiful* spirit: it looks simply to our Saviour's will, and tries as it may to be conformed to His likeness; thankfully availing itself of every help which His good Providence and gracious Spirit afford; shrinking, therefore, from all attempts to disparage the Old Testament, under pretence of exalting the New; or the Sacraments, in order to magnify the Word; or the example of the Church, and Saints of old, on the ground of each person being the best judge what edifies himself.

Against all such instances of presumption, the Faith recommended by the Apostle will set the plain words of our Blessed Saviour: "Whosoever shall break one of these least commandments, and shall teach men so, he shall be called the least in the Kingdom of Heaven: but whosoever shall do and teach them, the same shall be called great in the Kingdom of Heaven."

§ III. 10.

Justification by Faith exemplified in Abraham, and witnessed by David (Ch. iv. ver. 1—8).

(VER. 1.) *What shall we say then that Abraham our father, as pertaining to the flesh, hath found?*

Here an objector is supposed to say, "If all justification is by Faith in Christ, what becomes of the privileges promised in Scripture to Abraham's seed? What hath he found according to the flesh?" i.e. What good thing has been granted him for those who are literally His children? The question corresponds to those in ch. iii. 1.

(VER. 2.) *For if Abraham were justified by works, he hath whereof to glory; but not before God.*

This verse seems to stand in a parenthesis: "I say,

Abraham;" for if it could be once made out that he was justified by the merit of his own works, it would follow that he had "whereof to glory, but not before God;" something to rely upon, besides that treasure of mercy which is wholly and entirely laid up with God: and so the whole of the preceding argument would fail.

Abraham would naturally be referred to here by one objecting, on Judaical principles, because the Jews depended on their descent from Abraham; (see Isa. xli. 8; St. Matt. iii. 9; St. John viii. 33), because he is called "*the righteous man*" in Isaiah xli. 2, and because those "who *followed after righteousness*" were especially bidden to "look unto him" (Isa. li. 1, 2). That is, Abraham is represented to us, in the Old Testament, as a specimen of the way in which man may hope to find favour with God.

If, therefore, on the other hand, it can be proved that he was justified by faith and not by works, the controversy is at once ended. The Old Testament is proved to preach Christianity, and the Jew, on his own principles, must submit himself to the Gospel.

Before God.] Rather, "with God," as in St. John i. 1.

(VER. 3.) *For what saith the Scripture? Abraham believed God, and it was counted unto him for righteousness.*

This is the Apostle's answer to the objection in the first verse, the force of which had been explained in the second. "You ask, 'On the Christian scheme, what becomes of the promises to Abraham and his seed?' Why, what saith the

Scripture? Abraham believed God, and it was counted unto him for righteousness."

For what saith the Scripture?] The form of this question in the original is exactly that used in St. Luke xxiii. 22, and rendered there, " Why, what evil hath he done?"

Abraham believed God.] See Gen. xv. 6. This declaration of the inspired writer occurs after the *third* great trial of Abraham's faith; the first and second being the two commands to migrate, from Ur of the Chaldees into Haran (Acts vii. 2), and from Haran into Canaan (Gen. xii. 5). The third was, his continuing to trust in God's promise, though he still found himself, after so many years, in human appearance as far from its accomplishment as ever. The *perseverance*, in this case, was the great trial: there was no violent struggle required, no strong effort of self-denial for the time; but it was more like the ordinary, daily probation of us all, whether we will wait God's time contentedly and devoutly, though we have not our own will, nor see how we ever can have it. In one word, Abraham's faith was RESIGNATION; of which, though other instances, (especially the sacrifice of Isaac,) were more illustrious, yet this is singled out as especially proper to be a sample to all ages of justifying Faith.

It was counted unto him for righteousness.] The same words are used concerning Phinehas, and his zeal in executing judgment on Zimri and Cosbi, Psalm cvi. 31.

(VERS. 4, 5.) *Now to him that worketh is the reward not reckoned of grace, but of debt.*

But to him that worketh not, but believeth on him that justifieth the ungodly, his faith is counted for righteousness.

These two verses contain the Apostle's reasoning on the text which he had just quoted, which reasoning seems to turn chiefly on the use of the word "imputed."

Thus it stands: Those who are accepted by the Almighty, are accepted as Abraham was. But Abraham was accepted, not in virtue of his having strictly fulfilled the law, but of God's free mercy, *imputing* his faith to him for righteousness. The conclusion is evident. The sentiment of the two verses is exactly the same with ch. xi. 6.

To him that worketh.] The expression seems used in the same kind of sense as when we speak of a man's working in a vineyard, whose "reward," or rather "hire," (see St. Matt. xx. 8,) is not a matter of "grace" or favour, but strictly according to "the debt" incurred by the previous agreement.

Him that worketh not.] That is, who does not stand towards his Heavenly Master in the relation of one doing his day's work, so that in the evening the Master should be his debtor.

The ungodly.] From Josh. xxiv. 2, it should seem that this epithet might once have been applied even to Abraham in the literal sense. "Your Father dwelt on the other side of the flood in old time, even Terah, the father of Abraham, and the father of Nachor: *and they served other gods.*"

(VER. 6.) *Even as David also describeth the blessedness of the man, unto whom God imputeth righteousness without works.*

Even as David.] To confirm his account of Justification, St. Paul produces the witness of David, giving the same account of God's dealings generally, which Moses had given in the particular instance of Abraham. And certainly those Jews, who had any sort of candour in them, could not but acknowledge that Justification by Faith must be somehow reconcileable with their Law, when they found it confirmed both by Moses in the case of Abraham, and by David universally; thus uniting, in support of itself, the three names of which they were justly proudest.

(VERS. 6—8.) *Even as David also describeth the blessedness of the man, unto whom God imputeth righteousness without works,*

Saying, Blessed are they whose iniquities are forgiven, and whose sins are covered.

Blessed is the man to whom the Lord will not impute sin.

It is clear, on a comparison of these three verses, that "imputing righteousness without works" is the same thing as "forgiving sins," "covering iniquities," "not imputing sinfulness."

OBSERVATIONS ON § III. 10.

The Case of Abraham considered as the Pattern of Faith.

THERE is One perfect Model,—our Lord and Saviour, towards Whom we are bound to look up in all things.

Only in one respect He cannot be our pattern; that is, in regard of the right way of receiving the Mercy of God offered to sinners through Him. Our Lord, being wholly without sin, cannot, strictly speaking, be a pattern to sinners of the temper and frame of mind in which they must come to Him for Pardon.

Here, then, is to be admired the unwearied condescension of God our Heavenly Father, and the absolute perfection of His holy Word as a Rule and Guide of Life. In that one respect in which the Son of God, from the nature of the case, *could not* be our Example, we have expressly provided for us, and recommended to our devout imitation, the example of the holy Patriarch Abraham.

Only read or hear, *and consider*, the history of this Father of the faithful, as it is plainly set forth in the Book of Genesis. This will shew you what Faith means; not simply "*believing* God's general Promises," nor "*applying* them confidently to yourself," but "*living by* such belief as your rule." It is sincerely *resigning* yourself to God, body and soul, heart and understanding, to do and to suffer all His Will.

Particularly in that great concern of approaching God in Christ for pardon of our sins, this Faith, Trust, or Resignation will shew itself by our submitting, humbly and entirely, to the Way of Pardon which God has ordained: renouncing all notions of our own merit, and depending entirely on the Cross of Jesus Christ.

Here many will be apt to say, "Certainly, it is all very true; I see, by the light of common sense, that no sinner, how complete soever his repentance, can *claim* Pardon as naturally due to him, since we all owe God a perfect service; and were we even perfect at one moment, *that* could not pay the debt contracted by the imperfection of a former moment. And I see yet more plainly by Scripture, that the Blood of Jesus Christ is set forth as the only means of cleansing man from sin. Whenever I think of this, I assent to it; I never use any other plea in my applications to the Almighty for Pardon. What then is there wanting in my Faith?"

To a person asking such a question, answer might be made, It is yet possible that you have not the substance of true Faith? *How is it with you when matters do not go on to your mind?* If you allow yourself, then, to grumble and fret; if you do not habitually try to sacrifice your own will to the will of Him Who thoroughly knows and loves you; is it not plain that, whatever you may fancy, you do not *quite* acknowledge your own unworthiness? that still, in some unaccountable way, you reckon God Almighty your debtor, and yourself affronted, and ill-used, in not having your own way?

What is there in such Faith at all like the Faith of Abraham? For his whole life was a trial and exercise of Resignation, from his first call out of Ur of the Chaldees, to that greatest triumph over himself, the offering of his only son. Thus Resignation wrought with his works, and by his works was Resignation made perfect. And his name remains for ever a warning to all such as think to be justified by Faith, in the world to come, yet will not trust themselves heartily with their Saviour in the comparatively trifling concerns of this present evil world.

A like warning is to be found in the conduct of those who are held up in Scripture as *the* specimen and sample, if one may so speak, of *Unbelief;* opposed to Abraham, who was *the* specimen and sample of Faith: I mean, the disobedient Jews in the wilderness. With them our part must be, if we will not take it with faithful Abraham. See 1 Cor. x. 1—10; Hebrews iii. 7—iv. 11.

§ III. 11.

Justification by Faith not Invalidated, but Confirmed, by the Abrahamic Covenant of Circumcision (Ch. iv. 9—25).

(VERS. 9—12.) *Cometh this blessedness then upon the circumcision only, or upon the uncircumcision also? for we say that faith was reckoned to Abraham for righteousness.*

How was it then reckoned? when he was in circumcision, or in uncircumcision? Not in circumcision, but in uncircumcision.

And he received the sign of circumcision, a seal of the righteousness of the faith which he had yet being uncircumcised: that he might be the father of all them that believe, though they be not circumcised; that righteousness might be imputed unto them also:

And the father of circumcision to them who are not of the circumcision only, but who also walk in the steps of that faith of our father Abraham, which he had being yet uncircumcised.

The Apostle returns again to Abraham from this allusion to David: as if he had said, The case of Abraham not only enables us to determine that Justification, wherever vouchsafed, must be a free gift, but also that Circumcision is no necessary condition of it.

Circumcision . . . uncircumcision.] i.e. the *state* of a circumcised, or of an uncircumcised, person.

For we say, &c.] The word "For" may be understood as in ver. 3. See note there.

Not in circumcision, &c.] On comparison of Gen. xvi. 16 with Gen. xvii. 1, it appears that the mention of Abraham's Justification comes at least fifteen years before the Covenant of Circumcision. On this verse a pious commentator writes: "Would to God we were as full of faith, love, and integrity, *after* our *spiritual* circumcision (Baptism), as Abraham was *before* his *carnal* circumcision."

And he received, &c. Here the Apostle meets the difficulty. "Wherefore then serveth circumcision?"

The SIGN of circumcision.] Gen. xvii. 11, "It shall be a *token* of the Covenant between Me and you, and thy seed after thee."

That he should be the father, &c.] Gen. xvii. 4, "As for Me, behold, My Covenant is with thee, and thou shalt be *a Father of many nations:*" so vers. 5—7. "Father" means *spiritual* Father or pattern; *resembling* those to whom he is a Father, as Parents commonly resemble their own children. So St. John viii. 39, 44; 1 St. John iii. 2, 3, 9—11; Isaiah li. 1, 2.

Walk.] Literally, "walk *orderly*," by a line or rule marked out: see Acts xxi. 24; Gal. v. 25, vi. 16; Phil. iii. 16. The word is very expressive of the nature of Abraham's Faith, that it was not one great effort, but a matter of sober every-day practice.

In the steps.] " By a very scrupulous and careful imitation," 2 Cor. xii. 18; 1 St. Pet. ii. 21. Does not this make it the duty of Christians to observe and copy very devoutly the practical results and details of Abraham's Faith?

(VER. 13.) *For the promise, that he should be the heir of the world, was not to Abraham, or to his seed, through the Law, but through the righteousness of faith.*

Here St. Paul, in his consideration of Gen. xvii., passes from ver. 4 to ver. 8, that is, from the promise that he should be a Father of many nations, to the promise that he should possess the land of Canaan; which latter promise the Apostle teaches us to interpret by Abraham's being "heir of the world." Compare Ps. xxxvii. 9; St. Matt. v. 5; St. James ii. 5. The connection, therefore, of St. Paul's argument stands as follows:—" As the first promise to Abraham on his circumcision, that he should be father of many nations, so also the second, that he should be heir of the world, came not by any law," (was not earned by any merit of his,) "but only through God's gracious acceptation of his sincere faith instead of merit." (N.B. That promise also had been given to Abraham long before. See Gen. xii. 7; xiii. 14—17; and especially xv. 7, 18—21.)

(VERS. 14, 15.) *For if they which are of the Law*

be heirs, faith is made void, and the promise made of none effect:

Because the Law worketh wrath: for where no law is, there is no transgression.

"For if they only who are righteous by law,"—(that is, by perfect obedience to a divine law, in other words, by merit of their own,)—"be heirs, this is implicitly making void the faith which was first accepted" (Gen. xv. 6, 7) "as a qualification for heirship, and the promise which was then made," (compare Gal. iii. 17). "Because the Law, though not in its extent, yet in its actual result, worketh only wrath: giving more accurate knowledge of what is sin, but no clear revelation of Atonement, Sanctification, or everlasting Life."

(VER. 16.) *Therefore it is of faith, that it might be by grace; to the end the promise might be sure to all the seed; not to that only which is of the Law, but to that also which is of the faith of Abraham; who is the father of us all.*

"Therefore the expression, 'by Faith,' is used. Men are said to be justified 'by Faith,' rather than by Charity, Devotion, Holiness, or the like; that all the world might clearly understand Acceptance and Pardon to come of God's free grace, as promised to Abraham before his circumcision." For of all the names by which the Christian temper is denoted, *Faith* is that which points most directly to Christ as the only Fountain of Pardon and Grace, at the same time expressing entire renunciation of every kind of self-sufficiency.

To ALL the seed.] As if he had said, "Upon the whole, we may conclude that the spiritual seed of

Abraham, not his natural seed only, were chiefly intended in the promise." The following verses to the end of the chapter explain who are his spiritual seed.

Of us all.] That is, of all Christians, whether Jews or Gentiles.

(VER. 17.) (*As it is written, I have made thee a father of many nations,) before Him whom he believed, even God, Who quickeneth the dead, and calleth those things which be not as though they were.*

Who quickeneth the dead.] Alluding, perhaps, on the one hand, to the great trial of Abraham's Faith, the Sacrifice of Isaac; to which, as we know, he was encouraged by his Faith in a possible Resurrection (Heb. xi. 19); and, on the other hand, to God's wonderful work of mercy in quickening the Gentile world, dead in trespasses and sins (Eph. ii. 1); which to a Jewish eye was, as it were, " raising up of these stones children unto Abraham."

And calleth those things which be not as though they were.] This, again, may refer to the Promise of the birth of Isaac, on the one hand; on the other, to the calling of the heathen, which is described by the same expression (1 Cor. i. 28), "God hath chosen the things that are not, to bring to nought things that are."

(VERS. 18—21.) *Who against hope believed in hope, that he might become the father of many nations, according to that which was spoken, So shall thy seed be.*

And being not weak in faith, he considered not his own body now dead, when he was about an hundred years old, neither yet the deadness of Sarah's womb:

He staggered not at the promise of God through unbelief; but was strong in faith, giving glory to God;

And being fully persuaded that, what He had promised, He was able also to perform.

St. Paul, carried, as it were, away by a generous admiration of Abraham, expatiates on the details of his history, and shews how they enhanced the nobleness of his faith, when he was promised an heir through Sarah; then (vers. 23—25) transfers the whole to the case of devout Christians.

Against.] Rather, "beyond" hope.

That which was spoken.] Which had been spoken, when he was bidden to look up, and see if he could count the stars, Gen. xv. 6.

Now dead.] Heb. xi. 12, "Therefore sprang there even of one, and him *as good as dead*, so many as the stars of the sky in multitude."

Staggered not.] It is the same word in the Greek as Acts xi. 2, "They that were of the circumcision *contended* with Peter;" and Acts x. 20, "Go with them, *doubting* nothing." The strict meaning is, "He *disputed* not within himself against God's promise." Natural misgivings he had at first (see Gen. xv. 2, 3; xvii. 17, 18), but he did not indulge them by any temper of unbelief. *Involuntary* doubts, then, are consistent with acceptable Faith; but not doubts cherished, encouraged, and acted on.

(VER. 22.) *And therefore it was imputed to him for righteousness.*

Here the Apostle, like a Preacher at the end of a sermon, recurs to his text, repeating, and shortly applying it.

(VERS. 23, 24.) *Now it was not written for his sake alone, that it was imputed to him;*

But for us also, to whom it shall be imputed, if we believe on Him that raised up Jesus our Lord from the dead.

Raised up Jesus.] We have seen that the Resurrection of the Dead was a great point in Abraham's Faith, and every one knows that it is a chief point in ours. So the one faith resembles the other in *the thing believed*, as well as in the *kind of belief*.

(VER. 25.) *Who was delivered for our offences, and was raised again for our justification.*

For our justification.] That is, because we were justified, because our pardon was earned by His Death and Passion, God raised Him, our Surety and Representative, from the dead. The Resurrection sealed the Father's acceptance of the meritorious Sacrifice of the Son. For "if Christ be not raised, your Faith is vain; ye are yet in your sins," 1 Cor. xv. 17.

OBSERVATIONS ON § III. 11.

ABRAHAM is "the Father of us all," the Father of all true believers, "before God." Doubtless, God sees things as they really are, and, therefore, our relation to the holy Patriarch must be more than a mere figure of speech. It is grounded indeed on resemblance; but the privilege itself goes much further than that; and will be found, on serious thought, a matter of great admiration and thankfulness.

Let us consider it in this way:—(1.) What Abraham gains, by being the spiritual father of the Faithful; (2.) What they gain by being his children.

The first may be estimated in some way by reflecting how great the blessing is, if a man have but one child truely devout and dear to God. "The father of the righteous shall greatly rejoice, and he that begetteth a wise child shall have joy of him. Thy Father and thy Mother shall be glad, and she that bare thee will rejoice[a]." Conceive this blessing multiplied, as it were, by the whole number of faithful people, and you will have some idea of the privilege of him who is before God the Father of all believers.

God, in His mysterious bounty, promises to impute (if one may say so) to Abraham, the Christian Piety and Resignation of all the Saints, after the same manner as He imputes to a watchful and fond parent the improvement and good conduct of his children. For, indeed, the example of Abraham, diffused as it is by the Scripture through all times and countries, is continually doing the same sort of good as the example of a pious parent does to a child; and, indirectly, it may profit thousands who never, it may be, heard of his name, or have heard it without knowing his history. For if they follow some other pattern, which was itself immediately or remotely reflected from Abraham, they still are, by faith, his posterity, and every one of them adds to his reward.

How this comes to pass; *how* the successive conversions and advances of Christian men, in this lower world, can do any good to Abraham in his state of rest, as we cannot know, we must not enquire: but the fact seems unquestionable from holy Scripture, and the God of Abraham, to be sure, has abundant ways of accomplishing His word.

One thought, naturally suggested by our Lord's own manner of speaking, is the thought of Abraham welcoming his spiritual descendants, one by one, as they enter into their rest. Assuredly this was the expectation of the Jews in our Lord's time. The death of a good man, they thought, was passing into "Abraham's bosom." The happiness they looked forward to was, "sitting down with Abraham in the Kingdom of Heaven." It is obvious

---

[a] Prov. xxiii. 23, 24.

that our blessed Saviour's parables, while they refined and elevated this thought, by no means contradicted nor warned people against it; but rather gave men to understand that some such honour, as they supposed, was indeed shewn in the next world to the great Father and Pattern of them all.

Now here is held out peculiar encouragement to devout parents, watchful Masters, and all who, being entrusted with others, take care to be *exemplary* to their charge. *All* the faithful are blessed with Abraham, but these have a peculiar blessing. For, depend on it, it is not in vain that the following promise is set down in the Scripture, over and above God's other favours to Abraham:— "Abraham shall surely become a great and mighty nation, and all the nations of the earth shall be blessed in him. For I know him that he will command his children and his household after him; and they shall keep the way of the Lord, to do justice and judgment; that the Lord may bring upon Abraham that which He hath spoken of him."

May we not, in virtue of this sentence, humbly hope that such as follow Abraham in the quiet practice of household duties, will hereafter so far partake of his reward, that they, too, may recognise their children and children's children; their servants also, and *their* children, receiving their portion in the Paradise of God?

Further, since there are many persons who feel being childless as a great affliction; what if such consider that they may, by God's grace, obtain to be accounted before Him the Parents of all whom they, by good example or charitable influence of any kind, may help to win over to the way of holy obedience? They may feel lonely here, but He will give them a family in Heaven, "a place and a name better than of sons and of daughters;" just as He provided for the holy Patriarch an innumerable progeny, even all the faithful, over and above his children after the flesh.

Now, as to what we gain by being Abraham's spiritual children: first, it is a very clear instance of the high and consoling privilege of Communion between Saints on Earth and Saints in Paradise; which privilege, however disdained in our time, was so dear to the first and purest ages of Christians, that they gradually filled their year with Saints' Days, expressly for the devout exercise of that Communion.

And surely, in so doing, they acted in the spirit of the Apostolical commemorations of Abraham, and other ancient worthies. Surely the cold faithlessness of modern days, which would teach us to look at our Fathers gone before as no more to us than good historical examples; surely this temper of mind is reproved by St. Paul's representing Abraham as a real Father, by adoption, to us all, to be remembered as such, when we praise God in the Communion Service for "His servants departed this life in His faith and fear;" and more especially, perhaps, to be remembered by those (in this sinful world not a few), who either do not know their parents, or cannot remember them, but with pain and confusion of heart! Let such know that if they be faithful, Abraham is their Father, their spiritual Father, not in figure only, but by real appointment of Him, "of Whom the whole family of heaven and earth is named."

Were all the privileges here to be specified, which follow on our being in this sense the seed of Abraham, this would be in fact to go over the Patriarch's entire history. For "to Abraham and his seed were the promises made:"—the promise that the Lord would be their God, their shield, and exceeding great reward; the promise of the best that this world can give (for that is the spiritual meaning of the land of Canaan); and the promise of life and glory in the other world, implied in God's everlasting Covenant. So completely,—though as yet dimly, and in parable,—was the Gospel preached before to Abraham; and so perfect is the Unity which binds together the whole Church and Congregation of the Faithful, by virtue of Him who is the true Seed of Abraham, the Author and Finisher of our Fathers' Faith and ours.

§ III. 12.

Statement of Christian Privileges consequent on Justification (Ch. v. ver. 1—11).

(VER. 1.) *Therefore being justified by faith, we have peace with God through our Lord Jesus Christ.*

Peace with God.] St. Paul, having established the doctrine, proceeds now to point out some of its happy results. First, as to our *state* and *condition;* we were before enemies to God, now we have Peace with Him; according to the song of the Angels, when our Lord was born (St. Luke ii. 14). And therefore "the God of Peace" is one of the Titles by which St. Paul delighted to call the Almighty; and "Grace and Peace," as was observed before, is the ordinary salutation among Christians. And our Saviour is especially called "our Peace" (Eph. ii. 14). The proper meaning of the word is that God, for Christ's sake, looks on us not as enemies but as reconciled persons. Sometimes it is used to express *our own comfortable sense* of being so reconciled; as in St. John xvi. 33, "These things have I spoken unto you, that in Me ye might have Peace." In that sense, of course, it must be perceived by the person enjoying it; but, in the former and more proper sense, it "passeth all understanding." Many have it, and perceive it not; some, it is to be feared, think they perceive it, and are very far from having it. And in this sense, namely, as denoting God's being at peace with us, it is here declared to be a result of Justification. It is the state of Amity, following the Act of Pardon.

(VER. 2.) *By Whom also we have access by faith into this grace wherein we stand, and rejoice in hope of the glory of God.*

Access.] This is one of the words made sacred, as it were, by Apostolical use to express our Saviour's mercy, as a Mediator introducing us, to be forgiven by His offended Father. So St. Peter (1 Ep. iii. 18) says, "He once suffered for sins, the just for the unjust, *that He might bring us to God.*" "For through Him we both (Jews and Gentiles) have access, by one Spirit, unto the Father," (Eph. ii. 18; compare ch. iii. 12).

This grace.] "This favour or bounty of the Father."

And rejoice.] This is a second happy result of Justification: the first was, our being in a state of Pardon, and after it comes Cheerfulness, resulting from the reasonable hope which we consequently have of "the glory of God," that is, of everlasting life (see Rev. xxi. 11); or, more probably, God's approbation (see St. John xii. 43, and Rom. iii. 23, with the note there). N.B. This cheerful hope is the *natural* result of Justification and admission to Christian Privileges. But it is not always the *actual* result, bodily infirmities and mental perplexities intervening. In such a case, the dejection must be borne as one would bear a bodily disease: it is not to be charged on the conscience as a sin, nor is it a bad sign of our spiritual condition, except it be accompanied by known and habitual transgression.

(VERS. 3—5.) *And not only so, but we glory in tribulations also: knowing that tribulation worketh patience;*

And patience, experience; and experience, hope:
And hope maketh not ashamed; because the love of God is shed abroad in our hearts by the Holy Ghost which is given unto us.

Here St. Paul extends the ground of Christian cheerfulness: now that we belong to Christ's people, we may rejoice, not only in hope of future glory, but also in present tribulations and trials, knowing, &c. The turn of expression seems to intimate that what follows, to the end of ver. 5, was a kind of saying among Christians; possibly part of a chant or hymn, for it flows like the poetical parts of the Old Testament. The very same expression occurs, St. James i. 3, "My brethren, count it all joy when ye fall into divers temptations, *knowing this, that the trial of your faith worketh patience.*"

Experience.] That is, "the actual proof of the reality of your Faith." (Compare 2 Cor. ii. 9, xiii. 3; Phil. ii. 22.) "Affliction, borne sweetly and patiently, *tests* your Faith, which might otherwise deceive you; and then you may have the more reasonable hope." Does not this sufficiently disprove the notion that true faith is a peculiar kind of feeling or process in the heart, bringing with it its own evidence? For, were it so, there would be no occasion for affliction and patience to attest a man's faith to himself.

Hope maketh not ashamed.] That is, disappoints not. See ch. ix. 33, and x. 11, from Isaiah xxviii. 16, "Whosoever believeth on Him shall not be ashamed;" shall not find himself put to that confusion which men endure when their chief trusts fail. The reasoning here seems to be, That this hope, thus confirmed by affliction well endured, cannot disappoint we know, first, by the gift of the Holy Spirit, shed abroad in our hearts, as an earnest of the love of God (ver. 5); and secondly, by the consideration of what our Lord endured for us while we were yet aliens from Him (vers. 6—10).

Is shed abroad.] "He says not simply, It was *given*, but, It was *shed abroad* in our hearts; intimating the abundance of the gift. For He gave not heaven, and earth, and sea, but that which was more precious than all these,—that which made us angels instead of men, sons of God, and brethren of Christ; that is to say, He gave us the Holy Ghost. Now, were it not His will, our trial being over, to bestow on us some most glorious crown, He would not, before our trial, have endowed us with so great a blessing°."—(Compare Eph. i. 14; where the Holy Spirit is called the *earnest of our inheritance*).

(VER. 6.) *For when we were yet without strength, in due time Christ died for the ungodly.*

Without strength.] Sick, weak, and helpless; in our natural condition.

In due time.] According to the Prophets.

(VER. 7.) *For scarcely for a righteous man will one die: yet peradventure for a good man some would even dare to die.*

For scarcely.] As if he had written, "I say, *For the ungodly;* for it is much if any one submit to death even for a righteous person." (I make this allowance, because, now and then, we *do* see

---

° St. Chrysostom, Ninth Homily on Ep. to Rom., § 3.

people sacrificing their lives in a good man's cause.)

(VER. 8.) *But God commendeth His love toward us, in that, while we were yet sinners, Christ died for us.*

Commendeth.] So ch. iii. 5, " If our unrighteousness *commend* the righteousness of God;" that is, "set it forth to advantage, make it appear the more admirable."

(VER. 9.) *Much more then, being now justified by His blood, we shall be saved from wrath through Him.*

From wrath.] Rather, "*the* wrath," "the wrath to come," 1 Thess. i. 10.

(VER. 10.) *For if, when we were enemies, we were reconciled to God by the death of His Son, much more, being reconciled, we shall be saved by His life.*

Reconciled to God.] Compare 1 Cor. v. 18—20.

(VER. 11.) *And not only so, but we also joy in God through our Lord Jesus Christ, by Whom we have now received the atonement.*

And not only so, but we also joy, &c.] The construction is, " We shall be saved, being reconciled, &c.;" (as in ver. 10), " and not only reconciled, but also rejoicing, exulting, having a cheerful hope in God, &c." The Apostle recurs to the same two blessings which he had mentioned in the beginning of the chapter as the result of justification,—Peace with God (ver. 1), which is the same with reconciliation here; and Joy, or glorying, in hope, confirmed (among other things) by trouble patiently endured (ver. 2, 3).

The atonement.] That is, "the reconciliation" aforesaid: for atonement and reconciliation are the same word in the original; and "to atone," in old English, means "to set *at one* those who disagree."

OBSERVATIONS ON § III. 12. (Ch. v. ver. 1—11.)

THE foundation being thus laid,—that all who receive God's pardon receive it by Faith only without works, that is, through the merits of our Saviour only, and not through any desert of their own,—St. Paul proceeds to point out some of the privileges resulting from that gracious dispensation.

Now there are persons who look on it as the very first and chiefest of those privileges, that the person pardoned is assured, not only of his present interest in the Gospel, common to him with all Christians, but of his own final, everlasting salvation. Let us see how this doctrine agrees with the Apostle's way of speaking here. For this is the place where, of all others, one might expect a clear and distinct account of such assurance, supposing it a certain result and token of Justification. Here, where St. Paul is expressly enlarging on the happy and comfortable fruits of Justification, if absolute personal assurance be wanting, which, if real, would naturally be the very first mentioned, surely there arises a strong presumption that such assurance ought not to be insisted on as a necessary token of our being in a good way.

What, then, is the fact? In the first place, the expressions are all general: "*We* have peace with God," "*We* have access by faith," "*We* rejoice in hope," &c. *We*, i.e. the whole body of Christians, *as such; we*, of whom the next chapter fully proves, that we are still in danger of continuing in sin, of letting it rule in our mortal body, of yielding our members as instruments of unrighteousness. Such warnings and cautions would be needless, if a man's future conduct and condition were made sure to him from the first moment of justification.

Surely in this, as in all other points, the advice of the Church of England is sound and Scriptural, "We must receive God's promises, as they be *generally* set forth to us in holy Scripture;" not greatly anxious about appropriating them to ourselves in any other way than by following "that will of God, which we have expressly declared unto us in God's word."

In the next place, St. Paul says here, that the joy, or thankfulness of heart, which naturally belongs to a Christian's condition, is a joy felt "in hope of the glory of God," or "in hope of God's final approbation." Now, as the same St. Paul tells us a little further on (ch. viii. 24), "Hope that is seen is not hope; for what a man seeth, why doth he yet hope for?" The very notion of Hope, then, excludes that absolute certainty, which puts away all fear, and admits no chance of falling away.

Further; absolute positive assurance admits of no confirmation or increase: but the joy which St. Paul describes here is increased and confirmed by patient endurance of affliction. Patient endurance is a practical proof or trial, appointed to satisfy the conscience more and more, that the faith of the sufferer is genuine, and his hope such as will not disappoint him.

Who does not see at once that this is a very different state of mind from what some are taught to imagine and long for, both in themselves and in others, a state of mind in which people seem to themselves as certain of their future salvation as they are of their present existence? St. Paul's joy and glory, as represented in these verses, was far unlike this. It was a sober conviction of God's merciful purpose towards him, gradually strengthening with his patient continuance in well-doing.

Does any one think that his faith is more genuine than the faith of St. Paul, or that he has a right to expect a more comfortable hope than his? Why, then, should not Christians be content to measure their faith by their patient endurance, and other good works, as St. Paul did? Such a view may not at first sight overpower and dazzle, like the notion of absolute certainty. But, as it clearly tends to make men more watchful and humble, so, in the end, it will be found more cheering and consoling; not leading us to force ourselves into unnatural postures of mind, nor to keep up excitement of any sort; but sustaining and impelling us continually in the plain path of duty, which, after all, must be the only path of comfort and salvation.

Nor is this view at all inconsistent with the strong expressions of many good men, implying a kind of certainty of salvation, especially towards the latter part of their lives. Their certainty was still no more than a reasonable and assured hope. For Hope may be in all shades and degrees, from the sense of a faint possibility, such as is expressed in the Burial Service over the grave of such an one as may have repented for aught we know, to the joyful anticipation of an Apostle on the eve of martyrdom: "I have fought a good fight, I have finished my course, I have kept the faith: henceforth there is laid up for me a crown of righteousness." Yet the same Apostle, a while before, felt it needful to keep in remembrance the possibility of his being "a castaway," and to take precautions accordingly.

Doubtless, it is safer for ordinary Christians to imitate him in that sober, self-denying carefulness, rather than to aspire eagerly after his last triumphant assurance. Neither in this, nor in any other respect, is it well to seek too much of Heaven on earth. They who do so, are always in more or less danger of having their reward in earth and not in Heaven.

§ III. 13.

Correspondence between the Manner of our Fall in Adam, and that of our Recovery by Jesus Christ (Ch. v. ver. 12—21).

(VERS. 12—21.) *Wherefore, as by one man sin entered into the world, and death by sin; and so death passed upon all men, for that all have sinned:*

(For until the Law sin was in the world: but sin is not imputed when there is no law.

Nevertheless death reigned from Adam to Moses, even over them that had not sinned after the similitude of Adam's transgression, who is the figure of Him that was to come.

But not as the offence, so also is the free gift. For if through the offence of one many be dead, much more the grace of God, and the gift by grace, which is by one Man, Jesus Christ, hath abounded unto many.

And not as it was by one that sinned, so is the gift: for the judgment was by one to condemnation, but the free gift is of many offences unto justification.

For if by one man's offence death reigned by one; much more they which receive abundance of grace and of the gift of righteousness shall reign in life by one, Jesus Christ.)

Therefore as by the offence of one judgment came upon all men to condemnation; even so by the righteousness of one the free gift came upon all men unto justification of life.

For as by one man's disobedience many were made sinners, so by the obedience of one shall many be made righteous.

Moreover the law entered, that the offence might abound. But where sin abounded, grace did much more abound:

That as sin hath reigned unto death, even so might grace reign through righteousness unto eternal life by Jesus Christ our Lord.

This difficult passage follows, by way of general remark and deduction, from the view which had just been given of Justification by Faith and the privileges resulting thereon. It is one of the many places where it is peculiarly necessary to remember that St. Paul is writing a Letter, not a Treatise regularly arranged. We must expect, therefore, that he should occasionally interrupt himself, and insert explanations and remarks, such as a modern writer would subjoin in a note. The thirteenth and fourteenth verses of this chapter, as also the twentieth and twenty-first, appear to be insertions of this kind.

The course and order of the whole section may perhaps be truely stated as follows (ver. 12). " It appears, by what has been said, that there is a mysterious correspondency between the manner in which Sin and Death entered in, and prevailed in the world," (upon which prevalence, vers. 13, 14, is a *note*); "and the manner in which God vouchsafes to redeem and sanctify us: nay," (vers. 15—17) it is much *more* than *correspondency*. The favour of God, through Christ, and the effects of that favour, do *more* than answer to the curse on Adam, and effects of the Fall. Therefore (vers. 18, 19), the Apostle limits the comparison, for the present, to the circumstance that it was *one Act, of one Person,* which led to the whole in each of the two transactions: in other words, that Adam and CHRIST JESUS were respectively the Sureties and Representatives of all mankind.

As to the twentieth and twenty-first verses, they are evidently a kind of note likewise, to sum up briefly the purpose and effect of the Law, how it also magnifies God's mercy in the whole scheme of Justification as before explained.

Came into the world.] See Wisdom of Solomon, ii. 24, "Through envy of the Devil death came into the world." This was written, most probably, before the birth of our Saviour, and may shew how the Jewish Converts at Rome, to whom especially St. Paul was writing, had been used to think of Adam's fall, before they were Christians.

For that.] Rather, "on condition of which," "at the risk of which." All sinned, under the certain peril of death, the declared wages of sin, passing upon them. And death did pass upon them accordingly; as had been foretold in Gen. ii. 17, "In the day that thou eatest thereof thou shalt surely die."

All have sinned.] Compare c. iii. 23, "*All have sinned*, and come short of the glory of God."

The thirteenth and fourteenth verses appear to be what we should call a Note on the last clause of ver. 12. "Death passed upon all men, at the peril of which all men sinned. All, I say, sinned, at the known risk of the penalty of Death. How does that appear? Because, except where Law (which implies moral government, and of course a penalty), is known, sin is not accounted sin, properly speaking. But, that it *is* accounted sin in all mankind appears by the actual infliction of the penalty, Death; even upon those who would seem, at first sight, least liable to such penalty:—upon the generation between Adam and Moses, which had no covenant so *expressly* revealed for them to sin against, as Adam had revealed to him in Paradise."

Unto the Law.] Rather, "as far as Law reached;" meaning, that if there be any persons, or any portions of human life, to which Law does not reach, in them there can be no sin, properly so called; sin being, as is defined by St. John (1 Ep. iii. 4), "The Transgression of the Law." See before, ch. iv. 15, "Where no Law is, there is no transgression." St. Paul is not speaking in this verse of the Law of Moses only, but of all declarations of God's will, natural or revealed.

Of Adam's transgression.] The sinners between Adam and Moses sinned least in the likeness of Adam, because they had not the Word of God, forbidding what they did, under pain of His wrath, so distinctly revealed to them, as Adam had before, and as Jews and Christians have since.

A Figure of Him that was to come.] That is, of our Saviour, who is called, "the last Adam," and "the second Man" (1 Cor. xv. 45, 47). In what sense was Adam a Figure of our Lord? "Because," says St. Chrysostom, "as Adam caused death to all who sprang of him, though not themselves partakers of the forbidden fruit; so Christ, to all who are of Him, though in their past lives unrighteous, is become a warrant and surety of righteousness, His free gift to us all by His Cross."

But not as the offence, so also is the free gift.] Observe here the unaffected earnestness of the Apostle, stopping short, as it were, and correcting himself. For thus the sentence runs, connecting it with ver. 12. "As by one man sin and death came into the world, and passed unto all men; so—nay, not exactly so—*Not* as the offence, so also the free gift. Not exactly so, but in much greater perfection. Of which greater perfection one mark is what is mentioned, ver. 16, that, whereas *one offence* was enough to cause the Fall, the Restoration was after *numberless* offences. Another (ver. 17), That the reign of pardoned sinners in Life, through Christ, is much more *complete* than the reign of Death, by Adam.

The Grace of God.] That is, Pardon and Justification; "the *gift by grace*," that is, "the HOLY GHOST given unto us" (ver. 5). For that is called eminently, "*The* gift of God," Acts viii. 20; compare Acts x. 45, xi. 17. In Eph. iii. 7, it is, "The gift of the grace of God;" in Heb. vi. 4, it is, "The heavenly gift."

Not as it was by one that sinned, so is the gift.] Here St. Paul, like one writing eagerly, leaves out several words, to be supplied by the common sense of the reader. The whole meaning of this clause not being, "Not exactly as *the condemnation came* by one that sinned, so *did* the gift *come by one that was righteous;*" but in a way to set forth God's mercy still more wonderfully, which the latter part of the verse explains.

The judgment was by one.] That is, by one offence, namely, Adam's one act, in tasting the fruit of the forbidden tree.

By one man's offence death reigned by one.] In consequence of the transgression of Adam, death reigned over all, derived through the same Adam as the Father of all men.

The Offence of one . . . the Righteousness of one.] Rather, as it is in the margin, "*by one offence . . . by one righteousness.*"

Were made sinners.] Properly, "were *brought into court*," as it were; "were *presented before their Judge as sinners.*" The same word, in Acts xvii. 15, stands for "*conducted;*" in Heb. v. 1, for "*ordained;*" implying in each case something *formal* and *official.*

The Law.] Rather, *Law*, omitting the Article: That is, not simply the Law of Moses, but *any* positive Rule of Conduct whereof God is known to be Author. The *apparent* result of such a rule, introduced among creatures so sadly fallen as we are, might be merely to multiply offences; and no doubt was so in many cases. So much the more entire and signal was the triumph of Grace by Jesus Christ over the sin and guilt of disobeying known rules, as well as over the sin and guilt inherited by all mankind from Adam.

Entered.] Literally, "came in by-the-bye." In Gal. ii. 4, the same word stands for "came in privily." Here it implies that what is after mentioned, namely, the multiplying of offences, was something *by-the-bye*, not the *intent* of the Law.

That the offence might abound.] The word "*that*," here, as in many places, denotes the *result*, not the *purpose*, of what was done. As we say in common discourse, "Such a person went to such a place *to die;*" not meaning that he intended to die there, but that such was *actually the event* of his going. An instance may be found, St. Matt. ii. 23, "Joseph went and dwelt at Nazareth, *that it might be fulfilled* which was spoken by the Prophets:" not that he was thinking of the Prophecies, but he acted so that they were fulfilled. So here: the word "that" points out not the *purpose* but the *effect* of any divine Laws or Rules which might be laid on man in his lost state. The *result* would be, that sin would more abound. But from this, God took occasion to magnify the more His grace and mercy.

Through Righteousness.] There seems something very emphatical in the introduction of these words:

implying that Christ saves us not *in* but *from* our sins.

Observations on § III. 13.

Of Original Sin.

It is somewhat remarkable that in this Epistle, where St. Paul treats so much at large of the method of our salvation by Christ, he should go on so far before introducing the subject of *Original* Sin.

For first, he humbles the whole world by his unanswerable reproof of *actual* Sin. Then in the Name of Jesus Christ he offers the only way of deliverance. And not till *after that* does he recall to our thoughts the *source* of our corruption, and our *natural* impotency for good.

This order of teaching, so carefully observed by the Apostle, would seem to shew how men should order their meditations on the great truths of the Christian System; and how teach others (if such there be) for whose instruction they are responsible: Not to dwell, first and chiefly, on natural impotency, but on actual guilt: To acknowledge, indeed, with deep humiliation, that we are, one and all, born in iniquity; yet to bear in mind continually that, in our Lord and Saviour Christ Jesus, to Whom we are united by Holy Baptism, we have a present and effectual antidote to the mischief with which we are tainted. Thus, never separating in our thoughts Adam from Christ, the disease from the remedy, our own frailty from the power of Him Who is pledged to be our Strength and Protection, we shall neither forget our original sinfulness, nor make it an excuse for actual sin.

For these are the two opposite errors into which men are apt to fall. Some of us at all times, and almost all of us, with regard to those sins to which we feel no particular inclination, are disposed to *make light* of the fault and infection born in our souls and bodies. It is good, then, for all to be continually reminding themselves of it; and, with good Bishop Wilson, seriously to pray God that He would "give us a true knowledge of ourselves, of the corruption of our nature, and of the necessity of His gracious help to save us from ruin."

On the other hand, by a strange perverseness, when those sins come in our way to which we are so evidently inclined, that we cannot hide our ill tendency from ourselves, we are presently too apt to begin thinking of our original corruption, not as a ground of wholesome fear, but as a sort of excuse to quiet our consciences, and reconcile us to our own presumptuous sins.

There is always a deceiver at hand to help us in thus deceiving ourselves; to come in with such sayings as these: " Every man has his fault," " It is all in vain trying to be perfect," "We are born in a wicked world, and cannot go out of it," and the like.

Now the simple and short answer to all this is, that, whatever may be said of unregenerate Heathens, baptized Christians are in that condition, in which it is expressly promised, that, however sin may have abounded, grace shall much more abound. That is, however corrupt they may be, the Holy Spirit, offered in Christ's Ordinances, is more than able to purify and strengthen them. Thus every mouth is stopped, and the whole world of impenitent Christians especially made guilty before God.

How stands the case in regard of bodily disease, the punishment and effect of sin? A man's constitution has some hereditary taint: how will common sense direct him to deal with himself? To neglect the unsound tendency altogether, and just behave as if nothing at all were the matter with him? Or, if he cannot help thinking of it, yet to take liberties prejudicial to his health, under the pretence that, be he never so careful, the constitutional infirmity cannot be entirely cured? Nay, but to use all reasonable care in the way of watching, precaution, and palliation; that he may pass his time, if not in ease, yet in as little distress as possible.

It is much the same in regard of the soul's health;

except that the matter at issue is eternal, and that a certain and perfect recovery is offered, if the sick man will but persevere in obeying his infallible Physician.

§ IV.

OF SANCTIFICATION BY THE HOLY SPIRIT, THE NEXT INTENDED RESULT OF JUSTIFICATION (Ch. vi. 1—viii. 39).

I. *Sanctification enforced as a Duty, first, from the Typical Death, which all Christians undergo in Baptism* (Ch. vi. 1—14).

(VER. 1.) *What shall we say then? Shall we continue in sin, that grace may abound?*

That grace may abound.] This expression is repeated from the twentieth verse of the preceding chapter: "Where sin abounded, grace did much more abound." From it, St. Paul takes occasion to pass to the next great branch of his subject, the necessity of good works in those who are justified; to prevent that abuse, to which in all ages the doctrine of Pardon without Merit has been liable.

(VER. 2.) *God forbid. How shall we, that are dead to sin, live any longer therein?*

We who are dead unto sin.] That is, in respect of sin; so ver. 10, "He died unto sin once;" ch. vii. 4, "Ye are dead to the Law." The meaning is, It is as much out of the question for baptized and justified Christians to obey sin, as for a dead body to perform the actions of a living one. In respect of committing sin, they are to consider themselves dead and helpless, like a corpse. So also in Col. iii. 3, "Ye are dead, and your life is hid with Christ in God." In these and all similar places, not the actual but the natural result of admission into the Christian Covenant is intended: for example, in 1 St. John iii. 9.

(VER. 3.) *Know ye not, that so many of us as were baptized into Jesus Christ were baptized into His death?*

Know ye not.] This implies that the Romans, and all Christians, might be expected at once to enter into the notion of being "dead to sin;" a notion which, as the next verse intimates, was carefully taught by the very act of Baptism.

Baptized into Jesus Christ.] So in Gal. iii. 27, and in 1 Cor. x. 7, we read of the Jews being "baptized unto Moses," that is, admitted by Baptism into Communion with Moses and with Christ respectively. "To be baptized into His death," therefore, is "to be introduced by Baptism into a Participation of His Death;" not only by having it imputed to us, as it were, for Pardon of our sins, but also by actual conformity to it, in our *dying* to those sins for the future.

(VER. 4.) *Therefore we are buried with Him by baptism into death: that like as Christ was raised up from the dead by the glory of the Father, even so we also should walk in newness of life.*

We are buried with Him by Baptism.] Alluding to the original Form of that holy Sacrament, in which the baptized person was, as it were, *buried* for a moment under the water, and without delay *raised again.* Comp. Col. ii. 12; and the Baptismal Service of the Church of England, "Baptism doth *represent* unto us our profession, which is, to follow the example of our Saviour Christ, and to be made like unto Him; that as He died and rose again for us, so should we who are baptized die from sin and rise again unto righteousness." The force of such passages is much obscured among us by the general use of sprinkling instead of immersion,—a thing *allowed* rather than *encouraged* by the Church.

By the glory of the Father.] That is, most likely, "By His Divine Nature, which He receives of the Father, being from all Eternity GOD OF GOD, Light of Light, Very God of Very God." Comp. St. John xi. 40, where our Lord, speaking of the Resurrection of Lazarus, says, "Said I not unto thee, that if thou wouldst believe, thou shouldst see *the glory of God?*" raising the dead being a work appropriate to that most glorious Nature. And, therefore, Christ's raising Himself (St. John ii. 19) is proof of His being Very God.

Like as Christ . . . so we.] Compare 2 Tim. ii. 11, "If we be dead with Him, we shall also live with Him." This St. Paul cites as part of "a faithful saying;" that is, not improbably, a proverbial expression in use among the Primitive Christians.

(VER. 5.) *For if we have been planted together in the likeness of His death, we shall be also in the likeness of His resurrection.*

Planted together.] As if he had said, "*grafted into* Him by the likeness of His death," "by that Baptism which resembles His death."

We shall be also.] Or, "We *are to be* also" like Him, in leading a new life of holiness, by way of preparation for a Life of Glory like His in heaven.

(VER. 6.) *Knowing this, that our old man is crucified with Him, that the body of sin might be destroyed, that henceforth we should not serve sin.*

Our old man.] Our old, merely human, corrupt

Nature, such as we inherited it from Adam. Compare Ephes. iv. 22; Col. iii. 9.

Crucified with Him.] So Gal. ii. 20, "I am crucified with Christ; nevertheless I live, yet not I, but Christ liveth in me;" meaning that by the Virtue of Christ's Cross and Holy Spirit, communicated to us in Baptism, we have power to overcome sinful tendencies, so that sin shall utterly die away in us, and be powerless, like a man crucified and dead.

The body of sin.] That is, the whole power or substance of sin, made up of many bad habits and inclinations, as a man's body is of many limbs.

May be destroyed.] The word properly means, "made useless, inefficient, helpless, powerless;" in the Baptism Service it is "*abolished*," where after the Baptism prayer is made, according to the meaning of this verse, for the child or person just baptized, "that he, being dead unto sin, and living unto righteousness, and being buried with Christ in His death, may crucify the old man, and utterly abolish the whole body of sin; and that, as he is made partaker of the death of the Son of God, so he may be partaker of His resurrection."

(VERS. 7, 8.) *For he that is dead is freed from sin.*

Now if we be dead with Christ, we believe that we shall also live with Him.

These two verses seem to run into each other, thus, "He who is dead is in any case free from sin; but we who are dead *with* Christ trust also to live again in righteousness with Him."

Is freed.] This word is in opposition to "serving sin," or "being the slave of sin," in the verse before.

(VER. 9.) *Knowing that Christ being raised from the dead dieth no more; death hath no more dominion over Him.*

Death hath no more dominion over Him.] "Is no longer His Lord and Master." The figure of speech from slavery being kept up, as in vers. 6, 7.

(VER. 10.) *For in that He died, He died unto sin once: but in that He liveth, He liveth unto God.*

Once.] "Once for all; no more to return to corruption. In the same sense he says in Heb. ix. 27, 28, "It is appointed unto men *once* to die: . . . so Christ was *once* offered."

(VER. 12.) *Let not sin therefore reign in your mortal body, that ye should obey it in the lusts thereof.*

Your mortal body.] Opposed to the glorious, immortal body of our Lord Jesus Christ, which had been mentioned just before, vers. 9, 10. See the like opposition, with the like stress upon the word *mortal*, ch. viii. 11, and 2 Cor. iv. 11.

Thereof.] That is, of the body. The desires of the mortal body are the most prevailing instruments by which sin contrives to subdue Christians to slavery again. "*Purity*" is the great point on which evangelical freedom depends.

(VER. 13.) *Neither yield ye your members as instruments of unrighteousness unto sin: but yield yourselves unto God, as those that are alive from the dead, and your members as instruments of righteousness unto God.*

Yield.] Or "present." The word in the original has especial reference to a person's appearing before a superior. So 2 Tim. ii. 15, "Study to *shew* thyself approved unto God;" Col. i. 28, "That I may *present* every man perfect;" and see below, vers. 16, 19, "Let not sin, but God, be the Master, to whom, as servants anxious to be approved, you present your members and your whole selves."

(VER. 14.) *For sin shall not have dominion over you: for ye are not under the law, but under grace.*

Shall not have dominion.] Or, is not to be your master and owner. See ver. 9.

Ye are not under the Law, but under grace.] Not under a dispensation which only gives you *knowledge* of right and wrong, without giving you the grace of the Holy Spirit to do right. *You* have, or may have, that grace; therefore, it is in vain for you to plead that you are serving a hard Master against your will. You are delivered from that yoke which your Fathers were not able to bear.

The following is in short the substance of this whole section:—

VER. 1. The possible abuse of Justification is answered, (ver. 2), by considering the Christian's Death unto Sin, which (ver. 3) takes place at, and is signified by, Baptism: which Baptism implies (vers. 4, 5) a typical Resurrection too, upon consideration (vers. 6, 7), first, of the abolition of the tyranny of Sin implied in the typical Death, and (vers. 8—11) secondly, of the Death of Christ, into which we are baptized, being a death once for all, and his Life, an eternal one. Vers. 12, 13 are an earnest exhortation to live in purity, according to this faith; (ver. 14) the excuse of inability to resist temptation being now completely gone.

[*Here the MS. breaks off.*]

PROCESSIO SPIRITUS SANCTI.
The Doctrine of the Procession of the Holy Ghost.

The critical words in this controversy are:—

α. ἐκπορεύεσθαι, which is used only twice of the Holy Spirit; first in St. John xv. 26:—

ὅταν δὲ ἔλθῃ ὁ Παράκλητος, ὃν ἐγὼ πέμψω ὑμῖν παρὰ τοῦ Πατρός, τὸ Πνεῦμα τῆς ἀληθείας, ὃ παρὰ τοῦ Πατρὸς ἐκπορεύεται, ἐκεῖνος μαρτυρήσει περὶ ἐμοῦ.

When the Comforter is come, whom I will send unto you from the Father, even the Spirit of truth which proceedeth from the Father, He shall testify of Me.

And again in Rev. xxii. 1:—

καὶ ἔδειξέ μοι καθαρὸν ποταμὸν ὕδατος ζωῆς, λαμπρὸν ὡς κρύσταλλον, ἐκπορευόμενον ἐκ τοῦ θρόνου τοῦ Θεοῦ καὶ τοῦ Ἀρνίου.

And he shewed me a pure river of water of life, clear as crystal, proceeding out of the throne of God and of the Lamb.

That this last means the Holy Spirit, see St. John vii. 38, 39:—

ποταμοὶ ἐκ τῆς κοιλίας αὐτοῦ ῥεύσουσιν ὕδατος ζῶντος. τοῦτο δὲ εἶπε περὶ τοῦ Πνεύματος.

Out of his belly shall flow rivers of living water. But this He spake of the Spirit.

β. πνεῦμα itself; which, spoken of the Persons of the Holy Trinity, one amongst another, must be understood to indicate a real Personal Relation, I suppose; just as much as the words, Υἱός, or Πατήρ. So that the Spirit of the Son is as truly and properly "breathed" out from the Son, as the Son is "begotten" of the Father. That which invalidates the eternal "spiration" of the One, would seem to invalidate the eternal "filiation" of the Other.

If this be correct, then all passages which represent the Holy Ghost as the Spirit of Christ declare Him to proceed eternally from Christ. See, for example, Rom. viii. 9 :—

> ὑμεῖς δὲ οὐκ ἐστὲ ἐν σαρκὶ, ἀλλ' ἐν πνεύματι, εἴπερ Πνεῦμα Θεοῦ οἰκεῖ ἐν ὑμῖν. εἰ δέ τις Πνεῦμα Χριστοῦ οὐκ ἔχει, οὗτος οὐκ ἔστιν αὐτοῦ.
>
> *But ye are not in the flesh, but in the Spirit, if so be that the Spirit of God dwell in you. Now if any man have not the Spirit of Christ, he is none of His.*

Gal. iv. 6 :—

> ὅτι δέ ἐστε υἱοί, ἐξαπέστειλεν ὁ Θεὸς τὸ Πνεῦμα τοῦ Υἱοῦ αὐτοῦ εἰς τὰς καρδίας ὑμῶν, κράζον, Ἀββᾶ ὁ Πατήρ.
>
> *And because ye are sons, God hath sent forth the Spirit of His Son into your hearts, crying, Abba, Father.*

1 St. Pet. i. 11 :—

> ἐρευνῶντες εἰς τίνα ἢ ποῖον καιρὸν ἐδήλου τὸ ἐν αὐτοῖς Πνεῦμα Χριστοῦ.
>
> *Searching what, or what manner of time the Spirit of Christ which was in them did signify.*

St. John xx. 22 :—

> καὶ τοῦτο εἰπὼν, ἐνεφύσησε, καὶ λέγει αὐτοῖς· λάβετε Πνεῦμα ἅγιον.
>
> *And when He had said this, He breathed on them, and saith unto them, Receive ye the Holy Ghost.*

And, *perhaps,*

St. John xiv. 17 ; xv. 26 ; xvi. 13.
Acts ii. 17, 18, 33 (cf. Joel ii. 28, 29) ; v. 9 ; viii. 39 ; xv. 8 (cf. i. 24, for καρδιαγνώστης applied to Christ) ;
1 Cor. ii. 11 (cf. ver. 16) ; 2 Cor. iii. 17 ; 2 Thess. ii. 8.

γ. Διά (with a genitive) :—

St. John i. 3, 17 (?) :—

πάντα δι' αυτού εγένετο ... ή χάρις καὶ ή αλήθεια
διὰ Ἰησοῦ Χριστοῦ εγένετο.

*All things were made by Him . . . . grace and truth came
by Jesus Christ.*

Acts i. 2 :—

ἐντειλάμενος τοῖς ἀποστόλοις διὰ Πνεύματος Ἁγίου.

*After that He, through the Holy Ghost, had given commandments
unto the Apostles.*

Rom. v. 16—19 :—

ὡς δι' ἑνὸς ἁμαρτήσαντος .. οὕτω καὶ δι' ἑνὸς δικαιώματος ...

As by one that sinned . . . so by the obedience of One. . . .

1 Cor. viii. 6 :—

Ἰησοῦς Χριστὸς, δι' οὗ τὰ πάντα, καὶ ἡμεῖς δι' αὐτοῦ.

Jesus Christ, by whom are all things, and we by Him.

Gal. iv. 7 :—

κληρονόμος Θεοῦ διὰ Χριστοῦ.

An heir of God, through Christ.

Eph. ii. 18 :—

δι' αὐτοῦ ἔχομεν τὴν προσαγωγήν.

Through Him we have access.

Col. i. 16 :—

τὰ πάντα δι' αὐτοῦ καὶ εἰς αὐτὸν ἔκτισται.

All things were created by Him and for Him.

Titus iii. 6 :—

Πνεύματος ἁγίου, οὗ ἐξέχεεν ἐφ' ἡμᾶς πλουσίως διὰ
Ἰησοῦ Χριστοῦ.

*The Holy Ghost, which He shed on us abundantly through
Jesus Christ.*

&c., &c.

These expressions are allowed to prove that all the graces and gifts of the Holy Ghost, and the Holy Ghost Itself, so far as It is a grace and gift, flow down to us from the Father through the Son.

But there is an allowed analogy, or rather congruity, between the mutual relations of the Persons of the Blessed Trinity one amongst another, and the order in which They communicate Themselves to us.

As the Holy Ghost, then, is the gift of the Father by the Son, there is a congruity in that interpretation of the former sets of passages, which supposes Him to have His Being, i.e. to *proceed*, from the Father by the Son; which is what I suppose to be meant by the Latin form of the Nicene Creed.

The οἰκονομία points, as it were, to the θεολογία. (See a like argument in Hooker, E. P. l. v. c. 51, § 3 [a]).

Thus He will be strictly the Third Person, as the Son is the Second Person, by a kind of subordination which does not prejudice His equality.

This is offered for a taste of our Scriptural argument. For testimonies of the Fathers I will instance but in four :—St. AUGUSTINE, for the Latins; St. ATHANASIUS, St. CYRIL, and St. BASIL, for the Greeks.

[a] "And if some cause be likewise required why rather to this end and purpose the Son than either the Father or the Holy Ghost should be made man, could we, which are born the children of wrath, be adopted the sons of God through grace, any other than the natural Son of God being Mediator between God and us?"

α. See in ST. AUGUSTINE (inter alia) :—
   Tract. in Joan., 99, § 6—9.
   Contra Maximin. Arian., lib. 2, c. 14, § 1.
   De Trin., lib. 4, c. 29; lib. 5, c. 12; lib. 15, 45—47.

β. ST. ATHANASIUS (or rather, St. Dionysius of Alexandria) :—
   De Sententiâ Dionysii, § 17, t. i. 255 A., Ed. Ben. Paris, 1698. (This strikes me as a very decisive passage).

ST. ATHANASIUS himself :—
   Expositio Fidei, § 4, p. 102 A.
   Orat. 3, contra Arian., § 24.
   Ad Serap., I. Ep., § 1, p. 648 B, 649 B, D; § 6, p. 653 C; § 12, p. 661 C, D; § 14, p. 663 B; (Per Contr., § 16, p. 665 B); § 19; § 20, p. 669 B, C, D; § 21, ibid. E; § 23, p. 671 (διὰ τοῦ Υἱοῦ ἐν τῷ Πνεύματι); § 24, p. 673 B; (Image of the Son) C; § 25, ibid. E; § 26, p. 675 C; (ἴδιον τοῦ Λόγου) 676 A, C; (ἐπὶ, διὰ, ἐν) ibid. F, § 28; § 30; § 32.
   Ad Serap., III. Ep., § 1, p. 691 B; § 3, p. 692 D; § 4, p. 693 D; § 5, p. 694 D; § 6, p. 695 B.
   Ad Serap., IV. Ep., § 3, D, E.

γ. ST. CYRIL (ALEX.) :—
   Synod. Ep. ad Nestorium, § 10; and St. Cyril's Decl. ap. Theodoret, tom. v. 44 (ed. Schulze, 1774); Anathema ix.; (Per Contr., Theodoret, ibid. p. 47); St. Cyril, Defens., ibid. p. 48.
   In Joan., lib. X. t. iv. p. 910 A—p. 911 D.
   De S. Trin. Dial., t. v. p. 654 C, D; p. 655 A; p. 669 E; p. 671 C; p. 672 A, B; (E?); p. 674 E; p. 675 D; Dial. vii., p. 639 B, C, D; Dial. vii., p. 634 C; p. 637 A; p. 639 C, D, E; p. 640 D; p. 642 B; p. 647 D, E; p. 656 B (?); p. 657 C, D; p. 658 A.

δ. ST. BASIL :—
   De Spiritu Sancto, c. xvi. t. iii. p. 31 C; c. xvii. p. 36 E; c. xviii. p. 38 C and E; p. 39 A; c. xxvi. p. 53 E (ed. Paris, 1630).

APPENDIX ADDED BY EDITOR.

ST. AUGUSTINE.

Tract. in Joan., 99.

[Ed. Bened., vol. iii. p. 746, Paris, 1680.]

§ 6. Hic aliquis forsitan quærat, utrum et a Filio procedat Spiritus Sanctus. Filius enim solius Patris est Filius, et Pater solius Filii est Pater: Spiritus autem Sanctus non est unius eorum Spiritus, sed amborum. Habes ipsum Dominum dicentem, *Non enim vos estis qui loquimini sed Spiritus Patris vestri qui loquitur in vobis:* habes et Apostolum, *Misit Deus Spiritum Filii sui in corda vestra.* Numquid duo sunt, alius Patris alius Filii? Absit. *Unum enim corpus,* ait, cum significaret Ecclesiam; moxque addidit, *et unus Spiritus.* Et vide quomodo illic impleat Trinitatem. *Sicut vocati estis,* inquit, *in una spe vocationis vestræ. Unus Dominus;* hic utique Christum intelligi voluit: restat ut etiam Patrem nominet: Sequitur ergo, *Una fides, unum Baptizma; unus Deus et Pater omnium, qui super*

HERE, it is likely, some man may ask whether the Holy Ghost proceedeth also from the Son. For the Son is Son of the Father alone, and the Father is Father of the Son alone: but the Holy Ghost is not the Spirit of One of Them, but of Them both. Thou hast the Lord Himself saying, "For it is not ye that speak, but the Spirit of your Father that speaketh in you" (St. Matt. x. 20). Thou hast also the Apostle, "God hath sent the Spirit of His Son into your hearts" (Gal. iv. 6). Are they *two*, one of the Father, one of the Son? God forbid! For "one body," saith he (Eph. iv. 4—6), meaning the Church, and presently adds, "and one Spirit." And see how he there fills up the Trinity:—"As ye are called," saith he, "in one hope of your calling; one Lord,"—here of course he means Christ: it yet remains to name the Father; he proceeds therefore,—"One faith, one baptism, one God and Father of all, who is above

Processio Spiritus Sancti. 155

omnes, et per omnes, et in omnibus nobis. Cum ergo sicut unus Pater, et unus Dominus, id est Filius, ita sit et unus Spiritus, profecto amborum est: quandoquidem dicit ipse Christus Jesus, *Spiritus Patris vestri qui loquitur in vobis;* et dicit Apostolus, *Misit Deus Spiritum Filii sui in corda vestra.* Habes alio loco eundem Apostolum dicentem, *Si autem Spiritus ejus qui suscitavit Jesum ex mortuis, habitat in vobis;* hic utique Spiritum Patris intelligi voluit; de quo tamen alio loco dicit, *Quisquis autem Spiritum Christi non habet, hic non est ejus.* Et multa alia sunt testimonia, quibus hoc evidenter ostenditur, et Patris et Filii esse Spiritum, qui in Trinitate dicitur Spiritus Sanctus.

§ 7. Nec ob aliud existimo ipsum vocari proprie Spiritum; cum etiam si de singulis interrogemur non possimus nisi et Patrem et Filium Spiritum dicere; quoniam *Spiritus est Deus,* id est non corpus est Deus, sed Spiritus. Quod ergo communiter vocantur et singuli, hoc proprie vocari oportet all, and through all, and in us all." Seeing, therefore, as there is "one Father" and "one Lord" (Christ), so there is also one Spirit; without doubt He is the Spirit of both: since Christ Jesus Himself saith, "The Spirit of your Father which speaketh in you;" and the Apostle saith, "God hath sent the Spirit of His Son into your hearts" (Gal. iv. 6). Thou hast in another place the same Apostle saying, "But if the Spirit of Him that raised Jesus from the dead dwell in you" (Rom. viii. 11); here of course he meant the Spirit of the Father, of which Spirit however he saith in another place, "But whoso hath not the Spirit of Christ, he is none of His" (Rom. viii. 9). And there are many other proofs, by which that is evidently shewn to be the Spirit of the Father and the Son, which in the Trinity is called the Holy Spirit.

§ 7. And for no other cause do I consider Him to be distinctively called Spirit, while, if we be questioned concerning each Person severally, we cannot but affirm both Father and Son to be Spirit; since "God is a Spirit" (St. John iv. 24), that is, God is not body, but Spirit. What, therefore, They each in common are severally called, by that name behoved He to be called, who is not

tuit eum qui non est unus eorum sed in quo communitas apparet amborum. Cur ergo non credamus quod etiam de Filio procedat Spiritus Sanctus, cum Filii quoque ipse sit Spiritus? Si enim non ab eo procederet, non post resurrectionem se representans discipulis suis insufflasset dicens, *Accipite Spiritum Sanctum.* Quid enim aliud significavit illa insufflatio, nisi quod procedat Spiritus Sanctus et de ipso? Ad hoc pertinet etiam illud quod de muliere quæ fluxum sanguinis patiebatur, ait: *Tetigit me aliquis, Ego enim sensi de me virtutem exiisse.* Nam virtutis nomine appellari etiam Spiritum Sanctum, et eo loco clarum est, ubi Angelus dicenti Mariæ, *Quomodo fiet istud, quoniam virum non cognosco:* respondit, *Spiritus Sanctus superveniet in te, et Virtus Altissimi obumbrabit tibi:* et ipse Dominus, promittens eum discipulis ait, *Vos autem sedete in civitate quousque induamini virtute ex alto:* et iterum, *Accipietis,* inquit, *virtutem Spiritus Sancti supervenientem in vos: et eritis*

one of Them, but in whom appeareth the community of both. Then why should we not believe that the Holy Ghost proceedeth also from the Son, seeing the same is Spirit of the Son also? For did He not proceed from Him, He would not, when He presented Himself to His disciples after His resurrection, have breathed upon them, saying, "Receive ye the Holy Ghost" (St. John xx. 22). For what else did that insufflation signify, but that the Holy Ghost proceedeth from Him also? To this pertaineth that also which He said concerning the woman who had the flux of blood, "Some person hath touched Me, for I perceive that virtue is gone out of Me" (St. Luke viii. 46). For that the Holy Ghost is likewise called by that term, "virtue," is manifest also in that place where, when Mary said, "How shall this be, seeing I know not a man?" The Angel answered, "The Holy Ghost shall come upon thee, and the Virtue of the Highest shall overshadow thee" (St. Luke i. 35). And the Lord Himself, promising Him to His disciples, saith, "But tarry ye in the city, until ye be endued with virtue from on high" (St. Luke xxiv. 19). And again, "Ye shall receive," saith He, "the virtue of the Holy Ghost coming upon you,

Appendix added by Editor. 157

mihi testes. De hac virtute credendus est dicere evangelista, *Virtus de illo exibat et sanabat omnes.*

§ 8. Si ergo et de Patre et de Filio procedit Spiritus Sanctus; cur Filius dixit, *De Patre procedit?* Cur putas nisi quemadmodum ad eum solet referre et quod ipsius est, de quo et ipse est? Unde illud est quod ait, *Mea doctrina non est mea, sed ejus qui me misit.* Si igitur intelligitur hic ejus doctrina, quam tamen dixit non suam sed Patris; quanto magis illic intelligendus est et de ipso procedere Spiritus Sanctus, ubi sic ait, *De Patre procedit,* ut non diceret De me non procedit? A quo autem habet Filius ut sit Deus (est enim de Deo Deus) ab illo habet utique ut etiam de illo procedat Spiritus Sanctus; ac per hoc Spiritus Sanctus ut etiam de Filio procedat, sicut procedit de Patre, ab ipso habet Patre.

§ 9. * * * Spiritus autem

and ye shall be witnesses unto Me" (Acts i. 8). Of this Virtue the Evangelist must be believed to speak, in saying, "There went out Virtue from Him, and healed them all."

§ 8. If, then, the Holy Ghost proceedeth both from the Father and from the Son, wherefore said the Son, "Proceedeth from the Father"? (St. John xv. 26). What should be the reason, thinkest thou, except as He is wont to refer what belongeth to Himself to Him from whom He hath Himself His being? Whence that saying, " My doctrine is not Mine, but His that sent Me" (St. John vii. 16). If, then, it is here understood to be *His* doctrine, notwithstanding that He saith it is *not* His, but the Father's;— how much more must we then understand the Holy Spirit to proceed from Him also, where, speaking of the Spirit "proceeding from the Father," He is careful *not* to say, Proceedeth *not* from Me? Now from whom the Son hath it that He is God (for He is God of God), from the same hath He it, that from Him also should proceed the Holy Ghost; and consequently the Holy Ghost hath it from the Father Himself, that He should proceed from the Son also, as He proceedeth from the Father.

§ 9. * * * But the Holy

Sanctus non de Patre procedit in Filium, et de Filio procedit ad sanctificandam creaturam; sed simul de utroque procedit; quamvis hoc Filio Pater dederit, ut quemadmodum de se, ita de illo quoque procedat.

Ghost doth not proceed from the Father into the Son, and from the Son proceed to the creature, to sanctify the same; but proceedeth at once from both; albeit it is by the Father's gift to the Son that He should proceed as from the Father Himself, so from the Son also.

ST. AUGUSTINE.

Contra Maximinum Arianum, lib. ii. c. 14, § 1.

[Ed. Bened. (Paris, 1694), tom. viii. p. 703.]

Quæris a me, "Si de substantia Patris est Filius, de substantia Patris est etiam Spiritus Sanctus, cur unus Filius sit, et alius non sit Filius"? Ecce respondeo sive capias, sive non capias. De Patre est Filius, de Patre est Spiritus Sanctus: sed ille genitus, iste procedens: ideo ille Filius est Patris, de quo est genitus; iste autem Spiritus utriusque, quoniam de utroque procedit. Sed ideo cum de illo Filius loqueretur, ait, *De Patre procedit:* quoniam Pater processionis ejus est auctor, qui talem Filium genuit, et gignendo ei dedit ut etiam de ipso procederet Spiri-

You ask me this question: "If the Son is of the Substance of the Father, and the Holy Spirit is also of the Substance of the Father, why is one a Son, the other not a Son?" Here is my answer, whether you can take it in or no. The Son is of the Father, the Holy Ghost is of the Father; but the former as *begotten*, the latter as *proceeding:* therefore the one is the Son of the Father, of Whom He is begotten; the other is the Spirit of each, since He proceedeth from each. But when the Son was speaking of Him, He said, "He proceedeth from the Father," for this reason:—because the Father is the author of His procession, having begotten such a Son, and having, in begetting Him, given unto Him that the Holy Ghost should

tus Sanctus. Nam, nisi procederet et de ipso, non diceret discipulis, *Accipite Spiritum Sanctum;* eumque insufflando daret, ut a se quoque procedere significans, aperte ostenderet flando, quod spirando dabat occulte.

proceed from Him. For, were it not that the Holy Spirit proceeded from Him, He would not say to His disciples, "Receive ye the Holy Ghost;" and bestow Him by breathing, meaning by this to shew them that He proceeded from Himself also, the breathing being the outward sign of that which He gave by an inward inspiration.

ST. AUGUSTINE.

De Trinitate, lib. iv. § 29, being part of c. xx.

[Ed. Bened. (Paris, 1694), t. viii. p. 829.]

Sicut ergo Pater genuit, Filius genitus est: ita Pater misit, Filius missus est. Sed quemadmodum qui genuit et qui genitus est; ita et qui misit et qui missus est unum sunt; quia Pater et Filius unum sunt. Ita etiam Spiritus Sanctus unum cum eis est; quia hæc tria unum sunt. Sicut enim natum esse est Filio, a Patre esse; ita mitti est Filio, cognosci quod ab illo sit. Et sicut Spiritui Sancto donum Dei esse, est a Patre procedere, ita mitti, est cognosci quia ab illo procedat. Nec possumus dicere quod Spiritus Sanctus et a Filio

Therefore, as the Father begat, and the Son was begotten, so the Father sent, and the Son was sent. But even as He who begat and He who is begotten are one; so He who sent and He who was sent are one; because the Father and the Son are one. So also the Holy Spirit is one with Them; because these Three are one. For as the being born is to the Son equivalent to being of the Father, so the being sent is to the Son equivalent to being known to be of Him. And as to the Holy Spirit, the being the gift of God is equivalent to proceeding from the Father; so the being sent is equivalent to being known to proceed from Him. Nor can we say that the Holy Ghost doth not proceed from the Son also; for it can-

non procedat: neque enim frustra idem Spiritus et Patris et Filii Spiritus dicitur. Nec video quid aliud significare voluerit, cum sufflans in faciem discipulorum ait, *Accipite Spiritum Sanctum*. Neque ille flatus corporeus, cum sensu corporaliter tangendi procedens ex corpore, substantia Spiritus Sancti fuit; sed demonstratio per congruam significationem, non tantum a Patre, sed et a Filio procedere Spiritum Sanctum.

* * * Quod ergo ait Dominus, *Quem ego mittam vobis a Patre;* ostendit Spiritum et Patris et Filii. Quia etiam cum dixisset, *Quem mittet Pater*, addidit, *in nomine meo;* non tamen dixit, Quem mittet Pater a me: quemadmodum dixit, *Quem ego mittam vobis a Patre:* videlicet ostendens quod totius divinitatis, vel, si melius dicitur, deitatis, principium Pater est. Qui ergo a Patre procedit et Filio, ad eum refertur a quo natus est Filius.

not be said in vain that this same Spirit is the Spirit both of the Father and of the Son. Nor do I see what else can be the meaning of the passage, where breathing on the face of His disciples, He said, "Receive ye the Holy Ghost." We do not for one moment mean that that bodily breath, palpable, and proceeding from the Lord's body, was the *substance* of the Holy Ghost; but it was a proof, by way of congruity, that the Holy Ghost proceedeth from the Son as well as from the Father.

* * * When therefore the Lord said, "Whom I will send unto you from the Father" (St. John xv. 26), He shewed that He was the Spirit both of the Father and of the Son. Because, after saying, "Whom the Father will send," He added, "in My name." But He said not, "Whom the Father will send from Me;" as He said, "Whom I will send unto you from the Father:" clearly indicating that the Father is the origin of the whole Divinity, or, if the word be preferable, of the whole Godhead. He therefore who proceedeth from the Father and the Son, is referred to Him (as origin) of whom the Son is begotten.

IBID., lib. v. sec. 12 (cap. xi.), p. 839.

* * * Ergo Spiritus Sanctus ineffabilis est quædam Patris Filiique communio; et ideo fortasse sic appellatur, quia Patri et Filio potest eadem appellatio convenire. Nam hoc ipse proprie dicitur, quod illi communiter : quia et Pater spiritus et Filius spiritus, et Pater sanctus et Filius sanctus. Ut ergo ex nomine quod utrique convenit, utriusque communio significatur, vocatur donum amborum Spiritus Sanctus.

* * * Therefore the Holy Ghost is a kind of ineffable communion of the Father and of the Son; and therefore perhaps derives the name of "Spirit," because this term may be applied equally to Father and to Son. For He is properly said to be *that* which They are in common : because the Father is spirit, and the Son is spirit; and the Father is holy, and the Son is holy. As, therefore, by that name which suits each, the communion of each with the other is signified, so the gift of Both is called the Holy Spirit.

IBID., lib. xv. sec. 45, 46, 47, p. 998.

Mr. Keble refers his reader to all three sections. They are too long to be re-produced without abridgement.

After citing the same Scriptures as were cited in the other extracts, to shew that the Holy Ghost is spoken of as the Spirit of the Father, and as the Spirit of the Son; and that the Son gave Him to His disciples both on Easter Day and on the day of Pentecost; St. Augustine proceeds to reconcile the Scriptures which speak of the Son *bestowing*, with those that speak of Him *receiving*, the Spirit :—

Propter hoc et Dominus ipse Jesus Spiritum Sanctum non solum dedit ut Deus, sed etiam accepit ut homo; propterea dictus et plenus gratiâ et Spiritu Sancto. Et manifestius de illo

For this reason the Lord Jesus Himself not only gave the Holy Spirit as God, but also received Him as Man : wherefore He was said to be full of grace and of the Holy Spirit (St. John i. 14; St. Luke

scriptum est in Actibus Apostolorum: *quoniam unxit eum Deus Spiritu Sancto*. Non utique oleo visibili, sed dono gratiæ, quod visibili significatur unguento quo baptizatos ungit Ecclesia. Nec sane tunc unctus est Christus Spiritu Sancto quando super eum baptizatum velut columba descendit: tunc enim corpus suum, id est, Ecclesiam suam præfigurare dignatus est, in quâ præcipue baptizati accipiunt Spiritum Sanctum: sed istâ mysticâ et invisibili unctione tunc intelligendus est unctus, quando Verbum Dei caro factum est. * * *

In eo etiam quod de illo scriptum est, quod acceperit a Patre promissionem Spiritus sancti et effuderit, utraque natura monstrata est, et humana scilicet et divina: accepit quippe ut homo, effudit ut Deus. Nos autem accipere quidem hoc donum possumus pro modulo nostro, effundere autem super alios non utique possumus; sed ut hoc fiat, Deum super eos, a quo hoc efficitur, invocamus.

iv. 1). And still more plainly is it written of Him in the Acts of the Apostles (x. 38), that "God anointed Him with the Holy Ghost;" not, of course, with visible oil, but with the gift of grace, which is signified by the visible chrism with which the Church anoints those who are baptized. Nor do we mean that Christ was *then* anointed with the Holy Ghost, when the Spirit descended on Him as a dove at His baptism: for *then* He deigned to prefigure His mystical body, that is His Church, in which the baptized pre-eminently receive the Holy Ghost: but we must conceive Him to have received that mystical and invisible unction when the Word of God was made flesh. * * *

In the passage where it is written of Him that He received from the Father the promised gift of the Holy Ghost, and shed it forth, each of His two natures is exhibited, His human and His divine nature; for He received it as Man, and shed it as God. Now we can receive this gift according to our measure; but pour it forth on others, of course we cannot: but that this may be done, we make our prayer for them to God, by whom it is bestowed.

St. Augustine then shews (§ 47) that neither the *Generation* of the Son, nor the *Procession* of the Spirit, are in

the sphere of *time;* and that we must not apply to the Spirit the word *begotten* (which belongs to the Son alone), nor the word *unbegotten* (which belongs to the Father alone). And in the concluding words of the section, he again (as above, lib. iv. § 29) carefully reconciles the doctrine of the *Double Procession* with the doctrine of the *Monarchia;* as follows :—

Quapropter, qui potest intelligere sine tempore generationem Filii de Patre, intelligat sine tempore processionem Spiritus Sancti de utroque. Et qui potest intelligere in eo quod ait Filius, *Sicut habet Pater vitam in semetipso, sic dedit Filio vitam habere in semetipso;* non sine vitâ existenti jam Filio vitam Patrem dedisse, sed ita eum sine tempore genuisse ut vita quam Pater Filio gignendo dedit, coæterna sit vitæ Patris qui dedit; intelligat sicut habet Pater in semetipso ut de illo procedat Spiritus Sanctus, sic dedisse Filio ut de illo procedat idem Spiritus Sanctus, et utrumque sine tempore; atque ita dictum Spiritum Sanctum de Patre procedere ut intelligatur, quod etiam procedit de Filio,

Wherefore, whoever can understand how the generation of the Son of the Father is before all time, may equally well understand how the procession of the Holy Spirit from Both, is before all time also. And as you can understand the passage where the Son saith, "As the Father hath life in Himself, so hath He given to the Son to have life in Himself" (St. John v. 26), to mean, not that the Son was lifeless until the Father gave Him life, but that the Father begat Him so independently of all time, that the life which the Father gave to the Son in begetting Him, was coeternal with the life of the Father who gave it; so you can understand that even as the Father hath it in Himself that the Spirit should proceed from Him, so He granted to the Son that this same Spirit should proceed from Him also; and in each case independently of time. And again the affirmation that the Holy Spirit proceeds from the Father, must be understood to mean that the fact of His proceeding from

de Patre esse Filio. Si enim quicquid habet de Patre habet Filius, de Patre habet utique ut ex illo procedat Spiritus Sanctus. Sed nulla ibi tempora cogitentur, quæ habent prius et posterius; quia omnino nulla ibi sunt. Quomodo ergo non absurdissime Filius diceretur amborum, cum sicut Filio præstat essentiam sine initio temporis, sine ulla mutabilitate naturæ de Patre generatio; ita Spiritui Sancto præstet essentiam, sine ullo initio temporis, sine ullâ mutabilitate naturæ, de utroque processio? Ideo enim cum Spiritum Sanctum genitum non dicamus, dicere tamen non audemus ingenitum, ne in hoc vocabulo vel duos Patres in illa Trinitate, vel duos qui non sunt de alio quispiam suspicetur. Pater enim solus est non de alio, ideo solus appellatur ingenitus, non quidem in Scripturis, sed in consuetudine disputantium, et de re tantâ sermonem qualem valuerint proferentium. Filius autem de Patre natus est; et Spiritus Sanctus de Patre principaliter, et ipso sine ullo temporis intervallo dante, communiter de utroque procedit. Di-

the Son also, is a gift from the Father to the Son. For if the Son hath from the Father all that He hath, then, of course, He hath it from the Father that the Holy Spirit proceedeth from Him. But all this must be conceived as independent of time, unconditioned by *before* and *after;* for no such terms have place in the matter. Most absurd, then, would it be to say that the Spirit was Son of Both, seeing that, as the Son derives His being, without beginning of time, without change of nature, from His generation from the Father, so the Spirit derives His being, without beginning of time or change of nature, from His procession from Both. For this reason, while we refuse to speak of the Holy Spirit as begotten, we dare not speak of Him as *unbegotten*, lest by using this term we should seem to imply two Fathers in the Trinity, or two Self-existent Ones. For the Father is the only self-existent one; therefore He alone is said to be *unbegotten*, not indeed in Scripture, but in theological language, when men wish to use terms befitting so great a theme. But the Son is born of the Father; and the Holy Ghost proceedeth *from the Father principally,* and—the Father granting this before all time—from Both in common. He would

ceretur autem Filius Patris et Filii, si, quod abhorret ab omnium sanorum sensibus, eum ambo genuissent. Non igitur ab utroque est genitus sed procedit ab utroque amborum Spiritus.

be termed, however, the Son of Father and Son, if (a horrible supposition) He had been begotten of Both. Therefore He is not begotten of Father and Son, but proceedeth from each of Them, being the Spirit of Both.

ST. ATHANASIUS.

De Sententiâ Dionysii, § 17.

[Ed. Bened., Paris, 1698, tom. i. p. 254 F.]

This Epistle of St. Athanasius is an animated defence of his predecessor in the See of Alexandria, Dionysius, when the Arians claimed him as favouring their views. In the following passage, St. Athanasius is quoting words of Dionysius, to shew that he was perfectly orthodox as to the indivisibility of the Godhead.

"τῶν ὑπ' ἐμοῦ λεχθέντων ὀνομάτων ἕκαστον ἀχώριστόν ἐστι καὶ ἀδιαίρετον τοῦ πλησίον· Πατέρα εἶπον, καὶ πρὶν ἐπαγάγω τὸν Υἱὸν, ἐσήμανα καὶ τοῦτον ἐν τῷ Πατρί· Υἱὸν ἐπήγαγον, εἰ καὶ μὴ προειρήκειν τὸν Πατέρα, πάντως ἂν ἐν τῷ Υἱῷ προείληπτο· ἅγιον Πνεῦμα προσέθηκα, ἀλλ' ἅμα καὶ πόθεν καὶ διὰ τίνος ἧκεν ἐφήρμοσα. Οἱ δὲ οὐκ ἴσασιν, ὅτι μήτε ἀπηλλοτρίωται Πατὴρ Υἱοῦ ᾗ Πατήρ· προςκαταρκτικὸν γάρ ἐστι τῆς συναφείας τὸ ὄνομα· οὔτε ὁ Υἱὸς ἀπῴκισται τοῦ Πατρός· ἡ γὰρ Πατρὸς προσηγορία δηλοῖ τὴν κοινωνίαν· ἔν τε

"The Names I have mentioned cannot be separated or divided one from another. I named the Father; and before I made mention of the Son, I indicated Him in the Father. I made mention of the Son; and even if I had not previously spoken of the Father, He would have been anticipated in the Son. I added the Holy Ghost; but in doing so, I implied both Him from whom, and Him through whom He came. But those heretics know not that the Father, as Father, cannot be estranged from the Son; for the name is of itself suggestive of their conjunction. Nor is the Son removed from the Father; for the name of Father declares

ταῖς χερσὶν αὐτῶν ἐστι τὸ Πνεῦμα, μήτε τοῦ πέμποντος, μήτε τοῦ φέροντος δυνάμενον στέρεσθαι. Πῶς οὖν ὁ τούτοις χρώμενος τοῖς ὀνόμασι μεμερίσθαι ταῦτα καὶ ἀφωρίσθαι παντελῶς ἀλλήλων οἴομαι;"

Καὶ μετ' ὀλίγα ἐπάγει λέγων· "οὕτω μὲν ἡμεῖς εἴς τε τὴν Τριάδα τὴν Μονάδα πλατύνομεν ἀδιαίρετον, καὶ τὴν Τριάδα πάλιν ἀμείωτον εἰς τὴν Μονάδα συγκεφαλαιούμεθα."

Their fellowship. And in Their hands is the Spirit, incapable of being parted from Him who sends, or from Him who bears Him. How then can I, while using these names, suppose it possible for them to be divided and separated one from the other?"

And shortly afterwards he (Dionysius) adds:—"Thus do we expand the Unity into the Trinity, without dividing it: and again sum up the Trinity into the Unity without diminishing it."

Expositio Fidei, § 4. [Ed. Bened., t. i. p. 102 A.]

Τὸ δὲ ἅγιον Πνεῦμα, ἐκπόρευμα ὂν τοῦ Πατρὸς, ἀεί ἐστιν ἐν ταῖς χερσὶ τοῦ πέμποντος Πατρὸς καὶ τοῦ φέροντος Υἱοῦ, δι' οὗ ἐπλήρωσε τὰ πάντα.

The Holy Ghost, being that which proceedeth from the Father, is ever in the hands (at the disposal) of the Father who sendeth, and of the Son who beareth Him, through whom He filled all things.

Contra Arianos, Oratio iii. § 24. [Ed. Bened., t. i. p. 573 E.]

Γράφει τοίνυν ὁ Ἰωάννης οὕτω λέγων· Ἐν τούτῳ γινώσκομεν ὅτι ἐν αὐτῷ μένομεν καὶ αὐτὸς ἐν ἡμῖν, ὅτι ἐκ τοῦ Πνεύματος αὐτοῦ δέδωκεν ἡμῖν. Οὐκοῦν διὰ τὴν διδομένην ἡμῖν τοῦ Πνεύματος χάριν ἡμεῖς τε ἐν αὐτῷ γινόμεθα, καὶ αὐτὸς ἐν ἡμῖν· καὶ ἐπειδὴ τὸ Πνεῦμα τοῦ Θεοῦ ἐστι, διὰ τούτου γινομένου ἐν ἡμῖν εἰκότως καὶ ἡμεῖς, ἔχοντες τὸ Πνεῦμα, νομιζό-

St. John writes thus: "Hereby know we that we dwell in Him, and He in us, because He hath given us of His Spirit" (1 John iv. 13). Therefore it is by reason of the grace of the Spirit given unto us that we come to be in Him and He in us. And since He is the Spirit of God, it is through His coming to be in us, that we accordingly, having the Spirit, are deemed to come to be in God. And thus is God in us.

μεθα ἐν τῷ Θεῷ γενέσθαι· καὶ οὕτως ἐστὶν ὁ Θεὸς ἐν ἡμῖν. Οὐκ ἄρα ὡς ἔστιν ὁ Τἱὸς ἐν τῷ Πατρί, οὕτω καὶ ἡμεῖς γινόμεθα ἐν τῷ Πατρί· οὐ γὰρ καὶ ὁ Τἱὸς μετέχων ἐστὶ τοῦ Πνεύματος, ἵνα διὰ τοῦτο καὶ ἐν τῷ Πατρὶ γένηται· οὐδὲ λαμβανων ἐστὶ τὸ Πνεῦμα, ἀλλὰ μᾶλλον αὐτὸς τοῖς πᾶσι τοῦτο χορηγεῖ· καὶ οὐ τὸ Πνεῦμα τὸν Λόγον συνάπτει τῷ Πατρί, ἀλλὰ μᾶλλον τὸ Πνεῦμα παρὰ τοῦ Λόγου λαμβάνει.

It is not then after the manner in which the Son is in the Father, that we come to be in the Father. For the Son does not partake of the Spirit in order that He may so come to be in the Father. Nor is He one who receiveth the Spirit, but rather Himself bestows Him upon all. And it is not the Spirit who connects the Word with the Father, but rather the Spirit is a recipient from the Word.

Ep. ad Serapion, I. § 1. [Ed. Bened., t. ii. p. 648 B.]

* * * ἐξελθόντων μὲν τινῶν ἀπὸ τῶν Ἀρειανῶν διὰ τὴν κατὰ τοῦ Τἱοῦ τοῦ Θεοῦ βλασφημίαν, φρονούντων δὲ κατὰ τοῦ ἁγίου Πνεύματος, καὶ λεγόντων αὐτὸ μὴ μόνον κτίσμα, ἀλλὰ καὶ τῶν λειτουργικῶν πνευμάτων ἓν αὐτὸ εἶναι, καὶ βαθμῷ μόνον αὐτὸ διαφέρειν τῶν ἀγγέλων. Τοῦτο δέ ἐστι πρὸς μὲν τοὺς Ἀρειάνους προσποιητὸς μάχη· ἀληθὴς δὲ ἀντιλογία πρὸς τὴν εὐσεβῆ πίστιν.

There are some who have left the ranks of the Arians because of their blasphemies against the Son of God, but have themselves entertained ideas injurious to the Holy Ghost, saying that He is not only a creature, but also one of the ministering spirits, differing from the angels in rank only. They affect to be combating the Arians; but their real contention is against the Christian faith.

IBID., p. 649 B.

Τούτων γὰρ καὶ θαυμάσειεν ἄν τις τὴν ἄνοιαν, ὅτι τὸν Τἱὸν τοῦ Θεοῦ μὴ θέλοντες κτίσμα εἶναι, καὶ καλῶς γε κατὰ τοῦτο φρονοῦντες, πῶς τὸ Πνεῦμα τοῦ Τἱοῦ κτίσμα κἂν ἀκοῦσαι ἠνέσχοντο; Καὶ γὰρ εἰ διὰ τὴν πρὸς τόν Πατέρα τοῦ Λόγου ἑνότητα,

One may well wonder at their folly; for, refusing to call the Son of God a creature, (and so far right,) how can they endure even to hear the Spirit of the Son called a creature? For if the Son's unity

οὐ θέλουσιν εἶναι τῶν γενητῶν αὐτὸν τὸν Υἱὸν *** διὰ τί τὸ Πνεῦμα τὸ ἅγιον, τὸ τὴν αὐτὴν ἔχον ἑνότητα πρὸς τὸν Υἱὸν, ἣν αὐτὸς ἔχει πρὸς τὸν Πατέρα, κτίσμα λέγουσι;

with the Father forbids them to regard Him as one of created beings, *** how can they call the Holy Spirit a creature, seeing that He has the same unity with the Son, that the Son has with the Father?

D.

*** Εἰ γὰρ ἐφρόνουν ὀρθῶς περὶ τοῦ Λόγου, ἐφρόνουν ὑγιῶς καὶ περὶ τοῦ Πνεύματος, ὃ παρὰ τοῦ Πατρὸς ἐκπορεύεται, καὶ τοῦ Υἱοῦ ἴδιον ὄν, παρ' αὐτοῦ δίδοται τοῖς μαθηταῖς καὶ πᾶσι τοῖς πιστεύουσιν εἰς αὐτόν.

For if they conceived rightly of the Word, they would conceive soundly of the Spirit, which proceedeth from the Father, and being a property of the Son, is from Him given to His disciples and to all who believe on Him.

IBID., § 6 [p. 653 C.]

Καὶ τὴν μὲν πᾶσαν θεολογίαν καὶ τὴν ἡμῶν τελείωσιν, ἐν ᾗ συνῆπτεν ἡμᾶς ἑαυτῷ καὶ δι' ἑαυτοῦ τῷ Πατρὶ, ἐν τούτῳ συμπληρῶν, παρήγγειλε τοῖς μαθηταῖς· "Πορευθέντες, μαθητεύσατε, πάντα τὰ ἔθνη, βαπτίζοντες αὐτοὺς εἰς τὸ ὄνομα τοῦ Πατρὸς, καὶ τοῦ Υἱοῦ, καὶ τοῦ ἁγίου Πνεύματος."

Wishing to sum up all theology, and the whole process of our initiation whereby He knits us in communion to Himself, and through Himself to the Father, He charged His disciples, "Go, make disciples of all nations, baptizing them into the Name of the Father, and of the Son, and of the Holy Ghost."

IBID., § 12 [661 C.]

Athanasius shews that Moses clearly distinguished the Holy Spirit from Angels. In Exod. xxxiii. 1—15, he declined the offered "Angel" as guide, and claimed that "the Presence" should go with them, by "the Presence" meaning the Holy Spirit, as Isaiah shews, lxiii. 11—14: "Where is He that brought them up out of the sea with the shepherd of His flock? where is He that put His Spirit within him?... As a beast goeth down into the valley, the Spirit of the Lord caused him to rest; so didst Thou lead Thy people."

Appendix added by Editor.

IBID., § 14 [p. 663 B.]

Ἡ γὰρ ἁγία καὶ μακαρία Τριὰς ἀδιαίρετος καὶ ἡνωμένη πρὸς ἑαυτήν ἐστι· καὶ λεγομένου τοῦ Πατρὸς, πρόσεστι καὶ ὁ τούτου Λόγος καὶ τὸ ἐν τῷ Υἱῷ Πνεῦμα. Ἐὰν δὲ καὶ ὁ Υἱὸς ὀνομάζηται, ἐν τῷ Υἱῷ ἐστιν ὁ Πατὴρ, καὶ τὸ Πνεῦμα οὐκ ἔστιν ἐκτὸς τοῦ Λόγου. Μία γάρ ἐστιν ἐκ τοῦ Πατρὸς χάρις δι' Υἱοῦ ἐν Πνεύματι ἁγίῳ πληρουμένη.

For the Holy and Blessed Trinity is indivisible and united in itself. And when mention is made of the Father, there is also included the Son of the Father, and the Spirit who is in the Son. And if the Son be named, in the Son we have the Father, nor is the Spirit separable from the Word. For there is one grace from the Father, fulfilled through the Son in the Holy Spirit.

Per contra, Mr. Keble refers us to § 16 [p. 665 B.], a passage which, taken alone, might seem to make against the doctrine of the double Procession:—

οὐδὲ γὰρ ὠνομάσθη ἐν ταῖς Γραφαῖς υἱὸς τὸ Πνεῦμα, ἵνα μὴ ἀδελφὸς νομισθῇ· οὐδὲ υἱὸς τοῦ Υἱοῦ, ἵνα μὴ πάππος νοοῖτο ὁ Πατήρ· ἀλλ' ὁ Υἱὸς, τοῦ Πατρὸς υἱὸς, καὶ τὸ Πνεῦμα τοῦ Πατρὸς πνεῦμα εἴρηται· καὶ οὕτως τῆς ἁγίας Τριάδος μία ἡ θεότης καὶ πίστις ἐστίν.

Never once in the Scriptures is the Spirit called Son, lest a Brother should be imagined; nor yet Son of the Son, lest the Father should be conceived to be a grandfather. But the Son is the Son of the Father, and the Spirit is said to be the Spirit of the Father. And thus we have one Godhead of the Holy Trinity and one faith.

IBID., §§ 19, 20, 21 [p. 669, B, C, D, E.]

τοῦ τοίνυν Πατρὸς φωτὸς ὄντος, τοῦ δὲ Υἱοῦ ἀπαυγάσματος αὐτοῦ, ἔξεστιν ὁρᾶν καὶ ἐν τῷ Υἱῷ τὸ Πνεῦμα, ἐν ᾧ φωτιζόμεθα. τῷ δὲ Πνεύματι φωτιζομένων ἡμῶν, ὁ Χριστός

The Father then being *light* (1 John i. 5), and the Son being His *brightness* (Heb. i. 3), we may see, in the Son, the Spirit in whom we are *illumined* (Eph. i. 17). Seeing then that we are illumined by the Spirit, it is Christ who illumines us in

ἐστιν ὁ ἐν αὐτῷ φωτίζων. πάλιν τε τοῦ Πατρὸς ὄντος πηγῆς, τοῦ δὲ Υἱοῦ ποταμοῦ λεγομένου, πίνειν λεγόμεθα τὸ Πνεῦμα. τὸ δὲ Πνεῦμα ποτιζόμενοι τὸν Χριστὸν πίνομεν. * * * ζωοποιουμένων δὲ ἡμῶν ἐν τῷ Πνεύματι ζῆν αὐτὸς ὁ Χριστὸς ἐν ἡμῖν λέγεται * * *

§ 20. Καὶ γὰρ ὥσπερ μονογενὴς ὁ Υἱός ἐστιν· οὕτω καὶ τὸ Πνεῦμα παρὰ τοῦ Υἱοῦ διδόμενον καὶ πεμπόμενον, καὶ αὐτὸ ἕν ἐστι καὶ οὐ πολλά, οὐδὲ ἐκ πολλῶν ἕν· ἀλλὰ μόνον αὐτὸ Πνεῦμα. Ἑνὸς γὰρ ὄντος τοῦ Υἱοῦ τοῦ ζῶντος Λόγου, μίαν εἶναι δεῖ τελείαν καὶ πλήρη τὴν ἁγιαστικὴν καὶ φωτιστικὴν ζῶσαν ἐνεργείαν αὐτοῦ καὶ δωρεάν, ἥτις ἐκ Πατρὸς λέγεται ἐκπορεύεσθαι, ἐπειδὴ παρὰ τοῦ Λόγου τοῦ ἐκ Πατρὸς ὁμολογουμένου ἐκλάμπει, καὶ ἀποστέλλεται, καὶ δίδοται.

Ἀμέλει ὁ μὲν Υἱὸς παρὰ τοῦ Πατρὸς ἀποστέλλεται· ὁ δὲ Υἱὸς τὸ Πνεῦμα ἀποστέλλει. καὶ ὁ μὲν Υἱὸς τὸν Πατέρα δοξάζει· τὸ δὲ Πνεῦμα δοξάζει τὸν Υἱόν. καὶ ὁ μὲν Υἱός φησιν, " Ἃ ἤκουσα παρα τοῦ Πατρὸς, ταῦτα καὶ λαλῶ εἰς τὸν κόσμον"· τὸ δὲ Πνεῦμα ἐκ τοῦ Υἱοῦ λαμβάνει. Καὶ ὁ μὲν Υἱὸς ἐν τῷ ὀνόματι τοῦ

Him (John i. 9). Again, the Father being a *fountain* (Jer. ii. 13), and the Son being called a *river* (Ps. lxv. 10), we are said to drink the Spirit (1 Cor. xiii. 13); and being made to drink of the Spirit, we drink Christ (1 Cor. x. 4).

* * * When we are being quickened by the Spirit, Christ Himself is said to live within us (Gal. ii. 20). * * *

§ 20. For as the Son is only-begotten, so the Spirit also, given and sent from the Son, is Himself too *one*, and not many nor made up of many; but one simple Spirit. For inasmuch as the Son, the living Word, is one, *one* also must needs be, perfect and complete, the sanctifying and illuminating living energy and gift of the Son, which is said to proceed from the Father; since from the Word, who is confessedly of the Father, He (the Spirit) shines forth, and is sent forth, and is given.

Clearly the Son is sent forth from the Father (John iii. 16); but the Son sends forth the Spirit (xvi. 7). And the Son glorifies the Father (xvii. 4); but the Spirit glorifies the Son (xvi. 14). And the Son saith, " What I have heard from the Father, that I speak also to the World" (viii. 26); but the Spirit receives of the Son (xvi. 14). And the Son came in the

Πατρὸς ἦλθε· "Τὸ δὲ Πνεῦμα τὸ ἅγιον," φησὶν ὁ Υἱὸς, "ὃ πέμψει ὁ Πατὴρ ἐν τῷ ὀνόματί μου." Τοιαύτην τάξιν καὶ φύσιν ἔχει τὸ Πνεῦμα πρὸς τὸν Υἱὸν, οἵαν ὁ Υἱὸς ἔχει πρὸς τὸν Πατέρα.

name of the Father; but "the Holy Spirit" (saith the Son) "which the Father will send in My name." Thus the Spirit hath a like rank and nature in relation to the Son, as the Son hath in relation to the Father.

IBID., § 23 [p. 671].

οὕτω δὲ σφραγιζόμενοι, εἰκότως καὶ κοινωνοὶ θείας φύσεως γινόμεθα, ὡς εἶπεν ὁ Πέτρος, καὶ οὕτω μετέχει πᾶσα ἡ κτίσις τοῦ Λόγου ἐν τῷ Πνεύματι.

Being thus sealed, we become consequently partakers also of the divine nature, as St. Peter said (1 Pet. i. 4); and thus all created beings partake of the Word in the Spirit.

§ 24 [p. 673 B.]

Εἰ δὲ ὁ Πατὴρ διὰ τοῦ Λόγου ἐν Πνεύματι ἁγίῳ κτίζει τὰ πάντα καὶ ἀνακαινίζει, ποία ὁμοιότης ἢ συγγένεια τῷ κτίζοντι πρὸς τὰ κτίσματα; * * *
Εἰκὼν τοῦ Υἱοῦ λέγεται καὶ ἔστι τὸ Πνεῦμα· "Οὓς" γὰρ "προέγνω καὶ προώρισε συμμόρφους τῆς εἰκόνος τοῦ Υἱοῦ αὐτοῦ." * * *

But if the Father creates and renews all things *through* the Word *in* the Holy Spirit, what homogeneity can there possibly be between the Creator and the things created? * * *
The Spirit is called, and is, an Image of the Son. For we read, "Whom He foreknew, He also did predestinate to be conformed to the Image of His Son" (Rom. viii. 29).

[§ 27 [p. 676 A, C.]

Εἰ δὲ τοῦτο μὲν ἀεὶ τὸ αὐτό ἐστι καὶ μεθεκτόν, τὰ δὲ κτίσματα μετέχοντά ἐστιν αὐτοῦ· οὐκ ἂν εἴη τὸ Πνεῦμα τὸ ἅγιον οὔτε ἄγγελος, οὔτε ὅλως κτίσμα, ἀλλ' ἴδιον τοῦ Λόγου, παρ' οὗ διδόμενον μετέχεται παρὰ τῶν κτισμάτων. * * * ἓν ὄν, μᾶλλον δὲ τοῦ Λόγου ἑνὸς ὄντος ἴδιον, καὶ τοῦ Θεοῦ ἑνὸς ὄντος ἴδιον καὶ ὁμοούσιόν ἐστι.
§ 28. Εἷς Θεὸς ἐν τῇ ἐκκλησίᾳ κηρύττεται, "ὁ ἐπὶ

But if this (the Spirit) is ever the same and communicable, and if created beings partake thereof; then the Holy Spirit cannot be either angel or created being, but a property of the Word, by whose donation He is communicated to created beings. * * *
* * * Being one, or rather a property of the Word who is one, He (the Spirit) is also a property of the one God and consubstantial with Him.

πάντων, καὶ διὰ πάντων, καὶ ἐν πᾶσιν." "'Επὶ πάντων" μὲν ὁ Πατήρ, ὡς ἀρχὴ καὶ πηγή· "διὰ πάντων" δὲ διὰ τοῦ Λόγου· "ἐν πᾶσι" δὲ ἐν τῷ Πνεύματι τῷ ἁγίῳ.

§ 30 (commenting on 1 Cor. xii. 4—6). ἃ γὰρ τὸ Πνεῦμα ἑκάστῳ διαιρεῖ, ταῦτα παρὰ τοῦ Πατρὸς διὰ τοῦ Λόγου χορηγεῖται.

(On John xiv. 23). Ἔνθα γὰρ τὸ φῶς, ἐκεῖ καὶ τὸ ἀπαύγασμα· καὶ ἔνθα τὸ ἀπαύγασμα, ἐκεῖ καὶ ἡ τούτου ἐνεργεία καὶ αὐγοειδὴς χάρις.

One God is preached in the Church, " Who is over all, and through all, and in all" (Eph. iv. 6). " Over all," the Father, as origin and fountain: "through all," through the Word : " in all," in the Holy Ghost. * * *

§ 30. For what things the Spirit distributes to each, these things are supplied from the Father, through the Word. * * * For where the light is, there is the brightness also. And where the brightness is, there also is its energy and radiant grace.

ST. CYRIL (OF ALEXANDRIA).

Synodal Epistle to Nestorius, § 10.

Ὅταν δὲ λέγῃ περὶ τοῦ Πνεύματος, Ἐκεῖνος ἐμὲ δοξάσει· νοοῦντες ὀρθῶς, οὐχ ὡς δόξης ἐπιδεᾶ τῆς παρ' ἑτέρου φαμὲν, τὸν ἕνα Χριστὸν καὶ Υἱὸν τὴν παρὰ τοῦ ἁγίου Πνεύματος δόξαν ἑλεῖν· ὅτι μηδὲ κρεῖττον αὐτοῦ καὶ ὑπὲρ αὐτὸν τὸ Πνεῦμα αὐτοῦ. ἐπεὶ δὲ εἰς ἔνδειξιν τῆς ἑαυτοῦ θεότητος ἐκέχρητο τῷ ἁγίῳ Πνεύματι, πρὸς μεγαλούργιλον, δεδόξασθαι παρ' αὐτοῦ φησιν, ὥσπερ ἂν εἰ καί τις λέγοι τῶν καθ' ὑμᾶς περὶ τῆς ἐνούσης ἰσχύος αὐτῷ τυχὸν, ἤγουν ἐπιστήμης τῆς ἐφ' ὁτῳοῦν, ὅτι δοξάσουσί με. εἰ γὰρ καὶ ἔστιν ἐν ὑποστάσει τὸ Πνεῦμα ἰδικῇ, καὶ δὴ καὶ

But when He saith concerning the Spirit, " He shall glorify Me," a sound divine does not explain it to mean that because He needed glory from another, Christ the only Son of God received glory from the Holy Spirit ; because His Spirit cannot be His superior.

But when, for the manifestation of His own Divinity, He used the Holy Spirit for the doing of great deeds, He speaks of Himself as glorified by Him; just as one of you might say of his strength haply or knowledge of any subject, "They will make me glorious." For though the Spirit has a specific personality, and may be conceived as

Appendix added by Editor.

νοεῖται καθ' ἑαυτό, καθὸ Πνεῦμά ἐστι, καὶ οὐχ Υἱός, ἀλλ' οὖν ἐστιν οὐκ ἀλλότριον αὐτοῦ. Πνεῦμα γὰρ ἀληθείας ὠνόμασται, καὶ ἔστι Χριστὸς ἡ ἀλήθεια· καὶ προχεῖται παρ' αὐτοῦ, καθάπερ ἀμέλει καὶ ἐκ τοῦ Θεοῦ καὶ Πατρός. ἐνεργήσαν τοιγαροῦν τὸ Πνεῦμα διὰ χειρὸς τῶν ἁγίων ἀποστόλων τὰ παράδοξα μετὰ τὸ ἀνελθεῖν τὸν Κύριον ἡμῶν Ἰησοῦν Χριστὸν εἰς τὸν οὐρανὸν, ἐδόξασεν αὐτόν. ἐπιστεύθη γὰρ ὅτι Θεὸς κατὰ φύσιν ἐστὶν, πάλιν αὐτὸς ἐνεργῶν διὰ τοῦ ἰδίου Πνεύματος. διὰ τοῦτο καὶ ἔφασκεν, ὅτι ἐκ τοῦ ἐμοῦ λήψεται καὶ ἀναγγελεῖ ὑμῖν. Καὶ οὔτι που φαμὲν, ὡς ἐκ μετοχῆς τὸ Πνεῦμά ἐστι σοφόν τε καὶ δυνατόν. πολυτέλειον γὰρ καὶ ἀπροσδεές ἐστι παντὸς ἀγαθοῦ. ἐπειδὴ δὲ τῆς τοῦ Πατρὸς δυνάμεως καὶ σοφίας, τοῦτ' ἐστιν Υἱοῦ, Πνεῦμά ἐστιν, αὐτόχρημά ἐστι σοφία καὶ δύναμις.

existing by Itself, as Spirit, not as Son, yet It is not alien to the Son. For It is called the Spirit of truth, and the truth is Christ. And It is shed forth from the Son, as, of course, also out of * God the Father. Therefore, when by the hand of the holy Apostles the Spirit wrought those wonderful works after our Lord Jesus Christ's return to heaven, It glorified Him. For Christ was "believed on in the world," as truly God, when He began again (at Pentecost) to work through His Spirit. Wherefore also He said, "He shall receive of Mine and shall shew it unto you." Again, we by no means say that the Spirit, by way of participation, is wise and powerful. For It is abundant and self-sufficing in all that is good. But being the Spirit of the Father's Power and Wisdom, (that is, of the Son,) the Spirit is in very deed wisdom and power.

Anathema IX. At the end of Cyril's letter to Nestorius *de excommunicatione.*

εἴτις φησὶ τὸν ἕνα κύριον Ἰησοῦν Χριστὸν δεδοξάσθαι παρὰ τοῦ Πνεύματος ὡς ἀλ-

If any one affirms that our one Lord Jesus Christ was glorified by the Spirit, in that He

---

* When the Greek Fathers speak of the Spirit coming from the Son, they use the preposition παρὰ (*from the side of*); when from the Father, they use the preposition ἐκ (from *as from a centre*). Unfortunately, this nice distinction cannot be neatly preserved in Latin or English.

λοτρίᾳ δυνάμει τῇ δι' αὐτοῦ χρώμενον, καὶ παρ' αὐτοῦ λαβόντα τὸ ἐνεργεῖν δύνασθαι κατὰ πνευμάτων ἀκαθάρτων καὶ τὸ πληροῦν εἰς ἀνθρώπους τὰς θεοσημείας, καὶ οὐχὶ δὴ μᾶλλον ἴδιον αὐτοῦ τὸ Πνεῦμα, φησί, δι' οὗ καὶ ἐνήργηκε τὰς θεοσημείας· ἀνάθεμα ἔστω.

used the power which He had through the Spirit as a borrowed power, and in that He from the Spirit received the power of expelling unclean spirits and accomplishing those miracles He wrought for mankind, and not rather that it was His own proper Spirit through which He worked His miracles,—let him be anathema.

ST. BASIL.
Liber de Spiritu Sancto, c. xvi.
[Ed. Bened., Paris, 1730, t. iii. p. 31 C.]

B. Καὶ οὕτω δ' ἂν τὸ συναφὲς καὶ ἀδιαίρετον κατὰ πᾶσαν ἐνέργειαν ἀπὸ Πατρὸς καὶ Υἱοῦ τοῦ Πνεύματος διδαχθείης. . . .

C. Οὐ μὴν ἐπειδὴ πρῶτον ἐνταῦθα τοῦ Πνεύματος ὁ Ἀπόστολος ἐπεμνήσθη, καὶ δεύτερον τοῦ Υἱοῦ, καὶ τρίτον τοῦ Θεοῦ καὶ Πατρός, ἤδη χρὴ καθόλου νομίζειν ἀντεστράφθαι τὴν τάξιν. Ἀπὸ γὰρ τῆς ἡμετέρας σχέσεως τὴν ἀρχὴν ἔλαβεν· ἐπειδὴ ὑποδεχόμενοι τὰ δῶρα, πρῶτον ἐντυγχανόμενον τῷ διανέμοντι· εἶτα ἐννοοῦμεν τὸν ἀποστείλαντα· εἶτα ἀνάγομεν τὴν ἐνθύμησιν ἐπὶ τὴν πηγὴν καὶ αἰτίαν τῶν ἀγαθῶν. Μάθοις δ' ἂν τὴν πρὸς Πατέρα καὶ Υἱὸν τοῦ Πνεύματος κοινωνίαν καὶ ἐκ τῶν δημιουργημάτων τῶν ἐξ ἀρχῆς.

B. Thus mayst thou learn the Spirit's conjunction and practical inseparability from the Father and the Son. . . .

C. Because the Apostle in this passage (1 Cor. xii. 4—6) mentions the Spirit first, and the Son second, and God the Father third, we must by no means infer generally that the order of the Trinity is inverted. For it was in respect of His relation to us that he began with the Spirit; since in receiving the gifts we first come into direct relation with the Distributor. Next, we think of Him Who sent the Spirit. And lastly, we ascend in thought to the fountain and author of good things. Thou mayst also learn the communion which the Spirit hath with the Father and the Son from the first creation of the world.

IBID., c. xvii. p. 36 E.

Εἰ δὴ τῷ Πνεύματι πρέπειν οἴονται μόνῳ τὴν ὑπαρίθμησιν, μανθανέτωσαν, ὅτι κατὰ τὸν αὐτὸν τρόπον, συνεκφωνεῖται τῷ Κυρίῳ τὸ Πνεῦμα, καθ' ὃν καὶ ὁ Υἱὸς τῷ Πατρί. Τὸ γὰρ ὄνομα Πατρὸς καὶ Υἱοῦ καὶ ἁγίου Πνεύματος ὁμοίως ἐκδέδοται. Ὡς τοίνυν ἔχει ὁ Υἱὸς πρὸς τὸν Πατέρα, οὕτω πρὸς τὸν Υἱὸν τὸ Πνεῦμα, κατὰ τὴν ἐν τῷ βαπτίσματι παραδεδομένην τοῦ λόγου σύνταξιν. Εἰ δὲ τὸ Πνεῦμα τῷ Υἱῷ συντέτακται ὁ δὲ Υἱὸς τῷ Πατρί, δηλονότι καὶ τὸ Πνεῦμα τῷ Πατρί.

But if they suppose that a subordinate place in the Trinity is proper for the Spirit only, let them bethink them that the Spirit is proclaimed with the Son, precisely as the Son is proclaimed with the Father. For the name of Father, and of Son, and of Holy Spirit is co-ordinately uttered. As the Son therefore stands related to the Father, so the Spirit stands related to the Son, according to the arrangement of the baptismal formula. But if the Spirit is classed with the Son, and the Son with the Father, then clearly the Spirit is classed with the Father.

IBID., c. xviii. (p. 38 E.)

Καὶ οὐκ ἐντεῦθεν μόνον τῆς κατὰ τὴν φύσιν κοινωνίας αἱ ἀποδείξεις, ἀλλ' ὅτι καὶ ἐκ τοῦ Θεοῦ εἶναι λέγεται· οὐχ ὡς τὰ πάντα ἐκ τοῦ Θεοῦ, ἀλλ' ὡς ἐκ τοῦ Θεοῦ προελθόν, οὐ γεννητῶς ὡς ὁ Υἱὸς, ἀλλ' ὡς πνεῦμα στόματος αὐτοῦ. πάντως δὲ οὔτε τὸ στόμα μέλος, οὔτε πνοὴ λυομένη τὸ Πνεῦμα, ἀλλὰ καὶ τὸ στόμα θεοπρεπῶς, καὶ τὸ Πνεῦμα οὐσία ζῶσα, ἁγιασμοῦ κυρία, τῆς μὲν οἰκειότητος δηλουμένης

Nor are these the only proofs of the Spirit's community of nature with the Father, but there is also the fact that He is said to be *of God:* not in the sense in which all things may be said to be *of God*, but as *proceeding* (προελθόν) out of God,—not by way of generation as the Son, but as Spirit of His mouth. But as by "mouth" we in nowise mean a bodily member, so by Spirit we in nowise mean dissolving breath; but we use the word "mouth" in a divine sense, and by Spirit we mean a living substance, with the prerog-

ἐντεῦθεν, τοῦ δὲ τρόπου τῆς ὑπάρξεως ἀρρήτου φυλασσομένου. ἀλλὰ καὶ Πνεῦμα Χριστοῦ λέγεται ὡς ᾠκειωμένον κατὰ τὴν φύσιν αὐτῷ. διὰ τοῦτο εἴ τις Πνεῦμα Χριστοῦ οὐκ ἔχει, οὗτος οὐκ ἔστιν αὐτοῦ. ὅθεν μόνον ἀξίως δοξάζει τὸν Κύριον, ἐκεῖνος γὰρ ἐμὲ δοξάσει, φησίν, οὐχ ὡς ἡ κτίσις, ἀλλ' ὡς Πνεῦμα τῆς ἀληθείας τρανῶς ἐκφαῖνον ἐν ἑαυτῷ τὴν ἀλήθειαν, καὶ ὡς Πνεῦμα σοφίας τὸν Χριστὸν τὴν τοῦ Θεοῦ δύναμιν καὶ τὴν τοῦ Θεοῦ σοφίαν ἐν τῷ ἑαυτοῦ μεγέθει ἀποκαλύπτον. καὶ ὡς Παράκλητος δὲ ἐν ἑαυτῷ χαρακτηρίζει τοῦ ἀποστείλαντος αὐτὸν Παρακλήτου τὴν ἀγαθότητα, καὶ ἐν τῷ ἑαυτοῦ ἀξιώματι τὴν μεγαλωσύνην ἐμφαίνει τὴν τοῦ ὅθεν προῆλθεν.

ative of sanctifying; so that the closeness of the relationship is hence discernible, while the mode of His being remains ineffable. But further, He is called the Spirit of Christ, as being by nature closely related to Him. Therefore we read, "If any man have not the Spirit of Christ, he is none of His." Whence only He worthily glorifies the Lord; for the Lord said, "He shall glorify Me;" not as a creature might, but as the Spirit of truth clearly in Himself shewing forth the truth, and as the Spirit of wisdom, revealing Christ, "the power of God and the wisdom of God," in His own grandeur. And as the Paraclete, He in Himself expresses the goodness of the Paraclete (the Son) who sends Him: and in His own dignity He shews the greatness of Him (the Son), from Whom He (the Spirit) *proceeded* (προῆλθεν—not ἐκπορεύεται).

IBID., c. xxvi. p. 53 E.

Δεύτερος δὲ νοῦς οὐδὲ αὐτὸς ἀπόβλητος, ὅτι ὥσπερ ἐν τῷ Υἱῷ ὁρᾶται ὁ Πατήρ, οὕτως ὁ Υἱὸς ἐν τῷ Πνεύματι.

Nor is that other meaning to be discarded, that as the Father is beheld in the Son, so is the Son beheld in the Spirit.

ANALYSIS OF ST. PAUL'S EPISTLES,
FROM MR. KEBLE'S INTERLEAVED GREEK TESTAMENT.

THE EPISTLE TO THE ROMANS.

DATE of the Epistle, plain from ch. xv. 25—28 compared with Acts xx. 3, xxiv. 17.

§ I. Salutation (i. 1—7).
§ II. Assurances of his interest in them (8—15).
§ III. Of Justification by Faith only (i. 16—v. 21).

- a. Subject of § III. proposed (i. 16, 17).
- β. Foundation of the Doctrine in the misery of men (i. 18—iii. 20);
  - a. of the Gentiles (i. 18—ii. 10);
  - b. of the Jews (ii. 11—iii. 8);
  - c. of both, summed up (iii. 9—20).
- γ. The misery of unregenerate man having been fully proved, the true method of justification is
  - a. stated (21—28);
  - b. guarded by some necessary practical corollaries afterwards to be explained at large (29—31);
  - c. confirmed and illustrated by the example of Abraham (iv. 1—5), the witness of David (6—9), and the circumstance that Abraham was justified before he was circumcised (10—25).
- δ. Statement of Christian Privileges consequent on Justification (v. 1—11).
  1. Peace with God (1).
  2. Access by Prayer as to a reconciled King (2).
  3. Καύχησις (whatever that may be),
     - a. in hope of the glory of God (2),
     - b. in tribulation for the present, as an earnest of salvation (3—11).
- ε. Correspondence between the manner of our Fall and that of our Recovery; by way of Corollary to what has been said (12—21).

He begins a comparison (12), but interrupts it in the

manner of one correcting himself (15): the case of our recovery being more than analogous to the fall, both in the *favour* of God [considered, 1. in itself (ἡ χάρις); 2. in the gift of the Holy Ghost (ἡ δωρεά); 3. in the restoration of what had been many times forfeited] (15, 16); and in the *effect* of it (17). Therefore he limits the comparison to the circumstance that it was *one act* (18) and *one person* (19) which led to the whole in each case. A note on the effect of the Law (20, 21).

§ IV. Of Sanctification by the Holy Spirit, the result and purpose of Justification (vi. 1—viii. 39).

  α. Enforced as a duty,
    a. from the typical death of Baptism (vi. 1—14);
    b. from the cessation of our servitude under the Law (vi. 15—vii. 6).
    c. The exact relation of the Law to the Gospel, in respect of practical obedience is explained by the bye (vii. 7—viii. 11).

  β. Recommended as a *privilege* (viii. 12—39).

  α. *a.* Possible abuse of Justification (vi. 1), answered from considering the Christian's "Death unto Sin" (2). Which takes place at, and is signified by, Baptism (3). Which Baptism implies a typical resurrection too (4, 5), upon consideration, 1st. of the abolition of the tyranny of sin, implied in the typical death; 2nd. of the death of Christ, into which we were baptized, being a death once for all, and His life an eternal one (8—11.) Earnest exhortation to Christians to live in purity according to this faith (12, 13); the excuse of impotency being completely gone (14).

    b. Sanctification enforced from our being not under a Law but under Favour (vi. 15—vii. 6).

    Conclusion proposed (15), made out from the true account of our situation which is not exactly freedom, but a change of Masters; so that our former obedience to sin is at least to be the measure of our new obedience to Christ (16—20).

    [Sanctification enforced] from the present fruit, and final end of the two (Law and Favour) (21—23): and from an analogy between our case and that of a person set free from a relative duty (e.g. of marriage) by death (vii. 1—6). The principle in such a case being laid down (1); exemplified (2, 3); applied to our case (4); drawn into the required practical conclusion (5, 6).

c. Note on the exact relation of the Law to the Gospel, and of our conditions under the two; by which the duty of obedience is all the more enforced (vii. 7—13).

The Law is far from evil; but so far it made our condition worse, that, giving us a more perfect knowledge of sin (7), without Gospel means of resisting it, it only shewed us our wretched condition, and did not deliver us from it: made out from the nature of Law and Sin, which are correlatives (8): from our experience of the difference between childhood and riper years (9, 10), more particularly in the case of express Laws (such as those of Moses) perverted by corrupt casuistry (11). Conclusion stated (12, 13).

To explain this, consider the peculiar frame and condition of a person having knowledge without grace (14—25). He is opposed to the Law he owns (14), to his own conduct (15), thereby approving the Law (16), to such an extent that it almost seems as if some evil power possessed him (17): his best efforts going only to the approbation, not the practice, of holiness (18—20); or as if there were two laws contradicting each other within him (21—25):—a condition the remembrance of which makes him cry out for mercy and thankfulness (24, 25).

Consider, also, on the other hand, the condition of a Christian (viii. 1—11). He, if sincere, is free from condemnation (1), being at any rate free from the law of sin (2); for the Gospel has found a way to condemn sin without destroying the sinner, but only reforming him (3, 4): for as naturally as those who are left unregenerate are earthly-minded, so naturally those who are in the Spirit are heavenly-minded (5). And as the one ends in death (which is explained in 7, 8), so the other in life and peace (6). And as an earnest of this our condition, we have the Spirit of God dwelling in us, else we are not Christians at all (9). Which, implying the peculiar presence of Christ, implies a death unto sin and new birth unto righteousness, like Christ's (10); and implying the presence of the Father, who raised Christ, implies the possibility of using our very bodies to His service, which is a figurative resurrection of those bodies. [And thus there is an end of the "Law in our members" mentioned in vii. (11).]

β. Sanctification recommended as the chief Privilege (12—39):

a. By its being a matter of life and death (13):

b. By the adoption we have received (14—16):

c. By the hope of everlasting inheritance with Christ (17), which is so blessed that our sufferings are not to be compared with it (18);—as is shewn by the earnestness with which it is longed for, 1st. by the whole world (19—22), 2nd. by the Elect (i.e. Christians) (23—25), 3rd. by the Spirit of God Himself, as the Inspirer of our prayers (26, 27).

d. By the certainty that to good Christians all things are good (28—39).

§ V. Of the Rejection of the Jews (ix. 1—xi. 36).

1. Lamented (ix. 1—5).
2. Guarded from certain objections (6—29).
3. Accounted for by their error about Justification (30—x. 21).
4. Shewn not to be entire (xi. 1—10).
5. Nor final (xi. 11—36).

1. Their rejection lamented (1—5).

2. *a.* God's dispensation with regard to the Jews vindicated from the charge of a failure of purpose (6—13), it being evident from the beginning that it was a dispensation of election. The case of Isaac and Ishmael (7, 9), and also of Jacob and Esau (10—13), proving that natural descent, in this case, did not convey a right to the promises (8).

β. God's dispensation with regard to the Jews vindicated from the charge of unrighteousness (14—29).

His mercy did not proceed from caprice, but in strict conformity to His own attributes, proved by reference to His declaration to Moses (15, 16). So also His justice in letting sinners fill up the measure of their sins, e.g. Pharaoh (17). Summed up (18).

Objection: How is all this reconciled, considering His Almighty Power (19)? Answer

a. We are incompetent judges (20, 21).

b. We *may* see some of the great purposes amid the manifestations of God's moral government over the wicked (22), and His mercy to the penitent (23). As in the present case, both among Jews and Gentiles (24), according to the prophecy of Hosea (25, 26) and of Isaiah among the Jews more particularly (27—29).

3. The unbelief of the Jews accounted for by their error about Justification (ix. 30—x. 21).

Their error stated, and contrasted with the notions of the Gentiles (30—32), shewn to have been foretold (33), had something in it which interested you for them (x. 1, 2): but yet *was* an error (3), as is shewn

a. by stating the true doctrine (4), and proving it out of the Scriptures, by taking Moses' account of the sanctions of the Law (5), and comparing it with what he says of the Gospel (6—10).

β. by the prophecies of Isaiah (11) and Joel (12), which also indicate the *universality* of the new revelation (12), and shew that the Apostles were right in preaching as they did to the Gentiles (14, 15). Objection: "The Gospel was but partially received." Answer: "This also was prophesied (16) in terms which point out, by the bye, the need of more Revelation (17). The very general publication of the Gospel (18) and its rejection by the Jews in spite of Moses' and Isaiah's warning (19 —21) are much stronger arguments on the other side.

4. The Rejection of the Jews not entire (xi. 1—10).

He deprecates such a notion from his natural patriotism (1): illustrates the real state of the case from what was said to Elijah (2—5): deprecates, in a parenthesis, any notion of merit, properly so called, which they might revert to on this statement of God's continued favour to them (6). Shews that if they (as a body) failed of the benefit of this mercy, it was the fault of their own callousness (7), which in former instances, typical of this, had met with similar results (8—10).

5. The Rejection of the Jews not *final* (11—36).

    a. The contrary may be argued from the very circumstances of it. It has been so ordered as to lead to the acceptation of the Gospel among the Gentiles: the very thing to excite them to a religious emulation (11): and in this the Gentiles are as much concerned as they: for if God's mercy is so great that the very fall of His ancient people is turned to our good, how much more their recovery, which has a natural tendency that way (12). And here is the reason why St. Paul, as Apostle of the Gentiles, spoke so highly of his peculiar ministry (cf. Eph. iii. 8; Rom. xv. 18, &c.), viz. to profit the Gentiles still more if by any means he might provoke the Jews to jealousy (13—15).

    β. The same thing may be argued from the holiness of the Patriarchs (16). In which, having used the word "branches," it suggests the Parable of the Olive, by means of which he meets the probable errors of the Gentile converts on the subject: shewing them how unnatural it was for them to be puffed up, or feel any party-spirit against the Jews, since it was only by their union to that Body from which the Jews had fallen, that they lived at all (17, 18); not by any partial favour as some might dream (19), but in regard of their unbelief and faith respectively (20).

    Therefore their rejection is a reason not for pride but fear, and that *à fortiori* (21). This practical lesson he sums up in 22, 23; and then returns to his argument, and puts it *à fortiori*, still using the Parable (24).

    Then leaving both the Parable and the argumentation, he speaks out as a Prophet, and announces the whole counsel of God in this matter (25); confirms it from Isaiah (26, 27); and shews how in this way God's ancient and present dispensations are reconciled (28—31), and all reduced to this one great principle, of convicting all of unbelief, to bring all to repentance and pardon:—the subject in fact of the former part of the Epistle (32). Finally he ends with a hymn of glory to God, for thus turning evil into good (33—36).

§ VI. Practical results from the former Parts (xiii. 1— xv. 13).

1. Christian Sobriety (xii. 1—8).
2. Christian Charity (9—21).
3. Christian Loyalty (xiii. 1—10).
4. Constant remembrance of the end (11—14).
5. Condescension to one another's notions of duty (xiv. 1 —xv. 13).

1. Of Christian Sobriety* (with reference to the peculiar condition of the Roman Church when he wrote).
To be practised for God's sake, a. in the *body* (1), for all the foolish and flattering world (2); β. in the *mind*, concerning oneself, in suiting one's own opinion to God's gifts (3), according to the analogy of the body (4, 5, and part of 6): whatever our office be (6, 7, and part of 8), and whatever virtue it most calls on us to practise (8).

2. Of Christian Charity, described by various signs in the manner of memoranda. Cf. 1 Cor. xiii., 1 Thess. v., 1 St. Pet. iv. 7, &c. (I do not discern his exact arrangement in these verses, 9—21).

3. Of Christian Loyalty (xiii. 1—10).
We must be loyal, for, a. Government is of God (1, 2): β. its purpose is most useful, to repress vice, and encourage goodness (3, 4); which is a reason binding on the conscience as well as self-love (5).
Corollary: the reasonableness of paying taxes (6), which stands on the same ground as any other debt (7); and it does not become a Christian to have any debt but Charity: which, as it can never be fully paid, so in proportion as it is sincerely paid, supersedes positive laws and renders them unnecessary (8—10).

4. Constant remembrance of the end (xiii. 11—14).
These duties enforced, a. by the shortness of the time; which ought to impress us more instead of less, than when we first thought of it (11); β. by the great change approaching,—as great as from night to day (12); which requires a corresponding preparation on our parts (13), according to our Lord's example (14).

5. Condescension to one another's notions of Duty (xiv. 1— xv. 13).

---

* Mr. Keble's note: " He begins with Christian Sobriety as Jer. Taylor in his ' Holy Living.' "

General rule (1), illustrated by the case of the Judaizers who scrupled about eating (2); in which there being two parties, the strong and the weak, he gives directions,

α. to both, not to judge (3).
    a. because of the impertinence of interfering between God and His servant (3, 4);
    b. because *both*, for aught you know, may be acting for God's sake, in conformity to the principle of religion; illustrated by the example of days as well as meats (5—9);
    c. because we are soon to be judged ourselves (10—13).

β. He gives directions to the strong, particularly, to avoid whatever may occasion sin in others (13). Their principle indeed is true,—that such uncleanness is only relative and fanciful (14); but it becomes them
    a. not *to press such food on their brother*, if he scruple it; considering 1st. the value of his soul (15); 2nd. the duty of preserving our Christian liberty from reproach (16); 3rd. the avowed triflingness of these things in comparison of the great things of peace, &c. (17—19, in which N.B. the Apostle's ingenuity in taking up, as it were, the words of an objection, and turning them to his own account).
    b. It becomes the strong even to abstain themselves, rather than cause sin in others, considering,
        1st. the small value of the good, and the greatness of the loss (20);
        2nd. the duty and virtue of self-denial in such cases (20, 21);
        3rd. that they lose by it no part of the appropriate blessing of Faith, which is not for show, but for a quiet conscience; a great and rare blessing (22): whereas he who eats in doubt, being tempted by them, is self-condemned (23).
        4th. That God gave them their strength for the very purpose: to support the weak, not to enjoy themselves (xvi. 1, 2).
        5th. That Christ throughout set them such an example (3), which being illustrated by a quotation, leads to some affectionate expressions suitable to St. Paul's purpose (4—6).

6th. Particularly in the Gospel dispensation, which, so far as it is an union of Jews and Gentiles, is a great example of the πρόσληψις [b] which he wants to have practised among Christians (7—12); and which, he finally insinuates, would be sure to obtain them a blessing (13).

§ VII. His own feelings and plans explained (xv. 14—33). He knows there was no absolute need of such an Epistle (14): but it came within the line of his peculiar duty (15, 16); in which he had been very successful (17—19), observing the rule of going to untried places by preference (20, 21); which was one obstacle to his visiting Rome (22). His present plan: to visit Rome (23, 24) on his way into Spain, after he had first been to Jerusalem with alms (25, 26), most reasonably contributed (27). Plan following this (28); his good hope of it (29); requests intercession as one in jeopardy (30—32). A benediction (33).

[b] Πρόσληψις, προσλαμβάνεσθαι :—words used by St. Paul in the sense of *welcoming others into our communion.*—[ED.]

[*The Sixteenth Chapter, containing the Salutations, is omitted in the Analysis.*—ED.]

THE FIRST EPISTLE TO THE CORINTHIANS.

Date of 1 Cor. is made out from ch. xvi. 8, by which it is clear that it was written at Ephesus, when St. Paul was intending to leave it for the journey mentioned in Acts xx.; one purpose of which was a collection for the poor of Jerusalem. From the opening of 2 Cor. (i. 8) I gather that this was written before the stir by Demetrius; and from 1 Cor. iv. 17, xvi. 10, *after* Timothy and Erastus had been sent into Macedonia, but *before* they arrived at Corinth (Acts xix. 22).

§ I. Salutation (i. 1—3) and thanksgiving for the proficiency of the Corinthians (4—9).

§ II. Reproof of the Corinthians for their schism and party-spirit (i. 10—iv. 21).

Charge stated (i. 10—12).
Amendment enforced *a.* on general considerations (i. 12—iv. 5).
b. on personal considerations (iv. 6—21).

a. a. Their disputes contrary to the singleness with which Christ should be loved and obeyed (i. 12—17)—enforced by St. Paul's practice in not baptizing.

β. The σοφία, which, being over-esteemed, led them to disputes, was no measure of right and wrong in the Gospel (17), which rather appeared folly to men left to themselves (18); as had been prophesied (19), and came to pass (20): God ordering it so, to expose the false wisdom which had led the world from God (21): and thus Christ's Cross, though it completely answers both the Jews' demand of power, and the Greeks' of wisdom, appears weakness to the one, and folly to the other (22—24). God's glory being thus shewn both in the frame of the Dispensation itself (25), and in the sort of persons who received it (26), and the world at the same time completely humbled before Him (27—29), and His Son, who is wisdom and all in all (30, 31). This train of thought illustrated by reference to his own way of instructing them (ii. 1—5); and followed up by a claim on the part of Christians of the true wisdom, long hid in God (6—9), revealed only by His Spirit (10—12), and taught by spiritual arguments to spiritual men (13—16).

γ. The point on which they disputed shewed great imperfection in Christianity, viz. the merit of their respective teachers (iii. 1—4), who were but several ministers of the same divine work (5—10), a work of exceeding awfulness and danger (10—17), and therefore requiring, in those who judge as well as in those who practise it, the greatest intellectual humility (18—20), and entire freedom from low and party views (21—23). The whole topic summed up by a brief statement of the true office of Christ's ministers, their duty, and the frame of mind concerning man's judgment (iv. 1—5).

b. Personal considerations, enforcing the general warning against conceit and party-spirit (iv. 6—21).

He declares that he had only used his own name and Apollos' before as a mode of conveying his argument, which was general, against those faults (6), (which indeed might at once be put down by the bare consideration of our accountableness) (7). And whereas they seem to have represented themselves as being in a high state of spiritual enjoyment (8), it might not be amiss for them to recollect the sufferings, inward and outward, which the Apostles were enduring the while (8—13); of which he at least might remind them without invidiousness, as he was their spiritual father (14, 15), with whom they would do well to sympathize more than they did (16). And to assist them in doing so, was one purpose of his sending Timothy (17); not that he did not mean to come himself, as some imagined (18), who would soon find in his presence how little *talking* signifies (19, 20). Surely, then, they would rather he came in affection than in anger (21). Thus he passes to his direction concerning the incestuous person.

§ III. Reproof of the Corinthians regarding the incestuous person (v.). The charge brought (1), and the temper which it should produce in them stated (2); a solemn excommunication directed (3—5). Three remarks:— *first*, on the absurdity of their conceit with such sin among them (6); *second*, the need of their purifying themselves, to keep a spiritual as well as external Easter (7, 8); *third*, a limitation of his exclusive sentence to those who were Christians, and so amenable to discipline (9—13): confirmed by the analogy of the law (13).

§ IV. Reproof of the Corinthians for going to law before heathens. From the mention of ecclesiastical judgment, he naturally passes to their civil suits, which he blames on two grounds:—*a*. as being in heathen courts, discreditable to their high calling, as if the meanest of them ought not to be able to determine such trifles (vi. 1—6). β. as implying bad passions somewhere or other among themselves, such as in fact they had renounced in baptism, and such as disqualified them for God's kingdom (7—11).

§ V. Caution against sensuality;—connected with the last section by the mention of such sins in ver. 9, 10 (vi. 12—20). Christian liberty to be modified by Christian prudence (12); remembering that as there are some animal enjoyments which are necessary, though but for the short space of this world, so there are others which are positively wrong, *first*, as breaking the relation between our bodies and Christ, which was sealed by His resurrection, and will be confirmed by ours (13, 14),—and wrong in the most insulting way (15), proved by the institution of marriage (16), and its analogy to our union with Christ (17):—wrong, *secondly*, as being committed against our own bodies (18), which are the temples of the Holy Ghost, and God's property by redemption (19, 20), due therefore entirely to His glory.

From which he passes naturally to answering some questions which the Corinthians had sent him about marriage (ch. vii.).

a. Perhaps generally, but certainly in their case, he recommends abstinence, but allows marriage, and forbids separation, except temporary, for devotional purposes (1—7).

β. Repeating the general principle (8, 9), he settles the point of divorce by an appeal to Christ's own words (10, 11).
γ. On his own authority he forbids separation on the part of the believer when married to an unbeliever (12, 13):—
  a. because the sanctity of the one extended after a manner to the other, proved, à fortiori, from what they knew concerning their children (14);
  b. (After providing for the case of the unbeliever wishing to separate) he shews it by the tone of the Gospel generally (15):
  c. From the chance of doing good to the soul of the other (16).
  [This takes him into a digression, in which he illustrates the general principle on which the above rule depended:—the principle of making the best of things as they are, instead of seeking outward changes (17, 20, 24); e.g. in circumcision (18, 19), in slavery (21—23).]
δ. By his own authority, in like manner, he settles the duty of parents in respect of giving their children in marriage or no (25—38).
  Not as matter of commandment, but as matter of prudence, he rather recommends virginity (25—28), not for any excellency in itself, but with a view to Christian quietness of mind (29—35); so that, although there is nothing sinful in marriage, yet on the whole the other is better (36—38).
ε. In the same way second marriages are not forbidden, yet not recommended to widows (39, 40).

§ VI. Of eating things offered to idols (viii. 1—xi. 1).
  a. The general principle clear:—that, an idol being nothing, nothing offered thereto was unclean in itself (viii. 1—6).
  β. But the greatest practical caution to be observed, both for our brother's sake (7—ix. 22),
  γ. and for our own (ix. 23—x. 23).
  δ. The whole authoritatively summed up.
  β. The practice of eating εἰδωλόθυτα not to be rashly sanctioned:
    a. Because the danger to our brother's soul is not to be balanced by the mere consciousness of superior knowledge (viii. 7—13). Error from which that danger

arises; viz. a lingering fancy of ceremonial uncleanness (7); in which, by the way, we participate, if we press the absolute duty of eating (8). Rather let us look at the thing with a view to our brother's good (9); for it is plain how with this error our liberty may mislead him (10); and so for our foolish vanity Christ's work is undone (11), and Christ affronted (12). Therefore we should rather give up the most innocent liberties than give such scandal (13).

 b. Because in such matters it is right to go by the rule which St. Paul had set himself: which is made clear, *first*, in the instance of maintenance (ix. 1—18); and, *secondly*, by a general statement (19—22).

  First. He asserts his Christian liberty, and Apostolical prerogative (1), especially over the Corinthians (2), which was enough to stop the mouths of objectors (3), as carrying with it a right to maintenance, for himself and his family (4, 5), proved (A) by the example of other Apostles (5, 6); (B) by analogy (7), as in the law of Moses (8—10); (C) by natural equity and gratitude (11); (D) by the allowance of the Corinthians in other cases (12); (E) by the express ordinance of God, both under the Law (13), and under the Gospel (14). Having thus proved his right, he states his practice and his wish, to decline it (15); his peculiar delight being not simply to preach the Gospel, which he did by direct commandment (16), but to preach it without cost to the Church, the pleasure of which was a reward to him, over and above his trust as a steward of the Word (17, 18).

  Secondly. What he did in the matter of maintenance was an instance of his general rule (19), as practised towards Jews—men who owned right and wrong (20),—and men who did not (21); and, as in this instance, towards the weak; for the good of others (22).

 γ. This care of the Apostle was necessary to him, and is so to us, for the salvation of our own souls, as well as others (23); which work—how great and difficult it is—he illustrates

a. from the Grecian games (24—27);
b. from the history of the Israelites in the wilderness (x. 1—11);
c. from both; inferring the need of mistrust of ourselves (12), trust in God (13), such prudent care against idolatry, as would keep us, who are by the Sacrament of the Lord's Supper one with Christ, from becoming one (not with idols, which are nothing, but) with demons, and so provoking God (14—22).

a. 24—27. We must not take liberties, because our calling is like one of the ἀγῶνες. For (A) not every one that runs, wins: (B) self-command is required in all things. Again, they are *un*like in one thing which strengthens the argument:—St. Paul himself (considering A) took all pains, and (considering B) was universally temperate.

b. x. 1—11. We must not take liberties, because we have the example of the Israelites set before us; who all shared in privileges corresponding to Baptism (1, 2), and to the Lord's Supper, both as to the bread (3) and as to the cup (4); yet most of them fell (5); to warn us that with all our privileges we are in danger of wrong desires (6), which will lead either to gross apostasy, as when the first generation of Israelites worshipped the calf (7), and the second joined the Midianitish women (8); or to inward presumption, as when these were slain by serpents (9); and murmuring, as those fell by the plague after the matter of Korah (10); all which had a double meaning, regarding us as well as them (11).

c. Application of the examples above quoted (12—22).

Our duty is to be afraid of ourselves (12); yet to trust in God's grace (13): And as to the particular matter before the Corinthians to avoid every sort of idolatry (14); which—how it was connected with idol-feasts—their own common sense would shew them (15), considering that by the Lord's Supper they communicate in Christ's Body and Blood (16) [that being the medium which makes them one with each other] (17); just as the Jews communicated in the sacrifices by the feast which took place after them (18)[a]. Considering this, they might see that though the idol was nothing (19), yet the evil which prompted the idolatry was; and that it was therefore inconsistent for God's communicants to partake of that feast (20, 21), and affronting to God also (22).

    δ. Summing up the whole of the Corinthians' duty in the matter of things offered to idols (23—xi. 1).

Allowing their Christian liberty, it is yet to be limited by expedience (23), and by others' good (23, 24). Their liberty made it lawful for them to eat freely of common food, as God's gift (25, 26), even at meals with unbelievers (27). But the limitations above-mentioned forbade them to do so if any one expressed a scruple (28); because it was God's gift, and therefore only to be used to His glory, (taking care however not to be entangled in such scruples themselves, their thanksgiving always shewing that they meant no dishonour to God by their liberty) (29, 30). Generally do all to God's glory (31) and man's edification (32), as St. Paul did, putting himself in everybody's place (33), imitating him as he did Christ (xi. 1).

§ VII. Of certain points which needed regulation in the public worship of the Corinthians (xi. 2—xiv. 40).
1. Of the dress of men and women (xi. 2—16).
2. Of the Eucharist (17—34).
3. Of the exercise of spiritual gifts (xii. 1—xiv. 40).
    (In which arrangement observe the delicacy of the Apostle touching, *first*, on what was least universally interesting; *secondly*, on what was most obviously wrong; and, *thirdly*, on what would be most trying to the prejudices of the Corinthians).

1. Generally speaking they were to be praised for their obedience (2); but it was worth while to remind them of the great principle of subordination, by which, as Christ is inferior to the Father touching His manhood, and as the Church looks up to Him as her Head, so the woman to the

---

[a] Mr. Keble's note:—"Nothing surely can be more express than these verses to shew that the proper notion of the Lord's Supper is that of a feast upon a Sacrifice."

man (3): which settles the point that men should pray uncovered (4), and women covered (5): which last (being, I suppose, the point in dispute) is sufficiently indicated by considering what we should think of their being shorn (6). The reason given is the Scriptural account of the origin of man and woman: the man directly in the image of God (7), the woman *from* (8) and *for* (9) the man: which makes a mark of subordination of this kind right: considering moreover the presence of the angels (10): [taking care, however, to make no distinction between the two sexes in respect of their Christian calling (11, 12)]. This reason is confirmed by an appeal to natural instinct (13—15). Finally, if people will be perverse, the custom established must be pleaded against them (16).

2. He warns them that he had a charge against them, by incurring which they turned the Church assemblies into evil (17); and laid themselves open to the imputation of schism (18); which, by the way, might well be believed, since even heresies would be permitted to try their stability (19). To specify this charge:—it was their hurrying way of rushing to the Lord's Supper as to a common feast (20, 21),—to the reproach of the Church, and confusion of the poor (22). To correct this let them only recollect the institution of this Supper (23—25), and that consequently, when they take it, they are bearing witness to Christ's death (26); from which it follows, that if they do it unworthily they are consenting with His murderers,— at least slighting His remains (27)[b]. The practical remedy is also evident:—let a man prove or try himself (28), considering that he condemns himself by the very act of communicating, if he do it unworthily (29); in correction of which God had sent on the Corinthians temporal judgments (30), according to His wont when Christian people forget their calling (31, 32). This in general: and as to the particular case, let them wait decently for one another (33), and reserve their regular meals for their own houses (34).

---

[b] I have allowed this word to stand, though very sure that Mr. Keble would have changed it, had he revised his Manuscript for the Press.—ED.

3. Of spiritual or supernatural gifts.
   a. A test given that false spirits might not deceive (xii. 2, 3).
   β. In the management of really supernatural endowments, remember the common origin of these gifts amidst all their diversity (4—11):
   γ. and their union, like members of the same body (12—27), which of course implies inequality (28—30).
   δ. Also, how worthless they are without charity (31—xiii. 4), which is quite distinct from them, both by its marks (5—7) and by its excellency (8—13).
   ε. Yet this is not to exclude the pursuit of spiritual gifts, in due subordination to charity (xiv. 1), with right apprehensions of their relative importance, e.g. preferring prophecy to speaking with tongues (1—25); and with strict regard to edification, decency, and order (26—40).

More in detail:—

   β. With regard to the miraculous endowments: different as they are, yet looking on them as gifts, they come from the same Spirit (xii. 4), as modes of service from the same Lord (5), as powers from the same God (6). And expediency (of which God is the judge) assigns and measures the gift (7). Some are taught the *reason*, some the *facts*, of religion (8): some have simple faith, some miracles (9): and so of others (10); yet all from the same Spirit dispensing all freely (11).

   γ. This arrangement of the Holy Ghost may be illustrated by considering the natural body; which bears an analogy to the mystical body of Christ in being (A) one, (B) with many members (12);—explained as to A in the Church (13):—the practical result enforced in terms drawn from the body (14—26), i.e. since the constitution of the body is that of a whole, made up of various and unequal parts (14), the minister (15) and the learner (16) must not complain as if they were not of the body, because they have not the higher offices, considering, *first*, that various functions require various members (17); *second*, that the arrangement of these is according to God's good pleasure (18); and *third*, that without this diversity the body would perish (19). And, on the other hand, since the body, though of such various parts, is still *one* (20), those in higher places or gifts must not disdain the weaker (21); as is intimated in the natural body by the need of the weakest (22), and the respect natural to the most uncomely parts (23); which is God's doing (24), to produce perfect sympathy in the body (25); and His purpose is there accomplished (26). The case being analogous in the Church [as had been shewn as to the *unity of the body* (A) in verse 13, and is shewn as to the *diversity of members* (B) in verses 27—30], the conclusion is evident, yet admitting of a reasonable care about the better (i.e. the more edifying) gifts (part of 31).

δ. Contains
  a. The proposal of "a way" which was such κατ' ἐξοχήν (31);
  b. The declaration of its excellency over tongues (xiii. 1), over prophecy, over faith of miracles (2), devotion of all our goods, martyrdom (3):
  c. The account of its marks (4—7):
  d. Of its excellency in respect of χαρίσματα, that it is eternal, they temporary (8), proved by their imperfect nature (9), which cannot remain in a perfect state (10), any more than the notions of a child in full age (11); —our present and future spiritual sight differing as a shadow and substance, or as our knowledge and God's —(12). Whereas there being three tempers which will be never out of date, charity is the greatest (13).
  e. On the relative value of the spiritual gifts one among another. As Charity is above them all, since we are to *pursue* it, and only to *desire* χαρίσματα; so the best of them are the gifts of instruction (xiv. 1); because in tongues we speak to God only, in prophecy to man also (2, 3): in tongues we edify ourselves, in prophecy the Church (4). Prophecy is therefore the higher gift, unless interpretation be added to tongues (which implies prophecy in some sort) (5); for so only can the speaking by tongues be addressed to the hearers, and bring them either information, or instruction (6). Consider the absurdity of music without distinct sounds (7, 8); and see whether tongues without interpretation

have not something of the same (9). Or—there being many languages with each its system of sounds (10)—consider the uselessness of speaking one of them to a foreigner (11); and let that teach you what sort of spiritual gifts you should prefer (12); and, if you have tongues, pray that you may interpret (13), else you bring no edification to others by your prayers in an unknown tongue (14). Therefore any one who had his choice should prefer uniting the two gifts (15), else neither is there any communion nor edification to their hearers in their *thanksgiving* (16, 17). This he confirms by a strong expression of his own feelings (18, 19). Then, prefacing his argument by an appeal to their common sense (20), he proves by a passage in Isaiah (21) that gifts, such as these of tongues, were meant, rather for the convincing unbelievers,—Prophecy for believers (22): and even so, when exercised among themselves, the latter would have most force even in convincing the unbelievers themselves (23—25).

4. Practical rules for the management of these gifts.
   α. Generally, when you come together with each his gift of instruction, let edification be the rule (26).
   β. Particularly as to tongues. Let not more than two or three speak in each assembly, and never without an interpreter (27, 28).
   γ. As to *Prophecy*, let two or three speak by turns (29), and give way to express revelations, if such be made (30), each taking his share in the common edification (31); and having the command of his own gift (32): God revealing Himself everywhere, even on these occasions, as a God not of confusion but of peace (33).
   δ. The women to refrain from public instruction according to nature and Scripture, and to wait till after church for explanation (35).
   ε. Authoritative enforcement of all these rules, upon consideration that the Corinthians were neither the mother-church nor the only one (36). Appeal in this behalf to the prophetic knowledge of such as were really prophets (37). And censure of such as would not recognize them (38).

5. Brief recapitulation of the whole,
    α. As to the temper with which the χαρίσματα should be regarded (39):
    β. As to the outward conduct of them (40).

§ VIII. Of the Resurrection of the Dead (ch. xv.).

1. Summary of the evidence of our Saviour's Resurrection (1—11).
2. Necessary connexion of His Resurrection with ours, and with all our hopes (12—19).
3. Order observed by the Almighty in the completion of this great work (20—28).
4. Witness borne to it through the whole of practical religion, which falls to the ground without it (29—34).
5. Answer, by analogy, to the objection, that we cannot understand the *manner* of the Resurrection, or the *kind* of Body we shall have (35—49).
6. Prophetic declaration of as much as is needful to be known on this subject: and practical application (50—58).

1. Reference to the Gospel as first preached among them (1); with a hint of its importance (2). The first point in it the doctrine of the Atonement (3); the second, the Resurrection (4), proved by six appearances, each briefly indicated (5—8), and the last to St. Paul himself, very remarkable in its results, comparing his former unworthiness with what the mercy of God had enabled him now to do (9, 10). But to return, such was the Gospel (11).
2. Inconsistency of the denial of the Resurrection by some of the Corinthians with our Lord's Resurrection (12); since, if there be no Resurrection, Christ is not raised (13); and our faith and pardon are void (14); and we are false witnesses in religion (15). This repeated, substituting the impossibility of a Resurrection for the falsity of it (16, 17); and adding the consideration of the lost condition (in such a case) of those dead in Christ (18), and the pitiable condition of Christians generally (19).
3. The fact of Christ's Resurrection, and its relation to ours, stated again triumphantly (20); with a short parenthesis shewing its congruity, that the manner of our recovery might answer to the manner of our fall, both being by man (21),

and both by *one* man (22); and if it be yet matter of faith, that is from no doubtfulness in the thing, but because God works it by degrees: first, His resurrection; then ours (23); then the final triumph, upon which His mediatorial kingdom ceases (24), the Saviour having limited that kingdom by the subjection of His enemies (25), of which the last is Death (26); and having also implied His subordination as Mediator to His Father by the word ὑπέταξεν (27); which subordination will be manifested, and God's immediate agency revealed in some signal way, at the end (28).

4. As the doctrine of the Resurrection harmonizes with God's dealings, so it is implied in the very notion of a Christian life: e.g. in Baptism [c] (29), in the sufferings of the Apostles (30—32), in not living at random (32), the tendency to which in such irreligious speculations (33), and in the wilful ignorance of religion in which some live (34), requires the most earnest warning on the Apostle's part (33, 34).

5. If people object that they cannot understand *how* this will be, or *what sort of body* will appear (35), they may be referred to what happens in sowing; in which, first, the seed must die (i.e. be dissolved) (36); then a change must take place, the greatness of which we know by the difference between a dry grain and a plant of wheat (37), and that change varying in different kinds and individuals according to the will of God (38): which, if it cause so great differences here in various living substances (39), we may well conceive a like or greater difference between earthly and heavenly bodies (40); and infinite differences of glory between these and those, and between those one amongst another, as in the lights of Heaven (40, 41). And this, which we might conceive by analogy, will be made good in fact. The risen body will differ from the mortal one, in corruption (42), glory, power (43), and in being a fit instrument, not of the

---

[c] Mr. Keble's note is as follows:—

βαπτιζόμενοι ὑπὲρ τῶν νεκρῶν.] May not the phrase mean, "Who are from time to time receiving Baptism *in behalf of*," i.e. in testimony on the side of, "the Dead," scil. that they rise again.... The argument resting upon the very significant reference made in the act of baptizing to the doctrine of the Resurrection, (cf. Rom. vi. 3, 4); and (as St. Chrysostom points out) on the profession of Faith in the Resurrection which seems to have been the last thing then required of the Catechumens.

soul only, but of the spirit, for there is a real difference (44), in reference to which Moses spoke as he did of the creation of man; and we Christians can fill up the analogy to which he only alluded (45), observing always that God's dealings proceed in this order: viz. that the natural comes first, the spiritual after (46); Adam first, Christ after (47); representing, respectively, men's earthly and their heavenly condition (48), and our future resemblance to the other (49).

6. Authoritative declaration of the Apostle, that, there being a congruity between the substance and the condition in which it is placed, and it being impossible for the corrupt, as such, to inherit incorruption (50), the quick, as well as the dead, must be changed (51). The change will be sudden; the signal, the last trump; and it will go along with the resurrection of the dead (52);—it being God's purpose to make us, even our bodies, incorruptible and immortal (54); to which also the old Prophets bear witness, Isaiah (54), and Hosea (55). On which passages let it be remarked, that as the "sting" of which they speak is sin, and the power of sin depends on the imperfect state of man without the Gospel (56), we—delivered as we are already from that—have nothing to do but to be thankful (57) and persevering, since we know for certain that none of our labour can be vain (58).

[*The Analysis of the Sixteenth Chapter is wanting in the MS.*—ED.]

THE SECOND EPISTLE TO THE CORINTHIANS.

DATE of this Epistle after Pentecost (1 Cor. xvi. 8) A.U. 808, A.D. 56. Probably in the autumn, to give time for the journeys of St. Paul himself (ii. 13, 14), and of Titus (vii. 6), mentioned in it. The place evidently some town in Macedonia (ix. 2).

§ I. Salutation (i. 1, 2).

§ II. Account of his own sufferings and proceedings quite or nearly ever since dispatching the former Epistle (i. 3—vii. 16), with many digressions.

1. Expression of the state of mind which his trials had produced (3—7).
2. Statement of the last of them (probably that in Acts xix.), and of his deliverance (8—10).
3. Request for their intercession, with the reason why he depended on it (11—14). He begs it (11) relying on what conscience told him (12), his present writing agreeing with his past and (perhaps) his future sentiments,—or (perhaps) his writings agreeing with Scripture and experience [d]—(13); and answering to what they had expressed (14).
4. Account of his change of purpose about coming to Corinth (15—ii. 2).

His purpose had been to pay them a second visit for their edification (15), passing by them into Macedonia, and returning, and so away to Judea (16). Nor was it mere lightness which made him forego this, his purposes not depending on himself (17):—[which leads him to observe parentheti-

[d] On the 13th verse Mr. Keble's note is:—"May it be imagined from this that St. Paul had been charged by some with writing private letters inconsistent with what he wrote to the Church, 'which they read; or rather,' says he, 'consented to on meeting with it.' (There is a turn in the words ἀναγινώσκετε, ἢ καὶ ἐπιγινώσκετε, which I cannot render.) Or perhaps the word ἀναγινώσκετε may refer them to the Scriptures, as ἐπιγινώσκετε to their own conscience."

cally how little reason they had in his preaching to suspect him of anything like caprice or wavering (18), the great doctrine of redemption through Christ (19), and the consequent promises of God in Him, continuing always the same (20); and we having, to confirm us, God's Spirit given by Himself, as an unction (21), a seal and an earnest of His love (22)]. But to return: it was not of caprice, but to spare them, that he gave up that purpose (23); [and he uses the word "spare" in no invidious meaning (24)]; i.e. being a "helper of their joy," he would not come to them in grief (ii. 1) which would only be spoiling his own best comfort (2).

5. The same account given of the severity of the former Epistle: which, having had its effect, the censure there directed might now be taken off (3—11). Accordingly he had written as he did, instead of coming; trusting to their affectionate feelings (3), himself in great affliction—which he mentions, not to grieve them, but to shew his love (4).— [For, as to the offender, he knew they participated in his grief concerning him (5); and accordingly their censures on him had been sufficient (6) for them now to forgive and cheer him (7); which he exhorts them to do (8); thus giving a fresh proof of the obedience which he had before tried (9); and ratifying the absolution, as before their excommunication (10), to counteract the devil's work—i.e., I suppose, temptation to despair—(11)].

6. Account of his perplexity at Troas, and of his departure for Macedonia: with an expression of thanks to God for using him in the Gospel (not by way of recommending himself); and of trust in the same God (12—iii. 6). He went to Troas, and had made a beginning (12), but was so disquieted at not meeting Titus with news from Corinth, that he went on into Macedonia (13). The recollection of which journey gives him occasion to thank God for His peculiar mercy towards him (14) in accepting his services as an Evangelist, whether successful or no (15, 16); which thanks he is bold to offer, being conscious of his sincerity (17). [This tone he takes, not as needing to introduce himself, or be introduced by others (iii. 1):—the Church of Corinth, which he had founded, being itself his credentials (2); a recommendation, as it were, in Christ's own hand, written with His Spirit on men's hearts (3).] To return: This con-

fidence he has towards God, not of himself, but in God entirely (4, 5):—in God, who has made him minister of a covenant better than that of Moses, the one, alone, leading to death, the other to life (6).

7. Digression on the comparative glory of the Mosaic and Christian Ministry (7—11).

[N.B. I have just called my ministry better than that of Moses (6); now that of Moses was exceeding glorious, as was indicated by the anecdote of the veil (7); how much more mine (8);—that bringing condemnation, the other pardon (9); the second quite eclipsing even the real glory of the first (10); and this confirmed by the eternity of the one, the transitoriness of the other (11).]

8. Tempers suited to this glorious ministry.

a. παρρησία (12—18).

Our hope naturally leads to free access to God (12), unlike that separation which was indicated by Moses' veil (13). And if they do not acknowledge this, the fault is, not in the Scripture in which the obscurity is done away, but in their hearts, which keep the veil on the Old Testament (14, 15). But as in Exodus, when Moses went in to God, he took off the veil (16), so where the Spirit of the Lord is there is liberty (17): and this privilege, leading to constant improvement in Christ's likeness, Christians have always (18).

β. Tempers suited to the Christian Ministry, continued. Disinterestedness (iv. 1—6).

As God has favoured us, so we continue in the exercise of His favour continually (iv. 1), having no self-ends, but doing all to commend ourselves to God (2). And if some perceive not, it is *their own* fault, and at their own risk (3), for allowing the evil spirit to blind them (4); not *ours*, who consider Christ only as the Master, ourselves your servants for Christ's sake (5): We having truly in our hearts to perceive the glory of the Creator of the world, as now revealed by Jesus Christ (6).

γ. A mind superior to affliction, and set only on pleasing God (7—v. 10).

True: we are afflicted for the present: but as one final cause of this is clear (7), so it is not an affliction we give way to (8, 9); and accordingly it conforms us to the likeness of our Lord's life as well as His death (10, 11): and works a good effect on you our converts (12). The Faith which the Prophets felt and taught, we feel and teach (13) with regard to the Resurrection particularly (14);—understanding so much of God's glorious purposes, as not to separate your spiritual interest from our own (15); desiring, rather, strength from tribulation (16), when we consider what our brief troubles are leading to (17); and compare things temporal with things eternal (18). Or thus: if our present body were destroyed, we know of an eternal one to follow (v. 1); therefore, even while here, we long for a better state (2), if we could but make sure of it (3); we long, I say, in spite of our natural dread of death (4), such being God's purpose towards us, and the meaning of the seal of His Spirit (5). To which add the consideration that whilst we are here, we are away from Christ (6); it being our condition here to walk by faith not by sight (7). Therefore we look death in the face, for the sake of meeting Christ (8): and our only ambition is to please Him (9): remembering the great day of judgment (10).

δ. The Fourth requisite for the Christian ministry: Devotion to the cause, arising from a deep sense of its importance (v. 11—vi. 10).

Having mentioned the Day of Judgment, he points out its effect on their labours (11); [appealing to God and them for the truth of what he said (11), not boastfully, but to help them in maintaining his cause (12); and whether he took that tone, or the tone of quietness, he had always the same thing in view (13):]—as also the effect of *Christ's great love* (14), the reasonableness of which is shewn both from the greatness of the need, and the natural result of the deliverance (15). The result is, no relationship, to us, continues merely human (16). And not to us alone, but even Christ is, as it were, in a new world (17), in which all is directly from God,—both Christ's Ministry and ours (18):—ours, I say, which is, as it were, His, both in respect of reconciliation, and of transmitting the ministry (19): We are therefore properly ambassadors; and this is our message:—" Be reconciled" (20): this our reason:—" He hath made," &c. (21).

To which message from God we add our own exhortations (vi. 1), confirming them by the consideration of the *time;* that it will not last for ever, as Isaiah hints (2): and preaching also by our conduct, avoiding offence for our office' sake (3); approving ourselves

a. by patience in sufferings, *inward* (4), and *outward*, both from others, and from our own self-denials (5);
β. by other Christian virtues (6);
γ. by Christian talents (7);
δ. by all means and the most opposite circumstances (7, 8);
ε. by the contrast between what we are and what we are supposed to be (8—10).

9. Earnest recommendation to keep themselves from close connexion with unbelievers, preceded and followed by expressions of deep affection (vi. 11—vii. 3).

You see how fluent my affection makes me (11). Indeed, I take more account of your true interest than you do yourselves (12). And the recompense I ask is, that you would enter into those feelings of mine (13): especially keep yourselves from union with unbelievers, considering what utter contradiction is involved in it (14, 15); and that most in your relation to God as Temples of His Spirit; which is proved from Leviticus (16). And the consequent duty of separation enforced by Isaiah (17). And the reward of being God's children proved by Jeremiah and others (18): which promises we having, are bound peculiarly to all purity (vii. 1). And with this reproof you will bear, considering my blameless behaviour toward you (2), and that I speak from true affection, having no pleasure in condemning you (3).

10. Statement of his proceedings resumed, and continued to the return of Titus (vii. 4—16).

He had been speaking of his affection, and this was especially his feeling now, through the comfort he had just received from them (4), after his restless troubles, inward and outward, in Macedonia (5); by the return of Titus (6), and most by his account of the repentance of the Corinthians (7). Which quite put an end to his regret for having written sharply to them (8), and made him glad that he grieved them to repentance (9):—a sort of grief not to be repented of, and therefore unlike the deadly sorrow men feel about worldly things (10). And the good effects of it were especially instanced in their case (11). Whence they might understand his true purpose in being so sharp with them (12), and the greatness of his comfort now, enhanced as it was by sympathy for the joy of Titus (13), and by finding that he was quite right in what he had said to him in their praise (14): Titus himself delighting to dwell on the particulars of his reception at Corinth (15): and St. Paul's confidence in the Corinthians being restored (16).

§ III. Concerning the collection for the poor Christians of Jerusalem (viii., ix.)

1. (viii. 1—ix. 5.) Exhortation to the Corinthians to be zealous in their contributions;

   α. by the example of the Macedonian Churches (viii. 1) enhanced by their poverty, as their joy by their affliction (2), carried beyond their means (3), and earnestly pressed on the Apostle by their entreaties (4); the whole amounting to a complete surrender of themselves beyond what could have been ever anticipated (5); and leading St. Paul especially to recommend Titus to follow up his good beginnings with the Corinthians on that subject (6).

   β. The same enforced by their own superiority in other gifts (7); [not by way of command (8)]; but in remembrance of the mercies of Christ (9); and by their forwardness in planning the contribution at first (10); which required an answering zeal now (11).

   γ. By the consideration of allowance made for unavoidable deficiencies (12).

   δ. By the equity of the thing, that each should alternately supply the other's need with his abundance (13, 14), and so fulfil the lesson given typically by the *manna* coming to all in equal measure (15).

   ε. By the consideration of the *persons* whom he had sent to them; 1. Titus, and his zeal for them (16, 17); 2. (supposed) St. Luke, and his high character as an evangelist (18), particularly indicated by his appointment as a συνέκδημος* (19), which was due to the Apostle's character (20, 21); 3. Another remarkable for his great

---

* A fellow-traveller, cf. Acts xix. 29.—ED.

f Mr. Keble's note: "It seems clear that the two other messengers were earnestness in the cause, and confidence in them* (22). Altogether they have the strongest claims: Titus, for St. Paul's sake; the others, for the Church's and Christ's (23). They are therefore worthy of all the encouragement the Corinthians can give them (24); not that the Corinthians want to be taught the duty itself (ix. 1), since their zeal for it has become exemplary to the Macedonians (2); but only to be ready (3), and not to disappoint and shame himself with his Macedonian friends (4). And this is the full account of his sending the brethren (5).

2. The whole to be regarded rather as a privilege than as a duty—applicable to time, as well as money (ix. 2—15).
   a. As enhancing the reward (5, 6).
   β. As pleasing God (7), who is able to give you such grace (8), and has promised in the Psalm to favour the profuse almsgiver (9), which he prays might be fulfilled in them (10).
   γ. As occasioning thanksgiving (11), over and above the immediate use (12): such donations being (as it were) a double sacrifice of praise for their Christian calling, 1. in the liberality of the thing itself (13), 2. in the intercession and affection of the persons benefited (14), to which St. Paul most heartily adds his thanksgiving (15).

§ IV. A strong personal remonstrance, in opposition to some usurping teacher or teachers, x. 1—xiii. 10.

   a. Commencing with a threat, grounded on an appeal to a prerogative which he had in common with all the Apostles (x. 1—6).
   β. Proceeding to special proofs of his own commission and integrity (x. 7—xii. 18).
   γ Applying all this to their present condition (xii. 19—xiii. 10).
   a. Some persons had sneered at his difference of tone, when absent and present (x. 1). He hopes they will not force him to use his power against those who charged him with worldly

---

unknown to the Corinthians, else they would have been named as Titus was. Apollos, therefore, was not one."

* "In them," i.e. in the Corinthians.—ED.

motives (2); for though *in* the world, his warfare was not of the world (3), as would appear on considering the instruments of it (4), subduing pride, and making Christ all in all in every man's mind (5); and prepared (if he could once see the Corinthians submitting) to avenge all other disobedience without delay (6).

β. So much for general considerations common to all Christ's ministers. If we descend now to those which are personal; whatever reason any man can give for thinking he has Christ's commission, St. Paul could give the same and more (7). [He ventures to boast in this way, knowing that the event will make it good (8), and will take away all pretence of his being bold only at a distance (9—11).] They fancied he shrank from the comparison[h]. It only shewed how they limited their views to themselves (12).

1st., then, he kept to his own appointed rule (13), which included the Corinthians (14); and sought to confirm them before he went further—especially into another's province[i] (15, 16). [Here he checks his own self-commendation with a prophetic text (17), and an application of it to his own case, and his adversaries (18).]

2ly. They should bear with his "folly," as it was called (xi. 1), considering his anxiety about them, whom he had espoused to Christ (2), and who, he now feared, would be seduced (3).

3ly. They should bear with it, considering that whatever claim, even to a totally new gospel, any other teacher might set up (4), still his (St. Paul's) claim to be equal to the highest Apostles (5) would stand; if not on his eloquence, yet on his knowledge, and indeed on all the experience they had had of him (6).

4ly. They should consider his having served them freely (7), at the expense of other churches (8), especially of Macedonia: and so he meant it should be (9), pledging himself by an oath (10), not for want of love (11), but to silence the objectors (12); [whom he pauses to describe

---

[h] Mr. Keble's note: "Perhaps the first half of the verse might be put in inverted commas, as being the assertion, not improbably, of St. Paul's rivals."

[i] Mr. Keble's note: "It is first an object to me to make Christians better; secondly, only, to make heathens Christians."

as pretenders to Apostleship (13), and imitators of Satan's hypocrisy (14, 15)].

5ly. If they compared him with the ψευδαπόστολοι, [a topic which they were not to believe he entered on willingly (16, 17), but which others made much use of (18), and those well received by them (19), for all their ill-usage of them (20), and which he had no occasion to recur to considering his authority], still he had, even humanly speaking, as strong claims as they (21), in respect both of descent (22) and of services and sufferings (23); of which instances are given, both external (24—27), and internal (28, 29): [The latter in part shewing his weakness, and therefore more willingly mentioned by him (30); for the sincerity of what he says, God is witness (31)]. And then, as if forgotten in its proper place, another instance comes in (32, 33).

6ly. The tacit comparison of the Apostle with the ψευδαπόστολοι is carried on from sufferings to visions and revelations: a topic on which he had an especial reason to fear vainglory (xii. 1). For after his trance fourteen years before, and visit, bodily or not, to Paradise and Heaven (2, 3, 4), [favours so great that they might be mentioned, as proving God's mercy to him, though he had nothing of his own but infirmities (5), and yet the less that was said of them (however true) the better, that people might not have overweening thoughts of him (6)], I say, after this trance, an affliction was sent him to check vainglory (7), which after three prayers (8) Christ declined to remove, to make him an example of resignation, which he cheerfully acquiesced in (9); as he did in whatever he endured for Christ's sake, being strongest when weakest (10).

7ly. Again expressing his unwillingness to speak so much of himself, and laying the blame on them (11), he says it could not at any rate be any deficiency in miracles or gifts, they had to complain of (12), they being at least as well off as the other churches (13), except in the one point of their not being allowed to contribute to him [which he meant should still be so (14) whether it lessened their love for him or no (15)].

8ly. And whereas it might be said that this refusal of his

was mere policy (16), he appeals to the conduct of his messenger, Titus, as well as his own, to shew his frank dealing with them (17, 18).

γ. Application of St. Paul's personal remonstrance to the present case of the Corinthians (xii. 19—xiii. 10).

He was not speaking to clear himself to them, but in God's presence for their good (19): fearing party-spirit among them, for their sake (20), and his own: fearing also imperfect repentance for profligacy of other kinds (21). This leads him to warn them that when he came this time he should proceed solemnly, as Christ had appointed (xiii. 1); neither former nor present sinners would he spare (2); accepting their challenge, and appealing to Christ's miraculous power within him (3); which abode in the midst of his outward weakness, as Christ's divine omnipotency did through His crucifixion (4); bidding them try themselves, standing in awe of their own great privilege of Christ's peculiar presence, if they had not quite forfeited it (5). At any rate, he trusted *he* had not (6). And whilst he spoke thus sharply, his prayer was that they might so repent, as to take away all need for displaying his power; though his credit might suffer thereby (7); for it might seem as if he had boasted falsely, his power not being shewn except when the vindication of the right of his Master required it (8). But still his joy was to have them go on so well and perfectly, and reform themselves so thoroughly, that he might appear as no more than another man (9). And this was the full account of his writing as he did, to avoid the necessity of spiritual censures when present (10).

§ V. Parting advice (11); salutation (12); and blessing (13).

THE EPISTLE TO THE GALATIANS.

§ I. SALUTATION (i. 1—5).

§ II. Protest against any new Gospel (i. 6—10).

§ III. Originality of St. Paul's Gospel shewn in answer to the undervaluers of his authority (i. 11—ii. 14).

§ IV. Statement and vindication of his doctrine of Justification (ii. 15—iv. 7).

§ V. Application of it to correct the practical errors of the Galatians (iv. 8—vi. 10).

§ VI. Conclusion, summing up the whole, and blessing them (vi. 10—18).

§ I. i. 1—5. Salutation, reminding them of his immediate call from God (1), indicating offence by the tone of his address (2), and remembering them of the great benefit which they had received in Christ's dying to deliver them from this evil world (3—5), to which they were disposed to return.

§ II. 6—10. Occasion of his writing: the rapid falling away to a new Gospel (6); though in fact there could be no such thing; unless these new preachers were some wonderful persons (7). Once and again, therefore, he anathematizes those who preached any new Gospel, be they who they might (8, 9): and accounts for his speaking so strongly from the consideration that he had long left off trying to please men, else he could not be an Apostle (10).

§ III. Proof of the originality of his Gospel by a review of his demeanour to the other Apostles.

α. From his Conversion to a certain journey to Jerusalem (11—24).

β. During the Conference occasioned by that journey (ii. 1—10).

γ. When St. Peter was at Antioch (11—14).

a. "My Gospel is not human (11), for it was received immediately from our Saviour (12), in confirmation of which, consider that any prejudices I might have of my own, would be all in favour of Judaizing; as is clear from my persecuting, as I did (13), and from my great progress in the old religion (14). And when I was converted, with such circumstances as shewed me to be one raised up specially (15) to preach the Gospel to the Heathen, I took no counsel of man (16). I was in Arabia, and at Damascus, not at all with the Apostles at Jerusalem (17). Three years after, I visited Peter (18), and saw James (19). [This statement I think of consequence enough to confirm it by an oath (20).] The rest of my time I spent in Syria and Cilicia (21), unknown to the Jews (22), except by report (23) and thanksgiving (24)."

β. On the second journey to Jerusalem here referred to (one being omitted, Acts xi. 30), Barnabas and Titus being witnesses (ii. 1), St. Paul had a divine command to compare his Gospel with what the other Apostles preached, privately to prevent hazard of souls (2). The rest gave the strongest proof of their agreement with him, by not even having Titus circumcised (3); but whatever was done, was done with a view to those errors which some insincere persons were trying to introduce (4), whom St. Paul resisted constantly (5). And in conference the very chief Apostles (a strong proof of God's not respecting persons) made no difference, added nothing to him (6). But seeing the peculiar trust and favour which had been conferred on him,—which they knew by the same signs as in St. Peter's case,—they made a compact with him and St. Barnabas, to divide the ministry between them (7—9); only with a caution to remember the poor of Jerusalem, which, as St. Paul reminds the Galatians, he was earnest in fulfilling (10).

γ. The strongest proof of St. Paul's independence was his resisting St. Peter at Antioch (11), whose error was, withdrawing himself from intercourse with the Gentiles for fear of offending some Jews (12); which misled the other Jews and St. Barnabas himself (13), and led to a strong remonstrance from St. Paul on the inconsistency of his conduct (14).

§ IV. Statement and Vindication.

a. The Doctrine of Justification stated as the ground of Christian Faith (15, 16).
β. Vindicated from the charge of immorality (17—20).
γ. Shewn inconsistent with the error of going back to the Law for righteousness (21—iii. 18).
δ. Reconciled with the Law by considering the Law's preparatory nature (19—iv. 7.

a. Such persons as St. Peter and I, with all our Jewish privileges (15), have found it necessary to become Christians, to obtain the pardon by faith in Christ, which can never be obtained by works of any law (16).
β. If those who seek pardon through Christ are still found impenitent, that is not the fault of the doctrine (17), but of the person acting so inconsistently (18); the very drift and meaning of the change from the Law taught by that Law), to the Gospel, being "a life unto God" (19); a crucifixion, with Christ, unto sin ; and a life, in Christ, by Faith (20).
γ. Inconsistency of the doctrine of *Pardon through faith in Christ* with the supposed necessity of the *Law*.
 1. If Pardon could be had by any Law (or other way), Christ's death was unnecessary (21);—a consideration which it was strange had not occurred to the Galatians, who had been so carefully taught the whole process of our Lord's crucifixion (iii. 1).
 2. Spiritual gifts being annexed to Justification, if the Galatians received the Spirit by faith without the Law, they were so justified (2), [a topic which strongly marks how preposterous their error was (3), and how they were throwing away the fruits of the sufferings too (4)]. But it was enough to ask the question again (5).
 3. Abraham was justified by faith (6), and your glory is to be sons (representatives) of Abraham ; therefore you must be justified so too (7). And this explains how all nations are blessed in him : i.e. by the admission of the Gentiles to favour, in a similar way (8). The blessing of Abraham therefore, i.e. Justification, is confined to the faithful (9); —those who depend on the Law being in fact under the curse annexed to the disobedient (10). And besides : whereas the man whom God accounts righteous is he

who lives by faith in an unseen reward (11); the Law provides no such principle, but a present temporal reward (12). In a word, so far was the Law from conveying the blessing of Abraham, that Christ was crucified on purpose to redeem men from the curse of it,—the manner of His death being such as to indicate this (13);—thus purchasing a right to justify all nations as Abraham was justified, and to seal that mercy with His promised Spirit (14).

4. This topic of Abraham's acceptance may be urged to disprove the need of the Law, in the following way:—

Even among human covenants, no alteration may take place without mutual consent (15). But God's covenant to Abraham was a free promise (not to all his seed, but to a chosen individual, viz. Christ, as was indicated by the Hebrew idiom זרע), to forgive all faithful and resigned persons for His sake (16). This the Law, 430 years after, cannot invalidate (17), the notion of a subsequent Law with fresh conditions, and a free promise at first, being incongruous (18).

δ. Objection: Is not this making the Law useless? Answer: The Law was (q. d.) an addition to the first scheme, to be a witness to the world against sin, and a check to it, till the appointed time should come,—administered, not by the Son of God Himself, but by angels (cf. Heb. ii. 2, &c.), and through a mediator (19); [which last circumstance implies that it was a proper covenant,—a mediator or umpire implying two parties: but if so, it could not make any change in the old covenant, except it were made between the same two parties: now the parties to the old Covenant were God and Christ, to the Mosaic, God and the Jews; therefore one only of the former was a party to the latter; therefore the former was not affected by the latter (20)]. And as the purpose of the Law is thus stated without any impeachment of the Promise, so the substance of it is a full confirmation of the Faith. For it does not profess to be the life-giving Law, else of course righteousness might have been won through it (21); but now it has expressly convicted all men of sin and imperfect means of recovery, to prepare the way for the Gospel (22): up to which time, it was a guard and restraint (23): and so acted (to change the image) as a kind of schoolmaster to bring us to Christ and His righteousness by faith (24): whose office was superseded when faith came (25). To enter into the spirit of this, remember the privilege of sonship (26), which you received at Baptism, having then been put as it were in Christ's place (27); and that without distinction of birth, station, or sex (28). Remember also the privilege of *heirship*, consequent upon the former by virtue of the promise to Abraham (29). And to understand the difference of our condition now and under the Law, consider these privileges as having been (as it were) in abeyance, like those of a child in infancy (iv. 1) under guardians at the father's discretion (2). So our privileges *were* no more than those of a slave, or a child learning his letters: those sensible rules or motives by which we were in a degree managed, being no more than an alphabet to higher things (3). But now that our Saviour has come, in all things like unto us, incarnate, and subject to the Law (4), we, being redeemed by Him, are fully adopted as *sons* (5), of which the Spirit of filial love is a seal (6); and thus the difference of Jews and Christians is that of servants and sons and heirs of God through Christ (7).

§ V. Application of the Doctrine of the Epistle to correct the practical errors of the Galatians (iv. 8—vi. 10).

    a. Inconsistency of the Gentile converts in thus receding to the Law.

"Your idolatry before was so far excusable, that it was accompanied with ignorance (8); but your present voluntary submission to that imperfect state admits of no such palliation (9), e.g. your observance of days (10) enough to excite my worst fears (11)."

    β. Appeal to their former feelings towards him (12—20).

"Why cannot you take my word, who was once in the same error? you have no cause to mistrust me, as if you had deserved ill of me (12). Though it was not deliberate kindness, but some infirmity which brought me among you, at first, as a missionary (13); yet nothing could exceed your respect for me (14), and devotion to me (15). You have not surely come to dislike me for telling you the truth (16). It is rather the flattery of those who want to persuade you that you want one thing to be full partakers of the Gospel, they hoping to make themselves your idols (17). But as to whatever might flatter you, if you had any right to it when I was among you, how childish in you to give it up merely because I am away (18)! Indeed, I feel towards you as to children in the birth (19):—and would I were with you! that I might suit my instructions to your immediate occasion, so perplexed am I (20)."

γ. Appeal (as it were an after-thought) to the history of Abraham, which is shewn to be typical (iv. 21—v. 1).

"To make the matter as clear as possible, I will explain to you the meaning of a portion of Genesis, which the admirers of the Law cannot gainsay (21)." The history of Abraham having two sons abridged (22, 23); explained to be the two Covenants—the Jewish (24) [to which in the case of Agar there is an allusion in the very name] (25), and Christian (26), according to the Prophecy of her supernatural fruitfulness (27). Isaac therefore is the representative of Christians (28); his being taunted by Ishmael, the type of their persecution from the Jews (29). The decree of Ishmael's expulsion the type of God's admitting the faithful only to justification (30). We being therefore children of the freewoman (31) must stand fast in our liberty (v. 1).

δ. *Importance* of the point of circumcision.

"Virtually you give up the liberty and the blessing of Christ by submitting to circumcision (2); for you bind yourselves to the whole Mosaic Law (3), breaking the Covenant of Justification by faith, and falling from God's favour (4), which we are taught by His Spirit to expect only by Faith (5); i.e. *practical* faith,—circumcision, uncircumcision, and every thing else, being then of no consequence (6). And so you had once begun to act: what has checked you? (7). Not He that called you, in any way (8); but it is an infusion of evil teachers (9), which I hope you will get rid of (10). Least of all, does it come from me, else why am I still persecuted, or any one else, by the Jews? (11). It were best to excommunicate such perverters at once (12)."

ε. Caution against abuse of Christian liberty, shewing by the way the true root of the error of the Galatians (13—25).

"Observe that when we talk of Christian liberty, we mean nothing at random, but a service of love (13). [I say 'service of love:' because, as far as the Law is binding, its accomplishment is secured by that one principle, which is indeed the same as Moses has delivered in other words (14); whereas in the disputes about it, you seem in danger of going to the extremest faults against it (15).] Or thus: once try to conduct yourselves by the Spirit, and your earthly tendencies will be kept in order of course (16); it being out of the question for those who have any principle of that kind to live at their own will and pleasure (17): and in such proportion as you permit the Spirit (as a kind friend) to guide you, you are freed from the penalties and restraints of Law (18). And the rule is clear enough: it consists in avoiding such and such things, as unchristian (19—21); and pursuing others as the blessings of the Spirit, and as sealing our release from condemnation by the Law (22, 23). And do not say this is impossible; for all Christians have received a power to keep themselves in order, and have pledged themselves to do so, in virtue of Christ's cross (24): They live by the Spirit,—how inconsistent in them not to walk by the Spirit!" [It was neglect therefore of practical holiness, and not of points of doctrine, which led the Galatians to their error] (25).

ζ. Caution particularly against vanity and consequent unkindness (v. 26—vi. 5). Especially is it unworthy of those who have such a rule, to be vainglorious, disputatious, envious (26); or to treat the real faults of others in any other but a spirit of meekness, considering ourselves (vi. 1). Rather it should make us submit to any inconveniences even when deserved by others, in imitation of Christ (2): the self-consequence which would hinder this, being a mere dream of one's own fancy (3); and the only true satisfaction one can have, arising from the sober approval of one's own conduct on examination, without comparison with others, or appeal to their judgment (4). This is evident from the simple doctrine of personal responsibility (5).

η. Recommendation of charity, especially to the teachers of the Gospel (6—10). The duty inculcated (6), on the ground that whatever might be fancied, there is no deceiving God, nor evading the rule of retribution (7); which proceeds, both for good and evil, in strict analogy with God's ordinary dealings (8); and therefore perseverance is only reasonable as in husbandry (9), as also vigilance in seizing all opportunities (10).

§ VI. Conclusion :—

In which he draws their attention to the importance of the subject; his strong sense of which was indicated by his writing so long a letter with his own hand (11). The point at issue being in fact no less than the virtue of the Cross of Christ: which those who preached the Judaizing doctrine wished to avoid conforming themselves to (12). It being clear that this was their real motive; for they did not pretend to keep the rest of the Law, but wanted to win men to their partial conformity, that they might keep themselves in countenance by their example (13). In opposition to whom, St. Paul declares his resolution to depend on nothing but the doctrine of the Cross (14); in comparison of which, all these outward distinctions were absolutely nothing (15). And on such as follow his rule he pronounces a blessing (16). And so, first hinting the peculiar unkindness of annoying him who had suffered so much for Christ (17), commends them to His grace, and bids them farewell (18).

THE EPISTLE TO THE EPHESIANS.

§ I. SALUTATION, and congratulation on the conversion of the Ephesians (i. 1—ii. 22).

§ II. Account of St. Paul's special interest in it (iii. 1—21).

§ III. Consequent exhortations :
To Unity (iv. 1—16). Purity (17—24). Government of the Tongue (25—v. 21). Relative duties (22—vi. 9). Universal goodness under the similitude of armour (10—18).

§ IV. Farewell, and blessing (19—24).

§ I. a. Salutation. The Ephesians addressed simply as Christians, and St. Paul described simply as an Apostle.—The Epistle may therefore be expected to be of most universal application (i. 1, 2).

β. Thanksgiving to God for calling us to be Christians (3—14). He gives glory to God for the abundance of spiritual blessings (3), corresponding to His final purpose, known to Him for ever, to make us good by making us Christians (4) ; I mean His purpose of adopting us by Jesus Christ (5) ; that His grace might be glorified in us. *a.* in our *acceptance* through Christ (6), and the forgiveness of our sins (7) ; *b.* in the wisdom and prudence of His *revelation* (8, 9), reserved for the later dispensation ;—the revelation, I mean, of Christ's mediatorship (9, 10) : in whom both we Jews, set apart by His purpose to believe first (11, 12), have a part, and also you Gentiles, by hearing, Faith and Baptism (13) ; so receiving the Spirit for an earnest of their inheritance, till all be fulfilled, and all to His glory (14).

γ. Intercession, corresponding to the former Thanksgiving (15—ii. 10).

The report of their Faith and Love (15) caused him to give continual thanks, and to pray (16) that they might have more and more knowledge of Christ (17), and of their Christian Privileges, here summed up in two heads (A and B):

A. The hope of their calling and rich inheritance (18),
B. Omnipotence of God on our side, evinced
    1st, in the resurrection and glorification of Christ (19—21) of which He graciously considers it the sum, that He is made Head of the Church (22, 23);
    2nd, in our resurrection, when dead in sin (ii. 1), [both Gentile (2) and Jew, having been of old alike under the power of the Devil, to please themselves (3), and alike delivered only by God's mercy through Christ (4)], our resurrection, I say, and ascension with Him (5, 6) the full effect of which will only be understood in another world (7).

    And N.B. all this is entirely a matter of free grace and favour (8), not earned by works, therefore not to be boasted of (9), as the very nature of the case shews: God made us for good works, therefore we can never make Him our debtor (10).

δ. Recommendation to compare often their former state with their present (11—22).

Consider your former condition as Gentiles and uncircumcised (11), without Mediator, Church, Covenant, Hope or God (12); and then your present,—brought near by the blood of Christ (13);—one of His attributes being to be our Peace, uniting us together, and doing away the enmity which separated between us and God (14); doing away also the law of express outward services, and substituting the law of love, so as to re-create both Jew and Gentile alike after His own image (15), and reconcile both to God by His Cross for ever (16). And not only hath He done this, but revealed it too (17), giving us alike access by the same Spirit unto the Father (18), so that now we are at home with God (19), part of that building of which the Apostles and Prophets are the foundation, and Jesus Christ the head-cornerstone (20): inasmuch as He keeps the whole in its place, so that it is gradually completed to be a fit temple by His divine power (21): in Him, I say, to crown these mercies, you are inserted by Christianity, to be an habitation for God (22).

§ II. Expression of St. Paul's peculiar interest in the Conversion of the Gentiles (iii. 1—21). [The whole section is parenthetical, inserted to enforce the practical admonitions which follow.]

Now St. Paul was at this time in prison for vindicating the right of the Gentiles to be Christians (iii. 1); as would well appear if they regarded the history of his ministry (2), especially the revelation made to him (to which he had formerly referred) (3); according to the state of their information on such points (4) to *him*, I say, and to the other Apostles, first of all men (5), the mystery of the conversion of the Gentiles (6) by the Gospel, of which he became a minister (7). An astonishing instance of God's power, on comparing the instrument with the message (8), revealing so deep a mystery, not only to all men (9), but also to angels (10); the message, I mean, of Christ's mediation purposed for ever (11), accomplished in our acceptance through Him (12):—the greatest encouragement to pray that no tribulation might make him faint (13), and that God would continue the gift of spiritual strength (14—16), of the presence of Christ by Faith (17), of Christian understanding (18, 19): for all which he gives glory to God (20, 21).

§ III. Exhortations consequent on the statement of Christian Privileges:

a. to Unity (iv. 1—16).

This your calling requires a corresponding demeanour (1) in the way of meekness (2), and particularly with a view to the preservation of Christian Unity (3), the reasonableness of which is plain on considering the identity of our hope (4), of our Mediator, and His ways of saving us (5), of our God (6). Yet in this unity there is great diversity, as Christ has pleased (7), according to the Psalmist's prophecy (8), [which, N.B., implies previous humiliation (9), and shews whom God delights to honour (10)], fulfilled in the various extraordinary offices and gifts communicated to the Church (11), with a view to the improvement of the whole (12), till they were come to true Christianity (13), and to defend us from religious jugglery (14); so that we may by truth and love grow like Him (15), from whom, incessantly, the happy growth proceeds (16).

β. To Purity (17—24).
Again, we must not walk at random, as the Gentiles do (17), with darkened minds (18), given up to uncleanness (19), whereas the very drift of Christian instruction is (20, 21) putting off the likeness to Adam (22), and an inward renewal (23) after the likeness of Christ (24).

γ. In particular, self-government towards others is enforced: In respect of *truth* (25). In respect of *anger*, which must be checked as soon as perceived (26), lest the Devil " impose on " us (27). In respect of *honesty* (28). In respect of unsound conversation, which particularly grieves the Holy Ghost (29, 30). In respect of *unkind words* (31), for which the temper of God in Christ must be substituted (32), as it is natural for darling children to imitate their parents (v. 1), and for those to walk in love for whom Christ offered Himself (2). In respect of *immodesty*, which should not be named (3) nor (especially) jested upon ; rather our discourse should tend to thanksgiving (4) ; considering the serious consequences of impurity (5), which is the very cause of God's wrath against the Heathen (6), with whom as such we have no more to do (7), we being turned from darkness to light (8), i.e. holiness, which is the natural result of the Spirit (9) ; and so approve what God loves (10), and expose what He hates (11). These sins being disgraceful to speak of, are best exposed by their contraries (12, 13), as is implied in the mention of light in a well-known formula (14). Be therefore very careful (15) considering the bad times (16), e.g. avoiding excess of wine, that the Spirit may dwell in you (18), [marking God's will (17)] delighting in Psalms (19), thanksgiving (20), mutual submission (21).

δ. Relative duties.
  a. Of the marriage relation (22—33).
    Duty of submission on the wife's part (22), considering the analogy between her relation to the husband, and that of the Church to Christ (23, 24). Of love on the husband's part, considering Christ's love for the Church (25), which (observe) was not a blind fondness, but such as tended most to *her purity* (26, 27), both being grounded on the very close connexion between them, like that of the head and members of the same body

(28—30); as is signified in the words of the institution of marriage (31), which had a deeper meaning, referring to Christ and the Church (32), but are mentioned now particularly, to enforce the duties of the conjugal love (33).

 b. Relative duties of Children and Parents.

  Of children from natural equity (vi. 1) from God's commandment (2), enforced by promise (3). Of Parents, not to provoke, but calmly to instruct (4).

 c. Of slaves and masters.

  Slaves must shew due respect (5) and sincerity as to God (6); which thought should also teach them to serve with good will (7), considering that God's rewards will be distributed impartially (8). Masters must rule by love rather: remembering His impartiality to whom they must give account.

 e. Concluding exhortation to entire Holiness: in a Parable from the Armour of the Roman soldiers (10—20).

  Universal duty of Christian courage (10), of such preparation for our spiritual warfare, as may be expressed by completely arming ourselves (11), most needful, considering that we have not men but spirits to contend with, and very powerful spirits (12): our only chance is to arm ourselves entirely (13): so to take our station, guided with truth (i.e. a notion of things as they are, not fancies). Armed on the breast with righteousness, i.e. good conduct (14): shod with Christian good temper[k] (15): Resignation to cover all (16): the doctrine of eternal life to keep off speculative objections: and the Word of God always ready to defend us as a sword (17): with continual prayer, and intercession (18), which last he particularly asks for himself (19, 20)[l].

§ IV. (21—24) For information as to himself they are referred to Tychicus (21, 22). And so he ends with a blessing on them (23), and on all good Christians (24).

---

[k] Mr. Keble's note: "The thing meant is, I suppose, the *good temper* of the Gospel, preparing us especially for minor difficulties."

[l] Mr. Keble's note: "This Section is perhaps the most poetical in St. Paul's writings. Compare with it Wisdom v. 17—20."

THE EPISTLE TO THE PHILIPPIANS.

THIS Epistle is, perhaps, (except those to the Thessalonians,) the most like a *private* letter of all St. Paul's Epistles to Churches. It naturally writes off in *Seven* Paragraphs:

§ I. Salutation, and assurance of his devout remembrance of them (i. 1—11).

§ II. Comfort in respect of his imprisonment: as to the progress of the Gospel: and as to the probability of his coming to them again (i. 12—26).

§ III. Admonition to them to keep up union and perseverance, and to live in the Spirit of Christ's Incarnation (i. 27—ii. 18).

§ IV. Arrangements which he was making to communicate with them (ii. 19—30).

§ V. Caution against debasers of the Gospel (iii. 1—iv. 1).

§ VI. Interference to reconcile two persons who had quarrelled, leading to an exhortation to cheerfulness and kindness (iv. 2—9).

§ VII. Thanks for their contributions, and farewell (iv. 10—23).

§ I. Salutation (1, 2); assurance of the thankful joy with which he remembered them as Christians, from his first acquaintance with them (3—5); and of his confidence in their perseverance (6); which they had well deserved by their recollection of, and sympathy with, him (7): also of his wish to see them (8), and his prayer for their increase in spiritual wisdom (9), till they become, practically, perfect in it (10), according to the natural result of Christ's Gospel (11).

§ II. (i. 12—26). With regard to himself, his imprisonment had tended to the furtherance of the good cause (12), being much talked of in the Prætorium and generally (13), and adding boldness to the efforts of the Christians (14); so that the very spite of his enemies exulting over his calamity served to disseminate the truth, as well as the honest efforts of his friends viewing it as a part of his testimony (15—17): a matter of joy to him in the event, in whatever spirit it was done (18). To him, I say, personally, as it gave him more and more hope of his final acceptance, by their intercession and God's sanctification (19), through courage and resignation to life and death (20); which two being compared, though for himself he would rather die, for their sake he consents, as it were, to live (21—24); and predicts that he shall do so, and see them again to their edification and comfort (25, 26).

§ III. This (comfort) would, however, depend on their conduct, their unanimity in the good cause particularly (27), and their fortitude in calamity,—the best earnest of salvation (28), and a special favour over and above their Christian calling (29),— in imitation of St. Paul himself (30). He adjures them, therefore, by all the privileges of Christianity (ii. 1) to be united (2), humble (3), waiting on one another (4), in imitation of Christ's temper (5), shewn in His leaving His first glory (6), and taking the form of a slave, as He did in becoming man (7); and suffering death, even Crucifixion (8), which was rewarded by His glorification (9); to be Lord over all in heaven, earth, and hell (10); and to be the Mediator through whom all glory should be given to God (11); which is the greatest reason for their persevering as they had done, sincerely, and in an awful sense of God's working in them (12, 13); without murmuring or disputing (14), innocent, as an example to a bad world (15), and that the Apostle might see the fruit of his labour in them at last (16):—labour which, if it ended in martyrdom, ought to be the greatest joy to them, as the thought of it was to him (17, 18).

§ IV. Not but he wanted the comfort of knowing how they were going on: and therefore he was going to send them Timothy (19), being the only person on whom he could depend for thorough sympathy with regard to them (20), all being more or less taken up with themselves (21). But *him* they knew by proof (22); and he should send him as soon as he was out of suspense as to himself (23), trusting himself to come soon (24). For the present he had sent Epaphroditus, qualified by his connexion both with him and with them (25), and earnestly longing to see them again after his illness (26); which, however severe, had been removed,—an especial mercy to St. Paul and him (27). Him he had now sent for their mutual comfort (28), recommending him to their special care (29), who had so nearly lost his life in waiting on Christ and Christ's minister (30).

§ V. (iii. 1—iv. 1.) Having cheered them up, he now proceeds to admonish them, rather wishing to use too much than too little care for their security (1). And his admonition is against the Judaizing teachers, and their mangling, which they called circumcision (2), whereas the true circumcision was only with Christians (3). And this he says the more emphatically, since he had the authority of one possessing in the highest degree the external Jewish advantages (4), in circumcision, birth, sect (5), zeal, obedience (6). Yet all these, and whatever else he had that seemed good, he was willing to give up for Christ, and that without hesitation, as chaff or refuse (7, 8). For Christ, I say, and that righteousness which can only be had of God by faith in Him (9), i.e. the actual knowledge of His Resurrection and Death, by living a life conformable to them (10), in hope of the resurrection (11), never once supposing that he had done enough : since the very purpose for which Christ had *overtaken* him was to put him in a state of continual exertion (12); he knew he had not got his crown (13), but was still racing towards the heavenly goal (14): let this temper be our test of Christian perfection ; and if we sincerely cherish it, God will rectify what is in us at variance with it (15). Only keep fast hold, practically and peacefully, of the good you have already got (16). Such being the Apostle's temper, he calls on his converts to imitate him and his imitators (17); for which caution there was great need, through the number of seducers, of whom he had warned them as enemies to the Cross (i.e. recommending base compliances to avoid persecution) (18): abandoned, selfish, impudent, earthly-minded (19). Whereas the city to which he invited them was heavenly, and would be revealed by the coming of our Lord (20), to raise and change our bodies according to His supreme sovereignty (21). And with this awful topic he concludes his affectionate exhortation to them, to stand fast as they were in the Lord (iv. 1).

§ VI. (iv. 2—9). Evodias and Syntyche to be reconciled (2). The husband (perhaps) of one of them to assist them ; considering how they had helped St. Paul (3). Let all live in Christian cheerfulness (4) and exemplary equity, in expectation of the Lord (5); without carefulness, throwing all that on God (6). So might they be sure of His peace to keep their hearts and thoughts (7). One care only should they have: to do all that is right (8), as he had taught them and set the example (9).

§ VII. (iv. 10—23). Assurance of his thankfulness for the renewal of their liberality, which in purpose wanted no renewing (10);—not on his own account, who had learned the lesson of contentment in wealth and poverty alike (11—13), but on theirs who had well done (14); as, indeed, they were the only converts from whom he accepted such aid at first (15), having been twice supplied in the three weeks he stayed at Thessalonica (16). His joy then was that their reward would be increased (17). For himself he had more than enough, and God would take it as a meet sacrifice (18), and would reward their need in like manner (19). Doxology (20). Farewell (21, 22). Benediction (23).

THE EPISTLE TO THE COLOSSIANS.

§ I. SALUTATION, and expression of St. Paul's interest in the Colossians, and thankfulness on account of them (i. 1—29).

§ II. Warning against mixing human inventions with the Gospel (ii. 1—23).

§ III. Exhortation to holiness generally (iii. 1—17).

§ IV. Relative duties (iii. 18—iv. 1).

§ V. Concluding cautions, messages, and salutations (iv. 2—18).

§ I. (i. 1—29). The Colossians being unknown to St. Paul personally, are addressed simply as Christians (1, 2). He assures them of the part they had, *a.* in his thanksgiving (3—8) : *β.* in his prayers (9—23) : *γ.* in the consolation of his troubles (24—29).

a. He remembered them always in his devotions with thanksgiving (3), since he has heard of their conversion and charity (4). Thanksgiving, I say, for their part in the hope of Heaven (5) :—that Gospel hope, upon which they were endeavouring to act (6), to which Epaphras had introduced them (7), who himself told St. Paul of them (8).

β. And as he gave thanks, so he prayed for their daily growth in Christian wisdom (9), and in Christian practice, the only way to that wisdom (10), especially in respect of resignation (11), and thankfulness in trouble for their Christian calling (12), i.e. for being turned from Satan to Christ (13), who is, *a.* our Redeemer (14), *b.* God's image; infinitely great, and so first-born[m] over all even in His human nature (15), according to His hereditary right as Creator of all (16), pre-existent, and preserver of all (17); and more peculiarly absolute over the Church, and first-born from the dead (His οἰκονομία thus bearing an analogy to His natural government) (18).

---

[m] Mr. Keble's Note: "I suppose the word has reference to *dignity* rather than *time*. Our Lord in His human nature is the πρωτότοκος of creation : and well may it be so, for by Him (in His Divine nature) all things were created."

All which depends on His being very God, inhabiting (as it were) very man[a] (19), and the chosen instrument, in some unspeakable way connected with His sufferings, of all reconciliation with God everywhere (20). And as their privilege was thus great in itself, so it was enhanced by the consideration of what they were called from; which made them a special instance of that reconciliation (21); to whom individually Christ's death, and the sanctification and salvation depending on it, were now ensured, if they only kept the faith (22, 23).

γ. The thought of this their faith gave him joy in his sufferings, and encouraged him to suffer on for the Church (24), of which by a special dispensation he had been made a minister (25), to make known more particularly the mystery of Christ as the Saviour of the Gentiles (26, 27); which he laboured to do, bringing it home to every man by God's help (28, 29).

§ II. (ii. 1—23). With regard to themselves especially they shared his anxiety, with all Christians whom he had not seen (1), for that comfort and growth in true wisdom (2) which is only to be had in Christ (3). Which last caution he added against deceivers by plausible argument (4):—having much approved their beginning, in respect both of good order and of firmness (5), and only wishing them to continue and go on, upon the one foundation they had received (6, 7). They must therefore be on their guard *generally* against any encroachments which human philosophy might make on the Gospel (8). For as Christ has in Him the fulness of God (9); so have Christians, as such, already the fulness of Christ, the sovereign of all (10) by spiritual circumcision (11), i.e. Baptism, which is also a spiritual burial and resurrection (12); conveying even to Heathens a new life with Christ by forgiveness (13); the charge against us being blotted out, or nailed to the Cross, and so cancelled (14): and the evil spirits openly led in triumph (15). And in the assertion of their Christian liberty, they were particularly to be on their guard against doctrines of the ritual observance of meats and days (16), [on this principle, that the shadow gives way to the substance (17)], or of voluntary ritual observance, or "Angel-worship;" calling itself humility, and

---

[a] Mr. Keble's Note: "From the common usage with regard to this word (εὐδόκησε) I could fancy that πᾶν τὸ πλήρωμα might be the nominative case; and in that way the sentence flows on better to the next infinitive, ἀποκαταλλάξαι."

being presumption (18); and fundamentally wrong, in that it swerves, more or less, from Christ the only Mediator (19). It was contrary to the perfection of their Christian calling (20) to be subject to such trifling (21), transitory, human rules (22); which, in a show of austere wisdom, pervert fasting from its right use, and make it ritual instead of moral ° (23).

§ III. (iii. 1—17). From the particular errors mentioned above, and considered as inconsistent with the condition of a Christian, the Apostle passes to the delineation of that temper which alone suits the Christian privileges; which consists in seeking (1) and minding (2) heavenly, not earthly things: in being dead here, and our true life with Christ in Heaven (3): yet with a sure hope of meeting Him in glory (4). Parts of this dispensation will be,

1st. The mortification of our impure desires (5), which draw down God's anger on the Heathen (6); as the Colossians, recollecting their own days of Heathenism, might too well know (7).

2nd. Correction of irascible passions, especially in respect of angry words (8).

3rd. Speaking the truth to one another: which is especially required by our change from the likeness of Adam (9) to that of Christ (10), a change common to one as much as another (11).

4th. Cultivation of good feelings, gentleness, &c. (12), especially forgiveness in imitation of Christ (13); and to crown all, charity (14).

5th. Habitual reference of all things to the peace (or approbation) of God with thankfulness (15).

6th. Christian conversation and meditation, assisted by divine poetry and music (16).

7th. Mingling all we do with Christian motives, and Christian thankfulness.

§ IV. (iii. 18—iv. 1). E.g. Let wives practise on this principle

---

° Mr. Keble's Note: "Perhaps the verse might be rendered:—'Which things have a show (not the substance) of wisdom in affected voluntary service and humility, and unsparing use of the body, not in any real respect shewn to it in regard of surfeit (or, in the way of guarding against surfeit) of the appetite.' ἐν ἐθελοθρησκείᾳ, κ.τ.λ. being *opposed* to ἐν τιμῇ, κ.τ.λ., and not the latter exegetic of the former. . . . Thus the passage, at the same time that it does away with *ritual*, confirms and inculcates *moral* Fasting.

obedience (18); husbands, love and sweetness (19); children, submission (20); parents, condescension (21); slaves, loyalty in sight and out of sight (22), not feeling themselves degraded, as knowing that they serve the Lord (23), and shall be paid their wages by Him, whether for good (24) or for evil (25). Let masters treat their slaves *fairly;* remembering their own subjugation to God (iv. 1).

§ V. (iv. 2—18). Farewell admonitions,

1st. To pray with perseverance, attention, and thankfulness (2), especially for the Apostle, that he might do his duty (3, 4).

2nd. To use all Christian wisdom, with a view particularly to the Gentiles (5), especially in their conversation, the rule of which is exactly given (6). Reference for further information to Tychicus (7, 8), and to Onesimus (9).

Salutations from his Jewish helpers (10, 11), and from Epaphras (12), according to his particular interest in them (13): and from other Gentile companions of the Apostle (14). Salutation to Laodicea (15). The letter to Laodicea and Colossæ should be mutually read (16). Message to Archippus (17). Farewell (18).

THE FIRST EPISTLE TO THE THESSALONIANS.

§ I. (i., ii., iii.) EXPRESSIONS of love and encouragement.
§ II. (iv., v.) Good advice for the future.
§ I. *a.* Salutation (i. 1).
  β. Assurance that their conduct was matter of thanksgiving to him (i. 2—ii. 13).
  γ. Encouragement from considering the present state of Christianity in Judea, and with regard to the Jews (ii. 14—16).
  δ. Expression of his feelings with regard to his visiting them, and on receiving Timothy's report of them (ii. 17—iii. 13).

  β. It was matter of daily thanksgiving to him to think of them (2) for their Christian conversation (3), the manner of their calling having made as deep an impression on him (4, 5), as he hoped his conduct had on them (5). Particularly for their joy in affliction (6), by which they had become patterns to the Greek Christians (7), and indeed in every place (8), men preventing St. Paul with the accounts of their conversion to Christianity, which is here designated by serving the true God, and waiting for Jesus Christ (9, 10). And as he had joy in thinking of them, so they could not have forgotten the reality of his addresses to them (ii. 1), evinced *a.* by his boldness just after persecution (2); *b.* by the sincerity of motive and demeanour which he maintained (3), answering to the trust which the Omniscient reposed in him (4); without flattery, covetousness (5), or vainglory: whatever pretext the Apostolical authority might afford (6): with fostering gentleness (7), ready to give up all for them (8); as was especially shewn by the labour to which he submitted (9); *c.* by his Christian conversation with them (13) so paternal (11), and constantly urging improvement (12).

  This, then, was his joy, to recollect how they received the Gospel and acted on it (13).

γ. It was worth remarking that the conduct of the Macedonian Christians answered to that of the Jewish, as well as their trial (14); whose adversaries, following up their murder of Christ and His Prophets, were now hindering the conversion of the Gentiles; but he, by the Spirit of Prophecy foresaw the end (15, 16).

δ. According to these affectionate feelings he had been longing to see them ever since their parting (17), and had twice attempted it, but was hindered by persecution (18), for he looked to them for an increase of glory at the great day (19, 20). Therefore he could not rest without sending Timothy (iii. 1, 2) to comfort them by the assurance of his (St. Paul's) steadiness, and that of his companions (3), whose trials were no more than he had foretold (4). However, they led him to send and inquire of their perseverance (5). Now Timothy had brought a good account (6), and had comforted him and revived him with their perseverance (7, 8). His joy before God was beyond all thanks (9), as well as his wish to see them and improve them (10): for which in the end he prays (11), as well as for their continual growth and final endurance (12, 13).

§ II. (iv. and v.) Good advice for the future.

1. As to constant improvement (iv. 1) in what they knew already (2). But it was worth while to mention particularly,—
2. *Purity* (3):—recommended as a duty to our own bodies, and requiring much Christian wisdom (εἰδέναι) (4); as necessary to keep us from the sad condition of Gentiles (5); as part also of our duty to our neighbour, and implying fraud and unfairness if transgressed: which is sure to draw down God's anger (6), as most contrary to our Christian calling (7). N.B. Contempt of this warning is contempt of God, as surely as He has put His Holy Spirit in His Apostles (8).
3. *Brotherly Love:* in which God had given them such grace (9), that they only needed exhortation to improve (10), especially in respect of quietness and industry (11), with a view to others' edification and their own independence (12).
4. Consideration of the Last Day: with a view,
   α. to comfort concerning the dead (iv. 13—18),
   β. to constant watching (v. 1—11).

THE FIRST EPISTLE TO THE THESSALONIANS. 233

    a. One immediate effect of Christian principles is to modify our sorrow for the dead (13); whose return with Jesus follows surely from His Death and Resurrection (14); to which St. Paul by divine inspiration here adds the circumstance, that the resurrection of the dead will take place *along with* the glorification of the living (15); the course of which great day being, 1st. the Descent of the Lord, 2nd. the Resurrection of the dead in Christ (16), 3rd. the ascension of them with the living (in Christ) to meet Him, and be with Him for ever (17). This he leaves with them as matter of comfortable exhortation (18).

    β. (v. 1—11). If any one ask "when?" you know the answer (1), that no one knows (2), the destruction of the careless being to come on them suddenly and unerringly (3); but let it not be so to Christians (4), who are children of Light (5), whose part therefore is wakefulness and sobriety (6); the contrary evils being only of night and darkness (7), whereas we are bound to soberness and watching in Christian armour (8), remembering God's purpose to save us (9), and Christ's death for us (10). Such are the topics of comfort and instruction which Christians have always ready for one another (11).

5. General maxims of Christian conduct, and conclusion. Particular sympathy due to Christ's ministers (12); and love, which goes along with a spirit of mutual peace (13). *From* them [Christ's ministers] in particular all long-suffering is due (14). Revenge forbidden. Charity inculcated (15). Edify yourselves with joy (16), prayer (17), thanksgiving (18); and others by not doing anything to damp the fire of the Holy Ghost (19), by respecting all the means of grace, yet distinguishing, in the use of them, between right and wrong (20—22).

    Final blessing (23): uttered with confidence (24). Request for intercession (25) and salutation (26), and request that the Epistle be made public (27). Farewell (28).

THE SECOND EPISTLE TO THE THESSALONIANS.

§ I. SALUTATION, and congratulation on their faith and patience, with anticipation of the final result (i. 1—12).

§ II. Correction of an error with regard to our Saviour's coming, with prediction of an Apostasy first (ii. 1—17).

§ III. Farewell: with a kind of postscript relating to the idleness of some of their poor (iii. 1—18).

§ I. (i. 1—12.) Salutation (1, 2); expression of delight at their growth in faith and love (3), and patience, which was matter of exultation to him everywhere (4); and which he would have them consider as an earnest of future reward (5) and redress (6), at Christ's visible coming (7) to take vengeance of His and God's enemies (8), i.e. everlasting perdition (9); as also to be glorified in His friends, and to prove the Apostle's witness to all (10). To this consummation, and the intermediate improvement necessary, all his intercessions had respect (11), for the mutual glory of Christ and Christians (12).

§ II. (ii. 1—17.) Speaking of the coming of Christ, it was desirable they should be warned against exciting imaginations, whether grounded on supposed new revelations, or on interpretations of Apostolic words or writings of its immediate approach (1, 2). It will not come till the predicted Apostasy have taken place, and "the Man of Sin" (whatever it means) be revealed (4): whose *first* mark will be, magnifying himself against all gods to such a degree, as to set himself in their place in God's Temple (4): his *second*, that a certain "let" or hindrance, which as yet hindered him (else he was already beginning to work in the dark), would be taken away. [This hindrance he had mentioned to them, and therefore it was enough to refer to it now] (5—7). His *third* mark will be, that, once revealed, he will continue in being until the coming of our Lord, then to be destroyed (as it should seem) suddenly (8). His *fourth*, that he will come with false miracles (9) and immoral sophistry, to deceive those who will not love the truth (10): God letting such imposture loose among them (11), finally to expose that temper among them which makes people unbelievers because they are sinners (12). [Whatever, therefore, the prophecy means, those who are truly well-meaning cannot be involved in its censure.]

But committing these things to God, one thing is certain: that we owe Him constant thanks for those whom, in His purpose of saving them (13), He has called to be Christians (14). One thing they have to do: to stand fast in the Apostolic truth (15). And may the Saviour and Father give them comfort and firmness so to do (16, 17).

§ III. (iii.) Having preferred his usual request for their intercession (1), more particularly needed from the troubles he was exposed to at Corinth (2), and expressed his confidence in God (3) and in them (4), and given them a blessing (5), he bethinks himself of what he had heard of some men's disorderly conduct among them, and directs them to discountenance it (6), recollecting the example he himself had set (7), how he had supported himself by his own labour (8), waiving his right for example's sake (9); recollecting also the rule he had given, that the idle should not eat the Church's bread (10). This warning he repeats, in consequence of information of the idleness and vain curiosity of some of them (11), to whom in the name of Christ he recommends quietness and industry (12); and warns the rest not to be weary in any work of charity (13): specially, if they saw the above warning slighted, to be shy of such a person, out of brotherly kindness, not enmity (14, 15). Blessing of Peace (16), which is a token of St. Paul himself, being in his own handwriting (17). Farewell (18).

THE FIRST EPISTLE TO TIMOTHY.

§ I. SALUTATION and purpose of the Epistle (i. 1—20).
§ II. Rules concerning Christian Worship (ii. 1—15).
§ III. Rules about Ordination (iii. 1—15).
§ IV. Rules about Preaching (iii. 16—iv. 16).
§ V. Rules about Christian Discipline, with regard to sex, age, station (v. 1—25).
§ VI. Method of dealing with men in regard to their condition in life (vi. 1—11, 17—19).
§ VII. Farewell, as of one entrusting another with a precious charge (vi. 12—16, 20, 21).

§ I. Consists of *four* Paragraphs.
  α. Salutation (1, 2).
  β. Declaration of the purpose of the Epistle (3, 4, 18—20).
  γ. A long parenthesis, pointing out, 1st. some of the principles on which that purpose might be answered (5—11).
  δ. 2nd. The ground of St. Paul's personal authority (11—17).

  β. In pursuance of St. Paul's intention in leaving Timothy as a sentinel against perverse doctrine (i. 3), especially that sort which only pampers curiosity (4), he now proceeds [pointing out, by the way, the principles on which those errors might be guarded against, and his own authority to do so (as a great instance of mercy,)] to give him some further directions in harmony with what Timothy had before been told (18), relating to faith and a good conscience; the connexion between which is evidenced in the fall of some (19), especially Hymenæus and Alexander (20).

  γ. It may be observed by the way that such errors arise entirely from people's neglecting the end of the Apostle's injunction—Christian practice (i. 5, 6); which is particularly absurd in one who would explain the Law, since he can neither understand his own principles nor conclusions (7); e.g. he does not seem to be aware that Law is a parenthesis; and—being a relative term to the great corruption

of our nature (9, 10) [and then only good when practised (8)]
—is now naturally merged in the Gospel, which sets itself
against the same things more effectually (11).

δ. And for this St. Paul's words might be taken, since he had
been specially intrusted with the Gospel (11) out of Christ's
favour (12), for all his former enmity in consideration of his
ignorance (13); and had been admitted into the full benefit
of the Gospel (14) [which he most thankfully acknowledges
(15)], as a pattern to believers (16), for which he gives God
glory (17).

§ II. Rules concerning Christian Worship.

a. Of public prayer: it should contain intercession and thanksgiving for all—even heathens (ii. 1), especially for governors
(2), considering the end of their appointment and the will
of God (3), for the salvation and instruction of all (4). For,
generally speaking, the latter is necessary to bring us to the
one Mediator (5) and Redeemer (6): the doctrine which
St. Paul was particularly appointed to preach to the Gentiles (7).

β. The men everywhere should come to it pure, meek, and
free from worldly anxiety (8).

γ. The women in decent, not fine, apparel (9), their good
works being their best ornament (10): to learn humbly (11),
not to teach (12), considering men's priority, 1st. in creation
(13), 2nd. in understanding, shewn by his not having been
deceived, even at the Fall, as the woman was (14); for which,
however, God immediately provided a remedy^p, if women
are not wanting to themselves (15).

§ III. (iii. 1—15). Rules of Ordination, a. of Priests (1—7),
β. of Deacons (8—13), followed by an explanation of
the reason why St. Paul was so anxious to write on the
subject (14, 15).

a. The thing to be kept in view as a principle, in ordination of
Priests, is the intrinsic nobleness of the work (1), requiring

---

^p Mr. Keble's Note: "By means of that child-bearing, which was men-
tioned in the sentence passed on her," Gen. iii. 16. St. Chrysostom refers
the "faithful saying" to this, but Mr. Keble points out that in other passages the phrase πιστὸς λόγος seems to point to what follows.

great blamelessness in the way of temperance [q], kindness (2), gentleness, disinterestedness (3), a good probation at home (4, 5), experience (6), a good name even among infidels (7).

β. On the like sort of grounds to take care of the blamelessness (8, 9), and sufficient trial (10) of *Deacons:* the qualities of the wives[r] (11), and their own domestic authority (12), considering the advantage it is to a person to have exercised this office well (13). [All this St. Paul wrote, to make sure of Timothy's having sufficient directions, in case—contrary to his hope—he should be detained far from him (14, 15).]

§ IV. (iii. 16—iv. 16). Rules of public instruction.

The first thing is a clear view of the fundamental truths, which are summed up (16); then of the errors of our own sphere, such as the Spirit had foretold should come on the publication of the Gospel, amounting to apostasy through the instigation of evil spirits (iv. 1), acting by means of reckless men (2); e.g. enforcing celibacy and distinction of meats,

---

[q] 1 Tim. iii. 2, *the husband of one wife.* Folded in the Greek Testament at this place was a paper, in Mr. Keble's handwriting, marked "Copy," and dated "Penzance, Dec. 28, 1862." . . . "The last time I had occasion to consider it, I was convinced that the texts" (this text and verse 12, and Tit. i. 6) "meant to enforce monogamy as a condition ordinarily to be for the offices there mentioned. And I believe this is the sense of almost all antiquity. But neither could I conceal from myself that this might be part of the general preference of the cœlibate, which our Lord and St. Paul so plainly express. And as the Church, both in the East and among ourselves, has waived receiving that as a positive precept for Clergymen, so I presume we must understand our own Church (for the Eastern Church, I believe, does not in this go along with us) to interpret St. Paul's words here not as a peremptory law for all times and circumstances, but as a recommendation to be followed except for some grave cause; like the caution which accompanies it in Titus, that a man should not be ordained if he have unconverted or unruly children: or that other, that he should not be a novice. On these grounds or the like, I have kept silence when perhaps I might have had a right to interfere, but I should have thought it hard and wrong to do so, the parties being already committed. Had I been consulted beforehand, I suppose I should have said what I have now written: but I am sure I should have also said as earnestly as I could, that as things are among us, such an engagement, once made, should be kept as sacredly as any other, unless there be consent, spontaneous on both sides, to separate (cf. 1 Cor. vii. 5). May God give a right judgment and a great blessing to the persons, whoever they are, on whose behalf you ask the question."

[r] Mr. Keble does not notice the question whether γυναῖκας here may not rather mean *Deaconesses.*—ED.

contrary to God's creation and purpose (3); whereas all God's creatures are good, received thankfully (4), and are sanctified by His permission at first, and by prayer on each occasion (5). It is by such reference to first principles, both in our teaching and in our studies, that we shall do our duty well (6); declining irreverent and silly discussions, and entering on nothing which does not promote our own personal holiness (7), considering that as surely as exercise is the way to bodily health for a short time, so is piety to happiness in both worlds (8); or in other words—as is truly said among Christians (9):—"what signify toil and shame to those who have a living God to trust in, a Saviour to all, but to the believers more especially" (10). These are the views of the relative importance of things, which must be continually inculcated (11). As to the manner of doing so (in which the great danger in youth is that of being contemned), it depends, 1st. upon exemplary goodness (12); 2nd. upon devotion to pastoral care (13); 3rd. upon attention to gifts and talents in the limited sense (14). Give yourselves up to those, so as to be exemplarily improving (15); with care and perseverance; and you and your hearers will, as far as lies in you, be safe (16).

§ V. Rules of Discipline (v. 1—25).

a. How to correct old and young men (1) and women (2): which reminds the Apostle of the institution of Deaconesses, for which he recommends persons really destitute (3); since those who have children should have brought them up so as to ensure their support in their old age (4); and real destitution implies application to the Almighty (5),—a sort of life infinitely above that of *pleasure* (6). [N.B. These charges the Apostle gives, the better to ensure their fidelity, though nature herself might enforce them sufficiently (7, 8).] But to proceed, as to the Widows: their age and character are specified (9, 10). Young persons not so well qualified, since more exposed to temptation from pleasure (11, 12), idleness and foolish talking (13); they had better leave themselves open to domestic engagements till the danger of scandal is over (14, 15). This subject is ended by repeating the caution of the fourth verse, more particularly to the relatives of the widows (16).

β. In the government of the Clergy,
   a. Distinguish the more deserving by temporal encouragements (17), according to both Law and Gospel (18).
   b. Proceed openly both in receiving charges (19) and in rebuking offenders (20).
   c. In your own conduct (considering yourself as a minister of discipline) avoid partiality (21), precipitancy in ordination especially, and every sort of impiety (22), making health the only cause of indulgence in diet (23); and remembering that there are judgments in store for secret as well as open sins (24, 25).

§ VI. Method of dealing with men according to their condition in life (vi. 1—10).

Slaves must be especially instructed in the duty of obedience, if it were only for the credit of the Gospel (1). And the more if their masters be Christians too (2). Opposite doctrines can only proceed from vanity and ignorance engendering a spirit of controversy, and producing envy, strife, evil-speaking, uncharitable suspicions (3, 4), and whatever else is the occupation of wrong-headed men who make a trade of religion (5). [Not but that religion —with content—is the best bargain a man could make (6), since nothing else will follow us into the other world (7). It is common sense, therefore, to be satisfied with the least of this world's goods (8); especially considering the temptations to which love of wealth exposes one (9), and the many that have been ruined by it (10)].

§ VII. Parting Charge (11—16).

You see what you are to avoid: now what you are to practise is every Christian grace (11), with all possible earnestness, considering your peculiar obligations (12); to which is now added a charge in the presence of God and Christ (13), and in reference to the Day of Judgment (14), the approach of which is sure as the attributes of Almighty God (15, 16).

Postscript, adding something both to § VI. and to § VII.
(vi. 17—21).

§ VI. To the rules about content should be added especial charges to the rich against pride and idolatrous trust in wealth (17), and in favour of all sorts of charity and public spirit (18), with a view to the other world (19).

§ VII. To the parting charge is added a caution especially against the pretended "knowledge" or "enlarged views" of that time, as being full of profaneness, 1st. in unmeaning subtleties of ingenious sound, 2nd. in objections (20); a caution enforced by the sad experience of the heresy into which it had led some (21).

THE SECOND EPISTLE TO TIMOTHY.

§ I. GENERAL encouragements, implying rather low spirits in him to whom they are addressed (i. 1—ii. 13).

§ II. Directions or maxims of episcopal behaviour generally (ii. 14—26).

§ III. Maxims relating particularly to an approaching degeneracy among Christians (iii. 1—iv. 5).

§ IV. Commissions and statements relating to St. Paul himself (iv. 6—22).

§ I. *a.* Salutation (i. 1, 2), referring especially to the promise, and using the endearing word, ἀγαπητῷ.

β. Timothy is encouraged

a. by the thankful remembrance had of his family (3—5), as also by the affection shewn in the Apostle's prayers and wish to see him:

b. by the remembrance of the special grace he had received, a great warrant against cowardice (6, 7):

c. by the remembrance of the nobleness of the Gospel, and God's eternal purpose towards Christians revealed in it (8—10):

d. by St. Paul's example (11, 12).

γ. Timothy is directed to provide for the continuance of the truth by an abstract of St. Paul's preaching (13), the better to ensure that precious deposit; and so fulfil the purpose of the Spirit dwelling in them (14); the more necessary considering the spirit of defection which had been shewn in Asia (15): [to which Onesiphorus formed a noble exception] (16—18). The times therefore required energy in maintaining God's bounty—the Gospel (ii. 1); and care in selecting those who might continue it (2).

δ. Fresh encouragement needed upon the former directions (3—13). In doing these duties, tribulation is to be expected; as in warfare (3). Therefore disengage your mind from earthly things (4), and remember not only to be on the right side, but also to labour in the right spirit (5). So will your reward be *eminent* (6),—a matter greatly to be considered (7): as well as the very substance of our Gospel, the resurrection of Christ (8), and its flourishing in spite of our sufferings (9). St. Paul is full of confidence and perseverance (10), and holds by the group of Christian proverbs, "If we be dead," &c. (11—13).

§ II. (ii. 14—26). Such are the true topics of Christian instruction, avoiding dangerous disputes (14), sparing no pains in sound interpretation (15); but shunning profane and unpractical enquiries, as sure to lead to irreligion (16), and to spread: of which an instance is given (17, 18); [not that the foundation of Christian faith is shaken: it stands upon the joint security of God's promise and our loyal obedience (19); but as in a family, some vessels must be put to mean uses, so here (20). However, the way is clear for each man to get himself an honourable place,—it is merely shunning whatever is profane (21)]. Again, Timothy is directed to shun youthful lusts, and follow every kind of virtue (22); to deprecate that sort of inquiry which shews an irregular, undisciplined mind (23), and so produces strife, most unapt for a servant of the Lord (24), whose great business is to instruct in meekness, and never despair of any one* (25, 26).

§ III. (iii. 1—iv. 5.) Particularly you should be aware of the immorality to be expected in the times of the Gospel, so exactly answering to that of Heathenism (1—4), with the additional mark of hypocrisy, most to be avoided of all (5). One practice of these bad Christians especially stigmatized: that of insinuating themselves into domestic society, and leading weak people astray (6); not without the fault of those people themselves in giving the reins to their fancy and curiosity, under show of seeking the truth (7): to which, in fact, these teachers are as much opposed as the Magicians were to Moses: having, in fact, entirely corrupted their sense of religious truth (8): and will by-and-by appear as plainly as in the case of Moses (9).

Meantime do you, remembering my example, my sufferings, and deliverances (10, 11), [the common case of all who would

---

* Mr. Keble's Note on ii. 26. "Qu. Might εἰς τὸ ἐκείνου θέλημα be taken with ἀνανήψωσι,—putting a comma at αὐτοῦ, and referring ἐκείνου to Θεός in ver. 25. The ordinary use of ἐκείνου would seem to enforce this." [The meaning will then be, "That they may recover themselves out of the snare of the devil (who have been taken captive by him) unto obedience to God's will." —ED.]

be good Christians, as long as bad men will be wilful, and corrupt themselves and others (12, 13)], continue in your good beginnings taught by God Himself (14). For that may be truly said of one who from his youth has learned the Holy Scriptures of the Old Testament,—out of which one may learn Christian truth enough to save his soul (15). This we know, because all Scripture is inspired for our use (16), and so, that out of it a minister may learn all his duty (17).

So much for your personal duty: as to your ministerial, you are adjured by the remembrance of God's judgment (iv. 1) to be regular and instant in all sorts of pastoral care (2); and the more, as we must expect men to be at times impatient of sound doctrine, and led by their own fancies in multiplying teachers (3), the natural result of which is, that they like fables better than truth (4). Let it, therefore, be your care to wake up for suffering and doing all your work (5).

§ IV. Personal commissions, &c. (6—22).

I am the more earnest in pressing these duties on you, because I am so soon to go (6), looking with comfort to the past (7), and with hope to the future (8). Make haste and come (9), for I am alone (10) all but Luke, and want Mark in particular (11); Tychicus too being gone (12).

Remember and bring my manuscripts from Troas (13). Be on your guard henceforth against Alexander, remembering his behaviour to me (14, 15).

And be not faint-hearted about me: for you know how, although forsaken of men, I was delivered from my former imprisonment, to do more of God's work here (16, 17): and now I shall have a happier deliverance (18). Salutations (19).

[I am the more earnest about your coming, as my two other friends, Erastus and Trophimus, are away: and it is ill voyaging in winter (20, 21). Salutations from Rome (21). Farewell (22).]

THE EPISTLE TO TITUS.

This Epistle contains six Paragraphs :—

§ I. Salutation (i. 1—4).
§ II. Particular purpose of Titus' commission (5—16).
§ III. Instructions how to execute it; in respect of men's different ages (ii. 1—8).
§ IV. In respect of station, as to *slaves* (9—15), as to *subjects* (iii. 1—8).
§ V. In respect of disputes and heretics (9—11).
§ VI. Miscellaneous directions, and farewell (11—15).

§ I. St. Paul, in virtue of his Apostolical work (i. 1), end (2), and commission (3), sends his blessing to Titus (4).

§ II. Having left him in Crete to appoint elders (5), he tells him what outward marks an elder should have (6), what inward vices he should be free from (7), and what virtues possess (8). Especially how single-hearted he should be in teaching, with a view both to exhortation and rebuke (9); particularly the last, greatly needed by Jewish teachers (10), most destructive and unprincipled (11), according to Epimenides' character of the Cretans: who, being liars, and stupified by sensuality and sloth (12), required no timorous treatment (13) to withdraw them from profane superstition and Pharisaism (14): and teach them that the real difference of things is in us, and not in them (15); and that none are so bad as the hypocrites in heart (16).

§ III. Instructions how to teach in respect of men's *ages* (ii. 1—8). Sound doctrine (opposed to what was described in chap. i.) to be the measure of teaching (1), e.g. as to old men (2), old women (3), young women (4, 5), young men (6), among whom Titus was to be an especial pattern (7, 8).

§ IV. How to teach in respect of *stations* (ii. 9—iii. 8).

a. For slaves (ii. 9—15).

Their duty as to temper (9), as to honesty (10), for the credit of the Gospel, whose salutary appearance (11) is accompanied with perfect moral teaching (12), and glorious sanctions, having respect to our Lord's final coming (13), and past mercies (14). All this to be taught with authority (15).

β. For subjects (iii. 1—8).

Their duty is active obedience (1), especially in respect of the Sixth and Ninth Commandments (2); and is enforced by the remembrance of the sins from which Christianity delivers man (3); through no merit of our own, but entirely through Christ (4, 5), both in baptism and in following gifts of the Spirit (5, 6), and in our final hope (7). Impress these things, not controversially, that men may have the more will and leisure for practice (8).

§ V. Apostolical charge how a Bishop should deal with disputes, &c. (9—11), what matters (9) and what persons (10, 11) time is not to be spent with. N.B. This and the section before seem to point out the right way of dealing with Reformers, in the bad sense of the word.

§ VI. Commands about Titus' coming (12), about supplying ministers of the Gospel on their travels (13), recommended as a common case (14). Farewell (15).

THE EPISTLE TO PHILEMON.

§ I. SALUTATION (1—3).
§ II. Commendation of Philemon (4—7).
§ III. Recommendation of Onesimus (8—21).
§ IV. Farewell (22—24).

III. Waiving his own authority (8), he pleads his age and his bonds (9), his consideration of Onesimus as a child (10), reformed (11), and restored to Philemon (though ill-spared) for Philemon's own sake (12—14). To which are added God's special Providence appearing in the matter (cf. Gen. xlv. 5) (15, 16), and his own strong feeling, expressed by his willingness to take Onesimus's debt on himself (17—21).

NOTES ON THE GREEK TESTAMENT.

ΤΟ ΚΑΤΑ[a] ΜΑΤΘΑΙΟΝ ΑΓΙΟΝ ΕΥΑΓΓΕΛΙΟΝ.
The Gospel according to St. Matthew.

CHAP. I.—VER. 1.

Βίβλος γενέσεως Ἰησοῦ Χριστοῦ, υἱοῦ Δαβὶδ, υἱοῦ Ἀβραάμ.
The Book of the generation of Jesus Christ, the Son of David, the Son of Abraham.

Βίβλος γενέσεως.] Heb. סֵפֶר תּוֹלְדֹת Gen. v. 1.

Βίβλος.] Cf. Herod. ii. 100. It appears from Ezra (ii. 62) and Nehemiah (vii. 64) that the Jews preserved their genealogies carefully.

υἱοῦ ... υἱοῦ.] Agrees in both places with Ἰησοῦ. Cf. Gen. xxxvi. 2 (*Aholibamah the daughter of Anah the daughter of Zibeon*), compared with v. 24 [which shews that Anah was a man][b]; cf. also St. Luke iii. 23—33.

Abraham and David,—why particularly mentioned.

VER. 5.

Σαλμὼν δὲ ἐγέννησε τὸν Βοὸζ ἐκ τῆς Ῥαχάβ.
And Salmon begat Booz of Rachab.

If this Rahab was the harlot mentioned in Joshua, (as is most likely, from comparing this verse with the mention of Thamar, Ruth, and Bathsheba,) we may probably suppose that some generations are omitted here, as in ver. 8, since there is an interval of at least 300 years between Joshua and David.

VER. 8.

Ἰωρὰμ δὲ ἐγέννησε τὸν Ὀζίαν.
And Joram begat Ozias.

Three generations: why omitted? They are Azariah, Joash, and Amaziah. The explanation in the text is literally true, according to that Hebrew idiom, by which Isaiah predicted to

---

[a] κατά.]—Query whether Schleusner's quotation from Gal. i. 11 be much to the purpose; but that from 1 St. Peter iv. 14, κατὰ μὲν αὐτοὺς βλασφημεῖται κατὰ δὲ ὑμᾶς δοξάζεται, seems to justify us in translating it 'by.'

[b] *Note.*—The reader is requested to observe that whatever is enclosed in square brackets [. . . .] has been inserted by the Editor.

Hezekiah that his children should be carried away captive; whereas they were his far descendants. Probably these generations were omitted, on account of the wickedness of the three kings, in some genealogy from which this was copied; so Cain is not mentioned in the Book of Chronicles, nor Simeon in the Blessing of Moses, Deut. xxxiii.

VER. 11.
Ἐπὶ τῆς μετοικεσίας Βαβυλῶνος.
About the time they were carried away to Babylon.

N.B. ἐπὶ for Time.
St. Mark ii. 26, ἐπὶ Ἀβιάθαρ.
St. Luke iii. 2, ἐπ' ἀρχιερέων.
St. Luke iv. 27, ἐπὶ Ἐλισσαίου.
Acts xi. 28, ἐπὶ Κλαυδίου Καίσαρος.

Μετοικεσία an Euphemismus which seems to favour the notion of this being an extract from a Jewish record, and so does the way in which some MSS. have it, vid. Griesb. p. 5, n. o.

μετοικεσίας.] Heb. גָּלָה. i.e. 1 Chron. v. 22; Ezech. xii. 11.

VER. 12.
Μετὰ δὲ τὴν μετοικεσίαν Βαβυλῶνος, Ἰεχονίας ἐγέννησε τὸν Σαλαθιήλ· Σαλαθιὴλ δὲ ἐγέννησε τὸν Ζοροβάβελ.
And after they were brought to Babylon, Jechonias begat Salathiel; and Salathiel begat Zorobabel.

Consider how to reconcile this with Jer. xxii. 30 (*Write ye this man childless*). 1. Hammond proposes *adoption;* 2. but perhaps the passage in Jeremiah is misunderstood. LXX. renders it ἐκκήρυκτον, instead of ἄτεκνον. (I think 1 Chron. iii. 17, 19 —*the sons of Jeconiah, Assir, Salathiel his son, &c.*—favours the scheme of *adoption.*) And this agrees with the opinion of most commentators, that St. Matthew meant to give our Lord's legal descent from David; St. Luke His natural descent. Concerning the genealogies, see Grotius.

VER. 17.
Πᾶσαι οὖν αἱ γενεαὶ ἀπὸ Ἀβραὰμ ἕως Δαβὶδ, γενεαὶ δεκατέσσαρες.
So all the generations from Abraham to David are fourteen generations.

All the generations in the list; not all the actual generations.

Ver. 18.

Μνηστευθείσης γὰρ τῆς μητρὸς αὐτοῦ Μαρίας τῷ Ἰωσήφ, πρὶν ἢ συνελθεῖν αὐτούς.

When as His mother Mary was espoused to Joseph, before they came together.

Between marrying and betrothing there was generally some time; Deut. xx. 7, (*Hath betrothed a wife, and hath not taken her*). Force of γὰρ, *namely that* . . .

συνελθεῖν.] Frequent. apud Thucyd. and Aristot.

Ver. 19.

Ἰωσὴφ δὲ ὁ ἀνὴρ αὐτῆς, δίκαιος ὤν, καὶ μὴ θέλων αὐτὴν παραδειγματίσαι, ἐβουλήθη λάθρα ἀπολῦσαι αὐτήν.

Then Joseph her husband, being a just man, and not willing to make her a publick example, was minded to put her away privily.

δίκαιος.] perhaps here, "merciful." So צְדָקָה means ἐλεημοσύνη in Deut. xxiv. 13 (*It shall be righteousness unto thee before the Lord*); Dan. iv. 27 (*In LXX. and Vulg., Redeem thy sins by almsgiving*).

δίκαιος.] Deut. xxiv. 13 (as above).

Ps. cxii. 9, *Hath given to the poor; his righteousness remaineth for ever.*

Ps. cxlv. 16, 17, *Thou openest thine hand . . . righteous in all His ways.*

Isa. lviii. 7, 8, *Deal thy bread to the hungry . . . thy righteousness shall go before thee.*

Matt. vi. 1, *Your alms:* marg. "*righteousness.*"

παραδειγματίσαι.] Numb. xxv. 4.

Jer. xiii. 22, בְּגָלִי [*Their veils were taken away.*—Ed.]

Ezech. xxviii. 17, *I will lay thee before kings that they may see thee,*—παραδειγματισθῆναι.

Heb. vi. 6, *Put Him to an open shame.*

Ver. 20.

Ταῦτα δὲ αὐτοῦ ἐνθυμηθέντος . . . μὴ φοβηθῇς παραλαβεῖν. . . .

While he thought on these things . . . Fear not to take unto thee. . . .

For the strict law in this case, cf. Deut. xxii. 13—20, by which the supposed criminal would be punished with death. παραλαβεῖν Heb. לָקַח, Gen. iv. 19 (*Lamech took unto him two wives*); Hosea i. 2, (*so take thee a wife,* LXX. λάβε).

ἐνθυμηθέντος.] Acts x. 19 (*While Peter thought on the vision*).

Ver. 21.

Καὶ καλέσεις τὸ ὄνομα αὐτοῦ ΙΗΣΟΥΝ.

And thou shalt call his name JESUS.

ΙΗΣΟΥΝ. So מוֹשִׁיעַ of Alexander the Great, Isa. xix. 20 (*There shall be an altar to the Lord ... in Egypt ... He shall send them a Saviour*). Enquire whether the word has any reference to Jehovah : which would much illustrate what is said of Emmanuel.

Ver. 22 and 23.

Τοῦτο δὲ ὅλον γέγονεν, ἵνα πληρωθῇ τὸ ῥηθὲν....

Now all this was done, that it might be fulfilled which was spoken....

Ἰδοὺ ἡ παρθένος ἐν γαστρὶ ἕξει, καὶ τέξεται, υἱὸν, καὶ καλέσουσι τὸ ὄνομα αὐτοῦ Ἐμμανουήλ· ὅ ἐστι μεθερμηνευόμενον, Μεθ' ἡμῶν ὁ Θεός.

Behold, a virgin shall be with child, and shall bring forth a son, and they shall call his name Emmanuel, which being interpreted is, God with us.

Force of ἵνα. Isa. vii. 14. Occasion of the prophecy. New Testament quotes from Septuagint. Figure in καλέσουσι ("*They shall call His name,*" a Hebraism for "*He shall be*"). How fulfilled in Christ. Cf. Jer. xxxi. 22 (... *a new thing in the earth, A woman shall compass a man*).

Ver. 25.

Καὶ οὐκ ἐγίνωσκεν αὐτὴν, ἕως οὗ ἔτεκε τὸν υἱὸν αὐτῆς τὸν πρωτότοκον.

And knew her not till she had brought forth her firstborn son.

Force of ἕως οὗ, cf. xx. 44, *Sit thou ... till I make thine enemies;* xxviii. 20, *I am with you alway, even unto the end;* 2 Sam. vi. 23, *Michal had no child unto the day of her death.*

Chap. II.—Ver. 1.

Τοῦ δὲ Ἰησοῦ γεννηθέντος ἐν Βηθλεὲμ τῆς Ἰουδαίας ἐν ἡμέραις Ἡρώδου τοῦ βασιλέως, ἰδοὺ μάγοι ἀπὸ ἀνατολῶν παρεγένοντο εἰς Ἱεροσόλυμα.

Now when Jesus was born in Bethlehem of Judæa in the days of Herod the king, behold, there came wise men from the east to Jerusalem.

Why of Judæa, cf. Jos. xix. 15 (another Bethlehem in Zebulon).

Time of this after the Purification, probably a year and twelve days from the Nativity, cf. S. Luc. ii. 22 (Purification 40 days after birth), and ver. 16 of this chapter.

Who and what Herod was? Who were the Magi? Dan. i. 20 (*The magicians and astrologers*, Chald. אַשָּׁפִים); ii. 2, &c. Why ἀνατολῶν (so Virgil, 3 Geor. 437, "Solis ad ortus"). Perhaps they came from Tarshish, Isa. lx. 9, (*The isles shall wait for me, the ships of Tarshish*); Ps. lxxii. 10, *The Kings of Tarshish and of the isles shall bring presents;* Jackson. Lightfoot thinks from Arabia, which had been subject to David and Solomon, and was included in the promise of the land of Canaan.

Ver. 2.

Εἴδομεν γὰρ αὐτοῦ τὸν ἀστέρα ἐν τῇ ἀνατολῇ.

For we have seen his star in the east.

Refers to prophecy of Balaam, Num. xxiv. 17, *There shall come a Star out of Jacob.* Quotation from Chalcidius on Plato's Timæus [a].

ἐν τῇ ἀνατολῇ.] Perhaps *in its rising;* "in the East" is commonly plural (ἀνατολαῖς), Hammond. Lightfoot thinks the star was the light that appeared to the shepherds.

Ver. 4.

Τοὺς ἀρχιερεῖς καὶ γραμματεῖς τοῦ λαοῦ.

And when he had gathered all the chief priests and scribes of the people together.

Who were the ἀρχιερεῖς and γραμματεῖς? (1.) ἀρχιερεῖς were either the persons who had been from time to time turned out of their offices by the Romans, of whom Josephus mentions many; or the heads of the twenty-four courses of priests instituted by David (1 Chron. xxiv.). (2.) γραμματεῖς, whose office was double, 1. to expound the law by preaching; 2. to copy it.

τοῦ λαοῦ,] to distinguish them from such as Baruch, who were scribes to individuals.

---

[a] [The passage in the Platonist Chalcidius (Commentary on the *Timæus*, vii. 125) is that beginning, "Est quoque alia sanctior et venerabilior historia, quæ perhibet ortu Stellæ cujusdam, non morbos mortesque denunciatos, sed descensum DEI venerabilis, ad humanæ conservationis rerumque mortalium gratiam."—ED.]

Ver. 6.

Καὶ σὺ Βηθλεέμ, γῆ 'Ιούδα, οὐδαμῶς ἐλαχίστη εἶ ἐν τοῖς ἡγεμόσιν 'Ιούδα.

And thou Bethlehem, in the land of Juda, art not the least among the princes of Juda.

Refer to Micah v. 2 (Heb. i.), not translated as by LXX. Variation of word ἡγεμόσιν. The Hebrew here is, אַלְפֵי יְהוּדָה צָעִיר אַתָּה לִהְיוֹת, which LXX. literally render ὀλιγοστὸς εἶ τοῦ εἶναι ἐν χιλιάσιν 'Ιούδα. But Lightfoot proposes an ingenious rendering, "It is a small thing for thee to be among the thousands," &c., which reconciles it with St. Matthew; for χιλιάς may very well be put for ἡγεμών, as "a thousand" means probably a certain district, like our word "hundred," cf. 1 Sam. xxiii. 23, *I will search throughout all the thousands of Judah.*

Ver. 10.

Ἐχάρησαν χαρὰν μεγάλην σφόδρα.

They rejoiced with exceeding great joy.

μεγάλην σφόδρα.   Hebraismus.

Ver. 11.

προσήνεγκαν αὐτῷ δῶρα, χρυσὸν καὶ λίβανον καὶ σμύρναν.

They presented unto him gifts, gold, and frankincense, and myrrh.

Cf. Ps. lxxii. 10, 15, *To him shall be given of the gold of Sheba: prayer also shall be made for him;* Isa. lx. 6, ... *they shall bring gold and incense.* Enquire into the symbolical interpretation.

Ver. 12.

Καὶ χρηματισθέντες κατ' ὄναρ.

And being warned of God in a dream.

χρηματισθέντες.] St. Luke ii. 26, *It was revealed unto him (Simeon);* Acts x. 22, *Cornelius .... was warned from God;* Heb. viii. 5, *Moses was admonished of God;* xi. 7, *Noah, warned of God;* xii. 25, *refused him that spake,* χρηματίζοντα; sæpe apud Jerem. LXX.

Ver. 15.

Ἐξ Αἰγύπτου ἐκάλεσα τὸν υἱόν μου.

Out of Egypt have I called my son.

Hosea xi. 1, *When Israel was a child, &c.* An instance of the whole nation of Israel being a type of Christ. Cf. Isa. xix. 1,

The Lord rideth on a swift cloud and shall come into Egypt; and the idols shall be moved at His presence; but query?—See Milton's Hymn on the Nativity ("Nor is Osiris seen," &c.).

Ver. 16.

'Ανεῖλε πάντας τοὺς παῖδας τοὺς ἐν Βηθλεὲμ καὶ ἐν πᾶσι τοῖς ὁρίοις αὐτῆς, ἀπὸ διετοῦς καὶ κατωτέρω.

And slew all the children that were in Bethlehem, and in all the coasts thereof, from two years old and under.

ὁρίοις.] Regionibus. Ita LXX. Exod. and elsewhere, pro נְבוּל [borders in sense of territories].

ἀπὸ διετοῦς κ.τ.λ.] Cf. 1 Chron. xxvii. 23, *David took not the number of them from twenty years old, and under;* 2 Chron. xxxi. 16, *From three years old, and upwards.*

Ver. 18.

Φωνὴ ἐν 'Ραμᾶ ἠκούσθη, θρῆνος καὶ κλαυθμὸς καὶ ὀδυρμὸς πολύς, 'Ραχὴλ κλαίουσα τὰ τέκνα αὐτῆς· καὶ οὐκ ἤθελε παρακληθῆναι, ὅτι οὐκ εἰσί.

In Rama was there a voice heard, lamentation, and weeping, and great mourning, Rachel weeping for her children, and would not be comforted, because they are not.

Jer. xxxi. 15; Gen. xxxv. 19. Rachel was buried in Bethlehem, which was six miles from Ramah, and in the tribe of Benjamin; and it was at Ramah that the prophecy received its primary accomplishment in point of time, when Nebuzaradan there disposed of the captives taken at Jerusalem, Jer. xl. 1.

αὐτῆς.] Not strictly hers, except so far as she had a common interest in all Jacob's family. We must understand it as a strong poetical expression of the grief of the Israelitish mother.

'Ραχήλ.] Who died there, in labour of Benjamin, called by her, Benoni.

Ver. 19.

Τελευτήσαντος δὲ τοῦ 'Ηρώδου.
But when Herod was dead. . . .

For the account of Herod's cruelty in murdering his own son, &c., cf. Jos. *Antiq.* xvi. xi. 7; *Bell.* i. xxxii. 7.

Ver. 20.

Τεθνήκασι γὰρ οἱ ζητοῦντες τὴν ψυχὴν τοῦ παιδίου.
For they are dead which sought the young child's life.

οἱ ζητοῦντες.] N.B. Change of number,—"*they* who sought." Lightfoot thinks Herod and his son Antipater are meant; Antipater, from other anecdotes of his jealous and cruel disposition, seems very likely to have abetted the massacre.

Ver. 23.

Ὅπως πληρωθῇ τὸ ῥηθὲν διὰ τῶν προφητῶν, Ὅτι Ναζωραῖος κληθήσεται.
That it might be fulfilled which was spoken by the prophets, He shall be called a Nazarene.

κληθήσεται.] A Hebraism meaning no more than "he shall be;" cf. places where רָבָר is put for things, and ὀνόματα for persons, vid. Hammond. Ναζωραῖος may mean Christ's Divinity, as Nazir, the Branch of righteousness; or else it may mean His low and despised condition and country. Cf. Jackson, vol. ii. 401—416 [ed. 1673]; cf. prophecies of Caiaphas and Pharaoh ("Thou shalt see my face," &c.) as instances of words receiving a meaning far other than was intended. Name *Nazarene* used reproachfully by the Jews, was in fact an accomplishment of those prophecies which called Christ "the Branch," and of Samson's type of Him as a Nazarite. Isa. xi. 1, *A Branch* (נֵצֶר *netser*) *shall grow out of his roots.* But the word for Branch is צֶמַח, *tsemach*, in Isa. iv. 2; Jer. xxiii. 5, xxxiii. 15; Zech. vi. 12.

Why προφητῶν, not singular.

CHAP. III.—Ver. 1.

Ἐν δὲ ταῖς ἡμέραις ἐκείναις παραγίνεται Ἰωάννης ὁ βαπτιστὴς κηρύσσων ἐν τῇ ἐρήμῳ τῆς Ἰουδαίας.
In those days came John the Baptist preaching in the wilderness of Judæa.

Prophecies fulfilled.

Occurred when Jesus was at Nazareth, about thirty years old. Cf. Numb. iv. 3, *From thirty years old and upwards . . . to do the work in the Tabernacle.*

κηρύσσων.] The prophet's office.

ἐν τῇ ἐρήμῳ.] The place; viz. "The country," *rure.*

καὶ λέγων.] The preaching.—All distinguished in the Prophecy.

Ver. 2.

Καὶ λέγων, Μετανοεῖτε· ἤγγικε γὰρ ἡ βασιλεία τῶν οὐρανῶν.

And saying, Repent ye: for the kingdom of heaven is at hand

Force of μετανοεῖτε, and of βασιλεία τῶν οὐρανῶν. Meaning of μετάνοια opposed to μεταμέλεια. Lightfoot gives three reasons for the use of the word: 1. To do away Justification by legal works; 2. To meet the opinion of the sounder Jews, who put repentance and the reign of Christ together; 3. To hinder them from thinking bare confession enough.

ἡ βασιλεία τῶν οὐρανῶν.] Its triple meaning; why τῶν οὐρανῶν in the plural.

Ver. 3.

Φωνὴ βοῶντος ἐν τῇ ἐρήμῳ, Ἑτοιμάσατε τὴν ὁδὸν Κυρίου.

The voice of one crying in the wilderness, Prepare ye the way of the Lord.

Quoted from LXX., proof of Christ's Divinity from it.

Ver. 4.

Τὸ ἔνδυμα αὐτοῦ ἀπὸ τριχῶν καμήλου καὶ ζώνην δερματίνην περὶ τὴν ὀσφὺν αὐτοῦ· ἡ δὲ τροφὴ αὐτοῦ ἀκρίδες καὶ μέλι ἄγριον.

His raiment of camel's hair, and a leathern girdle about his loins; and his meat was locusts and wild honey.

Mal. iv. 5, *I will send you Elijah the prophet;* St. Matt. xvii. 12, 13, *Elias is come already and they knew him not;* St. Luke v. 17, *He shall go before Him in the spirit and power of Elias;* St. Matt. xi. 14, *If ye will receive it, this is Elias;* 2 Kings i. 8, *He was an hairy man and girt with a girdle of leather;* 1 Kings xvii. 6, *The ravens brought him bread and flesh*, xix. 6; Lev. xi. 22, *Ye may eat the locust after his kind;* 1 Sam. xiv. 25, *Came to a wood; and there was honey upon the ground.*

Ver. 5.

Ἐξεπορεύετο πρὸς αὐτὸν Ἱεροσόλυμα καὶ πᾶσα ἡ Ἰουδαία.

Then went out to him Jerusalem and all Judæa.

Cf. 1 Kings xviii. 19—39, *Now therefore send and gather to me all Israel, &c.*

Ver. 6.

Καὶ ἐβαπτίζοντο ἐν τῷ Ἰορδάνῃ ὑπ' αὐτοῦ.

And were baptized of him in Jordan.

Baptism a custom among the Jews.

Ver. 7.

Ἰδὼν δὲ πολλοὺς τῶν Φαρισαίων καὶ Σαδδουκαίων ἐρχομένους ἐπὶ τὸ βάπτισμα αὐτοῦ, εἶπεν αὐτοῖς, Γεννήματα ἐχιδνῶν, τίς ὑπέδειξεν ὑμῖν φυγεῖν ἀπὸ τῆς μελλούσης ὀργῆς.

But when he saw many of the Pharisees and Sadducees come to his baptism, he said unto them, O generation of vipers, who hath warned you to flee from the wrath to come?

Who were the Pharisees and Sadducees? and etymology of the two words.

Lightfoot refers both to the time of Ezra. Peculiar doctrines, peculiar vices; how they are the representatives of two classes of sinners.

γεννήματα ἐχιδνῶν.] Meaning, Children of the old Serpent.

τῆς μελλούσης ὀργῆς.] Mal. iv. 6, *He shall turn the heart of the fathers . . . lest I come and smite the earth with a curse.*

Ver. 8.

Ποιήσατε οὖν καρποὺς ἀξίους τῆς μετανοίας.

Bring forth therefore fruits meet for repentance.

Ποιήσατε οὖν καρποὺς.] A Hebraism? cf. ch. vii. 17—19, *Every good tree brought forth good fruit, &c.;* xiii. 23, *He that received seed into the good ground, &c.*

ἀξίους, cf. Thuc. iv. 34; ἄξια τῆς προσδοκίας.

Ver. 9.

Καὶ μὴ δόξητε λέγειν ἐν ἑαυτοῖς, Πατέρα ἔχομεν τὸν Ἀβραάμ. λέγω γὰρ ὑμῖν, ὅτι δύναται ὁ Θεὸς ἐκ τῶν λίθων τούτων ἐγεῖραι τέκνα τῷ Ἀβραάμ.

And think not to say within yourselves, We have Abraham to our father: for I say unto you, that God is able of these stones to raise up children unto Abraham.

Cf. Phil. iii. 4, εἴ τις δοκεῖ, κ.τ.λ., *If any man thinketh that he hath, &c.* But cf. Luke iii. 8, *Begin not to say within yourselves we have Abraham to our father, &c.* (where ἄρξησθε is redundant). For the Hebrew see Lightfoot, [" We do not say the Baptist played on the sound of these two words, בניא Benaia, children, and אבניא Abenaia (stones)."—ED.] Cf. Rom. ii, iii, iv. Probably a mystical meaning in λίθων τούτων, but cf. St. Luke xix. 40, *If these should hold their peace the stones would cry out;* and on the other hand, Isa. li. 1, *Look unto the Rock whence ye are hewn.*

Ver. 10.

Ἤδη δὲ καὶ ἡ ἀξίνη πρὸς τὴν ῥίζαν τῶν δένδρων κεῖται.
And now also the axe is laid unto the root of the trees.

Cf. Ps. lxxx. 8—16, *Thou hast brought a vine out of Egypt ... it is burned with fire, it is cut down;* Isa. v. 1—7, *My well-beloved hath a vineyard in a very fruitful hill, &c.*

Ver. 11.

Οὗ οὐκ εἰμὶ ἱκανὸς τὰ ὑποδήματα βαστάσαι· αὐτὸς ὑμᾶς βαπτίσει ἐν Πνεύματι ἁγίῳ καὶ πυρί.
Whose shoes I am not worthy to bear : he shall baptize you with the Holy Ghost, and with fire.

τὰ ὑποδήματα βαστάσαι.] A Hebrew proverb. Cf. Ps. cviii. 9. [Edom is only fit to hold my shoe as a slave while I wash my feet.—Ed.]

ἐν πνεύματι ἁγίῳ καὶ πυρί.] Cf. Acts ii. 3 ; Hooker [V. lxix. 5, "In this the Apostles' later Baptism, there was as well a visible descent of fire, as a secret miraculous infusion of the Spirit."]

Difference of Christ's Baptism and John's. Cf. 1 Reg. ubi sup., but query. [The reference seems to be to 1 Kings xviii. 19—39, quoted in note on ver. 5.—Ed.]

Ver. 12.

Οὗ τὸ πτύον ἐν τῇ χειρὶ αὐτοῦ, καὶ διακαθαριεῖ τὴν ἅλωνα αὐτοῦ, καὶ συνάξει τὸν σῖτον αὐτοῦ εἰς τὴν ἀποθήκην, τὸ δὲ ἄχυρον κατακαύσει πυρὶ ἀσβέστῳ.
Whose fan is in his hand, and he will throughly purge his floor, and gather his wheat into the garner; but he will burn up the chaff with unquenchable fire.

Cf. Isa. v. 24, *As the fire devoureth the stubble and the flame consumeth the chaff...;* xli. 15, 16, *I will make thee a new sharp threshing instrument...;* Ps. i. 4, *Like the chaff which the wind driveth away;* lxxxiii. 13, *As the stubble before the wind.* Parable of the Tares. Cf. Louth, ad loc. Esaiæ, ap. Præl. [describing the drag which oxen drew over the corn-sheaves spread on the floor.—Ed.]

οὗ ... αὐτοῦ.] Hebraism.

Vers. 10—12. The decisive nature of Messiah's rule strongly marked in these three verses. Cf. Isa. x. 23, *The Lord shall make a consumption, even determined, in the midst of all the land;* Rom. ix. 28, *He will finish the work and cut it short, &c.*

Ver. 15.

Ἄφες ἄρτι· οὕτω γὰρ πρέπον ἐστὶν ἡμῖν πληρῶσαι
πᾶσαν δικαιοσύνην.

*Suffer it to be so now: for thus it becometh us to fulfil
all righteousness.*

ἄρτι.] Heb. נָא [like the Latin *amabo*, or our "With your leave." Ed.]

δικαιοσύνην.] That Christ should be baptized was a point of righteousness, i.e. legal righteousness, because the High Priest was initiated by baptism and anointing, Exod. xl. 12—16; and because He was to be a pattern to us,—Lightfoot. All those things which under that more imperfect ministry were required of men to their being approved by God. Hammond, on Rom. i. 2.

Ver. 16.

Ἀνεῴχθησαν αὐτῷ οἱ οὐρανοὶ, καὶ εἶδε τὸ Πνεῦμα τοῦ Θεοῦ
καταβαῖνον ὡσεὶ περιστερὰν, καὶ ἐρχόμενον ἐπ᾽ αὐτόν·

*The heavens were opened unto him, and he saw the Spirit of God
descending like a dove, and lighting upon him.*

εἶδε probably refers to John; see St. John i. 32, *I saw the Spirit descending, &c.* **ὡσεὶ** need not mean bodily likeness,—alludes probably to the Cherubim and Shechinah.

Ver. 17.

Καὶ ἰδοὺ φωνὴ ἐκ τῶν οὐρανῶν λέγουσα, Οὗτός ἐστιν ὁ υἱός
μου ὁ ἀγαπητὸς, ἐν ᾧ εὐδόκησα.

*And lo a voice from heaven, saying, This is my beloved Son,
in whom I am well pleased.*

ἰδοὺ, Hebraism; **ἀγαπητὸς**, cf. Arist. Rhet. p. 36, [Διὸ καὶ οὐκ ἴση ζημία, ἄν τις τὸν ἑτερόφθαλμον τυφλώσῃ καὶ τὸν δύ᾽ ἔχοντα· ἀγαπητὸν γὰρ ἀφῄρηται,—"The loss of an eye is a far greater injury to a one-eyed man than to a two-eyed man; for it is his *only one* that is taken away." Arist. Rhet. i. 7, 41.—Ed.]; 2 Sam. xii. 25, *He called his (Solomon's) name Jedidiah (beloved of the Lord)*; Isa. xlii. 1, *Mine elect in whom my soul delighteth;* (quoted Matt. xii. 18).

CHAP. IV.—Ver. 2.

Καὶ νηστεύσας ἡμέρας τεσσαράκοντα καὶ νύκτας τεσσαράκοντα, ὕστερον ἐπείνασε.

*And when he had fasted forty days and forty nights, he was
afterward an hungred.*

So Moses and Elias.

Ver. 3.

Καὶ προσελθὼν αὐτῷ ὁ πειράζων.
And when the tempter came to him.

So ὁ βαπτίζων, as a proper name. Cf. Exod. xvi. *Behold, I will rain bread from heaven;* Ps. lxxviii. *He rained down manna upon them to eat;* cv. *He satisfied them with the bread of heaven.*

Ver. 4.

Ἀλλ' ἐπὶ παντὶ ῥήματι ἐκπορευομένῳ διὰ στόματος Θεοῦ.
But by every word that proceedeth out of the mouth of God.

Cf. Deut. viii. 3. כָּל־מוֹצָא פִי־יְהוָה, *omne quod egreditur ex ore Dei.* Ps. lxxxix. 34 (Heb. 35), *The thing that is gone out of my lips.*

Ver. 6.

Τοῖς ἀγγέλοις αὐτοῦ ἐντελεῖται περὶ σοῦ, καὶ ἐπὶ χειρῶν ἀροῦσί σε.

He shall give his angels charge concerning thee, and in their hands they shall bear thee up, &c.

Quoted from Ps. xci. 11, 12.

Εἰ υἱὸς εἶ τοῦ Θεοῦ.] A proof of Christ's Divinity; [for it shews that the Tempter understood Christ to claim it.—ED.]

Ver. 7.

Οὐκ ἐκπειράσεις Κύριον τὸν Θεόν σου.
Thou shalt not tempt the Lord thy God.

Quoted from Deut. vi. 16.

Ver. 10.

Κύριον τὸν Θεόν σου προσκυνήσεις καὶ αὐτῷ μόνῳ λατρεύσεις.
Thou shalt worship the Lord thy God, and Him only shalt thou serve.

Quoted from Deut. vi. 13.

Ver. 13.

Καὶ καταλιπὼν τὴν Ναζαρέτ.
And leaving Nazareth.

Why did He leave Nazareth? Ans. St. Luke iv. 24, *No prophet is accepted in his own country;* St. John iv. 44, *For Jesus himself testified that no prophet hath honour in his own country.*

Ver. 15.
Γαλιλαία τῶν ἐθνῶν.
Galilee of the Gentiles.

ἐθνῶν.] Because it was near Tyre and Sidon, &c. Cf. Isa. ix. 1,—[rendered thus by Louth :—" But there shall not hereafter be darkness in the land which was distressed: In the former time He debased the land of Zebulon and the land of Naphtali: But in the latter time He hath made it glorious: Even the way of the sea beyond Jordan, Galilee of the nations."—ED.] Cf. also 2 Kings xv. 29, [which explains how the Assyrians had formerly distressed these northern tribes.—ED.]

Ver. 18.
Περιπατῶν δὲ ὁ Ἰησοῦς παρὰ τὴν θάλασσαν τῆς Γαλιλαίας, εἶδε δύο ἀδελφούς.
And Jesus, walking by the sea of Galilee, saw two brethren.

First preachers came out of Galilee, cf. Gen. xlix. 21, *Naphtali . . . giveth goodly words;* Deut. xxxiii. 19, *And of Zebulon he said: They shall call the people unto the mountain; there shall they offer sacrifices of righteousness.*

Final cause of their being chosen out of a low condition, 1 Cor. i. 26, *Not many wise men after the flesh, not many mighty, not many noble, are called.*

Ver. 19.
Ἁλιεῖς ἀνθρώπων.
Fishers of men.

Cf. ch. xiii. 47—50, (Parable of the Net). So Æsch. Agam. 361, Γάγγαμον ἄτης πανάλωτου. [The net of an all-enclosing destiny.]

Ver. 23.
Διδάσκων ἐν ταῖς συναγωγαῖς αὐτῶν.
Teaching in their synagogues.

ἐν ταῖς συναγωγαῖς.] Observe the regularity of Christ's *manner* of preaching. He did all things decently and in order.

Ver. 24.
Ἡ ἀκοὴ αὐτοῦ.
His fame.
Καὶ ἐθεράπευσεν αὐτούς.
And he healed them.

ἀκοή.] A Hebraism, [the word "hearing" being used in sense of "*tidings*," as שֵׁמַע is frequently.—ED.]

On this verse, which is the first mention of a miracle, explain the nature of miracles, and refer to Paley's answer to Hume. δαιμονιζομένους. [Mr. Keble seems to have intended to add a note on this word at some future time.—Ed.]

CHAP. V.—VER. 1.

Ἰδὼν δὲ τοὺς ὄχλους ἀνέβη εἰς τὸ ὄρος· καὶ καθίσαντος αὐτοῦ, προσῆλθον αὐτῷ οἱ μαθηταὶ αὐτοῦ·

And seeing the multitudes, he went up into a mountain: and when he was set, his disciples came unto him.

Chap. V. Just before this Sermon He seems to have elected His Apostles; see St. Luke vi. 13, [*He called unto Him His disciples, and of them He chose twelve.*]

τὸ ὄρος.] The Sermon is on the mount, perhaps, to parallel the Law; and opens with Beatitudes, to parallel the Psalms. Not the Disciples only, but all Christians are concerned in it; (for whether the Disciples were ordained is doubtful, and if certain would make no difference). Cf. c. vii. 28, *The people were astonished at his doctrine.*

First Section of Sermon, Beatitudes, ver. 3—12.

Each Beatitude both present and future, vid. Hammond, Pract. Cat., lib. ii. § i. [" He went up to the Mount to intimate the matter of this Sermon to be the *Christian Law*, as you know the *Jewish Law* was delivered in a Mount. . . . Every one of these Graces hath matter of *present* blessedness in it. . . . There is also assurance of *future* blessedness to all those that have attained to those several Graces."—Ed.]

VER. 3.

Μακάριοι οἱ πτωχοὶ τῷ πνεύματι· ὅτι αὐτῶν ἐστιν ἡ βασιλεία τῶν οὐρανῶν.

Blessed are the poor in spirit: for theirs is the kingdom of heaven.

Vid. c. xviii. 4, *Whosoever shall humble himself as this little child, the same is greatest in the kingdom of heaven;* St. James ii. 5, *Hath not God chosen the poor of this world rich in faith, and heirs of the kingdom?* Humility runs through all the rest of these beatitudes, alternately respective to God and man.

Hammond in his *Practical Catechism* observes that "*humility is the seed-plot of all;*" from whence we proceed to *mourning* for sin, which respecteth God; *meekness*, which respecteth our neighbour; *hungering and thirsting* after righteousness, which is to be had of God; *mercifulness* towards man; *purity* respecting God; *peaceableness*, respecting man; persecution for God's sake. (lib. ii. § 1.)

VER. 4.

Μακάριοι οἱ πενθοῦντες· ὅτι αὐτοὶ παρακληθήσονται.

Blessed are they that mourn: for they shall be comforted.

Ps. cxxvi. 5, *They that sow in tears shall reap in joy;* 2 Cor. vii. 10, *Godly sorrow worketh repentance to salvation;* Eccles. vii. 2, 3, *Better to go to the house of mourning than to the house of feasting...*

VER. 5.

Μακάριοι οἱ πραεῖς· ὅτι αὐτοὶ κληρονομήσουσι τὴν γῆν.

Blessed are the meek: for they shall inherit the earth.

Ps. xxxvii. 11, *The meek shall inherit the earth.* As the fifth commandment contains the same promise, we may collect a particular reference to the duty of obedience.

VER. 6.

Μακάριοι οἱ πεινῶντες καὶ διψῶντες τὴν δικαιοσύνην· ὅτι αὐτοὶ χορτασθήσονται.

Blessed are they which do hunger and thirst after righteousness: for they shall be filled.

πεινῶντες καὶ διψῶντες. The first for sanctification, and the second for pardon; cf. St. John iv. 34, *My meat is to do the will of Him that sent Me;* Ps. cxix. 55, 56, [? Hammond refers to Ps. xlii. 1, *As the hart panteth after the water brooks, &c.*—ED.]

VER. 7.

Μακάριοι οἱ ἐλεήμονες· ὅτι αὐτοὶ ἐλεηθήσονται.

Blessed are the merciful: for they shall obtain mercy.

Ps. xxxvii. 25, ... *yet have I not seen the righteous forsaken, nor his seed begging bread;* c. vi. 14, 15, *If ye forgive men their trespasses, your heavenly Father will also forgive you, &c.*

VER. 8.

Μακάριοι οἱ καθαροὶ τῇ καρδίᾳ· ὅτι αὐτοὶ τὸν Θεὸν ὄψονται.

Blessed are the pure in heart: for they shall see God.

Purity opposed, 1. to carnality; 2. to hypocrisy. Heb. xii. 14, ... *holiness, without which no man shall see the Lord;* 1 St. John ii. 2, 3, ... *we shall see Him as He is. And every man that hath this hope in Him purifieth himself.*

Ver. 9.

Μακάριοι οἱ εἰρηνοποιοί·
Blessed are the peacemakers.

Cf. St. James iii. 18, *The fruit of righteousness is sown in peace of them that make peace;* Ephes. ii. 14, *He is our peace, who hath made both one.* 'Sons of God' means imitators of Him, Ephes. v. 1, *Be ye therefore followers of God, as dear children.*

Ver. 10.

Μακάριοι οἱ δεδιωγμένοι ἕνεκεν δικαιοσύνης.
Blessed are they which are persecuted for righteousness' sake.

Cf. St. Matt. xix. 29, 30, *Every one that hath forsaken ... the last shall be first;* St. Luke xxii. 28—30, *Ye are they which have continued with Me in My temptations, &c.;* which shews that this, like the other Beatitudes, hath its accomplishment in both worlds.

Ver. 12.

Χαίρετε καὶ ἀγαλλιᾶσθε, κ.τ.λ.
Rejoice and be exceeding glad, &c.

See the command obeyed in Acts v. 41, *Rejoicing that they were counted worthy to suffer shame for His name.*

St. Luke (vi. 23) has σκιρτήσατε. Cf. St. James v. 10, 11, *Take the prophets ... for an example, &c.;* Acts vii. 52, *Which of the prophets have not your fathers persecuted?* St. Luke xiii. 33, 34, *It cannot be that a prophet perish out of Jerusalem. O Jerusalem, which killest the prophets, &c.*

Ver. 13.

Ὑμεῖς ἐστε τὸ ἅλας τῆς γῆς· ἐὰν δὲ τὸ ἅλας μωρανθῇ, ἐν τίνι ἁλισθήσεται; εἰς οὐδὲν ἰσχύει ἔτι ...
Ye are the salt of the earth: but if the salt have lost his savour, wherewith shall it be salted? It is thenceforth good for nothing, &c.

Second Section. Christians must be exemplary, 13—16.

"Sal vulgo animi aut orationis indolem, hic hominum genus denotat. Insulsum apud Latinos simile quiddam τοῦ μωρανθῇ, sonat." Query whether this at all hints at the world's being saved for the elect's sake? Cf. Gen. xviii. [Abraham's intercession for Sodom] and St. Matt. xxiv. 22, *For the elect's sake those days shall be shortened;* ἰσχύει illustrated from Gal. v. 6, *Neither circumcision availeth* (ἰσχύει) *anything.*

VER. 14.

Οὐ δύναται πόλις κρυβῆναι ἐπάνω ὄρους κειμένη.
A city that is set on an hill cannot be hid.

ὄρους.] The Church is likened to a mountain by Isaiah ii. 2, *The mountain of the Lord's house shall be established;* and Micah iv. 1, *The mountain of the house of the Lord shall be established.*

VER. 15.

Ἀλλ' ἐπὶ τὴν λυχνίαν.
But on a candlestick.

Cf. Apuleius ap. Wetstein. [Tom. i. p. 292, "Novaculam sub pulvinar abscondit, lucernamque modio contegit." Metamorph. V.]

VER. 16.

Οὕτω λαμψάτω τὸ φῶς ὑμῶν ἔμπροσθεν τῶν ἀνθρώπων, ὅπως ἴδωσιν ὑμῶν τὰ καλὰ ἔργα, καὶ δοξάσωσι τὸν πατέρα ὑμῶν τὸν ἐν τοῖς οὐρανοῖς.

Let your light so shine before men, that they may see your good works, and glorify your Father which is in heaven.

Ambiguity in the English word *let;* still no encouragement to vainglory. δοξάσωσι, to glorify by obedience; 1 Cor. x. 31, *Whatsoever ye do, do all to the glory of God.*

VER. 17.

Third Section. Christ did not abolish but perfected the Law, 17—20.

Μὴ νομίσητε ὅτι ἦλθον καταλῦσαι τὸν νόμον ἢ τοὺς προφήτας· οὐκ ἦλθον καταλῦσαι, ἀλλὰ πληρῶσαι.

Think not that I am come to destroy the law, or the prophets: I am not come to destroy, but to fulfil.

Difference between νόμον and προφήτας. Force of καταλῦσαι to be taken as an indication of that of πληρῶσαι, which is probably an αὔξησις of μὴ καταλῦσαι, and means 1. fully to establish; 2. fully to explain; 3. fully to obey; 4. fully to accomplish, the old dispensation; as it was, 1. a covenant; 2. a revelation; 3. a law; 4. a shadow of good things to come. And in this way the word "perfect" seems no unfit rendering of πληρῶσαι; not necessarily implying any defect in the substance of the moral law, but only in the delivery and explanation of it. Cf. Heb. vii. 19, *The Law made nothing perfect, but the bringing in of a better hope did.*

Ver. 18.

Ἀμὴν γὰρ λέγω ὑμῖν, ἕως ἂν παρέλθῃ ὁ οὐρανὸς καὶ ἡ γῆ, ἰῶτα ἓν ἢ μία κεραία οὐ μὴ παρέλθῃ ἀπὸ τοῦ νόμου, ἕως ἂν πάντα γένηται.

For verily I say unto you, Till heaven and earth pass, one jot or one tittle shall in no wise pass from the law, till all be fulfilled.

Ἀμήν.] Kept in most versions. ["*Amen*" instead of the "*verily*" of the English Version.—ED.] Cf. 2 Cor. i. 20, *All the promises of God in Him are Yea, and in Him Amen;* Rev. iii. 14, *These things saith the Amen.*

ἕως ἄν, κ.τ.λ.] Cf. c. xxiv. 34, 35, *This generation shall not pass, &c.*

ἰῶτα.] An imperfect letter.

κεραία.] A dash of the pen.

Ver. 19.

Ὃς ἐὰν οὖν λύσῃ μίαν τῶν ἐντολῶν τούτων τῶν ἐλαχίστων, καὶ διδάξῃ οὕτω τοὺς ἀνθρώπους, ἐλάχιστος κληθήσεται ἐν τῇ βασιλείᾳ τῶν οὐρανῶν· ὃς δ' ἂν ποιήσῃ καὶ διδάξῃ, οὗτος μέγας κληθήσεται ἐν τῇ βασιλείᾳ τῶν οὐρανῶν.

Whosoever therefore shall break one of these least commandments, and shall teach men so, he shall be called the least in the kingdom of heaven: but whosoever shall do and teach them, the same shall be called great in the kingdom of heaven.

Schleusner, under the word λύω, expounds this "shall interpret;" but the use of καταλύω above contradicts this; and besides, under the word ἐλάχιστος, Schleusner contradicts himself.

From the reference to doing and teaching, the faults of the Scribes may probably be gathered, for (1) their doctrinal righteousness was imperfect, they taught men to break the commandments, cf. ch. xv. 1—20, and the rest of this chapter; (2) their practice came not up to it, cf. ch. xxiii. (*Woe unto you Scribes and Pharisees . . .*) and passim.

Ver. 20.

Λέγω γὰρ ὑμῖν, Ὅτι ἐὰν μὴ περισσεύσῃ ἡ δικαιοσύνη ὑμῶν πλεῖον τῶν γραμματέων καὶ Φαρισαίων, οὐ μὴ εἰσέλθητε εἰς τὴν βασιλείαν τῶν οὐρανῶν.

For I say unto you, That except your righteousness shall exceed the righteousness of the scribes and Pharisees, ye shall in no case enter into the kingdom of heaven.

περισσεύσῃ—εἰσέλθητε.] Very strong expressions. Note here

what (I believe) Bp. Taylor says, that the Jews held that if but two men were to enter into the kingdom of heaven, one would be a Scribe, and the other a Pharisee. Also the ἀκρίβεια of the Pharisees, Acts xxvi. 5, *After the most straitest sect of our religion I lived a Pharisee.*

VER. 21.

Fourth Section. Six instances of perfecting the Law, 21—48.

Ἠκούσατε ὅτι ἐρρέθη τοῖς ἀρχαίοις, Οὐ φονεύσεις, ὃς δ' ἂν φονεύσῃ, ἔνοχος ἔσται τῇ κρίσει.

Ye have heard that it was said by them of old time, Thou shalt not kill; and whosoever shall kill shall be in danger of the judgment.

Not διὰ τῶν ἀρχαίων. Where I find the word in the New Testament, it governs a dative of the person addressed.

τῇ κρίσει.] The provincial courts established by Moses, see Deut. xvi. 18, *Judges and officers shalt thou make thee in all thy gates ... throughout thy tribes, and they shall judge the people;* cf. also Exod. xxi. 12, *He that smiteth a man ... shall be surely put to death;* Deut. xix. 11, 12, (*The avenger of blood*).

VER. 22.

Ἔνοχος ἔσται τῇ κρίσει.
Shall be in danger of the judgment.
Ἔνοχος ἔσται τῷ συνεδρίῳ·
Shall be in danger of the council.

κρίσις seems here to mean more than meets the ear.

συνέδριον.] Cf. Numb. xi. 16, *Gather me Seventy men of the Elders of Israel.*

Μωρέ.] A very strong word in Hebrew. Cf. Joshua vii. 15, *He hath wrought folly in Israel* (נְבָלָה, *flagitium*); 2 Sam. iii. 33, *Died Abner as a fool dieth?* (נָבָל); Ps. xiv. 1, *The fool* (נָבָל) *hath said in his heart ...*

VER. 23.

Ἐὰν οὖν προσφέρῃς τὸ δῶρόν σου ἐπὶ τὸ θυσιαστήριον.
Therefore if thou bring thy gift to the altar.

Application to the Holy Communion.

VER. 27.

Ἠκούσατε ὅτι ἐρρέθη τοῖς ἀρχαίοις, Οὐ μοιχεύσεις·
Ye have heard that it was said by them of old time, Thou shalt not commit adultery.

First error (verse 21), making the civil law the measure; second (in this verse), leaving out bad desire from the list of sins.

Ver. 29.

Εἰ δὲ ὁ ὀφθαλμός σου ὁ δεξιὸς σκανδαλίζει σε.
And if thy right eye offend thee.

σκανδαλίζει.] Corresponds to the Hebrew מוֹקֵשׁ, a *snare*, from יקשׁ, *bent, ἐν τῇ παγίδι ἐπικαμπὲς ξύλον*, " Respiciunt hæc de oculo dicta versum 28, cap. v.;" Grot.

Ver. 31.

Ἐρρέθη δὲ, Ὅτι ὃς ἂν ἀπολύσῃ τὴν γυναῖκα αὐτοῦ, δότω αὐτῇ ἀποστάσιον.
It hath been said, Whosoever shall put away his wife, let him give her a writing of divorcement.

Connected with the thought of the two preceding verses. So ch. xix. 10, *If the case of the man be so with his wife, it is not good to marry.*

Cf. Deut. xxiv. 1, *When a man hath taken a wife . . . let him write her a bill of divorcement;* St. Matt. xix. 8, *Moses because of the hardness of your hearts suffered you to put away your wives.* Possibly the law might be made less lax, as well as Polygamy forbidden, as the world was more fully peopled. Also marriage was now to put us in mind of the union betwixt Christ and his Church.

Ver. 32.

Παρεκτὸς λόγου πορνείας.
Saving for the cause of fornication.

λόγου.] So *ratione*, in Latin.

Ver. 33.

Οὐκ ἐπιορκήσεις, ἀποδώσεις δὲ τῷ Κυρίῳ τοὺς ὅρκους σου·
Thou shalt not forswear thyself, but shalt perform unto the Lord thine oaths.

This is the only commandment of the first Table which Christ expounds. The Jews were less deficient in it. The last clause of the verse relates to vows, cf. Numb. xxx. 2, *If a man vow a vow unto the Lord, or swear an oath to bind his soul with a bond, he shall not break his word, &c.* The error in expounding was mentioning only the highest act [omitting the many other ways in which the Lord's Name may be taken in vain.—Ed.]

Ver. 34.

Ἐγὼ δὲ λέγω ὑμῖν, Μὴ ὀμόσαι ὅλως·
But I say unto you, Swear not at all.

Cf. St. James v. 12, *Above all things, my brethren, swear not, neither by heaven, &c.* But all swearing is not forbidden. Cf. ch. xxvi. 63, 64 [where Christ accepts the oath administered to Him]; 2 Cor. xi. 31, *The God and Father of our Lord Jesus Christ knoweth that I lie not;* i. 18, *As God is true, &c.*

Ver. 35.

Μήτε ἐν τῷ οὐρανῷ, ὅτι θρόνος ἐστὶ τοῦ Θεοῦ· μήτε ἐν τῇ γῇ, ὅτι ὑποπόδιόν ἐστι τῶν ποδῶν αὐτοῦ·

Neither by heaven, for it is God's throne; nor by the earth, for it is his footstool.

It was idolatry to swear by anything without reference to God: cf. Deut. vi. 13, *Thou shalt fear the Lord thy God ... and shalt swear by His Name;* Ps. xvi. 4. *Their drink offerings of blood will I not offer, nor take up their names into my lips.* And to swear lightly by anything was therefore profaneness, as it included a reference to His Name; this is expressed in our Lord's reasons here. On θρόνος and ὑποπόδιον, cf. Isa. lxvi. 1, *Heaven is my throne, and the earth is my footstool, &c.*

Ver. 37.

Τὸ δὲ περισσὸν τούτων ἐκ τοῦ πονηροῦ ἐστιν.

For whatsoever is more than these cometh of evil.

ἐκ τοῦ πονηροῦ has a double sense, as in the Lord's Prayer; but the result is the same [whether we understand it to mean *the Evil One* or *evil*.—Ed.]

Ver. 38.

Ἠκούσατε ὅτι ἐρρέθη, Ὀφθαλμὸν ἀντὶ ὀφθαλμοῦ, καὶ ὀδόντα ἀντὶ ὀδόντος·

Ye have heard that it hath been said, An eye for an eye, and a tooth for a tooth.

Cf. Exod. xxi. 24, *Thou shalt give life for life, eye for eye, tooth for tooth, hand for hand.* The error here, was interpreting a judicial precept in a moral sense.

Ver. 39.

Ἐγὼ δὲ λέγω ὑμῖν μὴ ἀντιστῆναι τῷ πονηρῷ·

But I say unto you, That ye resist not evil.

ἀντιστῆναι.] To withstand by way of retaliation.

Ver. 40.

Καὶ τῷ θέλοντί σοι κριθῆναι καὶ τὸν χιτῶνά σου λαβεῖν.

And if any man will sue thee at the law and take away thy coat.

κριθῆναι.] Cf. Job ix. 3, *If he will contend with Him* (κριθῆναι μετ' αὐτοῦ); so ἀδελφὸς μετὰ ἀδελφοῦ κρίνεται, *brother goeth to law with brother;* 1 Cor. vi. 6.

VER. 41.

Καὶ ὅστις σε ἀγγαρεύσει μίλιον ἕν.
And whosoever shall compel thee to go a mile.

ἀγγαρεύσει.] Cf. Herod. viii. 98 [description of the Persian couriers. So ἄγγαρον πῦρ, *the courier flame of the beacon*] Æsch. Agam. 282.

This passage shews how individual Christians should endure slight oppressions from their governors.

μίλιον.] A Latin word.

VER. 42.

Τῷ αἰτοῦντί σε δίδου·
Give to him that asketh thee.

Indiscriminate charity clearly not commanded here, and therefore by parity of reasoning, indiscriminate submission not implied in the other cases. Cf. 1 Tim. v. 9 [not to relieve widows indiscriminately]; St. John xviii. 20, 21 [our Lord refusing to be questioned by the High Priest]; Acts xvi. 37 [St. Paul's protest at Philippi]; xxii. 25, *Is it lawful for you to scourge a man that is a Roman;* and the whole case of St. Paul before Felix and Festus. Query, What is the limit? Answer, That nothing be done but upon public grounds, and no violence offered upon any grounds. That war is not forbidden, see St. Luke iii. 14 [the Baptist's words to the soldiers], and the case of Cornelius. That capital punishments are not forbidden, see Rom. xiii. 4, *He beareth not the sword in vain, for he is the minister of God.*

VER. 43.

Ἠκούσατε ὅτι ἐρρέθη, Ἀγαπήσεις τὸν πλησίον σου, καὶ μισήσεις τὸν ἐχθρόν σου.
Ye have heard that it hath been said, Thou shalt love thy neighbour, and hate thine enemy.

Cf. Lev. xix. 18, *Thou shalt not avenge, nor bear any grudge against the children of thy people, but thou shalt love thy neighbour.* Brother among the Jews meant of the same blood; Deut. xv. 12, *If thy brother, an Hebrew man or Hebrew woman, be sold;* xxiii. 20, *unto a stranger thou mayest lend upon usury, but unto thy brother thou shalt not.* Neighbour meant one of the same Religion. Among Christians, Neighbours are all mankind; Brothers, fellow Christians, 2 Pet. i. 7, *To brotherly kindness add charity.* But Neighbour is used more largely in the Old Testament for him who is next to thee. Cf. 2 Sam. ii. 16 (*They caught every one his fellow*). And therefore our Saviour extends it in Luke x. [parable of Good Samaritan] ; cf. also Exod. xxii. 21, *Thou shalt not vex a stranger;* xxiii. 9, 4, 5, *If thou meet thine enemy's ox or ass going astray, thou shalt restore it to him.* On the other hand, are the cases of the seven nations of Canaan (Josh. iii. 10), Amalek, Moab, and Ammon, but the distinction is manifest.

VER. 44.

'Αγαπᾶτε τοὺς ἐχθροὺς ὑμῶν, εὐλογεῖτε τοὺς καταρωμένους ὑμᾶς, καλῶς ποιεῖτε τοὺς μισοῦντας ὑμᾶς, καὶ προσεύχεσθε ὑπὲρ τῶν ἐπηρεαζόντων ὑμᾶς, καὶ διωκόντων ὑμᾶς·

Love your enemies, bless them that curse you, do good to them that hate you, and pray for them which despitefully use you and persecute you.

Observe, thought, word, and deed are here specified, also slight injuries are to be borne with, as appears from the word ἐπηρεαζόντων. Cf. Arist. Rhet. ii. 2 [ἔστι γὰρ ὁ ἐπηρεασμὸς ἐμποδισμὸς ταῖς βουλήσεσιν οὐχ ἵνα τι αὐτῷ ἀλλ' ἵνα μὴ ἐκείνῳ,—thwarting from petty spite].

VER. 45.

Τὸν ἥλιον αὐτοῦ ἀνατέλλει.
For he maketh his sun to rise.

Cf. v. 9. ἀνατέλλει, used actively to express the Hebrew verb in Hiphil [*caused to rise*], an usual Hellenism.

VER. 46.

Οὐχὶ καὶ οἱ τελῶναι τὸ αὐτὸ ποιοῦσι ;
Do not even the publicans the same?

τελῶναι.] Very offensive by trade, political situation, character.

VER. 47.

Τί περισσὸν ποιεῖτε ;
What do ye more than others?

περισσόν.] Cf. Arist. Rhet. i. 6 [καὶ τὰ ἴδια, καὶ ἃ μηδείς, καὶ τὰ περιττά,—*things peculiar, original, and extraordinary*].

VER. 48.

Ἔσεσθε οὖν ὑμεῖς τέλειοι, ὥσπερ ὁ πατὴρ ὑμῶν ὁ ἐν τοῖς οὐρανοῖς τέλειός ἐστι.
Be ye therefore perfect, even as your Father which is in heaven is perfect.

τέλειοι respondet τῷ "ἅγιοι," cf. Lev. xx. 26, *And ye shall be holy unto Me; for I the Lord am holy.* τελειόω means "to consecrate."

Three reasons [for sanctifying our affections] are given in these verses [45—48],—to be like God, to be unlike bad men, to receive a reward; and to be like God comes first and last.

CHAP. VI.—VER. 1.

Προσέχετε τὴν ἐλεημοσύνην ὑμῶν μὴ ποιεῖν ἔμπροσθεν τῶν ἀνθρώπων.

Take heed that ye do not your alms before men.

Sub. ἑαυτοῖς. Subintelligitur sæpe τὸν νοῦν, semper autem, quantum scio, cum dativo, non cum infinitivo, jungitur.

δικαιοσύνην, apud Griesbach; [see note on i. 19 *supra*.—ED.]

παρὰ τῷ πατρί, laid up for you with your Father.

VER. 2.

Μὴ σαλπίσῃς ἔμπροσθέν σου, ὥσπερ οἱ ὑποκριταὶ ποιοῦσιν ἐν ταῖς συναγωγαῖς καὶ ἐν ταῖς ῥύμαις.

Do not sound a trumpet before them, as the hypocrites do in the synagogues and in the streets.

σαλπίσῃς, to be taken metaphorically; συναγωγαῖς, forsan non technica [need not be understood in its technical sense, but for any place where men congregate.—ED.] "When they gave alms in the Synagogue, they had it openly proclaimed and published what they gave; and an open proclaiming in the streets, for the calling of the poor to gather the corner of the field they had left them,"—Lightfoot. [N.B. I have looked in vain for this passage in Lightfoot. His note, *in loco*, alludes to the Alms-chest in every synagogue, and a proclamation (of what nature uncertain) in connexion with it; and also to proclamations in harvest-time, specifying what fields, or corners of fields, were open to gleaners. Possibly Mr. Keble gives the substance of this note from memory.—ED.]

VER. 5.

Φιλοῦσιν ἐν ταῖς συναγωγαῖς καὶ ἐν ταῖς γωνίαις τῶν πλατειῶν ἑστῶτες προσεύχεσθαι.

They love to pray standing in the synagogues and in the corners of the streets.

φιλοῦσιν, are accustomed. They were bound by tradition to

be much in prayer. Lightfoot says they prayed in the Synagogues in the time of public prayer, but apart from the rest.

ἑστῶτες.] The Jews used to *stand* when they prayed, cf. Mark xi. 25, *when ye stand praying;* Luke xviii. 11, 13 (parable of Pharisee and Publican); Job xxx. 20, *I say unto Thee . . . I stand up, and Thou hearest not;* Gen. xviii. 22, *Abraham stood yet before the Lord;* Jer. xv. 1, *Though Moses and Samuel stood before Me;* and xviii. 20, *I stood before Thee to speak good for them.* Query whether the three last texts do not imply that *standing* is the peculiar gesture for intercession, and therefore used by the Priest in the Communion Service. So Tertullian uses *statio* as a name for the place of prayer [*De Orat.* xix., &c.—ED.]

Ver. 6.

Σὺ δὲ ὅταν προσεύχῃ, εἴσελθε εἰς τὸ ταμιεῖόν σου, καὶ κλείσας τὴν θύραν σου, πρόσευξαι τῷ πατρί σου τῷ ἐν τῷ κρυπτῷ.
But thou, when thou prayest, enter into thy closet, and when thou hast shut thy door, pray to thy Father which is in secret.

This is consistent with *common* prayer; see ch. xviii. 19, *If two of you shall agree on earth as touching anything that they shall ask, it shall be done for them.*

Ver. 7.

Προσευχόμενοι δὲ μὴ βαττολογήσητε, ὥσπερ οἱ ἐθνικοί·
But when ye pray, use not vain repetitions, as the heathen do.

βαττολογήσητε.] Cf. Ecclus. vii. 14, *Make not much babbling when thou prayest,* e.g. [the Latin Office of] the Roman Catholics.

ὥσπερ οἱ ἐθνικοί.] As in the many names they gave their gods: πολυώνυμε, &c. See also Acts xix. 34, *All with one voice about the space of two hours cried out, Great is Diana of the Ephesians;* Ter. [*Heaut.*, v. i. "Ohe, jam desine deos obtundere," &c.]

Our Liturgy not liable to this charge, cf. Luke xxii. [the thrice-repeated prayer in Gethsemane]; xviii. 1, *Men ought always to pray, and not to faint;* Acts xii. 5, *Prayer was made without ceasing of the Church for him;* Thess. v. 17, *Pray without ceasing;* Col. iv. 2, *Continue in prayer.* And consider, 1, the relief afforded by the variation of the Service; 2, the pregnant meaning of the prayers repeated; 3, the fact of the best men having most delighted in them.

ἔθνος and λαός, cf. Acts xxvi. 17, 23, where "the people"—God's people—are opposed to the Gentiles.

Ver. 8.

Οἶδε γὰρ ὁ πατὴρ ὑμῶν, ὧν χρείαν ἔχετε, πρὸ τοῦ ὑμᾶς αἰτῆσαι αὐτόν.

Your Father knoweth what things ye have need of, before ye ask him.

Cf. Juv. [x. 347, "Permittes ipsis expendere numinibus, quid Conveniat nobis," &c.]

Gr. Poeta ap. Platon., [Ζεῦ βασιλεῦ, τὰ μὲν ἐσθλὰ καὶ εὐχομένοις καὶ ἀνεύκτοις Ἄμμι δίδου· τὰ δὲ δεινὰ καὶ εὐχομένοις ἀπαλέξειν].

Ver. 9.

Οὕτως οὖν προσεύχεσθε ὑμεῖς· Πάτερ ἡμῶν ὁ ἐν τοῖς οὐρανοῖς, ἁγιασθήτω τὸ ὄνομά σου.

After this manner therefore pray ye: Our Father, which art in heaven, Hallowed be thy name.

Observe, I. That this was chiefly formed from old Jewish Prayers.

II. That it was for a form, and not merely a directory; for, 1. This is the literal sense of the words: 2. The customs of the Jews would lead the Apostles to take them so: for authority in Old Testament for a set form, *vide* Numbers vi. 22—27 [form of Blessing]; Deut. xxi. 8 [form of Expiation]; xxvii. 13—15, [form of Curses on Ebal]; and the whole Book of Psalms: 3. Possibly this may account for His delivering it twice; but the differences of the two are such as to make us suppose that the first was public, the other private.

III. That each petition, like each commandment, is the head of a class, and they admit of a similar general division,—the glory of God and the good of mankind.

Πάτερ.] Isa. lxiii. 16, *Doubtless Thou art our Father;* lxiv. 8, *But now, O Lord, Thou art our Father;* Mal. i. 6, *If then I be a father, where is mine honour?* 1. As Creator; 2. As Father of Jesus Christ; for from Christ's prayers, and from the Apostolical blessings, it is probable that this prayer is specially addressed to God the Father.

ἡμῶν.] Teaches, 1. difference between us and Christ in sonship; 2. humility; 3. charity.

Vide Talmud ap. Lightfoot, "Orantem oportet semper se cum Ecclesia consociare, nequis oret numero singularis."

ὁ ἐν τοῖς οὐρανοῖς.] ὁ vocativum.

ὄνομα.] 1. The Majesty of God Himself; 2. Anything whereupon His Name is called, and which has so far come to represent it to our minds.

ἁγιασθήτω,] i.e. to separate; vide Deut. vii. 6, *A holy people ... chosen to be a special people;* xxvi. 18, 19, *A peculiar people ... holy unto the Lord;* xix. 2, *Thou shalt separate three cities:* compared with Jos. xx. 7, *And they appointed Kedesh, &c.*, where קָדֵשׁ (to appoint) corresponds to הִבְדִּיל (to separate) in the former verse. Consider also the use of κοινός in Acts x., *common or unclean;* Heb. x. 29, *an unholy thing.* The petition then means, Mayest Thou be served and glorified in opposition to irreligion, and that with incommunicable service, in opposition to Idolatry, and, may Thy holy things, places, persons, &c., be treated with peculiar reverence by us, and amongst the rest ourselves, who are a λαὸς περιούσιος.

VER. 10.

Ἐλθέτω ἡ βασιλεία σου· γενηθήτω τὸ θέλημά σου,
ὡς ἐν οὐρανῷ, καὶ ἐπὶ τῆς γῆς.

Thy kingdom come. Thy will be done in earth, as it is in heaven.

God's kingdom has been already explained. Of His will, *vide* ch. vii. 21, *Not every one that saith unto Me, Lord, Lord, &c.*; how it is done in heaven, Ps. ciii. 21, *Ye ministers of His that do His pleasure;* cf. also what He said in His agony.

VER. 11.

Τὸν ἄρτον ἡμῶν τὸν ἐπιούσιον δὸς ἡμῖν σήμερον·

Give us this day our daily bread.

ἐπιούσιος ab ἐπιούσια ab περιούσιος ap. LXX. a περιουσίᾳ; means sufficient for *being;* ἐπὶ τὴν οὐσίαν, Mede.

VER. 12.

Καὶ ἄφες ἡμῖν τὰ ὀφειλήματα ἡμῶν, ὡς καὶ ἡμεῖς ἀφίεμεν
τοῖς ὀφειλέταις ἡμῶν·

And forgive us our debts, as we forgive our debtors.

ὀφειλέται cum ἁμαρτωλοί, commutatur St. Luke xiii. 2, "*sinners,*" 4, "*debtors*" in the margin.

ἀφίεμεν.] Opponitur τῷ κρατεῖν, cf. Ecclus. xxviii. 2, *He that revengeth ... he will surely keep his sins; forgive thy neighbour ... so shall thy sins also be forgiven.* Unforgiving persons, using the petition, curse themselves.

Ver. 13.

Καὶ μὴ εἰσενέγκῃς ἡμᾶς εἰς πειρασμόν, ἀλλὰ ῥῦσαι ἡμᾶς ἀπὸ τοῦ πονηροῦ. ὅτι σοῦ ἐστιν ἡ βασιλεία καὶ ἡ δύναμις καὶ ἡ δόξα εἰς τοὺς αἰῶνας. ἀμήν.

And lead us not into temptation, but deliver us from evil: For thine is the kingdom, and the power, and the glory, for ever. Amen.

Cf. St. Matt. xxvi. 41, *Pray that ye enter not into temptation* (πειρασμόν). God does not tempt, St. James i. 13, *Neither tempteth He any man;* but He suffers men to be tempted, sometimes by way of trial, as the children of Israel in the wilderness; sometimes by way of punishment, e.g. Balaam; this clause applies to both.

ὁ πονηρός,] or τὸ πονηρόν? May mean both, being said of sin and of punishment. As to the Doxology, it is wanting in the Greek and Latin Doctors, and in the manuscripts B. and D., and its insertion may be easily accounted for by its appearing in the Liturgy of the Greek Church. There is authority for the "Amen," 1 Cor. xiv. 16, *How shall he . . . say Amen at thy giving of thanks?*

Ver. 14.

Ἐὰν γὰρ ἀφῆτε τοῖς ἀνθρώποις τὰ παραπτώματα αὐτῶν, ἀφήσει καὶ ὑμῖν ὁ πατὴρ ὑμῶν ὁ οὐράνιος·

For if ye forgive men their trespasses, your heavenly Father will also forgive you.

Our Lord gives a reason for *this* petition, because it was the only one omitted by the Jews.

Ver. 16.

Ὅταν δὲ νηστεύητε, μὴ γίνεσθε ὥσπερ οἱ ὑποκριταί, σκυθρωποί· ἀφανίζουσι γὰρ τὰ πρόσωπα αὐτῶν.

Moreover when ye fast, be not, as the hypocrites, of a sad countenance: for they disfigure their faces.

Christ takes it for granted that Christians will fast.

Is is spoken against the Pharisees, cf. St. Luke xviii. 12, *I fast twice a week.*

The Jews had four public yearly fasts: see Levit. xxiii. 26 [for one of them, the Day of Atonement. For mention of all the four, see] Zech. viii. 19, *The Fast of the fourth month, and the Fast of the fifth, and the Fast of the seventh, and the Fast of the tenth.* From Zech. viii. 5 (*When ye fasted and mourned in the fifth and seventh month those seventy years*), it seems that two of these were appointed in Babylon.

ἀφανίζουσι, perhaps they *cover* or *hide*, cf. Ezek. xxiv. 17, 22, *Make no mourning ... cover not thy lips;* or possibly, They produce paleness, cf. Lexicog.; πρόσωπα may mean *looks.* Cf. Hab. i. 5, and Acts xiii. 41, *Behold, ye despisers, and wonder, and perish.* [ἀφανίσθητε, which may mean, be astonished or dismayed.—ED.]

VER. 17.

Σὺ δὲ νηστεύων ἄλειψαί σου τὴν κεφαλὴν, καὶ τὸ πρόσωπόν σου νίψαι·

But thou, when thou fastest, anoint thy head, and wash thy face.

Cf. Ps. civ. 15, *Oil to make his face to shine;* from which and similar passages, it follows that Christ is not here commanding men to pretend to be feasting, but only to go on as usual.

VER. 18.

Ὁ πατήρ σου ὁ βλέπων ἐν τῷ κρυπτῷ.

Thy Father which seeth in secret.

Cf. Isa. xlv. 15, *Verily Thou art a God that hidest Thyself;* where God is called אֵל מִסְתַּתֵּר, and by LXX. Θεὸς καὶ οὐκ ᾔδειμεν.

VER. 19.

Μὴ θησαυρίζετε ὑμῖν θησαυροὺς ἐπὶ τῆς γῆς, ὅπου σὴς καὶ βρῶσις ἀφανίζει, καὶ ὅπου κλέπται διορύσσουσι καὶ κλέπτουσι·

Lay not up for yourselves treasures upon earth, where moth and rust doth corrupt, and where thieves break through and steal.

From this to the end may be considered as an explication of the tenth Commandment, and of the fourth petition in the Lord's Prayer. διορύσσουσι does not necessarily mean digging through, though probably its first use in this sense came from the custom of hiding treasure in a field. βρῶσις may mean rust in corn, and then we shall have the two chief cares of the body referred to here, the Food in βρῶσις, and Raiment in σής. Cf. Sapph. ap. Pind. Schol. in Pyth. iv. 407, [ὅτι Διὸς παῖς ὁ χρυσός, κεῖνον οὐ σὴς οὐδὲ κὶς δάπτει.—ED.]

VER. 22.

Ἐὰν οὖν ὁ ὀφθαλμός σου ἁπλοῦς ᾖ, ὅλον τὸ σῶμά σου φωτεινὸν ἔσται·

If therefore thine eye be single, thy whole body shall be full of light.

Explained, ἁπλοῦς means "liberal," 2 Cor. viii. 2, *The riches of their liberality* (ἁπλότητος); Rom. xii. 8, *He that giveth with simplicity* (ἁπλότητι); cf. Arist. Eth. [I cannot find this reference.— ED.] The connexion of this and the following verse, with what comes before and after, is probably best made out by considering the meaning of "an evil eye," and of ἁπλότης in other parts of the New Testament. Cf. Arist Eth. vi. 12 [διὰ τὸ ἔχειν ἐκ τῆς ἐμπειρίας ὄμμα ὁρῶσιν ὀρθῶς]; and i. 6 [where human good is defined to be doing the proper work of the soul well.—ED.]

φωτεινόν.] Cf. Ephes. v. 8, *Now are ye light in the Lord;* 1 St. John i. 6, 7, *If we walk in the light as He is in the light.* . . . Covetousness is "the lust of the eye," Hammond.

VER. 23.

Ἐὰν δὲ ὁ ὀφθαλμός σου πονηρὸς ᾖ.
But if thine eye be evil.

ὀφθαλμὸς πονηρὸς.] So רָע is opposed to בָּרָה; and so ἄφθονος means "liberal." Cf. St. Mark vii. 22, *An evil eye;* St. Matt. xx. 15, *Is thine eye evil, because I am good.*

VER. 24.

Οὐδεὶς δύναται δυσὶ κυρίοις δουλεύειν· ἢ γὰρ τὸν ἕνα μισήσει, καὶ τὸν ἕτερον ἀγαπήσει· ἢ ἑνὸς ἀνθέξεται, καὶ τοῦ ἑτέρου καταφρονήσει. οὐ δύνασθε Θεῷ δουλεύειν καὶ μαμμωνᾷ.

No man can serve two masters: for either he will hate the one, and love the other; or else he will hold to the one, and despise the other. Ye cannot serve God and mammon.

Here our Lord anticipates the objection, Why cannot I receive both worlds? Also observe that the δοῦλος was required to give a more undivided service to his master than servants now are, and therefore more nearly answering to the case of one governed by avarice, or by true religion. τοῦ ἑνὸς — τοῦ ἑτέρου; *hujus—illius.* Mammon is a Syriac name for riches; it seems to have been occasionally used as a proper name.

VER. 25.

Διὰ τοῦτο λέγω ὑμῖν, Μὴ μεριμνᾶτε τῇ ψυχῇ ὑμῶν, τί φάγητε, καὶ τί πίητε.

Therefore I say unto you, Take no thought for your life, what ye shall eat, or what ye shall drink.

Cf. Phil. iv. 6, *Be careful for nothing;* 1 Pet. v. 7, *Casting all your care on Him.* μετεωρίζεσθαι, ap. St. Luc. xii. 29. Occurrit Christus tacitæ objectioni : saltem de necessariis hisce prospiciam.

Ver. 26.

Ὁ πατὴρ ὑμῶν ὁ οὐράνιος τρέφει αὐτά· οὐχ ὑμεῖς μᾶλλον διαφέρετε αὐτῶν ;
Your heavenly Father feedeth them. Are ye not much better than they ?

Emphatice πατήρ.

μᾶλλον is redundant, cf. St. Mark vii. 36, μᾶλλον περισσότερον ; 2 Cor. vii. 13, περισσοτέρως δὲ μᾶλλον.

Ver. 27.

Τίς δὲ ἐξ ὑμῶν μεριμνῶν δύναται προσθεῖναι ἐπὶ τὴν ἡλικίαν αὐτοῦ πῆχυν ἕνα ;
Which of you by taking thought can add one cubit unto his stature ?

Zaccheus was μικρὸς τῇ ἡλικίᾳ. St. Luke xix. 3, *He was little of stature.* But it may mean *time;* cf. Ps. xxxix. 5, *Thou hast made my days as an handbreadth.*

Ver. 28.

Καταμάθετε τὰ κρίνα τοῦ ἀγροῦ.
Consider the lilies of the field.

Example of Christ's way of teaching; by familiar instances.

Ver. 29.

Οὐδὲ Σολομὼν ἐν πάσῃ τῇ δόξῃ αὐτοῦ περιεβάλετο ὡς ἓν τούτων.
Even Solomon in all his glory was not arrayed like one of these.

Cf. 1 Kings x. [The queen of Sheba's visit to Solomon].

" Homerus omnes flores vocavit λείρια." Pollux ap. Scult. in Poli Synopse.

Ver. 30.

Εἰ δὲ τὸν χόρτον τοῦ ἀγροῦ.
Wherefore, if God so clothe the grass of the field.

Discrimen, τοῦ ξύλου, and τοῦ χόρτου.

Ver. 33.

Ζητεῖτε δὲ πρῶτον τὴν βασιλείαν τοῦ Θεοῦ καὶ τὴν δικαιοσύνην αὐτοῦ, καὶ ταῦτα πάντα προστεθήσεται ὑμῖν.
But seek ye first the kingdom of God, and his righteousness; and all these things shall be added unto you.

Cf. 1 Kings iii. 11, *Because thou hast asked . . . for thyself under-*

standing to discern judgment. . . . I have also given thee that which thou hast not asked, both riches and honour.

Observe here, 1. The express promise; cf. 1 Tim. vi. 6, *Godliness with contentment is great gain;* 8, *. . . having food and raiment, let us be therewith content;* iv. 8, *Godliness is profitable unto all things, having promise of the life that now is, and of that which is to come;* Heb. xiii. 5, 6, *Be content with such things as ye have, for He hath said, I will never leave thee, nor forsake thee; so that we may boldly say, The Lord is my helper;* on which, *vide* Taylor, "Holy Dying," 236 [d].

2. It is given by way of προσθήκη [supplementally].

VER. 34.

Μὴ οὖν μεριμνήσητε εἰς τὴν αὔριον· ἡ γὰρ αὔριον μεριμνήσει τὰ ἑαυτῆς. ἀρκετὸν τῇ ἡμέρᾳ ἡ κακία αὐτῆς.

Take therefore no thought for the morrow, for the morrow shall take thought for the things of itself. Sufficient unto the day is the evil thereof.

Cf. the history of the manna [Exod. xvi. 19, &c., *And Moses said, Let no man leave of it till the morning. Notwithstanding . . . some of them left of it until the morning, and it bred worms, and stank*].

κακία for κακότης.

CHAP. VII.—VER. 1.

Μὴ κρίνετε, ἵνα μὴ κριθῆτε.
Judge not, that ye be not judged.

κρίνω *id quod* κατακρίνω. Rom. ii. 1, *Wherein thou judgest another, thou condemnest thyself;* explained by καταλαλῶ, St. James iv. 11, *He that speaketh evil of his brother, and judgeth his brother.* But in 1 Cor. iv. 5 (*Judge nothing before the time, &c.*) it seems to be forbidden in a sense which excludes premature praise, and in general their disposition to judge of others. In Rom. xiv. 10, *Why dost thou judge thy brother? or why dost thou set at nought thy brother?*

It is opposed to ἐξουθενεῖν in a way which seems to indicate

---

[d] [Ch. v. § 5 (*Against Despair*), "I find that the Spirit of God taught the writers of the New Testament to apply to us all in general, and to every single person in particular, some gracious words which God in the Old Testament spake to one man upon a special occasion, in a single and temporal instance. Such are the words which God spake to Joshua, *I will never fail thee nor forsake thee.*"—ED.]

that one means *moral*, and the other *intellectual* contempt. In St. James ii. 13 (*he shall have judgment without mercy that hath shewed no mercy*) κρίσις is opposed to ἔλεος, and the whole passage is directed against προσωποληψία, and the not judging of others by a mild rule, like that of the Gentiles, but by a severe rule, like that of the law. The judgment threatened is both of this world and of the next.

VER. 2.

Ἐν ᾧ γὰρ κρίματι κρίνετε, κριθήσεσθε· καὶ ἐν ᾧ μέτρῳ μετρεῖτε, ἀντιμετρηθήσεται ὑμῖν.

For with what judgment ye judge, ye shall be judged; and with what measure ye mete, it shall be measured to you again.

This is a proverb, and so our Lord used several proverbs. Cf. ch. x. 24, *The disciple is not above his master;* xix. 24, *It is easier for a camel to go through the eye of a needle, &c.*

VER. 3.

Τί δὲ βλέπεις τὸ κάρφος τὸ ἐν τῷ ὀφθαλμῷ τοῦ ἀδελφοῦ σου, τὴν δὲ ἐν τῷ σῷ ὀφθαλμῷ δοκὸν οὐ κατανοεῖς;

And why beholdest thou the mote that is in thy brother's eye, but considerest not the beam that is in thine own eye ?

κάρφος used by Herod. for chaff. This also was proverbial, and answers to Hor. Sat. I. iii. 67, "Eheu Quam temere in nosmet legem sancimus iniquam;" and "Cum tua pervideas oculis male lippus inunctis," Ibid. 25. "Mos nimirum erat Christo dicta de rebus humanis usurpari solita ad divina transferre." Grot.

VER. 5.

Ἔκβαλε πρῶτον τὴν δοκὸν ἐκ τοῦ ὀφθαλμοῦ σου.

First cast out the beam out of thine own eye.

Not only as a matter of moral propriety, but as a necessary qualification for judging rightly. Grot.

VER. 6.

Μὴ δῶτε τὸ ἅγιον τοῖς κυσί· μηδὲ βάλητε τοὺς μαργαρίτας ὑμῶν ἔμπροσθεν τῶν χοίρων.

Give not that which is holy unto the dogs, neither cast ye your pearls before swine.

This is a qualification of the former precept, say Hammond and Grotius; *quod dicit,*—There are some men so proud and malicious (like dogs), or so stupid and sensual (like swine), that they will only reject your charity, which ought to be the most effectual admonition, and persecute your persons, which ought to be most dear*. In the first clause, there is an allusion to the impurity of dogs. Cf. Exod. xvi. 31, *Ye shall cast it to the dogs;* Deut. xxiii. 18, *The price of a dog...;* Rev. xxii. 15, *For without are dogs and sorcerers;* Phil. iii. 2, *Beware of dogs;* ch. xv. 26, *It is not meet to take the children's bread, and to cast it to dogs.*) In the second to that of *swine.* Cf. Lev. xi. 7, and Deut. xiv. 8, *The swine... cheweth not the cud; he is unclean to you.* Both are united, Isa. lxvi. 3, *He that sacrificeth a lamb, as if he cut off a dog's neck; he that offereth an oblation, as if he offered swine's blood;* 2 St. Peter ii. 22, *The dog is turned to his own vomit again, and the sow... to her wallowing.*

Here ends the eighth section of the Sermon, which may be regarded as an exposition of the ninth commandment. [See Hammond, *Pract. Cat.*, lib. iv. § 1.]

VERS. 7—27.

Since the precepts hitherto given are difficult, Christ now shews how we may get strength to perform them, that is, by prayer, 7—11; by observing the golden rule, 12; by a manful resolution to abide in our Christian calling, whatever it cost, 13, 14; by a prudent choice and use of guides, for which he points out a text, 15—20; lastly, by a thorough sense that religion is nothing without practice, 21—27.

VER. 7.

Αἰτεῖτε, καὶ δοθήσεται ὑμῖν· ζητεῖτε, καὶ εὑρήσετε· κρούετε, καὶ ἀνοιγήσεται ὑμῖν.

Ask, and it shall be given you; seek, and ye shall find; knock, and it shall be opened unto you.

Repetition here denotes the duty of perseverance, cf. St. Luke xi. 9—13, *Ask, and it shall be given you, &c.;* St. James v. 16, *The effectual fervent prayer of a righteous man availeth much;* and i. 5, *If any of you lack wisdom, let him ask God, that giveth to all men liberally;* cf. [Second Collect in] Baptismal Service.

* Mr. Keble seems to have had Hammond's paraphrase open before him :— "For this matter of reprehending others (all holy advices and admonitions out of God's word), because they are a very precious deed of Charity, take care they be not cast away upon those that are incorrigible."—ED.

Ver. 8.

Πᾶς γὰρ ὁ αἰτῶν λαμβάνει.
For every one that asketh receiveth.

As to the non-fulfilment of the promise on some occasions, see Taylor on *The Return of Prayer;* St. James i. 6, *Let him ask in faith, nothing wavering;* iv. 3, *Ye ask and receive not, because ye ask amiss.*

Ver. 9.

Ἢ τίς ἐστιν ἐξ ὑμῶν ἄνθρωπος, ὃν ἐὰν αἰτήσῃ ὁ υἱὸς αὐτοῦ ἄρτον, μὴ λίθον ἐπιδώσει αὐτῷ;
Or what man is there of you, whom if his son ask bread, will he give him a stone?

τίς.] "Siquis;" cf. St. Luke xi. 5, τίς ἐξ ὑμῶν ἕξει φίλον ... ; v. 11, τίνα δὲ ὑμῶν τὸν πατέρα αἰτήσει ὁ υἱός; St. James iii. 13, τίς σοφὸς καὶ ἐπιστήμων ... ; ch. xii. 11, τίς ἔσται ἐξ ὑμῶν ... ; xxiv. 45, τίς ἄρα ἐστὶν ὁ πιστὸς δοῦλος ... ; Hag. ii. 3, τίς ἐξ ὑμῶν ὃς εἶδεν τὸν οἶκον ... ἐάν post relativum redundat; v. 19, ὃς ἐὰν λύσῃ ... ; x. 14, ὃς ἐὰν μὴ δέξηται ὑμᾶς ... ; 42, ὃς ἐὰν ποτίσῃ. ...

Ver. 11.

Εἰ οὖν ὑμεῖς πονηροὶ ὄντες ... δώσει ἀγαθὰ τοῖς αἰτοῦσιν αὐτόν.
If ye then, being evil ... give good things to them that ask him?

πονηρός.] Grudging, as in the phrase ὀφθαλμὸς πονηρός, according to Hammond; but Qu. cf. Job xv. 14, 15, *What is man that he should be clean, &c.*

ἀγαθά.] scil. Spiritus Sanctus. Cf. St. Luke xi. 13, *How much more shall your heavenly Father give the Holy Spirit to them that ask Him;* and St. James i. 5, *If any of you lack wisdom, &c.*

Ver. 12.

Πάντα οὖν ὅσα ἂν θέλητε ἵνα ποιῶσιν ὑμῖν οἱ ἄνθρωποι, οὕτω καὶ ὑμεῖς ποιεῖτε αὐτοῖς·
Therefore all things whatsoever ye would that men should do to you, do ye even so to them.

Cf. Isocrates ad Nicoclem, pp. 71, 76 [οὕτως ὁμίλει ταῖς πόλεσι πρὸς τὰς ἥττους, ὥσπερ ἂν τὰς κρείττους πρὸς σεαυτὸν ἀξιώσειας,—So deal with the lesser states as thou wouldst have the greater states deal with thee; ἃ πάσχοντες ὑφ' ἑτέρων ὀργίζεσθε, ταῦτα τοῖς ἄλλοις μὴ ποιεῖτε: What you resent at the hands of others, that do not to others.—Ed.] But observe that the rules there do not, by a good deal, come up to our Saviour's precept, for the universal one is negative only, the other is a peculiar precept addressed to the representatives of a king. Cf. Miller's Bampton Lectures, p. 136, and Gibbon. It was often quoted by Severus[1]. Hammond calls it an extension of the eighth commandment. [See *Pract. Cat.*, lib. iv. § 2.] Cf. Rom. xiii. 8, *Owe no man anything, but to love one another;* Gal. v. 14, *All the law is fulfilled in one word, even in this, Thou shalt love thy neighbour as thyself.*

Ver. 13.
Εἰσέλθετε διὰ τῆς στενῆς πύλης·
Enter ye in at the strait gate.

A precept of Christian strictness. Hammond [*Pract. Cat.*, as above]. Life is "a gate," "a way," because we only pass through it. Christian life a strait gate, because ἐσθλοὶ μὲν γὰρ ἁπλῶς, &c. Cf. Hesiod Op. et Dies. 287—290 [τὴν μέντοι κακότητα καὶ ἰλαδόν ἐστιν ἑλέσθαι ῥηϊδίως· ὀλίγη μὲν ὁδός, μάλα δ' ἐγγύθι ναίει· τῆς δ' ἀρετῆς ἱδρῶτα θεοὶ προπάροιθεν ἔθηκαν ἀθάνατοι· μακρὸς δὲ καὶ ὄρθιος οἶμος ἐπ' αὐτήν καὶ τρηχὺς τὸ πρῶτον. The line from Bias, partly quoted above, is, Ἐσθλοὶ μὲν γὰρ ἁπλῶς, παντοδαπῶς δὲ κακοί,—*There is but one way for the good, but many for the wicked.*—Ed.]

Ver. 14.
Ὅτι στενὴ ἡ πύλη, καὶ τεθλιμμένη ἡ ὁδὸς ἡ ἀπάγουσα εἰς τὴν ζωήν, καὶ ὀλίγοι εἰσὶν οἱ εὑρίσκοντες αὐτήν.
Because strait is the gate, and narrow is the way, which leadeth unto life, and few there be that find it.

The Jews thought that in the time of the Messiah all would be good.

ὅτι might possibly mean "how." [Mr. Keble had in his mind the Vulgate, "Quam angusta porta!" but this was based on MSS. which read τί instead of ὅτι.—Ed.]

Ver. 15.
Προσέχετε δὲ ἀπὸ τῶν ψευδοπροφητῶν, οἵτινες ἔρχονται πρὸς ὑμᾶς ἐν ἐνδύμασι προβάτων, ἔσωθεν δέ εἰσι λύκοι ἅρπαγες.
Beware of false prophets, which come to you in sheep's clothing, but inwardly they are ravening wolves.

---

[1] [Spartianus, in the Augustan History, speaking of Alex. Severus, says, "Clamabatque sæpius, quod a quibusdam sive Judæis sive Christianis audierat et tenebat: idque per præconem, cum aliquem emendaret, dici jubebat: Quod tibi fieri nonvis, alteri ne feceris. Quam sententiam usque adeo dilexit, ut et in palatio et in publicis operibus præscribi juberet."—Ed.]

Cf. 2 St. Peter ii. 1, *But there were false prophets also among the people, even as there shall be false teachers among you.* Elijah's mantle was in Greek, μηλωτής (sheep-skin), 1 Kings xix. 13, *He wrapped his face in his mantle;* 2 Kings ii. 13, *He took up the mantle of Elijah;* cf. Zech. xiii. 4, *Neither shall they wear a rough garment to deceive.*

λύκοι ἅρπαγες.] Cf. Acts xx. 29. The caution is against professing Christians, cf. v. 21, *Not every one, &c.* (N.B. The distinction between the show of godliness and the power.)

VER. 16.

Ἀπὸ τῶν καρπῶν αὐτῶν ἐπιγνώσεσθε αὐτούς· μήτι συλλέγουσιν ἀπὸ ἀκανθῶν σταφυλὴν, ἢ ἀπὸ τριβόλων σῦκα;
Ye shall know them by their fruits. Do men gather grapes of thorns, or figs of thistles?

Here it is disputed whether Christ means the fruits of the *doctrine* or their *lives*. I apprehend the former, as discernible from the latter. Cf. 2 Tim. iii. 5, *Having a form of godliness, but denying the power thereof;* and quæ habet Grot. ad loc. [Grotius instances the evil fruits of heresy: "Perpessiones defugiunt; allectant eos qui in vitiis hærent, præsertim opulentiores; quæstiones movent nihil facientes ad profectum pietatis," &c.—ED.] These men had sheep's clothing; yet their fruits were bad: i.e. not being notoriously wicked, and in outward show gracious and reverent, they yet wanted the love of God.

τριβόλων.] Lat. ap. Virg. [Geor. i. 153, "Lappæque tribulique, interque nitentia culta Infelix lolium]. Cf. Article VII. [Of Good Works, "Which are the fruits of faith."]

VER. 18.

Τὸ δὲ σαπρὸν δένδρον.
A corrupt tree.

σαπρόν.] Bad, as the English "corrupt."

VER. 19.

Πᾶν δένδρον μὴ ποιοῦν καρπὸν καλὸν, ἐκκόπτεται καὶ εἰς πῦρ βάλλεται.
Every tree that bringeth not forth good fruit is hewn down, and cast into the fire.

Cf. St. John xv. 6, *If a man abide not in Me, he is cast forth as a branch, and is withered;* ch. iii. 10, *And now also the axe is laid unto the root of the trees, &c.*

Ver. 20.

Ἄραγε ἀπὸ τῶν καρπῶν αὐτῶν ἐπιγνώσεσθε αὐτούς.
Wherefore by their fruits ye shall know them.

If it had been ἆρα γε with a question, it would have been a most triumphant conclusion; and I take ἄρα γε, affirmatively, to carry a similar meaning.

Ver. 21.

Οὐ πᾶς ὁ λέγων μοι, Κύριε, Κύριε, εἰσελεύσεται εἰς τὴν βασιλείαν τῶν οὐρανῶν·
Not every one that saith unto me, Lord, Lord, shall enter into the kingdom of heaven.

St. John xiii. 13, *Ye call Me Master and Lord, and ye say well;* St. Luke vi. 46, *Why call ye Me, Lord, Lord, and do not the things which I say?* ch. xxv. 11, *Lord, Lord, open to us.*

Ver. 22.

Πολλοὶ ἐροῦσί μοι ἐν ἐκείνῃ τῇ ἡμέρᾳ, Κύριε Κύριε, οὐ τῷ σῷ ὀνόματι προεφητεύσαμεν, καὶ τῷ σῷ ὀνόματι δαιμόνια ἐξεβάλομεν, καὶ τῷ σῷ ὀνόματι δυνάμεις πολλὰς ἐποιήσαμεν;
Many will say to me in that day, Lord, Lord, have we not prophesied in thy name? and in thy name have cast out devils? and in thy name done many wonderful works?

First express mention of the day of judgment.

προεφητεύσαμεν.] Probably taken here literally.

τῷ σῷ ὀνόματι.] Cf. St. Mark xvi. 17, *In My Name shall they cast out devils;* Acts iii. 6, *In the Name of Jesus Christ of Nazareth;* ix. 34, *Æneas, Jesus Christ maketh thee whole;* xix. 5, *Baptized in the Name of the Lord Jesus.* Argument hence for the excellency of Christ's Person.

δυνάμεις.] Effect for cause. [Cause for effect (?).—ED.]

Here observe, 1. How much the evidence of the Apostles is strengthened by the care shewn in the New Testament not to set up miracles as signs of God's favour. Cf. St. Luke x. 20, *In this rejoice not that the spirits are subject unto you, but rather rejoice because your names are written in heaven.*

2. Difference of χάρις and χάρισμα, cf. 1 Cor. xiii. [Praise of Faith, Hope, and Charity, compared with *gifts* of tongues, &c.]; case of Balaam and Judas, and of the old Prophet in 1 Kings xiii. [all of whom had *gifts* without *grace*]. Applied to the present time it suggests an especial caution not to regard success, eloquence, &c., as signs of God's favour.

Ver. 23.

Καὶ τότε ὁμολογήσω αὐτοῖς, ὅτι οὐδέποτε ἔγνων ὑμᾶς·
And then will I profess unto them, I never knew you.

ὁμολογήσω.] Heb. *ἔγνων* [יָדַע, as in Ps. i. 6, *The Lord knoweth (approveth) the way of the righteous.*—ED.] Cf. St. John x. 14, *I know My sheep, and am known of Mine;* Rom. viii. 29, *Whom He did foreknow, He also did predestinate;* 1 Cor. viii. 3, *If any man love God, the same is also known of Him.*

Ver. 24.

Πᾶς οὖν ὅστις ἀκούει μου τοὺς λόγους τούτους, καὶ
ποιεῖ αὐτούς.
Therefore whosoever heareth these sayings of mine, and doeth them.

Cf. St. James i. 22, *Be ye doers of the word, and not hearers only;* St. John xiii. 17, *If ye know these things, happy are ye if ye do them;* 1 St. John ii. 3, seqq. *Hereby do we know that we know Him, if we keep His commandments;* iii. 7, *He that doeth righteousness is righteous;* and *passim*.

Here consider how the demand of perfect holiness is reconcileable with the redemption from the Law and free Grace. Consider, 1. God demands it as a *condition*, not as a *price*. (Observe that in the first covenant our holiness was not *per se*, but by the mercy of God, the consideration and price of eternal life.) 2. He gives His Holy Spirit, which was not under the Law.

Ver. 28.

Ἐξεπλήσσοντο οἱ ὄχλοι ἐπὶ τῇ διδαχῇ αὐτοῦ·
The people were astonished at his doctrine.

Cf. St. John vii. 46, *Never man spake like this man;* St. Luke iv. 22, *All bare Him witness, and wondered at the gracious words.*

Ver. 29.

Ἦν γὰρ διδάσκων αὐτοὺς ὡς ἐξουσίαν ἔχων, καὶ
οὐχ ὡς οἱ Γραμματεῖς.
For he taught them as one having authority, and not as the scribes.

Cf. St. Matt. xxi. 23, &c., *By what authority doest Thou these things?* &c.; They had been used to say, Let us wait for a Prophet. Cf. 1 Mac. iv. 46, *They laid up the stones . . . until there should come a prophet to shew what should be done with them;* xiv. 41, *Until there should arise a faithful prophet.* But He taught with more authority than even the highest prophet, viz. in *His own* Name; cf. Heb. iii. 5, 6, *Christ as a Son over His own house;* and with perfect innocence.

CHAP. VIII.—VER. 1.

Καταβάντι δὲ αὐτῷ ἀπὸ τοῦ ὄρους, ἠκολούθησαν αὐτῷ ὄχλοι πολλοί.

When he was come down from the mountain, great multitudes followed him.

St. Matthew puts the Doctrine first, and then the Miracles; vid. ch. iv. 23, *Teaching in their synagogues . . . and healing all manner of sickness.*

VER. 2.

Καὶ ἰδοὺ, λεπρὸς ἐλθὼν προσεκύνει αὐτῷ λέγων.

And, behold, there came a leper and worshipped him.

Probably this miracle happened the year before the Sermon on the Mount, in one of our Lord's incidental excursions from Capernaum. For St. Luke places the centurion's servant's cure immediately after the Sermon. ἰδοὺ does not fix the order of the cure; cf. ch. ix. 2, *And behold they brought unto Him a man sick of the palsy.*

αὐτῷ repeated, a Hebraism; but cf. Soph. Œd. Tyr. 276-7, καὶ ταῦτα τοῖς μὴ δρῶσιν εὔχομαι θεοὺς μήτ' ἄροτον αὐτοῖς γῆς ἀνιέναι τινά . . . etiam Thucydides iv. 93, τῷ δὲ Ἱπποκράτει . . . ὡς αὐτῷ ἠγγέλθη . . . πέμπει, &c.

λεπρὸς.] Cf. Levit. xiii., xiv., and Deut. xxiv. 8, 9, for the law concerning lepers.

It was a type of sin. Cf. Ps. xxxviii. 3, *There is no soundness in my flesh because of Thine anger;* Isa. i. 6, *No soundness in it, but wounds, and bruises, and putrifying sores:* and consider, 1. no creature so unclean as man, perhaps none other, living [e]; 2. It was the greatest and most lasting uncleanness; 3. It continued after cleansing; 4. It was purified when the person owned himself entirely unclean; 5. The High Priest shared not in it; Aaron was not leprous, Uzziah was.

VER. 3.

Θέλω, καθαρίσθητι.

I will; be thou clean.

Cf. ch. vii. 29, *As one having authority.*
Cf. Gen. i. 3, φῶς γενέσθω, *Let there be light.*

[e] I leave these words as I find them.—ED.

Ver. 4.

Καὶ λέγει αὐτῷ ὁ Ἰησοῦς, "Ορα μηδενὶ εἴπῃς· ἀλλ' ὕπαγε, σεαυτὸν δεῖξον τῷ ἱερεῖ, καὶ προσένεγκε τὸ δῶρον ὃ προσέταξε Μωσῆς, εἰς μαρτύριον αὐτοῖς.

And Jesus saith unto him, See thou tell no man; but go thy way, shew thyself to the priest, and offer the gift that Moses commanded, for a testimony unto them.

Observe Christ's respect for the Law, and also His humility. The Jews thought leprosy came from the hand of God immediately; cf. 2 Kings v. 7, *Am I a God, to kill and to make alive?* ch. xi. 5 [Christ's appeal to the cleansing of lepers in reply to the Baptist's message].

αὐτοῖς, either "the priests," governed of μαρτύριον, or "the lepers," governed of προσέταξε;—or the whole may be taken with λέγει αὐτῷ, i.e. He said it in witness of His being the Son of God.

Query, whether the office of binding and loosing sins be not typified by this ordinance of Moses?

Ver. 5.

Προσῆλθεν αὐτῷ ἑκατόνταρχος παρακαλῶν αὐτόν.

There came unto him a centurion, beseeching him.

ἑκατόνταρχος shews that a soldier's business is lawful. Cf. St. Luke iii. 14 [the Baptist and the soldiers]; Acts x. 1, *A centurion ... a devout man, and one that feared God.* Probably the soldier might have heard of the cure of the nobleman's son, recorded St. John iv. 53. According to St. Luke, the centurion sent elders of the Jews.

Ver. 6.

Ὁ παῖς μου βέβληται ἐν τῇ οἰκίᾳ παραλυτικός.

My servant lieth at home sick of the palsy.

βέβληται] is very expressive of the man's helplessness. Cf. v. 14, βεβλημένην καὶ πυρέσσουσαν; St. Mark vii. 30, βεβλημμένην ἐπὶ τῆς κλίνης; Rev. ii. 22, βάλλω αὐτὴν εἰς κλίνην.

Ver. 8.

Οὐκ εἰμὶ ἱκανὸς ἵνα μου ὑπὸ τὴν στέγην εἰσέλθῃς·

I am not worthy that thou shouldest come under my roof.

ἱκανός.] Cf. ch. iii. 11, οὗ οὐκ εἰμὶ ἱκανὸς τὰ ὑποδήματα βαστάσαι.

Ver. 9.

Καὶ γὰρ ἐγὼ ἄνθρωπός εἰμι ὑπὸ ἐξουσίαν, ἔχων ὑπ' ἐμαυτὸν στρατιώτας·
For I am a man under authority, having soldiers under me.

q. d. Thou canst do this as readily, and with as full right, and more certain success, as my superiors can command me, or I mine inferiors. It is an argument *à fortiori*. If I can do this, who am ὑπὸ ἐξουσίαν, how much more Thou.

Ver. 10.

Οὐδὲ ἐν τῷ Ἰσραὴλ τοσαύτην πίστιν εὗρον.
I have not found so great faith, no, not in Israel.

Why should our Lord have expected Faith in Israel? Answer from prophecy more particularly.

Ver. 11.

Ὅτι πολλοὶ ἀπὸ ἀνατολῶν καὶ δυσμῶν ἥξουσι, καὶ ἀνακλιθήσονται μετὰ Ἀβραὰμ καὶ Ἰσαὰκ καὶ Ἰακὼβ ἐν τῇ βασιλείᾳ τῶν οὐρανῶν.
That many shall come from the east and west, and shall sit down with Abraham, and Isaac, and Jacob, in the kingdom of heaven.

A prophecy of the calling of the Gentiles. The Jews often represented the Kingdom of Heaven as a feast, in Abraham's bosom; cf. St. Luke xvi. 22, *Was carried by the Angels into Abraham's bosom;* Gen. xxviii. 14, *In thee . . . shall all the families of the earth be blessed;* St. Luke xxii. 29, 30, *That ye may eat and drink at My table in My kingdom;* Isa. xxv. 6, 7, *In this mountain shall the Lord of hosts make unto all people a feast of fat things.*

There is a euphemism in ἀνακλιθήσονται.

Why are these three named particularly? 1. Because God was called their God; 2. Because Canaan was promised to them; 3. Because they were the heads of the nation. And the Gentiles are seated next to them, as the centurion's faith was preferred to that of Israel.

Ver. 12.

Οἱ δὲ υἱοὶ τῆς βασιλείας ἐκβληθήσονται εἰς τὸ σκότος τὸ ἐξώτερον· ἐκεῖ ἔσται ὁ κλαυθμὸς καὶ ὁ βρυγμὸς τῶν ὀδόντων.
But the children of the kingdom shall be cast out into outer darkness: there shall be weeping and gnashing of teeth.

Lightfoot (*in loco*) represents this as a prophecy of the *final* rejection of the Jews: but qu?

τὸ σκότος τὸ ἐξώτερον best illustrated by ch. xxv. 10—12 [the exclusion of the foolish Virgins]; and v. 30, *Cast ye the unprofitable servant into outer darkness.*

The prophecy began to be signally accomplished, Acts xiii. 46—51 [Paul and Barnabas turning from the Jews to the Gentiles at Antioch].

υἱοὶ τῆς βασιλείας.] Cf. Rom. ix. 4, 5, *Israelites, to whom pertaineth the adoption and the glory, &c.* Perhaps βρυγμὸς may express cold.

VER. 14.
Πενθερὰν αὐτοῦ.
His wife's mother.

Peter was married. Cf. 1 Cor. ix. 6, *Have we not power to lead about . . . a wife, as well as . . . Cephas?*

VER. 16.
Ὀψίας δὲ γενομένης προσήνεγκαν αὐτῷ δαιμονιζομένους πολλούς.
When the even was come, they brought unto him many that were possessed with devils.

ὀψία is an adjective; it marks our Lord's unwearied benevolence. God probably permitted so many δαιμονιζομένους, to shew Christ's power.

VER. 17.
Αὐτὸς τὰς ἀσθενείας ἡμῶν ἔλαβε, καὶ τὰς νόσους ἐβάστασεν.
Himself took our infirmities, and bare our sicknesses.

ἐβάστασεν.] Cf. St. John xx. 15, *If thou have borne him hence;* 1 St. Pet. ii. 24, *His own self bare our sins;* Heb. v. 1, 2, *Who can have compassion, &c.;* iv. 15, *Touched with the feeling of our infirmities;* Isa. liii. 4, *Surely He hath borne our griefs;* St. Mark vii. 34, *He sighed, and saith unto him, Ephphatha;* St. Luke vii. 13, *He had compassion on her, and said unto her, Weep not;* St. John xi. 33, 35, 38, *He groaned in the spirit, and was troubled . . . Jesus wept . . . again groaning in Himself;* from which it may seem not improbable that the place is applied here to express our Lord's divine sympathy.

The Rabbins call Christ "the Leper of the house of Rabbi:" Lightfoot (Hor. Heb. *in loco*), who renders ἐβάστασεν, "who is able to remove" our sorrows. But add Christ's agony to the texts quoted above. Observe that, as Christ's healing disease was typical of His taking away sin, so this prophecy has a double sense, 1. miracles, 2. redemption.

Ver. 19.

Καὶ προσελθὼν εἷς Γραμματεύς.
And a certain scribe came, and said unto him.

εἷς pro τὶς, fere cum genitivo apud Atticos.

Ver. 20.

Αἱ ἀλώπεκες φωλεοὺς ἔχουσι, καὶ τὰ πετεινὰ τοῦ οὐρανοῦ κατασκηνώσεις· ὁ δὲ υἱὸς τοῦ ἀνθρώπου οὐκ ἔχει, ποῦ τὴν κεφαλὴν κλίνῃ.
The foxes have holes, and the birds of the air have nests; but the Son of man hath not where to lay his head.

Here Christ speaks to the man's thoughts, who was probably worldly in his purpose.

ὁ υἱὸς τοῦ ἀνθρώπου] denote our Lord's divine nature, His Messiahship, His humility. Cf. Ps. viii. 4, *What is man ... and the Son of man, that Thou visitest him?* lxxx. 17, *The Son of man whom Thou madest so strong for Thyself;* Dan. vii. 13, *One like the Son of man.*

Ver. 21.

Ἕτερος δὲ τῶν μαθητῶν αὐτοῦ εἶπεν αὐτῷ, Κύριε, ἐπίτρεψόν μοι πρῶτον ἀπελθεῖν καὶ θάψαι τὸν πατέρα μου.
And another of his disciples said unto him, Lord, suffer me first to go and bury my father.

Clement of Alexandria says this was Philip [Strom. iii. c. 4, κἂν συγχρήσωνται τῇ τοῦ κυρίου φωνῇ λέγοντος τῷ Φιλίππῳ, Ἄφες τοὺς νεκρούς, &c.—ED.]

θάψαι, some say, means, "live on to my Father's death." Cf. Job xiv. 13, *Oh that Thou wouldest hide me in the grave ...;* from which it seems that burying was a great duty among the Jews.

Ver. 22.

Ἄφες τοὺς νεκροὺς θάψαι τοὺς ἑαυτῶν νεκρούς.
And let the dead bury their dead.

νεκρούς.] Possibly a proverbial expression, cf. St. Luke ix. 60. Compare Ephes. ii. 1, *You hath He quickened who were dead in trespasses and sins.* Perhaps an allusion to the uncleanness contracted by touching the dead, which was certainly unfit for Christ's peculiar people; evidently there is the figure like that in Revelation (xxii. 18), "If any man shall add unto these things, God shall add unto him the plagues that are written in this book," &c. The dead were unclean; the priest might not touch them, Lev. xxii. 4, 8, *Whoso toucheth anything that is unclean, &c.* Clement quotes a precept of Pythagoras, ἀπέχεσθαι τῶν θνησιμαίων [Pædag. ii. 1?]. Bad men were spiritually dead; cf. Ephes. ii. 5, *When we were dead in sins;* Rom. viii. 11, *He that raised up Christ . . . shall quicken your mortal bodies.*

VER. 27.
Ποταπός ἐστιν οὗτος;
What manner of man is this?

Ποταπός, qualis, quantus; ποδαπός, *cujas* in Latin. Cf. St. Mark xiii. 1, 2; ποταποὶ λίθοι, 2 Pet. iii. 11, ποταποὺς δεῖ ὑπάρχειν ὑμᾶς. . .

VER. 28.
Καὶ ἐλθόντι αὐτῷ εἰς τὸ πέραν εἰς τὴν χώραν τῶν Γεργεσηνῶν, ὑπήντησαν αὐτῷ δύο δαιμονιζόμενοι ἐκ τῶν μνημείων ἐξερχόμενοι.
And when he was come to the other side into the country of the Gergesenes, there met him two possessed with devils, coming out of the tombs.

Perhaps these Gergesenes might be a remnant of the old Canaanites; they were certainly many of them Gentiles. St. Mark and St. Luke mention only one possessed, but he might be superior in rank or in misery. They used to live in tombs; the eastern tombs would easily admit of this; cf. the account of the Resurrection.

VER. 29.
Τί ἡμῖν καὶ σοί, Ἰησοῦ υἱὲ τοῦ Θεοῦ; ἦλθες ὧδε πρὸ καιροῦ βασανίσαι ἡμᾶς;
What have we to do with thee, Jesus, thou Son of God? art thou come hither to torment us before the time?

τί ἡμῖν καὶ σοί.] Difference between the Hebrew and Latin phrase [מַה־לִּי וָלָכֶם, *Quid mihi tecum.*] The latter expresses contempt; the former, complaint.

πρὸ καιροῦ.] Cf. 2 St. Pet. ii. 4, *If God spared not the angels that sinned . . . reserved unto judgment;* Jud. 6, *The angels . . . He hath reserved in everlasting chains, under darkness, unto the judgment of the great day.*

VER. 30.
Ἦν δὲ μακρὰν ἀπ' αὐτῶν ἀγέλη χοίρων πολλῶν βοσκομένη.
And there was a good way off from them an herd of many swine feeding.

οὐ μακράν is what one would expect; but the meaning is the

same. μακράν would mean "at some distance;" οὐ μακράν, "within reach." Swine forbidden, cf. Deut. xiv. 8, *The swine, because it divideth the hoof, yet cheweth not the cud, it is unclean unto you; ye shall not eat of their flesh;* but it was eaten very commonly. Probably these *swine* were to be smuggled into Judæa.

VERS. 31, 32.

Ἐπίτρεψον ἡμῖν ἀπελθεῖν εἰς τὴν ἀγέλην τῶν χοίρων.
καὶ εἶπεν αὐτοῖς, Ὑπάγετε.
Suffer us to go away into the herd of swine.
And he said unto them, Go.

This does not make Christ the author of sin; for He only refrained from hindering what they asked; it shewed His Divinity. The devil had a double spite to gratify here; against the owners, and against our Lord Himself. This miracle justified the Law of Moses to the Gentiles, who were wont to sneer at this precept. Perhaps it might shew the punishment of wallowing like swine in sensual lusts; viz. being delivered into the power of the devil. And He shewed His power over evil spirits; their malice, and the blessing to us of the restraint He keeps over them. See the history of Job.

VER. 34.

Παρεκάλεσαν ὅπως μεταβῇ ἀπὸ τῶν ὁρίων αὐτῶν.
They besought him that he would depart out of their coasts.

St. Luke v. 8, *Depart from me, for I am a sinful man, O Lord.* Observe the different manner in which our Lord treated St. Peter in the verse quoted above, and these Gergesenes in the text. The one He took at their word, and departed from them, the other not.

CHAP. IX.—VER. 1.

Ἦλθεν εἰς τὴν ἰδίαν πόλιν.
And came into his own city.

τὴν ἰδίαν πόλιν.] Sc. Capernaum; v. St. Mark ii. 1, *He entered into Capernaum after some days.*

VER. 2.

Καὶ ἰδὼν ὁ Ἰησοῦς τὴν πίστιν αὐτῶν εἶπε τῷ παραλυτικῷ,
Θάρσει τέκνον, ἀφέωνταί σοι αἱ ἁμαρτίαι σου.
And Jesus seeing their faith said unto the sick of the palsy, Son, be of good cheer; thy sins be forgiven thee.

τὴν πίστιν αὐτῶν.] Sc. of the men and of the sick person himself. Observe here the effect of a faithful intercession. Disease was the one effect of all sin, and the particular punishment of some sins among the Jews. Cf. Deut. xxviii. 21, 22, 27, 60 [the diseases which disobedience should entail on the Israelites]. Cf. etiam Isa. xxxiii. 24, *The inhabitant shall not say, I am sick; the people that dwell therein shall be forgiven their iniquity;* cf. also Numb. v.; 1 Cor. v. 5, *To deliver such an one to Satan, for the destruction of the flesh, that the spirit may be saved.*

In saying, "Thy sins," &c., Christ gave assurance that the disease should be healed, and pointed out the origin of it, and of scourges generally. Cf. Rev. xxi. 4, *There shall be no more death,* . . . *neither shall there be any more pain.*

ἀφέωνται is *per diæresin* for ἀφεῖνται, scil. the Attic perfect. Some hold it to be imperative; but cf. St. Luke vii. 47, λέγω σοι ἀφέωνται αἱ ἁμαρτίαι αὐτῆς; 1 St. John ii. 12, γράφω ὑμῖν ὅτι ἀφέωνται, &c. Again, the ἵνα of v. 6 may be referred to what went before, I said it in order that, &c. Thus He declared 1. His own power as Christ; 2. the doctrine of Justification.

Ver. 3.

Καὶ ἰδοὺ τινὲς τῶν γραμματέων εἶπον ἐν ἑαυτοῖς, Οὗτος βλασφημεῖ.
And, behold, certain of the scribes said within themselves, This man blasphemeth.

Cf. ch. xxvi. 64, *Hereafter shall ye see* . . . *Then the High Priest rent his clothes, saying, He hath spoken blasphemy.*

Ver. 4.

Καὶ ἰδὼν ὁ Ἰησοῦς τὰς ἐνθυμήσεις αὐτῶν εἶπεν.
And Jesus knowing their thoughts said.

Cf. 1 Sam. xvi. 7, *The Lord looketh on the heart;* 1 Kings viii. 39, *Thou only knowest the hearts of all the children of men;* 1 Cor. ii. 10, 11, *The Spirit searcheth all things.* . . . Hence we obtain presumptive proof of our Lord's divinity from these words.

Ver. 5.

Τί γάρ ἐστιν εὐκοπώτερον, εἰπεῖν, Ἀφέωνταί σοι αἱ ἁμαρτίαι· ἢ εἰπεῖν, Ἔγειραι καὶ περιπάτει;
For whether is easier, to say, Thy sins be forgiven thee; or to say, Arise, and walk?

Quod dicit, I know you count it an easy thing and deride it, what I have just said. But it is in fact a greater miracle of divine mercy than the other, and as a proof that I possess it on earth, I now make use of the other.

Perhaps τί may mean, "how," "why," "in what respect." Cf. St. Chrys. iii. 331, 12, 13 (ed. Sav.), where he uses τί for πότερον. [Hom. xiv. 4, in 1 Corinth., τί τοίνυν εὐκολώτερον, ἐφίεσθαι πολλῶν χρημάτων, ἢ μείζονα εἶναι τῆς ἐπιθυμίας ταύτης;—ED.]

VER. 6.
Ὁ υἱὸς τοῦ ἀνθρώπου.
The Son of man.

ὁ υἱὸς τοῦ ἀνθρώπου.] Cf. Dan. vii. 13, *Behold, One like the Son of man came with the clouds of heaven, and came to the Ancient of Days;* and Ps. lxxx. 17, *Let Thy hand be upon the man of Thy right hand, upon the Son of man whom Thou madest strong for Thyself.*

VER. 8.
Ἰδόντες δὲ οἱ ὄχλοι ἐθαύμασαν, καὶ ἐδόξασαν τὸν Θεόν.
But when the multitudes saw it, they marvelled, and glorified God.

Observe the different feelings with which different bystanders viewed our Lord's miracles *here* and in ver. 33 (*The multitudes marvelled, saying it was never so seen in Israel*), compared with ver. 34, *The Pharisees said, He casteth out devils through the prince of the devils;* and ch. viii. 34, *When they besought Him that He would depart out of their coasts.*

VER. 9.
Εἶδεν ἄνθρωπον καθήμενον ἐπὶ τὸ τελώνιον, Ματθαῖον λεγόμενον.
He saw a man, named Matthew, sitting at the receipt of custom.

Probably there was a custom-house on the sea-shore.

Whether Levi was Matthew is disputed, principally on the ground of his relationship to Alphæus not being mentioned in the catalogues of Apostles. v. Grotius *ad loc.*, and Michaelis. Some suppose him to have been St. Jude, and the ἀρχιτελώνης, under whom St. Matthew was.

VER. 10.
Καὶ ἐγένετο αὐτοῦ ἀνακειμένου ἐν τῇ οἰκίᾳ, καὶ ἰδοὺ πολλοὶ τελῶναι καὶ ἁμαρτωλοί.
And it came to pass, as Jesus sat at meat in the house, behold, many publicans and sinners. . . .

In the house of Levi. Cf. St. Mark ii. 15, *As Jesus sat at meat in his house;* St. Luke v. 29, *Levi made Him a great feast in his own house.*

ἁμαρτωλοί.] Like other words in ηλός and ωλός, expresses the habit; so σιγηλός, φειδωλός, κ.τ.λ. Such persons would be with the Gentile Publicans, 1. As having no scruples in associating with the unclean; 2. As being without any character to lose.

VER. 12.

Οὐ χρείαν ἔχουσιν οἱ ἰσχύοντες ἰατροῦ, ἀλλ' οἱ κακῶς ἔχοντες.

They that be whole need not a physician, but they that are sick.

Hence we see for what end we may converse with sinners, i.e. to make them better; but if there be no chance of that, we are to break with them; cf. ch. xviii. 17, *If he neglect to hear the Church, let him be unto thee as an heathen and a publican:* or if there be a greater chance of making other men worse, cf. 1 Cor. v. 9—13, ... *With such an one, no, not to eat.* Antisthenes made the like excuse when reproached for the like conduct; and Diogenes, to justify himself for not living in Lacedæmon [Diog. Laert. *Antisthenes,* vi. 6, ὀνειδιζόμενος ποτὲ ἐπὶ τῷ πονηροῖς συγγίνεσθαι, καὶ οἱ ἰατροί, φησι, μετὰ τῶν νοσούντων εἰσιν, ἀλλ' οὐ πυρέττουσι; Stobæus S. xi., says of Diogenes, οὐδὲ γὰρ ἰατρὸς, εἶπεν, ὑγείας ὢν ποιητικὸς ἐν τοῖς ὑγιαίνουσι διατριβὴν ποιεῖται.—ED.]

VER. 13.

Ἔλεον θέλω, καὶ οὐ θυσίαν.

I will have mercy, and not sacrifice.

Hosea vi. 6, *For I desired mercy, and not sacrifice;* 1 Sam. xv. 22, *To obey is better than sacrifice;* Ps. iv. 5, *Offer the sacrifice of righteousness;* Isa. i. 11—14, *To what purpose is the multitude of your sacrifices unto Me, saith the Lord;* lxvi. 3, *He that killeth an ox is as if he slew a man, &c.* Distinction of moral and positive duties here clearly marked out.

οὐ ... ἀλλά.] "Magis quam" ["not *that* but *this,*" meaning "*this* more than *that*"]. Cf. St. John vii. 16, *My doctrine is not Mine, but His that sent Me.*

πορευθέντες μάθετε, Hebraism [צְאוּ לִמְדוּ.—ED.]

Observe, the eating with the heathens was strictly a breach of the ceremonial law.

Ver. 14.

Διατί ἡμεῖς καὶ οἱ Φαρισαῖοι νηστεύομεν πολλά, οἱ δὲ μαθηταί σου οὐ νηστεύουσι;

Why do we and the Pharisees fast oft, but thy disciples fast not?

Cf. ch. xi. 18, 19, *John came neither eating nor drinking.* John's disciples fasted for prayer, their master being in prison. St Luke v. 33, *Why do the disciples of John fast often, and make prayers?* Acts xii. 5, *Peter was kept in prison, but prayer was made without ceasing of the Church unto God for him.* Besides that, his discipline was more austere than Christ's; probably to shew the different genius of the Old and New Testament.

The disciples of John would fast often, because of their master's imprisonment.

Ver. 15.

Μὴ δύνανται οἱ υἱοὶ τοῦ νυμφῶνος πενθεῖν, ἐφ' ὅσον μετ' αὐτῶν ἐστιν ὁ νυμφίος; ἐλεύσονται δὲ ἡμέραι ὅταν ἀπαρθῇ ἀπ' αὐτῶν ὁ νυμφίος, καὶ τότε νηστεύσουσιν.

Can the children of the bride-chamber mourn, as long as the bridegroom is with them? But the days will come, when the bridegroom shall be taken from them, and then shall they fast.

Cf. St. John iii. 29, *He that hath the bride is the bridegroom, &c.;* Hos. ii. 16, *Thou shalt call Me Ishi (husband), and shalt call Me no more Baali (Lord)*; Rev. xxi. 9, *Come hither, I will shew thee the Bride, the Lamb's wife.*

οἱ υἱοὶ τοῦ νυμφῶνος.] A Hebraism [בְּנֵי־הַחֻפָּה], St. John xvii. 12, *The son of perdition.* So perhaps Judges xiv. 20 [Samson's wife was given to his companion, whom he had used as his friend]; scilicet *υἱοὶ* vocantur in aliquid destinati, alicui addicti aut adjuncti.

The disciples were not persecuted while Christ was with them. In consequence of this saying, the Church kept Easter-Eve as a great fast.

Ver. 16.

Οὐδεὶς δὲ ἐπιβάλλει ἐπίβλημα ῥάκους ἀγνάφου ἐπὶ ἱματίῳ παλαιῷ.

No man putteth a piece of new cloth unto an old garment, for that which is put in to fill it up taketh from the garment.

Quod dicit,—This service of Christian fasting is yet too precious for My half-educated disciples. 1 Cor. iii. 1, 2, *I have fed you with milk, and not with meat, &c.;* Heb. v. 12—14, *Every one that useth milk is unskilful in the word of righteousness; for he is a babe.*

VER. 17.

Οὐδὲ βάλλουσιν οἶνον νέον εἰς ἀσκοὺς παλαιούς.

Neither do men put new wine into old bottles.

Perhaps there is here an allusion to that figure by which Christ in many places represented the change of dispensations, i.e. calling the New Testament the *new wine*. Cf. St. John ii. (the miracle at Cana); St. Luke xxii. 18, *I will not drink of the fruit of the vine until the kingdom of God shall come.*

VER. 18.

Ἰδοὺ, ἄρχων ἐλθὼν προσεκύνει αὐτῷ, λέγων, "Ὅτι ἡ θυγάτηρ μου ἄρτι ἐτελεύτησεν·

There came a certain ruler, and worshipped him, saying, My daughter is even now dead.

Ἄρχων.] Scil. ἀρχισυνάγωγος. His business was to preside in the assemblies, to appoint who should read, &c.; St. Mark v. 22, and St. Luke viii. 41 (Jairus, "a ruler of the synagogue").

ἄρτι.] "By this time."

VER. 20.

Καὶ ἰδοὺ γυνὴ αἱμορροοῦσα δώδεκα ἔτη, προσελθοῦσα ὄπισθεν.

And, behold, a woman, which was diseased with an issue of blood twelve years, came behind him.

She was afraid, partly because she was in a state of legal uncleanness.

VER. 21.

Ἔλεγε γὰρ ἐν ἑαυτῇ, Ἐὰν μόνον ἅψωμαι τοῦ ἱματίου αὐτοῦ, σωθήσομαι.

For she said within herself, If I may but touch his garment, I shall be whole.

Cf. Zech. viii. 23, *Ten men shall take hold of the skirt of him that is a Jew, saying, . . . God is with you.* She made a mistake in attributing the miracles of Christ to some natural power independent of His will, but was right in expecting all power from Him whom God anointed with the Holy Ghost, and with power all over, as the High Priest was anointed with oil.

VER. 22.
Ἡ πίστις σου σέσωκέ σε.
Thy faith hath made thee whole.

This was a common saying among the primitive Christians, and was objected to them by Celsus, as a sign of unreasoning assent; but Origen answered him.

VER. 23.
Ἰδὼν τοὺς αὐλητὰς καὶ τὸν ὄχλον θορυβούμενον.
And saw the minstrels and the people making a noise.

The custom of lamenting the dead with pipes came from the Gentiles. No sign of it in the Old Testament; but only of a kind of mournful chant, θρῆνος, begun by old women, and followed by the wailing, κοπετός, of the whole company. But music at a funeral is mentioned among ἄκαιρα by the son of Sirach [Ecclus. xxii. 6, *A tale out of season is as musick in mourning*].

τὸν ὄχλον θορυβούμενον.] It was reckoned a great act of charity to be present at a funeral, and a kind of entertainment was also made. Lightfoot, *in loc.*

VER. 24.
Οὐ γὰρ ἀπέθανε τὸ κοράσιον, ἀλλὰ καθεύδει.
For the maid is not dead, but sleepeth.

Ita St. John xi. 11, *Our friend Lazarus sleepeth;* 1 Cor. xv. 6, *Some are fallen asleep;* and 18, *They also which are fallen asleep in Christ;* 1 Thess. iv. 13—15 (*Concerning them which are asleep*). Christ might mean, 1. To leave the matter ambiguous before the people; 2. To give evidence of the immateriality of the soul against the Sadducees; 3. To instruct us that death to the Christian is no more than a sleep.

VER. 25.
Ὅτε δὲ ἐξεβλήθη ὁ ὄχλος, εἰσελθὼν ἐκράτησε τῆς χειρὸς αὐτῆς, καὶ ἠγέρθη τὸ κοράσιον.
But when the people were put forth, he went in, and took her by the hand, and the maid arose.

ἐξεβλήθη.] Cf. ver. 38, ὅπως ἐκβάλῃ ἐργάτας εἰς τὸν θερισμόν; ch. xii. 20, ἐκβάλῃ εἰς νῖκος τὴν κρίσιν; and 35, ἐκ τοῦ ἀγαθοῦ θησαυροῦ ἐκβάλλει τὰ ἀγαθά; St. John x. 4, ὅταν τὰ ἴδια πρόβατα ἐκβάλῃ; Rev. xiv. 15, 16, ἔβαλεν τὸ δρέπανον. He touched her as if she were really but asleep.

Ver. 27.

'Ελέησον ἡμᾶς, υἱὲ Δαβίδ.

Thou Son of David, have mercy on us.

Observe, these blind men thought our Lord to be Christ, and He confirmed their faith by answering to the name. How is this consistent with His studious concealment of that truth? He wished people to find it out for themselves, instead of its being openly declared by Him; and He would not let these make Him known. (Cf. Isa. xxxv. 5, *The eyes of the blind shall be opened;* xlii. 7, *To open the blind eyes, &c.*) This is plain, (1) from ver. 30, (2) from His not healing them till they were in the house.

Ver. 30.

Καὶ ἐνεβριμήσατο αὐτοῖς ὁ 'Ιησοῦς, λέγων, 'Οράτε μηδεὶς γινωσκέτω.

Jesus straitly charged them, saying, See that no man know it.

ἐνεβριμήσατο.] Gave signs of indignation, for many had before made Him known.

Ver. 33.

Οὐδέποτε ἐφάνη οὕτως ἐν τῷ 'Ισραήλ.

It was never so seen in Israel.

The last clause seems to refer to the wonderful events of the whole day. Cf. xii. 22, seq. *The blind and dumb both spake and saw, and all the people were amazed.*

Ver. 35.

Καὶ περιῆγεν ὁ 'Ιησοῦς τὰς πόλεις πάσας καὶ τὰς κώμας διδάσκων ἐν ταῖς συναγωγαῖς αὐτῶν, καὶ κηρύσσων τὸ εὐαγγέλιον τῆς βασιλείας, καὶ θεραπεύων πᾶσαν νόσον καὶ πᾶσαν μαλακίαν ἐν τῷ λαῷ.

And Jesus went about all the cities and villages, teaching in their synagogues, and preaching the gospel of the kingdom, and healing every sickness and every disease among the people.

Difference of κηρύσσων and διδάσκων, λόγος and διδαχή; the one to believers, the other to infidels. Acts v. 42, *They ceased not to teach and preach Jesus Christ;* xv. 35, *Teaching and preaching the Word of the Lord;* 1 Tim. v. 17, *They who labour in the Word and doctrine;* 2 Tim. iv. 2, *Preach the Word ... with all longsuffering and doctrine.*

This passage shews that the Jews (and first Christians also) had country synagogues, like our country churches.

Ver. 36.

Ἰδὼν δὲ τοὺς ὄχλους, ἐσπλαγχνίσθη περὶ αὐτῶν, ὅτι ἦσαν ἐκλελυμένοι καὶ ἐρριμμένοι ὡσεὶ πρόβατα μὴ ἔχοντα ποιμένα.

But when he saw the multitudes, he was moved with compassion on them, because they fainted, and were scattered abroad, as sheep having no shepherd.

ἐσπλαγχνίσθη.] The ancients made the *bowels* the seat of pity, the heart of wisdom, the liver of jealousy, the gall of malice, &c.

ἐσκυλμένοι, ἐρριμμένοι.] The one by the vain and burthensome traditions, the other by the profligate neglect of their teachers. Or ἐκλελυμένοι, made to faint; cf. Heb. xii. 5, *Nor faint when thou art rebuked;* Gal. vi. 9, *We shall reap if we faint not.* Cf. Numb. xxvii. 17, *As sheep which have no shepherd;* 1 Kings xxii. 17, *I saw all Israel . . . as sheep that have not a shepherd.*

Ver. 37.

Ὁ μὲν θερισμὸς πολύς, οἱ δὲ ἐργάται ὀλίγοι.

The harvest truly is plenteous, but the labourers are few.

Cf. ch. iii. 12, *Gather his wheat into the garner;* xiii. 24 (Parable of Sower); St. Mark iv. 26 (Parable of seed growing secretly); St. John iv. 35, *There are yet four months, and then cometh harvest.* The expression implies the preparation of people's minds to receive the Messiah.

Ver. 38.

Δεήθητε οὖν τοῦ κυρίου τοῦ θερισμοῦ, ὅπως ἐκβάλῃ ἐργάτας εἰς τὸν θερισμὸν αὐτοῦ.

Pray ye therefore the Lord of the harvest, that he will send forth labourers into his harvest.

This verse is a great reason for the Ember-weeks.

τοῦ κυρίου τοῦ θερισμοῦ.] Cf. St. John xv. 1, *I am the true Vine, and My Father is the husbandman;* St. Matt. xxi. 35, *The husbandman took his servants, and beat one, &c.*

ἐκβάλῃ.] Cf. ch. xii. 35, *Bringeth forth good things . . . evil things;* St. John x. 4, *He putteth forth His own sheep.*

CHAP. X.—VER. 1.

Καὶ προσκαλεσάμενος τοὺς δώδεκα μαθητὰς αὐτοῦ, ἔδωκεν αὐτοῖς ἐξουσίαν πνευμάτων ἀκαθάρτων.

And when he had called unto him his twelve disciples, he gave them power against unclean spirits.

What He had just directed to be prayed for, He here accomplishes Himself. He had chosen the Apostles before (cf. St. Luke vi.); but till now they had not been with Him long enough to be qualified as evidences [sic, qu. witnesses?].

δώδεκα.] Cf. St. Luke xxii. 30, *Judging the twelve tribes;* Rev. xxi. 12, *Twelve gates, and at the gates twelve angels;* 14, *Twelve foundations, and in them the names of the twelve Apostles;* from which it would seem that there is an analogy here with the number of the tribes of Israel. Cf. also Rev. iv. 4, *And round about the throne were four-and-twenty seats;* and ch. xix. 28, *Ye which have followed Me, in the regeneration . . . twelve tribes of Israel.*

ἔδωκεν αὐτοῖς ἐξουσίαν.] A special instance of Divine power.

ἐξουσίαν πνευμάτων.] Scil. *against* them. Cf. ch. xii. 31 (blasphemy of, i.e. against, the Holy Ghost).

ἀκαθάρτων.] By way of antithesis to ἅγιον. Lightfoot suspects the cause of the number of unclean spirits to be the special curse now coming on the special impiety of the Jews.

VER. 2.

Τῶν δὲ δώδεκα ἀποστόλων τὰ ὀνόματά ἐστι ταῦτα· πρῶτος Σίμων ὁ λεγόμενος Πέτρος, καὶ Ἀνδρέας ὁ ἀδελφὸς αὐτοῦ.

Now the names of the twelve apostles are these; The first, Simon, who is called Peter, and Andrew his brother; James the son of Zebedee, and John his brother.

ἀπόστολοι.] Erant proprie non tantum legati, sed vicem magistri gerentes. It was a great mercy to give a catalogue of the Apostles.

πρῶτος.] *Ordine* non *gradu:* first called with Andrew, St. John i. 40, 41.

Πέτρος.] May mean either a foundation-rock, or a strong corner-stone. He was so, because of the Churches being both [Hebrew and Gentile] founded by his ministry; see Acts ii. and x. [the 3,000 on Pentecost, and the household of Cornelius].

VER. 3.

Ἰάκωβος ὁ τοῦ Ζεβεδαίου, καὶ Ἰωάννης ὁ ἀδελφὸς αὐτοῦ. Φίλιππος, καὶ Βαρθολομαῖος· Θωμᾶς, καὶ Ματθαῖος ὁ τελώνης· Ἰάκωβος ὁ τοῦ Ἀλφαίου, καὶ Λεββαῖος ὁ ἐπικληθεὶς Θαδδαῖος.

Philip, and Bartholomew; Thomas, and Matthew the publican; James the son of Alphæus, and Lebbæus, whose surname was Thaddæus.

The Apostles are mentioned here, as nearly as we can make out, in the order of their calling. Cf. St. John i. 37—51 [where we hear of the call of Andrew, John (?), Peter, Philip, Nathanael, supposed to be Bartholomew]. Alphæus is perhaps the same with Clopas; he was probably the husband of Mary's sister. Christ did not disdain His relations, though they were in general so ill-disposed to Him. Thaddæus comes from the same root; and is the same radically with הדה [to *praise;* whence "Judah" (see Gen. xxix. 35, *Now will I praise the Lord; therefore she called his name Judah*) altered to Thadai, תדי, to distinguish the faithful Jude from the traitor, according to Wetstein.—ED.]

VER. 4.

Σίμων ὁ Κανανίτης, καὶ Ἰούδας Ἰσκαριώτης ὁ καὶ παραδοὺς αὐτόν.

Simon the Canaanite, and Judas Iscariot, who also betrayed him.

"Canaanite," probably the Zealot; such were Phinees, Elias, the Maccabees. An account of their corruption is found in Josephus, Bell. Jud. IV. [c. iii. 9, 11, 12, and VII. c. viii. 1].

"Iscariot," probably from his town Iscarair-Kerioth (cf. Josh. xv. 25), quod autem de eodem loco apud Jerem. xliii. 41, Amos ii. 2, memoratur ait Schleusner, vereor ut res se habeat; illis enim locis mentio fit τοῦ קריות cujusdam Moabitici, hic autem Judaicam desideramus urbem. Cf. Cod. Cant. *in loco* et apud Joan. xii. 4 [the Cambridge MS. (D) omits "Simon's son," and reads, ἀπὸ Καρυώτου.—ED.].

VER. 5.

Εἰς ὁδὸν ἐθνῶν μὴ ἀπέλθητε, καὶ εἰς πόλιν Σαμαρειτῶν μὴ εἰσέλθητε.

Go not into the way of the Gentiles, and into any city of the Samaritans enter ye not.

εἰς ὁδὸν ἐθνῶν.] Cf. Sept. apud Jer. ii. 18 [τί σοι καὶ τῇ ὁδῷ Αἰγύπτου, &c.]; also as to the exclusion of the Gentiles *for the present,* cf. St. Matt. xv. 24 [the cure of the woman of Canaan's daughter]; St. Luke xxiv. 47, *That repentance and remission of sins should be preached among all nations, beginning at Jerusalem;* Acts ii. 39, *The promise is unto you, and to your children, and to all that are afar off;* xiii. 46, *It was necessary that the Word of God should first have been spoken to you;* Rom. ix. 10, *To the Jew first, and also to the Gentile;* compare Pensées de Pascal [Pt. II. Art. ix. des preuves historiques de la Religion].

εἰς πόλιν Σαμαρειτῶν.] Because the Samaritans were enough like Jews to give rise to a mistake. Cf. 2 Kings xvii. 41, *So these nations feared the Lord, and served their graven images;* cf. also Ezra iv., Nehemiah ii., iv., vi., and St. John iv. Christ wished (1) to make the world understand the greatness of the Jews' privileges; (2) to convince them of their sin; (3) to guard against offending them; cf. Rom. xv. 8, *Jesus Christ was a minister of the circumcision for the truth of God.*

VER. 6.

Πορεύεσθε δὲ μᾶλλον πρὸς τὰ πρόβατα τὰ ἀπολωλότα οἴκου Ἰσραήλ.

But go rather to the lost sheep of the house of Israel.

πρόβατα τὰ ἀπολωλότα.] Cf. St. Luke xv. [Parable of Lost Sheep]; St. John x. 15, *I lay down My life for the sheep;* Ezek. xxxiv. [Woe to the false shepherds]; Jer. iv., v., vi. [God's judgments on Judah]; Isaiah liii. 6, *All we like sheep have gone astray.*

VER. 7.

Πορευόμενοι δὲ κηρύσσετε, λέγοντες· Ὅτι ἤγγικεν ἡ βασιλεία τῶν οὐρανῶν.

And as ye go, preach, saying, The kingdom of heaven is at hand.

The same proclamation which John and Jesus had made.

VER. 8.

Ἀσθενοῦντας θεραπεύετε, λεπροὺς καθαρίζετε, νεκροὺς ἐγείρετε, δαιμόνια ἐκβάλλετε. δωρεὰν ἐλάβετε, δωρεὰν δότε.

Heal the sick, cleanse the lepers, raise the dead, cast out devils: freely ye have received, freely give.

νεκροὺς ἐγείρετε.] Probable reason for omitting these words in many MSS.

δωρεάν.] Whereas ye have not received your power of healing at large expense (as physicians) give also freely. Cf. 2 Kings v. (cure of Naaman); Gen. xiv. 22 (Abram refusing the King of Sodom's gifts); Dan. v. 17, *Let thy gifts be to thyself... yet I will read the writing;* Acts viii. 20, *Thy money perish with thee.*

Yet it was allowed them to receive sustenance; 1 Cor. ix. [the minister ought to live by the Gospel]; Gal. vi. 6, *Let him that is taught communicate unto him that teacheth;* Phil. iv. 15, *No church communicated with me ... but ye only.*

But sometimes they would forego it to spare the people, or for example's sake; Acts xx. 34, 35, *These hands have ministered unto my necessities, &c.:* or to avoid scandal, 2 Cor. xi. 7—12, *I have kept myself from being burdensome ... that I may cut off occasion from them which desire occasion.*

Ver. 9.

Μὴ κτήσησθε χρυσὸν, μηδὲ ἄργυρον, μηδὲ χαλκὸν
εἰς τὰς ζώνας ὑμῶν.

Provide neither gold, nor silver, nor brass in your purses.

κτήσησθε.] Apud St. Mark vi. 8, and St. Luke ix. 3, αἴρετε.

Cf. ch. vi. 34, *Take no thought for the morrow;* some things here are commanded for that journey only, some universally, some both, in different verses, e.g. ver. 5, latter part of ver. 8, and this ninth verse. Christ did not observe quite the letter of this commandment; cf. St. John xiii. 29, *Buy those things that we have need of;* nor the Apostles, 1 Thess. ii. 9, *Labouring night and day, because we would not be chargeable;* 2 Tim. iv. 12.

χαλκόν.] Sic "*æs,*" apud Latinos.

ζώνας.] Sic "*zonam perdidit,*" Horace, [Ep. II. ii. 40].

Ver. 10.

Μὴ πήραν εἰς ὁδὸν, μηδὲ δύο χιτῶνας, μηδὲ ὑποδήματα, μηδὲ
ῥάβδον· ἄξιος γὰρ ὁ ἐργάτης τῆς τροφῆς αὐτοῦ ἐστιν.

Nor scrip for your journey, neither two coats, neither shoes, nor yet staves: for the workman is worthy of his meat.

πήραν.] A scrip for provisions.

ῥάβδον.] For defence, probably, cf. St. Luke xxii. 36, *He that hath no sword, let him ... buy one.* Whence in St. Mark vi. 8 they are allowed ῥάβδον, not ῥάβδους, scil. for support; and σανδάλια, but not κτήσασθαι ὑποδήματα; there was a difference between σανδάλια and ὑποδήματα.

The latter part of the verse is Christ's charter for a provision for the support of the clergy.

VER. 11.

Εἰς ἣν δ' ἂν πόλιν ἢ κώμην εἰσέλθητε, ἐξετάσατε τίς ἐν αὐτῇ ἄξιός ἐστι· κἀκεῖ μείνατε, ἕως ἂν ἐξέλθητε.

And into whatsoever city or town ye shall enter, enquire who in it is worthy; and there abide till ye go thence.

Cf. Acts xvi. 15, *She besought us saying, ... Come into my house, and abide.*

VER. 12.

Εἰσερχόμενοι δὲ εἰς τὴν οἰκίαν, ἀσπάσασθε αὐτήν.

And when ye come into an house, salute it.

The Jewish salutation was, Peace be unto you; cf. Phil. iv. 7, *The peace of God which passeth all understanding.*

VER. 13.

Ἐὰν δὲ μὴ ᾖ ἀξία, ἡ εἰρήνη ὑμῶν πρὸς ὑμᾶς ἐπιστραφήτω.

If it be not worthy, let your peace return to you.

Cf. Acts xiii. 46, *Seeing ye judge yourselves unworthy.* Pothinus, Bishop of Lyons, being asked who was the God of the Christians, answered, "If thou beest worthy, thou shalt know." Cf. Ps. xxxv. 13, *My prayer returned into mine own bosom;* Isa. lv. 11, *My word ... shall not return unto Me void.*

VER. 14.

Ἐκτινάξατε τὸν κονιορτὸν τῶν ποδῶν ὑμῶν.

Shake off the dust of your feet.

The Jews accounted the dust of a heathen city impure. By shaking it off, the Apostles were to signify that they would have no more communication with them. Acts xiii. 51, *And they shook off the dust of their feet against them.*

VER. 15.

Ἀνεκτότερον ἔσται γῇ Σοδόμων καὶ Γομόρρων ἐν ἡμέρᾳ κρίσεως, ἢ τῇ πόλει ἐκείνῃ.

It shall be more tolerable for the land of Sodom and Gomorrha in the day of judgment, than for that city.

Cf. ch. xi. 23, 24, *And thou, Capernaum ... than for thee.*

VER. 16.

Γίνεσθε οὖν φρόνιμοι ὡς οἱ ὄφεις, καὶ ἀκέραιοι ὡς αἱ περιστεραί.
Be ye therefore wise as serpents, and harmless as doves.

Special care taken by Christ not to flatter His disciples. Imperative form for predictive, cf. Gen. iii. 1, *Now the serpent was more subtil.* ... The dove is said to have no gall [Hammond, *in loco.*—ED.]

VER. 17.

Παραδώσουσι γὰρ ὑμᾶς εἰς συνέδρια, καὶ ἐν ταῖς συναγωγαῖς αὐτῶν μαστιγώσουσιν ὑμᾶς.
They will deliver you up to the councils, and they will scourge you in their synagogues.

Cf. Acts iv. 12, *They brought him to the council;* xx. 22, 23, *Bonds and afflictions abide me;* 2 Cor. xi. 25, *Thrice was I beaten with rods, once was I stoned.*

Query whether they punished in their synagogues [Lightfoot and Wetstein adduce evidence that they did.—ED.] 1 Macc. vii. 12, *Then did there assemble unto Alcimus and Bacchides a company of scribes to require justice.*

VER. 18.

Καὶ ἐπὶ ἡγεμόνας δὲ καὶ βασιλεῖς ἀχθήσεσθε.
And ye shall be brought before governors and kings.

Cf. Acts xxiv.—xxvi. [Paul before Felix, and Festus, and Agrippa].

VER. 19.

Δοθήσεται γὰρ ὑμῖν ἐν ἐκείνῃ τῇ ὥρᾳ τί λαλήσετε.
For it shall be given you in that same hour what ye shall speak.

Cf. St. Luke xxi. 12—15, *I will give you a mouth and wisdom.* As in the case of Moses, Exod. iv. 11, *Go, and I will be with thy mouth, and teach thee what thou shalt say.* And in the case of Isaiah, vi. 7, 8, *Lo, this hath touched thy lips,* ... *send me;* and in the case of St. Peter, Acts ii., iii., x.; and in the case of St. Stephen, Acts vii., *Boldness, with fervent zeal, &c.,* or in Scripture language, "utterance."

VER. 21.

Παραδώσει δὲ ἀδελφὸς ἀδελφὸν εἰς θάνατον.
And the brother shall deliver up the brother to death.

This was among the signs of the Messiah. Cf. ch. xxiv. 10,

Then shall many be offended, and shall betray one another; 2 Tim. iii. 1—3, *Men shall be lovers of their own selves . . . false accusers.*

VER. 22.

Καὶ ἔσεσθε μισούμενοι ὑπὸ πάντων διὰ τὸ ὄνομά μου· ὁ δὲ ὑπομείνας εἰς τέλος, οὗτος σωθήσεται.

And ye shall be hated of all men for my name's sake: but he that endureth to the end shall be saved.

διὰ τὸ ὄνομά μου.] Cf. Acts v. 41, *Counted worthy to suffer shame for His Name;* i.e. because of Me by whose Name ye are called.

ὑπομείνας.] Scil. "endureth these troubles," or rather "abideth" simply. Partes temporis οὐχ ὑπομένουσι [Mr. Keble appears to mean that the word ὑπομένειν is not used of such *mere continuance* as we predicate of *time*, but implies hardship, like the Latin *durare.*—ED.] Virgil, "Durate, et vosmet rebus servate secundis," Æn., i. 207. Qu. is the "salvation" temporal or eternal? The question is principally dependent on another, namely, what is the *coming of the Son of man* in the next verse. In the meantime, it will be true in both senses.

ὁ δὲ ὑπομείνας εἰς τέλος.] Cf. ch. xxiv. 13 [where the phrase is repeated].

VER. 23.

Ὅταν δὲ διώκωσιν ὑμᾶς ἐν τῇ πόλει ταύτῃ, φεύγετε εἰς τὴν ἄλλην. ἀμὴν γὰρ λέγω ὑμῖν, Οὐ μὴ τελέσητε τὰς πόλεις τοῦ Ἰσραὴλ, ἕως ἂν ἔλθῃ ὁ υἱὸς τοῦ ἀνθρώπου.

But when they persecute you in this city, flee ye into another: for verily I say unto you, Ye shall not have gone over the cities of Israel, till the Son of man be come.

Observe here the permission given to use lawful means for safety, provided you do not forsake your duty; cf. Acts xiv. 5, 6, *When there was an assault . . . fled unto Lystra.* This should check them who are proud of persecutions.

τελέσητε.] Thuc. iv. 78, ἐκ τῆς Μελετίας ἀφώρμησεν, ἐς Φάρσαλόν τε ἐτέλεσε. So διανύειν is often used; so Florus [i. c. 18], "consummare Italiam" [h.e. *obire, peragrare* Italiam].

The coming of Christ means, 1. His coming to judgment; 2. (as is generally believed) that great type of it, the destruction of Jerusalem; 3. His coming to His Apostles by His Spirit; so Grotius here; 4. His coming into men's hearts by His power; so Beza. Consider which is most probable.

Ver. 24.

Οὐκ ἔστι μαθητὴς ὑπὲρ τὸν διδάσκαλον, οὐδὲ δοῦλος
ὑπὲρ τὸν κύριον αὐτοῦ.

The disciple is not above his master, nor the servant above his lord.

A proverb often used by Christ in different senses. Use made of it by the Church in Visitation of the Sick ["There should be no greater comfort to Christian persons, than to be made like unto Christ by suffering patiently," &c.]

Ver. 25.

Εἰ τὸν οἰκοδεσπότην Βεελζεβοὺλ ἐκάλεσαν, πόσῳ μᾶλλον
τοὺς οἰκιακοὺς αὐτοῦ ;

If they have called the master of the house Beelzebub, how much more shall they call them of his household ?

An allusion probably to the blasphemy of the Pharisees concerning His miracles. Beelzebub mentioned 2 Kings i. 2, *Go, inquire of Beelzebub, the god of Ekron.* Pliny [Hist. Nat., x. 28] speaks of Ζεὺς μυίαγρος; so Apollo Smintheus, from his driving away mice. בַּעַל is Baal or Belus, probably the sun, who, being put at the head of the false gods, his name was applied by the Jews to the head of the false dæmons.

πόσῳ μᾶλλον τοὺς οἰκιακούς.] This prophecy was fulfilled in Celsus calling the Christians γόητας. Lucian confounds them with such impostors as Peregrinus. Tacitus calls them, "convictos odio humani generis," and the religion, "exitiabilis superstitio," &c.

Ver. 26.

Μὴ οὖν φοβηθῆτε αὐτούς· οὐδὲν γάρ ἐστι κεκαλυμμένον, ὃ
οὐκ ἀποκαλυφθήσεται· καὶ κρυπτὸν, ὃ οὐ γνωσθήσεται.

Fear them not therefore: for there is nothing covered, that shall not be revealed ; and hid, that shall not be known.

For the whole Gospel must nevertheless be preached, and God will judge one day betwixt you and your persecutors.

Ver. 27.

Ὃ λέγω ὑμῖν ἐν τῇ σκοτίᾳ, εἴπατε ἐν τῷ φωτί· καὶ ὃ εἰς τὸ
οὖς ἀκούετε, κηρύξατε ἐπὶ τῶν δωμάτων.

What I tell you in darkness, that speak ye in light: and what ye hear in the ear, that preach ye upon the housetops.

ὃ λέγω ὑμῖν ἐν τῇ σκοτίᾳ.] In the parson's library.
This verse refers to the mysterious parts of Christianity kept

secret at first, e.g. the calling of the Gentiles. Christ is said to tell it them in their ears, in imitation of the Jewish προφήται, who had each his ὑποπροφήτης [or interpreter] into whose ear they whispered.

δῶμα means peculiarly a house-top; cf. Josh. ii. 6, *She had brought them up to the roof of the house;* Judges ix. 51, *They gat them to the top of the tower;* and xvi. 27, *There were upon the roof about three thousand men.*

VER. 28.

Καὶ μὴ φοβηθῆτε ἀπὸ τῶν ἀποκτεινόντων τὸ σῶμα, τὴν δὲ ψυχὴν μὴ δυναμένων ἀποκτεῖναι· φοβήθητε δὲ μᾶλλον τὸν δυνάμενον καὶ ψυχὴν καὶ σῶμα ἀπολέσαι ἐν γεέννῃ.

And fear not them which kill the body, but are not able to kill the soul: but rather fear him which is able to destroy both soul and body in hell.

ἀπολέσαι.] Plus quam ἀποκτεῖναι.

VER. 29.

Οὐχὶ δύο στρουθία ἀσσαρίου πωλεῖται; καὶ ἓν ἐξ αὐτῶν οὐ πεσεῖται ἐπὶ τὴν γῆν ἄνευ τοῦ πατρὸς ὑμῶν.

Are not two sparrows sold for a farthing? and one of them shall not fall on the ground without your Father.

According to Schleusner the ἀσσάριον was probably the tenth of a *Denarius*, and therefore originally the *As;* but in process of time one-tenth of sixteen *Asses.* Arbuthnot, p. 42, says, Cleopatra determined it to be one half the *As.*

Here the doctrine of God's *general* providence is asserted; and in the next place that of His *particular* providence. The Epicureans denied this altogether; the Peripatetics (Aristot. Eth., x. 494) spoke doubtingly of it [εἰ γάρ τις ἐπιμέλεια τῶν ἀνθρωπίνων ὑπὸ θεῶν γίνεται, ὥσπερ δοκεῖ, κ.τ.λ. lib. x. c. 9.—ED.] The Jews confined it to men. Plato, and Pindar, and Æschylus spoke of it gloriously.

VER. 30.

Ὑμῶν δὲ καὶ αἱ τρίχες τῆς κεφαλῆς πᾶσαι ἠριθμημέναι εἰσί.

But the very hairs of your head are all numbered.

According to the phrase, "Not a hair of his head shall perish," 1 Sam. xiv. 45; Acts xxvii. 34, *There shall not an hair fall from the head of any of you.* In Latin, to despise is, "*nullo numero habere.*"

Ver. 31.

Πολλῶν στρουθίων διαφέρετε ὑμεῖς.
Ye are of more value than many sparrows.

Cf. ch. vi. 26, *Behold the fowls of the air, &c.*

Ver. 32.

Πᾶς οὖν ὅστις ὁμολογήσει ἐν ἐμοὶ ἔμπροσθεν τῶν ἀνθρώπων, ὁμολογήσω κἀγὼ ἐν αὐτῷ ἔμπροσθεν τοῦ πατρός μου τοῦ ἐν οὐρανοῖς.
Whosoever therefore shall confess me before men, him will I confess also before my Father which is in heaven.

ὁμολογήσω ἐν αὐτῷ.] So נָגַד. περὶ σου in Ps. lxxxvii. 4, *Glorious things are spoken of thee.*

ἐν, redundant apud Nold. voc. בְּ. [The particle בְּ is redundant sometimes in Hebrew, and used to be called *Beth essentiæ.*—Ed.] Perhaps ὁμολογήσει may carry a notion of boasting.

Ver. 33.

Ὅστις δ' ἂν ἀρνήσηταί με.
But whosoever shall deny me.

Scil. renounce Me.

Ver. 34.

Οὐκ ἦλθον βαλεῖν εἰρήνην, ἀλλὰ μάχαιραν.
I came not to send peace, but a sword.

Not in intention, but in effect, from the perverseness of men. This was fulfilled, (1) in the grievous massacres and murders of the Jews; (2) in the quarrels among Christians and heathens, and among one another.

Ver. 35.

Διχάσαι ἄνθρωπον κατὰ τοῦ πατρὸς αὐτοῦ, καὶ θυγατέρα κατὰ τῆς μητρός.
To set a man at variance against his father, and the daughter against her mother.

Quoted from Micah vii. 6, *The son dishonoureth the father, the daughter riseth up against her mother, &c.*

Ver. 37.

Ὁ φιλῶν πατέρα ἢ μητέρα ὑπὲρ ἐμὲ, οὐκ ἔστι μου ἄξιος.
He that loveth father or mother more than me is not worthy of me.

St. Luke xiv. 26, *If any man come to Me, and hate not his father and mother, &c.;* so Abraham, Gen. xii. 1, *Get thee out of thy country, and from thy kindred.*

VER. 38.

Καὶ ὃς οὐ λαμβάνει τὸν σταυρὸν αὐτοῦ καὶ ἀκολουθεῖ
ὀπίσω μου, οὐκ ἔστι μου ἄξιος.

And he that taketh not his cross, and followeth after me, is not worthy of me.

λαμβάνει.] αἴρειν or βαστάζειν in the other Evangelists. The cross was used among the Romans and Persians; cf. Ezra vi. 11, *Let timber be pulled down from his house; and, being set up, let him be hanged thereon.* Christ here makes a reference to the kind of death which He was to undergo Himself; for all condemned malefactors bore their cross.

VER. 39.

Ὁ εὑρὼν τὴν ψυχὴν αὐτοῦ, ἀπολέσει αὐτήν· καὶ ὁ ἀπολέσας
τὴν ψυχὴν αὐτοῦ ἕνεκεν ἐμοῦ, εὑρήσει αὐτήν.

He that findeth his life shall lose it: and he that loseth his life for my sake shall find it.

So we know that many Christians were delivered from the slaughter at Jerusalem, but many apostates probably perished in it.

VER. 40.

Ὁ δεχόμενος ὑμᾶς, ἐμὲ δέχεται.

He that receiveth you receiveth me.

"Apostolus cujusque est quisque," Hebraicum dictum [a man's apostle, or proxy, is as himself (Hammond)]. Cf. St. John xx. 21, *As My Father hath sent Me, even so send I you;* 2 Cor. v. 20, *We pray you in Christ's stead;* Gen. xii. 3, *I will bless them that bless thee.*

VER. 41.

Ὁ δεχόμενος προφήτην εἰς ὄνομα προφήτου, μισθὸν προφήτου λήψεται· καὶ ὁ δεχόμενος δίκαιον εἰς ὄνομα δικαίου,
μισθὸν δικαίου λήψεται.

He that receiveth a prophet in the name of a prophet shall receive a prophet's reward; and he that receiveth a righteous man in the name of a righteous man shall receive a righteous man's reward.

Observe gradations of reward, as of punishment, in ver. 15. Here they are three, (1) παῖδες; (2) δίκαιοι; (3) προφῆται. The reward for receiving each is either, (1) the same with their own; or (2) that given on their account; as βλασφ. τ. π.[h]

Ver. 42.

Καὶ ὃς ἐὰν ποτίσῃ ἕνα τῶν μικρῶν τούτων ποτήριον ψυχροῦ μόνον εἰς ὄνομα μαθητοῦ.

And whosoever shall give to drink unto one of these little ones a cup of cold water only in the name of a disciple.

Observe μικρῶν synonymous with μαθητῶν. Cf. ch. xviii. 3, *Except ye be converted, and become as little children.*

CHAP. XI.—Ver. 1.

Μετέβη ἐκεῖθεν τοῦ διδάσκειν καὶ κηρύσσειν ἐν ταῖς πόλεσιν αὐτῶν.

He departed thence to teach and to preach in their cities.

ταῖς πόλεσιν αὐτῶν.] Cf. ch. xii. 9, *Their synagogue;* St. Luke iv. 15, *In their synagogues;* it means those of the Jews. Observe again the difference of διδάσκειν and κηρύσσειν [see note on iv. 23].

Ver. 2.

Ὁ δὲ Ἰωάννης ἀκούσας ἐν τῷ δεσμωτηρίῳ τὰ ἔργα τοῦ Χριστοῦ, πέμψας δύο τῶν μαθητῶν αὐτοῦ.

Now when John had heard in the prison the works of Christ, he sent two of his disciples.

ἐν τῷ δεσμωτηρίῳ.] Scil. apud Machærum. Why he was imprisoned there, see ch. xiv. 3 ["for Herodias' sake"]. He asks not for information, but to fulfil his office of herald; and to increase the faith of his disciples, who were rather jealous of our Lord. See ch. ix. 14 [the question about fasting]; St. John iii. 26 [the complaint that Christ baptized so many].

The name is taken probably from Ps. cxviii. 26, *Blessed is he that cometh.* Cf. the accounts of Christ's entry into Jerusalem.

Ver. 5.

Τυφλοὶ ἀναβλέπουσι ... καὶ πτωχοὶ εὐαγγελίζονται.

The blind receive their sight, ... and the poor have the gospel preached to them.

---

[h] [I have given the last four words exactly as they stand abbreviated in Mr. Keble's MS., being unable to conjecture their meaning, unless it be, "even as the punishment for blaspheming one who speaks *in the name of* the Holy Ghost, will be the same as that for blaspheming the Holy Ghost."—Ed.]

Cf. Isa. xxxv. 5, *Then the eyes of the blind shall be opened, &c.;* lxi. 1, *The Lord hath anointed me to preach, &c.*

πτωχοί.] Are perhaps taken in a spiritual sense. Observe here, by Christ's not answering their question immediately, how He deals with us in the matter of evidences. The raising the dead was more than was predicted. Christ's teaching the poor was most contrary to that of the scribes; for they said that the Holy Ghost only rested on a rich man. Cf. St. John vii. 48, 49, *Have any of the rulers ... believed on Him ?*

εὐαγγελίζονται.] Expresses a real effect, as passive words often do; q. d. "They receive the truth given them."

Ver. 6.

Καὶ μακάριός ἐστιν, ὃς ἐὰν μὴ σκανδαλισθῇ ἐν ἐμοί.
And blessed is he, whosoever shall not be offended in me.

See Ps. ii. 12, *Kiss the Son, &c.*

σκάνδαλον.] Is, (1) a gull-trap, (2) a snare, (3) a stone or block in the way. For the use of the word here, see ch. xiii. 21, *By-and-by he is offended;* xxvi. 31, 33, *All ye shall be offended.*

Ver. 7.

Κάλαμον ὑπὸ ἀνέμου σαλευόμενον;
A reed shaken with the wind ?

Here some find John's steadiness contrasted with the vacillation which the scribes were chargeable with.

Ver. 8.

Ἄνθρωπον ἐν μαλακοῖς ἱματίοις ἠμφιεσμένον;
A man clothed in soft raiment ?

"Soft," some say, silken.

Ver. 9.

Ναὶ, λέγω ὑμῖν, καὶ περισσότερον προφήτου.
Yea, I say unto you, and more than a prophet.

John was more than a prophet, if we take Maimonides' account of inspiration, for God Himself spake with him.

περισσότερον.] Cf. ch. v. 47, τί περισσὸν ποιεῖτε.

Ver. 10.

Ἰδού, ἐγὼ ἀποστέλλω τὸν ἄγγελόν μου πρὸ προσώπου σου,
ὃς κατασκευάσει τὴν ὁδόν σου ἔμπροσθέν σου.
Behold, I send my messenger before thy face, which shall prepare thy way before thee.

Cf. Mal. iii. 1, *Behold, I will send My messenger, and He shall prepare the way before Me; and the Lord whom ye seek shall suddenly come to His temple, even the Messenger of the Covenant;* where it is, *I will send . . . before My face* (Heb.) This, and the word "Lord" in great letters, though not Jehovah [but וְהָאָדוֹן], are strong in support of our Saviour's Divinity; Christ was "the Angel of the Covenant," probably, in Exod. xxiii. 20, (*Behold, I send an angel before thee*).

The prophecy is quoted according to sense, not sound. (1) For the prophet speaks to the people; here to Christ; (2) ἔμπροσθέν σου is added.

Cf. ch. iii. 3, *The voice of one crying, &c.* The herald's office is double,—to proclaim; and to make way; John fulfilled both.

Ver. 11.

Οὐκ ἐγήγερται ἐν γεννητοῖς γυναικῶν μείζων Ἰωάννου τοῦ Βαπτιστοῦ· ὁ δὲ μικρότερος ἐν τῇ βασιλείᾳ τῶν οὐρανῶν μείζων αὐτοῦ ἐστιν.

Among them that are born of women there hath not risen a greater than John the Baptist: notwithstanding he that is least in the kingdom of heaven is greater than he.

John is compared here with the other prophets before Christ; and in the discharge of his prophetic office.

μικρότερος.] q. d. ἐλάχιστος. Cf. St. Luke x. 24, *Many prophets and kings have desired, &c.*; Heb. xi. 40, *That they without us should not be made perfect;* St. Luke ix. 48, *He that is least among you all, the same shall be great.*

He was peculiarly great from his miraculous birth; from his clear knowledge of the Person of Christ; and from his peculiar relation to Him.

He was not so great as the least prophet under the Gospel, because (1) the Christian knew the mystery of godliness, of the truths of God Incarnate, &c.; (2) he could usually work miracles; (3) the Holy Ghost had special care to instruct the Christian prophet.

ὁ μικρότερος.] Scil. προφήτης. Cf. St. Luke vii. 28, *Among those born of women, there is not a greater prophet than John the Baptist.*

Ver. 12.

Ἀπὸ τῶν ἡμερῶν Ἰωάννου τοῦ Βαπτιστοῦ ἕως ἄρτι, ἡ βασιλεία τῶν οὐρανῶν βιάζεται, καὶ βιασταὶ ἁρπάζουσιν αὐτήν.

From the days of John the Baptist until now the kingdom of heaven suffereth violence, and the violent take it by force.

Cf. Exod. xix. 24, *Let not the priests and the people break through to come up unto the Lord.*

βασιλεία τῶν οὐρανῶν.] Did not properly begin till Christ's instalment in His regal office, by His resurrection and ascension.

ἀπὸ τῶν ἡμερῶν.] That is, from the beginning of His preaching, a reference to the admission of persons who would be thought least likely to obtain the kingdom, the publicans and Gentiles; see St. Matt. xxi. 31, xv. 28; in which case it must be a metaphor from a feast; or it is (as ἁρπάζουσιν seems to denote) a metaphor from a taken city. Learn hence that we ought to set about the work of religion with all our might, Josh. i. 6, *Be strong, and of a good courage.*

Ver. 13.

Πάντες γὰρ οἱ προφῆται καὶ ὁ νόμος ἕως Ἰωάννου προεφήτευσαν.

For all the prophets and the law prophesied until John.

Here the question is whether the stress should be laid on the verb προεφήτευσαν, or on the nominative cases, προφῆται and νόμος. If the former, the whole is a declaration of the greater clearness of the preaching of the Gospel, than of that of the Law. But qu. whether προφητεία in the New Testament does often mean obscure predictions? Therefore I should prefer the latter way, which would place the excellency of the Baptist's ministry in this, that the Law ended in him; and its defect in this, that the Gospel did not quite begin; so rendering a reason for both the assertions in ver. 11. Observe that where St. Luke introduces a discourse similar to this, he inverts the order of vers. 12, 13; St. Luke xvi. 16, *The law and the prophets were until John; since that time the kingdom of God is preached, and every man presseth into it.*

Ver. 14.

Εἰ θέλετε δέξασθαι, αὐτός ἐστιν Ἠλίας, ὁ μέλλων ἔρχεσθαι.

If ye will receive it, this is Elias, which was for to come.

Our Lord's manner of declaring this proves that He knew it

would be a hard doctrine for them to relish; for many had rejected John for his evidence of Christ, and all expected a literal, not a figurative, Elias. See a parallel expression in 1 Cor. xi. 16, *If any man seem to be contentious, we have no such custom.*

Cf. Mal. iv. 5, *Behold, I will send you Elijah the prophet, before the coming of the great and dreadful day of the Lord.*

The principal point of resemblance between John and Elijah seems to be the object of their mission, described in St. Luke i. 17, *To turn the hearts of the fathers to the children.* Both came in a time of general defection, the one to temporal, the other to spiritual, idolatry. Both were unsuccessful, except as to a remnant. There are also many points of resemblance in personal character and circumstances. Let it be considered particularly, whether the history of 1 Kings xviii. [the fire from heaven on Carmel] may not have a typical meaning. The Fathers expected a literal Elias, but it seems impossible to resist the arguments offered in Whitby (*ad locum*) to refute their notion. [Whitby's argument is based on St. Matt. xvii. 12, 13; and from Acts ii. 16 he shews that Mal. iv. 5 need not point to the *Second* Advent:— "The day of our Lord's *first* coming, considered as reaching to the destruction of Jerusalem, was indeed a very 'dreadful day.'" —ED.]

VER. 15.

'Ο ἔχων ὦτα ἀκούειν, ἀκουέτω.
He that hath ears to hear, let him hear.

One reason, perhaps, why this was so important a thing for them to know, was that, being so plainly told that the prophecy concerning Elijah was to be taken spiritually, not literally, they might be the readier to believe the same of those concerning Jesus.

For the phrase, ὦτα ἀκούειν, understand ὥστε; cf. ch. xiii. 9, *Who hath ears to hear, let him hear;* St. Luke viii. 8, Rev. ii. 7, et alicubi.

VER. 17.

Ηὐλήσαμεν ὑμῖν καὶ οὐκ ὠρχήσασθε· ἐθρηνήσαμεν ὑμῖν, καὶ οὐκ ἐκόψασθε.
We have piped unto you, and ye have not danced; we have mourned unto you, and ye have not lamented.

A wonderful instance of Christ's condescension, to draw an

illustration from children making believe, first to be at a feast, secondly to be at a funeral; sic Herbert, 405[1].

This seems to be authority for Boyle's "Reflections," and such books.

τίνι δὲ ὁμοιώσω.] An exordium common among the Jews.

ὁμοία ἐστὶ παιδαρίοις.] Not that the Jews were like those boys, but that the one transaction was like the other; cf. xiii. 24, 45, *The kingdom of heaven is like* ... For the thought, cf. Prov. xxix. 9, *If a wise man contendeth with a foolish man, whether he rage or laugh, there is no rest.* The proverb was used by the Talmudists, of God's different dealings with Ahaz, and with Amaziah. Buxtorf says, Christ represents the children as referring to the double use of pipes at feasts and at funerals; see ix. 23, *Saw the minstrels and the people making a noise.*

VERS. 18, 19.

Ἦλθε γὰρ Ἰωάννης μήτε ἐσθίων, μήτε πίνων. ...
ἦλθεν ὁ υἱὸς τοῦ ἀνθρώπου ἐσθίων καὶ πίνων ... καὶ ἐδικαιώθη
ἡ σοφία ἀπὸ τῶν τέκνων αὐτῆς.

John came neither eating nor drinking ...
The Son of man came eating and drinking ... But wisdom is
justified of her children.

In the difference between John and Jesus we may see the mercy of God, who would try all ways with the Jews; also an aptness to the message which each brought; also a warning to ourselves, not to judge others or plume ourselves on such distinctions.

Of the various interpretations of the last clause, those of Hammond and Maldonate seem to shew fairest, viz. Wisdom (i.e. the Gospel) has this overpowering argument to justify herself, that she is received by just the sort of people by whom the truth is likely to be received; cf. St. Luke vii. 29, *All the people ... justified God, being baptized with the baptism of John;* ver. 25, (*hidden these things from the wise and prudent, and revealed them*

---

[1] Possibly the allusion is to the lines on Affliction, in "the Church":—

"There is but joy and grief;
If either will convert us we are thine:
Some Angels used the first; if our relief
Take up the second, then thy double line
And several baits in either kinde
Furnish thy table to thy minde."—ED.

to babes); to which Maldonate adds, "and rejected by them by whom the truth was likely to be rejected;" taking τῆς σοφίας in a wider sense, "all to whom grace is offered." I think St. Luke vii. 29 confutes Whitby's notion that the clause is ironical, a continuation of the scoff of the Pharisees.

VER. 20.

Τότε ἤρξατο ὀνειδίζειν τὰς πόλεις.
Then began he to upbraid the cities.

ὀνειδίζειν.] Is quoted as used by Plato and Xenophon in the like sense.

VER. 21.

Οὐαί σοι, Χοραζὶν οὐαί σοι Βηθσαιδάν.
Woe unto thee, Chorazin! woe unto thee, Bethsaida!

Of Bethsaida were Philip, Andrew and Peter; and we hear particularly of the healing of a blind man there (St. Mark viii. 22—26), and of the feeding of the five thousand (St. Luke ix. 10—17). Tyre and Sidon were warned in the Old Testament by Ezekiel (xxvi. 2, and seq.), by Isaiah xxiii. 1 (the burden of Tyre), Jeremiah xxv. 22, xlvii. 4, and Zech. ix. 1—4. Their ruling sins seem to have been pride of worldly wisdom, and of wealth; as those of the Jews were of spiritual wisdom and wealth. But perhaps Christ mentioned them rather as being near, than as being like. This text most clearly implies the doctrine of different degrees of grace being to be measured by different opportunities of its external means; and to be followed, if rejected, by different degrees of punishment.

I do not see how Hammond's interpretation of a temporal judgment is consistent with the future tense in verses 22 and 24 (*It shall be more tolerable*). For the day of Sodom's and Tyre's temporal judgment had been long come; and ἡμέρα κρίσεως is never used in that sense that I know of; ἡμέρα ἐπισκοπῆς is. Tyre and Sidon were separated from the knowledge of Christ's mighty works by place, Sodom by time. They represent, therefore, both classes of those who are, without any fault of their own, insufficiently furnished with evidence of Him. The sentence passed in verse 22 is inconsistent with Grotius' notion of giving ἂν the sense of "perhaps;" Christ here exercises His attribute of knowing the hearts; cf. Ezra iii. 6, *Surely had I sent thee to them, they would have hearkened unto thee.*

Ver. 23.

Καὶ σύ, Καπερναούμ, ἡ ἕως τοῦ οὐρανοῦ ὑψωθεῖσα, ἕως ᾅδου καταβιβασθήσῃ· ὅτι εἰ ἐν Σοδόμοις ἐγένοντο αἱ δυνάμεις αἱ γενόμεναι ἐν σοί, ἔμειναν ἂν μέχρι τῆς σήμερον.

And thou, Capernaum, which art exalted unto heaven, shalt be brought down to hell: for if the mighty works, which have been done in thee, had been done in Sodom, it would have remained until this day.

Capernaum seems to have flourished in merchandise; but as this could be nothing comparable to the wealth of Tyre, I should rather take the passive participle, ὑψωθεῖσα, in a middle sense, "which exaltest thyself." Hammond well observes that ᾅδης is best construed not locally, but "the state of the dead;" Gen. xxxvii. 35, *I will go down into the grave, unto my son;* Ps. xvi. 10, Acts ii. 27, *Thou wilt not leave my soul in hell;* Rev. vi. 8, *A pale horse;* . . . *and hell followed with him.* And in the Apocrypha many times: cf. 1 Sam. ii. 6, *He bringeth down to the grave, and bringeth up;* Isa. xiv. 15, *Thou shalt be brought down to hell, to the sides of the pit;* lvii. 9, *Thou didst debase thyself, even unto hell.*

So Æsch. Sept. c. Theb. 327, οἰκτρὸν γὰρ πόλιν ὧδ᾽ ἀγυγίαν Ἀΐδᾳ προϊάψαι.

Ver. 25.

Ἐν ἐκείνῳ τῷ καιρῷ ἀποκριθεὶς ὁ Ἰησοῦς εἶπεν, Ἐξομολογοῦμαί σοι, πάτερ, κύριε τοῦ οὐρανοῦ καὶ τῆς γῆς, ὅτι ἀπέκρυψας ταῦτα ἀπὸ σοφῶν καὶ συνετῶν, καὶ ἀπεκάλυψας αὐτὰ νηπίοις.

At that time Jesus answered and said, I thank thee, O Father, Lord of heaven and earth, because thou hast hid these things from the wise and prudent, and hast revealed them unto babes.

ἀποκριθείς], in the sense of answering, is bad Greek, according to Phrynichus, apud Schleusner: ἀποκρινάμενος would be right, so the Hebrew עָנָה, to which ἀποκρίνεσθαι answers. It means here, *Continued his discourse;* ch. xxii. 1, *Jesus answered and spake unto them again by parables;* xxvi. 25, *Judas answered and said;* ver. 63, *The High Priest answered and said.*

The thought of the sin and misery of them who rejected Him, naturally brought to His mind the qualification and the blessedness of those who received Him, which He describes to the end of the chapter.

ἐξομολογοῦμαι] means (1) to confess sins, (2) to give thanks,

(3) to glorify, more generally; and this seems to be the meaning here.

The next clause is a Hebraism, *quod dicit*, ἀποκρύψας ταῦτα ἀπεκάλυψας; cf. Rom. vi. 17, *But God be thanked, that ye were the servants of sin, but ye have obeyed from the heart that form of doctrine which was delivered you.*

Let us all give glory to God, in imitation of our dear Lord, for framing His Gospel so that it should be hid from the self-sufficient and revealed unto babes. Keep me, O God, from being wise in mine own eyes, and proud in mine own sight; lest, while I am shewing the Light of Thy glorious Gospel to others, I become blind to it myself!

Read Cameron's note here (in Pole's *Synopsis*), and judge of the danger of following up a favourite hypothesis too far. To avoid the conclusion evidently following from this verse against irrespective Predestination, he says, "Non mirum [erat Deum mansuetis se potius quam superbis revelare, cujus ratio patet, nec opus tunc fuisset ad εὐδοκίαν Dei recurrere];" by which he contradicts a fundamental tenet of Christianity, and of his own scheme of it; for he allows that human reason of itself could discern sufficiently the great doctrine of "mysteries being revealed to the meek."

VER. 26.

Ναὶ, ὁ πατὴρ, ὅτι οὕτως ἐγένετο εὐδοκία ἔμπροσθέν σου.

Even so, Father: for so it seemeth good in thy sight.

Ναὶ more than any word seems to be the Greek of אָמֵן, and is here the seal of God the Son, set to the gracious dispensation of God the Father. εὐδοκία ἔμπροσθέν σου, Hebraism used in the Liturgies, juxta Grotium; יְהִי רָצוֹן לְפָנֶיךָ. Cf. 1 Cor. i. 21, εὐδόκησεν ὁ Θεός, *It pleased God by the foolishness of preaching to save them that believe.*

VER. 27.

Πάντα μοι παρεδόθη ὑπὸ τοῦ πατρός μου· καὶ οὐδεὶς ἐπιγινώσκει τὸν υἱὸν, εἰ μὴ ὁ πατήρ· οὐδὲ τὸν πατέρα τις ἐπιγινώσκει, εἰ μὴ ὁ υἱὸς, καὶ ᾧ ἐὰν βούληται ὁ υἱὸς ἀποκαλύψαι.

All things are delivered unto me of my Father: and no man knoweth the Son, but the Father; neither knoweth any man the Father, save the Son, and he to whomsoever the Son will reveal him.

A question is stirred up here whether πάντα mean persons or

things. What if we extend it to both, and say, that both the souls to be saved, and the ways of saving them, are expressly declared to be entrusted to Christ as the One Mediator? That the *neuter* (πάντα) may mean *persons*, cf. St. Matt. xviii. 11, *For the Son of man is come to save that which was lost*, where τὸ ἀπολωλός corresponds to εἰς τῶν μικρῶν τούτων of ver. 14; Heb. xii. 13, *Lest that which is lame be turned out of the way* (ἵνα μὴ τὸ χωλὸν ἐκτραπῇ); 1 St. John v. 4, *Whatsoever is born of God* (πᾶν τὸ γεγεννημένον ἐκ τοῦ Θεοῦ).

Grotius rather takes παρεδόθη in the sense of tradition; and perhaps that rendering may suit the context. In the second clause Christ's Divinity is certainly implied; and in the third, salvation exclusively through Him.

Adjuva, Domine, adjuva Sancte Spiritus, ut melius intelligam cæcâ hâc et profanâ mente, quid sibi velit versus hic mirabilis; per Jesum tuum carissimum. Amen.

VER. 28.

Δεῦτε πρός με πάντες οἱ κοπιῶντες καὶ πεφορτισμένοι,
κἀγὼ ἀναπαύσω ὑμᾶς.

Come unto me, all ye that labour and are heavy laden, and
I will give you rest.

δεῦτε.] An adverb.

κοπιῶντες καὶ πεφορτισμένοι.] An allusion here probably to the hard bondage in Egypt, which is often referred to as an emblem of our natural state.

VER. 29.

Ἄρατε τὸν ζυγόν μου ἐφ᾽ ὑμᾶς, καὶ μάθετε ἀπ᾽ ἐμοῦ, ὅτι
πρᾷός εἰμι καὶ ταπεινὸς τῇ καρδίᾳ· καὶ εὑρήσετε ἀνά-
παυσιν ταῖς ψυχαῖς ὑμῶν.

Take my yoke upon you, and learn of me; for I am meek and lowly
in heart: and ye shall find rest unto your souls.

Cf. Zech. ix. 9, *Rejoice greatly, O daughter of Zion; shout, O daughter of Jerusalem: behold, thy king cometh unto thee: he is just, and having salvation; lowly, and riding upon an ass, and upon a colt the foal of an ass.*

A yoke was a very common emblem of obedience among the Jews. Gen. xxvii. 40, *Thou shalt break his yoke from off thy neck;* Ps. ii. 3, *Let us break their bands asunder;* Jer. ii. 20, *I have broken thy yoke, and burst thy bands;* Acts xv. 10, *Why tempt ye*

God, to put a yoke upon the neck of the disciples. "Amat Christus loqui prophetarum verbis: extant hæc, apud Jer. vi. 16" [*Ask for the old paths ... and walk therein, and ye shall find rest for your souls*], Grotius.

Whether Christ propounds His own lowliness as an example or as an encouragement, comes much to the same thing; but it seems rather more to the purpose to take it as an example; and then it will point out the natural tendency of meekness and lowliness to give rest, and will connect it with ver. 25.

VER. 30.

'Ο γὰρ ζυγός μου χρηστὸς, καὶ τὸ φορτίον μου ἐλαφρόν ἐστιν.
For my yoke is easy, and my burden is light.

Observe the ἀστεῖον of the epithets: *light*, to burthen; and *benign, gracious*, to yoke. Read a sermon of Hammond's on the text. To reconcile it with the precepts of self-denial, and also with the doctrine of original sin, consider (1) the promises of the Spirit, (2) the love of God can make anything pleasant, (3) the hope of eternal life, (4) the natural tendency of virtue to reward itself. Chrysostom said, "Difficilius vitium virtute[b]." Let it be so to me, O God, for Jesus Christ's sake! Amen.

No excuse for infidelity, if God had never given us but this one chapter. For here we have, (1) The Evidences, both Prophecy and Miracles, vers. 2—15; (2) The different ways of God's dealing with man, and pretences on which they reject Him, vers. 16—19; (3) The punishment of wilful unbelief, vers. 20—24; (4) The reward and qualifications of the Christian, vers. 25—30.

[b] [Ὁρᾷς πῶς εὔκολον ἡ ἀρετὴ, δύσκολον δὲ ἡ κακία; Expos. in Ps. vii.—ED.]

WORKS by the late REV. JOHN KEBLE, M.A.

OCCASIONAL PAPERS AND REVIEWS on Sir Walter Scott, Poetry, and Sacred Poetry, Bishop Warburton, Rev. John Miller, Exeter Synod, Judicial Committee of Privy Council, Parochial Work, the Lord's Supper, Solomon, the Jewish Nation. By the late Rev. JOHN KEBLE, Author of "The Christian Year." Demy 8vo., pp. xx., 506, with Two Facsimiles from Common-place Book, cloth extra, 12s.

"More than one-third of the volume is taken up with original, and hitherto unpublished, papers of Mr. Keble, the remainder with reviews printed in the 'British Critic' and 'Christian Remembrancer,' and one of them on 'sacred poetry' in the 'Quarterly Review,' whilst edited by Mr. Keble's friend and biographer, the late Sir John Coleridge; to these are added three tracts called out by passing events, but events which are ever repeating themselves, a fact which invests these tracts with a permanent value.... The volume of 'Occasional Papers and Reviews' is not a mere collection of papers published, and hitherto uncollected, but of thoughts and judgments on past topics, which will possess an enduring value in the eyes of all who cherish the memory of John Keble, and will give to those who may not have known the author of 'The Christian Year,' the best means of estimating a character of singular simplicity and utter un-selfconsciousness.... No man surely ever lived who thought less of himself than the author of this volume.... This side of Mr. Keble's character, his humility, brought out in a letter contributed to this volume, is sketched with the rare felicity which marks almost all the writings of John Henry Newman, and by recollections of his own intercourse with Mr. Keble. To this letter is added a postscript by Dr. Pusey, so that in this posthumous volume we are again reminded of what the English Church and the world owes to the three Fellows of Oriel, who, more than thirty years ago, aroused the half-torpid, if not stagnant, religious life, not of England only, but of Christendom. By this publication, and by their own contributions to this volume, Dr. Pusey and Dr. Newman have not only added another column to the monument erected to Mr. Keble's memory, but have added to the depth of our obligation to themselves. Generations will pass away before the names, again blended in this volume, of Keble, Pusey, and Newman will be forgotten by the Christian Church."—*John Bull.*

"The volume before us appears at a singularly opportune time.... A reprint of Mr. Keble's Tracts will be read with even more eagerness and interest now than on the occasion of their first appearance. It must not be supposed this volume of remains contains nothing else than Mr. Keble's papers on the crisis of 1850. There is much else both of high interest and enduring value."—*Church Quarterly Review.*

"All the papers have this surpassing value, that, over and above their literary merits, they reveal a noble, devout, tender spirit, of a modest and chaste reserve almost astonishing. The paper on Warburton especially is an instance of how a saintly mind can apologize for and make the best of another mind which, though its masculine power and vigour are universally admitted, has been usually regarded as rough, coarse, and even worldly. We assure our readers that they have a great treat before them in the loving and reverent perusal of this collection of Keble's writings, many of them in a vein with which they had not perhaps connected their memory of Keble."—*Church Review.*

"Three of the papers contained in the volume are said to be from unpublished manuscripts. The first is a discussion of the proper meaning of the term, 'The Lord's Supper.' Keble here argues with considerable force that this name, according to Scriptural use, does not belong to the Holy Eucharist, but to the feast of charity. His quotations from the New Testament and from the early Fathers seem to support his position.

"The second paper is on the character and history of Solomon, with a view especially to the question of his final penitence. It is a production of great value, both for its scholarly research and for its freshness. The third paper is an abstract of what the author evidently intended to be a more extended treatise. Its title is 'The Jewish Nation, and God's Dealings with Them.' The author draws a parallel between the history of the Jews and that of our present and imperfect Christianity.

"It is a very ingenious attempt at analogy, and the result is, in most points, remarkably successful. It shews a careful study of the history of God's ancient people, and an accurate knowledge of the special defects in the Church of to-day.

"The preface to this volume is from the pen of Dr. Pusey. It is a warm and loving tribute to Keble's worth and saintliness. A letter written by John Henry Newman in answer to an inquiry as to the articles contributed by Keble to the 'British Critic,' of which Newman was at one time the editor, is also printed."—*New York Churchman.*

"They are prefaced by two letters of deep interest from Dr. Newman and Dr. Pusey. There is something extremely touching in the reunion, as it were, of the three old friends and fellow-labourers."—*Guardian.*

OXFORD AND LONDON: JAMES PARKER AND CO.

WORKS by the late REV. JOHN KEBLE, M.A. (continued).

LETTERS OF SPIRITUAL COUNSEL AND GUIDANCE. Third Edition, much enlarged, with a New Preface by R. F. WILSON, M.A. Post 8vo., cloth, 6s.

SERMONS, OCCASIONAL AND PAROCHIAL. 8vo., cloth, 12s.; also in 12 Parts (containing Three Sermons), 1s. each.

VILLAGE SERMONS ON THE BAPTISMAL SERVICE. 8vo., cloth, 5s.

ON EUCHARISTICAL ADORATION. Fifth Edition. WITH CONSIDERATIONS SUGGESTED BY A PASTORAL LETTER ON THE DOCTRINE OF THE MOST HOLY EUCHARIST. 24mo., 2s.

AN ARGUMENT AGAINST REPEALING THE LAWS WHICH TREAT THE NUPTIAL BOND AS INDISSOLUBLE. Second Edition, 8vo., 1s.

SEQUEL OF THE ARGUMENT AGAINST IMMEDIATELY REPEALING THE LAWS WHICH TREAT THE NUPTIAL BOND AS INDISSOLUBLE. 1857. 8vo., 4s.

SUNDAY LESSONS. THE PRINCIPLE OF SELECTION. Being No. XIII. of "Tracts for the Times." 8vo., 6d.

A LITANY OF OUR LORD'S WARNINGS. With SUGGESTIONS FOR THE USE OF IT. 1864. 16mo., 6d.

DIFFICULTIES IN THE RELATIONS BETWEEN CHURCH AND STATE. With a Preface by H. P. LIDDON, D.D., Canon of St. Paul's. Pp. 70, Demy 8vo., sewed, 1s.

THE STATE IN ITS RELATIONS WITH THE CHURCH. Reprinted from the "British Critic," October, 1839. With a Preface by H. P. LIDDON, D.D. 8vo., pp. 72, sewed, 1s.

LETTER TO A MEMBER OF CONVOCATION, deprecating a Royal Commission for dealing with the Prayer-Book. 8vo., 2d.

WORKS by the late REV. JOHN KEBLE, M.A. (continued).

ON THE REPRESENTATION OF THE UNIVERSITY OF OXFORD. A LETTER to SIR BROOK W. BRIDGES, Bart. 1852. 8vo., 6d.

A VERY FEW PLAIN THOUGHTS ON THE ADMISSION OF DISSENTERS TO THE UNIVERSITY. 1854. 8vo., 6d.

WOMEN LABOURING IN THE LORD. A SERMON preached at Wantage, 1863. Fcap. 8vo., 6d.

PENTECOSTAL FEAR. A SERMON preached at Cuddesdon on the Anniversary of the Theological College. 1864. 8vo., 1s.

ON THE MYSTICISM ATTRIBUTED TO THE EARLY FATHERS OF THE CHURCH. Being No. LXXXIX. of "Tracts for the Times." 8vo., sewed, 3s. 6d.

CATHOLIC SUBSCRIPTION TO THE XXXIX. ARTICLES, considered in reference to Tract 90, 1841. (Reprinted with Tract 90, with Dr. Pusey's Historical Preface.) 8vo., sewed, 1s. 6d.

SERMONS FOR THE CHRISTIAN YEAR. By the Rev. JOHN KEBLE, Author of "The Christian Year."

ADVENT TO CHRISTMAS. 8vo., cloth, 6s.	EASTER TO ASCENSION DAY. 8vo., cloth, 6s.
ASH-WEDNESDAY TO HOLY WEEK. 8vo., cloth, 6s.	ASCENSION DAY TO TRINITY SUNDAY inclusive. 8vo., cloth, 6s.
CHRISTMAS AND EPIPHANY. 8vo., cloth, 6s.	SERMONS FOR SAINTS' DAYS. 8vo., cloth, 6s.
HOLY WEEK. 8vo., cloth, 6s.	

There remain, to follow at intervals,

SEPTUAGESIMA TO LENT.	SERMONS for the TRINITY SEASON.

STUDIA SACRA. COMMENTARIES ON THE INTRODUCTORY VERSES OF ST. JOHN'S GOSPEL, AND ON A PORTION OF ST. PAUL'S EPISTLE TO THE ROMANS; with other Theological Papers by the Rev. JOHN KEBLE, M.A. 8vo., cloth, 10s. 6d.

OXFORD AND LONDON: JAMES PARKER AND CO.

BOOKS
PUBLISHED
BY JAMES PARKER AND CO.
OXFORD, AND 377, STRAND, LONDON.

Theological, &c.

THE LATE REV. JOHN KEBLE, M.A.
OCCASIONAL PAPERS AND REVIEWS, on Sir Walter Scott, Poetry, and Sacred Poetry, Bishop Warburton, Rev. John Miller, Exeter Synod, Judicial Committee of Privy Council, Parochial Work, the Lord's Supper, Solomon, the Jewish Nation. By the late Rev. JOHN KEBLE, Author of "The Christian Year." Demy 8vo., cloth extra, 12s.

"They are prefaced by two letters of deep interest from Dr. NEWMAN and Dr. PUSEY. There is something extremely touching in the reunion, as it were, of the three old friends and fellow-labourers."—*Guardian.*

STUDIA SACRA. COMMENTARIES on the Introductory Verses of St. John's Gospel, and on a Portion of St. Paul's Epistle to the Romans; with other Theological Papers by the late Rev. JOHN KEBLE. 8vo., cloth.
[*Just ready.*

THE BOOK OF COMMON PRAYER.
AN INTRODUCTION TO THE HISTORY OF THE SUCCESSIVE REVISIONS OF THE BOOK OF COMMON PRAYER. Crown 8vo., cloth, 12s.

THE FIRST PRAYER-BOOK OF EDWARD VI., compared with the Successive Revisions of the Book of Common Prayer; together with a Concordance and Index to the Rubrics in the several editions. Crown 8vo., cl., 12s.

OLD CATHOLIC RITUAL.
A CATHOLIC RITUAL, published according to the Decrees of the First Two Synods of the Old Catholics of the German Empire. Done into English and Compared with the Offices of the Roman and Old German Rituals. By the Rev. F. E. WARREN, B.D., Fellow of St. John's College, Oxford. Crown 8vo., cloth, 3s. 6d.

BISHOP CLEVELAND COXE.
APOLLOS; or, THE WAY OF GOD. A Plea for the Religion of Scripture. By A. CLEVELAND COXE. Crown 8vo., cloth, 5s.

THE LATE BISHOP WILBERFORCE.
ADDRESSES TO THE CANDIDATES FOR ORDINATION on the Questions in the Ordination Service. *Fifth Thousand.* Crown 8vo., cloth, 6s.

WORDS OF COUNSEL ON SOME OF THE CHIEF DIFFICULTIES OF THE DAY, bequeathed to the Church in the Writings of SAMUEL WILBERFORCE, late Lord Bishop of Winchester. Collected and arranged by the late THOMAS VINCENT FOSBERY, M.A. Second Edition, Crown 8vo., cloth, 7s. 6d.

SERMONS PREACHED ON VARIOUS OCCASIONS. With a Preface by the Lord Bishop of ELY. 8vo., cloth, 7s. 6d.

JEWISH INTERPRETATION.
THE FIFTY-THIRD CHAPTER OF ISAIAH ACCORDING TO THE JEWISH INTERPRETERS. I. Texts edited from Printed Books, and MSS., by AD. NEUBAUER. Price 18s. II. Translations by S. R. DRIVER and AD. NEUBAUER. With an Introduction to the Translations by the Rev. E. B. PUSEY, Regius Professor of Hebrew, Oxford. Post 8vo., cloth, 12s.

CONFIRMATION.
THE HISTORY OF CONFIRMATION. By WILLIAM JACKSON, M.A., Queen's College, Oxford; Vicar of Heathfield, Sussex. Crown 8vo., cloth, 4s.

(1177.4.100.)

THEOLOGICAL WORKS, &c. (continued).

REV. E. B. PUSEY, D.D.

DANIEL THE PROPHET. Nine Lectures delivered in the Divinity School of the University of Oxford. With a new Preface. By E. B. Pusey, D.D., &c. *Seventh Thousand.* 8vo., cloth, 10s. 6d.

THE MINOR PROPHETS; with a Commentary Explanatory and Practical, and Introductions to the Several Books. In Six Parts. 4to., sewed. Parts I.—V., 5s. each; Part VI., 6s.

Part I. contains Hosea—Joel, Introduction. | Part IV. Micah i. 13 to Habakkuk, Introduction.
Part II. Joel, Introduction—Amos vi. 6.
Part III. Amos vi. 7 to Micah i. 12. | Part V. Habakkuk, Zephaniah, Haggai.
Part VI. (completing the Work) Zechariah, Malachi.

The Six Parts in One Volume, complete. Cloth, 31s. 6d.

THE DOCTRINE OF THE REAL PRESENCE, as contained in the Fathers from the death of St. John the Evangelist to the 4th General Council. By the Rev. E. B. Pusey, D.D. 8vo., cloth, 7s. 6d.

THE REAL PRESENCE, the Doctrine of the English Church, with a vindication of the reception by the wicked and of the Adoration of our Lord Jesus Christ truly present. By the Rev. E. B. Pusey, D.D. 8vo., 6s.

The **COUNCILS of the CHURCH,** from the Council of Jerusalem to the close of the 2nd General Council of Constantinople, A.D. 381. By the Rev. E. B. Pusey, D.D. 8vo., cloth, 6s.

ELEVEN ADDRESSES DURING A RETREAT OF THE COMPANIONS OF THE LOVE OF JESUS, engaged in Perpetual Intercession for the Conversion of Sinners. By the Rev. E. B. Pusey, D.D. 8vo., cloth, 3s. 6d.

ON THE CLAUSE "AND THE SON," in regard to the EASTERN CHURCH and the BONN CONFERENCE: A LETTER to the Rev. H. P. Liddon, D.D., Ireland Professor of Exegesis, Canon of St. Paul's. By the Rev. E. B. Pusey, D.D., Regius Professor of Hebrew and Canon of Christ Church. 8vo., cloth, 5s.

THE EPISTLES AND GOSPELS.

A COMMENTARY ON THE EPISTLES AND GOSPELS IN THE BOOK OF COMMON PRAYER. Extracted from Writings of the Fathers of the Holy Catholic Church, anterior to the Division of the East and West. With an Introductory Notice by the Dean of St. Paul's. In Two Vols., Crown 8vo., cloth, 15s.

THE OLD TESTAMENT.

STORIES FROM THE OLD TESTAMENT. With Four Illustrations. Square Crown 8vo., cloth, 4s.

F. GODET.

GODET'S BIBLICAL STUDIES ON THE OLD TESTAMENT. Edited by the Hon. and Rev. W. H. Lyttelton. Fcap. 8vo., cloth, 6s.

VERY REV. JOHN W. BURGON, B.D., Dean of Chichester.

THE LAST TWELVE VERSES OF THE GOSPEL ACCORDING TO S. MARK Vindicated against Recent Critical Objectors and Established, by John W. Burgon, B.D., Dean of Chichester. With Facsimiles of Codex ℵ and Codex L. 8vo., cloth, 12s.

REV. CANON TREVOR, D.D., M.A.

THE CATHOLIC DOCTRINE OF THE SACRIFICE AND PARTICIPATION OF THE HOLY EUCHARIST. By George Trevor, D.D., M.A., Canon of York; Rector of Beeford. Second Edition, revised and enlarged. Crown 8vo., cloth, 10s. 6d.

THEOLOGICAL WORKS, &c. (continued). 3

THE LATE REV. J. KEBLE, M.A.
LETTERS OF SPIRITUAL COUNSEL AND GUIDANCE. By the late Rev. J. KEBLE, M.A., Vicar of Hursley. Edited, with a New Preface, by R. F. WILSON, M.A., Vicar of Rownhams, &c. Third Edition, much enlarged. Post 8vo., cloth, 6s.

ON EUCHARISTICAL ADORATION. By the late Rev. JOHN KEBLE, M.A., Vicar of Hursley.—With Considerations suggested by a Pastoral Letter on the Doctrine of the Most Holy Eucharist. Cheap Edition, 24mo., sewed, 2s.

THE LATE BISHOP OF BRECHIN.
AN EXPLANATION OF THE THIRTY-NINE ARTICLES. With an Epistle Dedicatory to the Rev. E. B. PUSEY, D.D. By A. P. FORBES, D.C.L., Bishop of Brechin. Second Edition, Crown 8vo., cloth, 12s.

A SHORT EXPLANATION OF THE NICENE CREED, for the Use of Persons beginning the Study of Theology. By ALEXANDER PENROSE FORBES, D.C.L., Bishop of Brechin. *Second Edition.* Crown 8vo., cloth, 6s.

THE LORD BISHOP OF SALISBURY.
THE ADMINISTRATION OF THE HOLY SPIRIT IN THE BODY OF CHRIST. The Bampton Lectures for 1868. By GEORGE MOBERLY, D.C.L., Lord Bishop of Salisbury. *2nd Edit.* Crown 8vo., cloth, 7s. 6d.

SERMONS ON THE BEATITUDES, with others mostly preached before the University of Oxford. By GEORGE MOBERLY, D.C.L. *Third Edition.* Crown 8vo., cloth, 7s. 6d.

REV. WILLIAM BRIGHT, D.D.
A HISTORY OF THE CHURCH, from the Edict of Milan, A.D. 313, to the Council of Chalcedon, A.D. 451. *Second Edition.* Post 8vo., 10s. 6d.

JOHN DAVISON, B.D.
DISCOURSES ON PROPHECY. In which are considered its Structure, Use, and Inspiration. By JOHN DAVISON, B.D. A New Edition. 8vo., cloth, 9s.

THE LATE ARCHDEACON FREEMAN.
THE PRINCIPLES OF DIVINE SERVICE; or, An Inquiry concerning the True Manner of Understanding and Using the Order for Morning and Evening Prayer, and for the Administration of the Holy Communion in the English Church. *A New Edition.* 2 vols., 8vo., cloth, 16s.

CATENA AUREA.
CATENA AUREA. A Commentary on the Four Gospels, collected out of the Works of the Fathers by S. THOMAS AQUINAS. Uniform with the Library of the Fathers. Re-issue. Complete in 6 vols. 8vo., cloth, £2 2s.

REV. DR. IRONS.
CHRISTIANITY AS TAUGHT BY S. PAUL. The Bampton Lectures for 1870. To which is added an Appendix of the Continuous Sense of S. Paul's Epistles; with Notes and Metalegomena. Second Edition, with New Preface, 8vo., with Map, cloth, 9s.

REV. I. GREGORY SMITH, M.A.
CHARACTERISTICS OF CHRISTIAN MORALITY. The Bampton Lectures for 1873. Second Edition, Crown 8vo., cloth, 3s. 6d.

BEDE'S ECCLESIASTICAL HISTORY.
BEDE'S ECCLESIASTICAL HISTORY OF THE ENGLISH NATION. A New Translation by the Rev. L. GIDLEY, M.A., Chaplain of St. Nicholas', Salisbury. Crown 8vo., cloth, 6s.

REV. D. WATERLAND, D.D.
A CRITICAL HISTORY OF THE ATHANASIAN CREED, by the Rev. DANIEL WATERLAND, D.D. Edited by the Rev. J. R. KING, M.A. Fcap. 8vo., cloth, 5s.

THE CONSTITUTIONS AND CANONS ECCLESIASTICAL OF THE CHURCH OF ENGLAND, Referred to their Original Sources, and Illustrated with Explanatory Notes. By MACKENZIE E. C. WALCOTT, B.D., F.S.A., Præcentor and Prebendary of Chichester. Fcap. 8vo., cloth, 4s.

THE PASTORAL RULE OF ST. GREGORY. Sancti Gregorii Papæ Regulæ Pastoralis Liber, ad Johannem Episcopum Civitatis Ravennæ. With an English Translation. By the Rev. H. R. BRAMLEY, M.A., Fellow of Magdalen College, Oxford. Fcap. 8vo., cloth, 6s.

THE DEFINITIONS OF THE CATHOLIC FAITH and Canons of Discipline of the first four General Councils of the Universal Church. In Greek and English. Fcap. 8vo., cloth, 2s. 6d.

DE FIDE ET SYMBOLO: Documenta quædam nec non Aliquorum SS. Patrum Tractatus. Edidit CAROLUS A. HEURTLEY, S.T.P., Dom. Margaretæ Prælector, et Ædis Christi Canonicus. Fcap. 8vo., cloth, 4s. 6d.

S. AURELIUS AUGUSTINUS, Episcopus Hipponensis, de Catechi- zandis Rudibus, de Fide Rerum quæ non videntur, de Utilitate Credendi. In Usum Juniorum. Edidit C. MARRIOTT, S.T.B., Olim Coll. Oriel. Socius. *New Edition.* Fcap. 8vo., cloth, 3s. 6d.

ANALECTA CHRISTIANA, In usum Tironum. Excerpta, Epistolæ, &c., ex EUSEBII, &c.; S. IGNATII Epistolæ ad Smyrnæos et ad Polycarpum; E. S. CLEMENTIS ALEXANDRI Pædagogo excerpta; S. ATHANASII Sermo contra Gentes. Edidit et Annotationibus illustravit C. MARRIOTT, S.T.B. 8vo., 10s. 6d.

CUR DEUS HOMO, or Why God was made Man; by ST. ANSELM. Translated into English, with an Introduction, &c. *Second Edition.* Fcap. 8vo., 2s. 6d.

THE BOOK OF RATRAMN the Priest and Monk of Corbey, commonly called Bertram, on the Body and Blood of the Lord. (Latin and English.) To which is added AN APPENDIX, containing the Saxon Homily of Ælfric. Fcap. 8vo. [*Nearly ready.*

OXFORD SERIES OF DEVOTIONAL WORKS. Fcap. 8vo.

The Imitation of Christ.
FOUR BOOKS. By Thomas A KEMPIS. Cloth, 4s.

Andrewes' Devotions.
DEVOTIONS. By the Right Rev. Father in God, LAUNCELOT ANDREWES. Translated from the Greek and Latin, and arranged anew. Antique cloth, 5s.

Taylor's Holy Living.
THE RULE AND EXERCISES OF HOLY LIVING. By BISHOP JEREMY TAYLOR. Antique cloth, 4s.

Taylor's Holy Dying.
THE RULE AND EXERCISES OF HOLY DYING. By BISHOP JEREMY TAYLOR. Antique cloth, 4s.

Taylor's Golden Grove.
THE GOLDEN GROVE; a Choice Manual, containing what is to be Believed, Practised, and Desired, or Prayed for. By BISHOP JEREMY TAYLOR. Printed uniform with "Holy Living and Holy Dying." Antique cloth, 3s. 6d.

Sutton's Meditations.
GODLY MEDITATIONS UPON THE MOST HOLY SACRAMENT OF THE LORD'S SUPPER. By CHRISTOPHER SUTTON, D.D., late Prebend of Westminster. A new Edition. Antique cloth, 5s.

Wilson's Sacra Privata.
THE PRIVATE MEDITATIONS, DEVOTIONS, and PRAYERS of the Right Rev. T. WILSON, D.D., Lord Bishop of Sodor and Man. Now first printed entire. Cloth, 4s.

Laud's Devotions.
THE PRIVATE DEVOTIONS of DR. WILLIAM LAUD, Archbishop of Canterbury, and Martyr. Antique cloth, 5s.

Spinckes' Devotions.
TRUE CHURCH OF ENGLAND MAN'S COMPANION IN THE CLOSET; or, a complete Manual of Private Devotions, collected from the Writings of eminent Divines of the Church of England. Floriated borders, antique cloth, 4s.

Ancient Collects.
ANCIENT COLLECTS AND OTHER PRAYERS. Selected for Devotional use from various Rituals. By WM. BRIGHT, D.D. Antique cloth, 5s.

Devout Communicant.
THE DEVOUT COMMUNICANT, exemplified in his Behaviour before, at, and after the Sacrament of the Lord's Supper: Practically suited to all the Parts of that Solemn Ordinance. 7th Edition, revised. Fcap. 8vo., toned paper, red lines, cloth, 4s.

EIKΩN BAΣIΛIKH.
THE PORTRAITURE OF HIS SACRED MAJESTY KING CHARLES I. in his Solitudes and Sufferings. Ant. cloth, 5s.

DEVOTIONAL.

THE SERVICE - BOOK OF THE CHURCH OF ENGLAND, arranged according to the New Table of Lessons. Crown 8vo., roan, 12s.; calf antique or calf limp, 16s.; limp morocco or best morocco, 18s.

ANNUS DOMINI. A Prayer for each Day of the Year, founded on a Text of Holy Scripture. By CHRISTINA G. ROSSETTI. 32mo., cloth, 3s. 6d.

DEVOTIONS BEFORE AND AFTER HOLY COMMUNION. With Prefatory Note by KEBLE. Sixth Edition, in red and black, on toned paper, 32mo., cloth, 2s.
The above, with the Service, 32mo., cloth, 2s. 6d.

INSTRUCTIONS ON THE HOLY EUCHARIST, AND DEVOTIONS FOR HOLY COMMUNION, being Part V. of the Clewer Manuals, by Rev. T. T. CARTER, M.A., Rector of Clewer. 18mo., cloth, 2s.

THE EVERY-DAY COMPANION. By the Rev. W. H. RIDLEY, M.A., Rector of Hambleden, Bucks. Fcap. 8vo., cloth, 3s.

THE LIFE OF JESUS CHRIST IN GLORY: Daily Meditations, from Easter Day to the Wednesday after Trinity Sunday. By NOUET. Translated from the French, and adapted to the Use of the English Church. *Third Thousand.* 12mo., cloth, 6s.

A GUIDE FOR PASSING ADVENT HOLILY. By AVRILLON. Translated from the French, and adapted to the use of the English Church. *New Edition.* Fcap. 8vo., cloth, 5s.

A GUIDE FOR PASSING LENT HOLILY. By AVRILLON. Translated from the French, and adapted to the use of the English Church. Fourth Edition. Fcap. 8vo., cloth, 6s.

MEDITATIONS FOR THE FORTY DAYS OF LENT. With a Prefatory Notice by the ARCHBISHOP OF DUBLIN. 18mo., cloth, 2s. 6d.

OF THE IMITATION OF CHRIST. FOUR BOOKS. By THOMAS A KEMPIS. A New Edition revised. On toned paper, with red border-lines, &c. Small 4to., cloth, 12s. Also, printed in red and black. Fcap., cloth, 4s.

THE INNER LIFE. Hymns on the "Imitation of Christ," by THOMAS A'KEMPIS; designed especially for Use at Holy Communion. By the Author of "Thoughts from a Girl's Life," &c. Fcap. 8vo., cloth, 3s.

DAILY STEPS TOWARDS HEAVEN; or, Practical Thoughts on the Gospel History, for every day in the year. With Titles and Characters of Christ. 32mo., roan, 2s. 6d. Large type edition, Crown 8vo., cloth, 5s.

EVENING WORDS. Brief Meditations on the Introductory Portion of our Lord's Last Discourse with His Disciples. 16mo., cloth, 2s.

THOUGHTS DURING SICKNESS. By ROBERT BRETT, Author of "The Doctrine of the Cross," &c. Fcap. 8vo., limp cloth, 1s. 6d.

THE PASTOR IN HIS CLOSET; or, A Help to the Devotions of the Clergy. By JOHN ARMSTRONG, D.D., late Lord Bishop of Grahamstown. *Third Edition.* Fcap. 8vo., cloth, 2s.

BREVIATES FROM HOLY SCRIPTURE, arranged for use by the Bed of Sickness. By the Rev. G. ARDEN, M.A., Rector of Winterborne-Came; Domestic Chaplain to the Right Hon. the Earl of Devon. *2nd Ed.* Fcap. 8vo., 2s.

SHORT READINGS FOR SUNDAY. By the Author of "Footprints in the Wilderness." With Twelve Illustrations on Wood. Third Thousand, Square Crown 8vo., cloth, 3s. 6d.

DEVOTIONS FOR A TIME OF RETIREMENT AND PRAYER FOR THE CLERGY. New Edition, revised. Fcap. 8vo., cloth, 1s.

EARL NELSON'S FAMILY PRAYERS. With Responsions and Variations for the different Seasons, for General Use. New and improved Edition, *large type*, cloth, 2s.

SERMONS, &c.

PAROCHIAL SERMONS. By E. B. PUSEY, D.D. Vol. I. From Advent to Whitsuntide. *Seventh Edition.* 8vo., cloth, 6s. Vol. II., 8vo., cl., 6s. ─── Vol. III. Reprinted from "Plain Sermons by Contributors to Tracts for the Times." Revised Edition. 8vo., cloth, 6s.

PAROCHIAL SERMONS preached and printed on Various Occasions, 1832—1850. By E. B. PUSEY, D.D. 8vo., cloth, 6s.

SERMONS preached before the **UNIVERSITY OF OXFORD** between A.D. 1859 and 1872. By E. B. PUSEY, D.D. 8vo., cloth, 6s.

LENTEN SERMONS preached chiefly to Young Men at the Universities, between A.D. 1868 and 1874. By E. B. PUSEY, D.D. 8vo., cloth, 6s.

ILLUSTRATIONS OF FAITH. Eight Plain Sermons, by the late Rev. EDWARD MONRO. Fcap. 8vo., cloth, 2s. 6d.

Uniform, and by the same Author,

PLAIN SERMONS ON THE BOOK OF COMMON PRAYER. Fcap. 8vo., cloth, 5s.

SERMONS ON NEW TESTAMENT CHARACTERS. Fcap. 8vo., 4s.

HISTORICAL AND PRACTICAL SERMONS ON THE SUFFERINGS AND RESURRECTION OF OUR LORD. 2 vols., Fcap. 8vo., cloth, 10s.

CHRISTIAN SEASONS.—Short and Plain Sermons for every Sunday and Holyday throughout the Year. Edited by the late Bishop of Grahamstown. 4 vols., Fcap. 8vo., cloth, 10s. Second Series, 4 vols., Fcap. 8vo., cloth, 10s.

SHORT SERMONS FOR FAMILY READING, following the Order of the Christian Seasons. By the Rev. J. W. BURGON, B.D., Dean of Chichester. 2 vols., Fcap. 8vo., cl., 8s. 2nd Series, 2 vols., Fcap. 8vo., cl., 8s.

PAROCHIAL SERMONS. By the late JOHN ARMSTRONG, D.D., Lord Bishop of Grahamstown. Fcap. 8vo., cl., 5s.

SERMONS FOR FASTS AND FESTIVALS. By the late JOHN ARMSTRONG, D.D. A new Edition. Fcap. 8vo., 5s.

SERMONS FOR THE CHRISTIAN YEAR. By the Rev. JOHN KEBLE, Author of "The Christian Year."

ADVENT TO CHRISTMAS. 8vo., cl., 6s.

ASH-WEDNESDAY TO HOLY WEEK. 8vo., cloth, 6s.

CHRISTMAS AND EPIPHANY. 8vo., cloth, 6s.

HOLY WEEK. 8vo., cloth, 6s.

EASTER TO ASCENSION DAY. 8vo., cloth, 6s.

ASCENSION DAY TO TRINITY SUNDAY inclusive. 8vo., cloth, 6s.

SERMONS FOR SAINTS' DAYS. 8vo., cloth, 6s.

There remain, to follow at intervals,

SEPTUAGESIMA TO LENT. | SERMONS FOR THE TRINITY SEASON.

VILLAGE SERMONS ON THE BAPTISMAL SERVICE. By the Rev. JOHN KEBLE, M.A., Author of "The Christian Year." 8vo., cloth, 5s.

THE AWAKING SOUL, as Sketched in the 130th Psalm. Addresses delivered at St. Peter's, Eaton-square, on the Tuesdays in Lent, 1877. By E. R. WILBERFORCE, M.A., Vicar of Seaforth, Liverpool, and Sub-Almoner to the Queen. Crown 8vo., limp cloth, 2s. 6d.

XX. SHORT ALLEGORICAL SERMONS. By the Rev. BEAUCHAMP K. W. PEARSE, M.A., Rector of Ascot, Staines, and Rev. WALTER AUGUSTUS GRAY, M.A., Vicar of Arksey, Yorkshire. *Fourth Edition*, Fcap., cloth, 2s. 6d. *Fifth Edition*, Fcap. 8vo., sewed, 1s.

SERMONS AND ESSAYS ON THE APOSTOLICAL AGE. By the Very Rev. ARTHUR PENRHYN STANLEY, D.D., Dean of Westminster, and Corresponding Member of the Institute of France. *Third Edition, revised.* Crown 8vo., cloth, 7s. 6d.

WORDS AT COMMUNION-TIME. Short Sermons preached at Celebrations of Holy Communion. By WALTER FRANCIS ELGIE, M.A., Curate in Charge of Otterbourne, Hants. Fcap. 8vo., cloth, 3s. 6d.

OXFORD LENT SERMONS, 1857, 8, 9, 65, 6, 7, 8, 9, 70. 8vo., cloth, 5s. each.

Works of the Standard English Divines,

PUBLISHED IN THE LIBRARY OF ANGLO-CATHOLIC THEOLOGY,

AT THE FOLLOWING PRICES IN CLOTH.

ANDREWES' (BP.) COMPLETE WORKS. 11 vols., 8vo., £3 7s.
    THE SERMONS. (Separate.) 5 vols., £1 15s.

BEVERIDGE'S (BP.) COMPLETE WORKS. 12 vols., 8vo., £4 4s.
    THE ENGLISH THEOLOGICAL WORKS. 10 vols., £3 10s.

BRAMHALL'S (ABP.) WORKS, WITH LIFE AND LETTERS, &c.
5 vols., 8vo., £1 15s. (Vol. 2 cannot be sold separately.)

BULL'S (BP.) HARMONY ON JUSTIFICATION. 2 vols., 8vo., 10s.
——————— DEFENCE OF THE NICENE CREED. 2 vols., 10s.
——————— JUDGMENT OF THE CATHOLIC CHURCH. 5s.

COSIN'S (BP.) WORKS COMPLETE. 5 vols., 8vo., £1 10s.

CRAKANTHORP'S DEFENSIO ECCLESIÆ ANGLICANÆ.
8vo., 7s.

FRANK'S SERMONS. 2 vols., 8vo., 10s.

FORBES' CONSIDERATIONES MODESTÆ. 2 vols., 8vo., 12s.

GUNNING'S PASCHAL, OR LENT FAST. 8vo, 6s.

HAMMOND'S PRACTICAL CATECHISM. 8vo., 5s.
——————— MISCELLANEOUS THEOLOGICAL WORKS. 5s.
——————— THIRTY-ONE SERMONS. 2 Parts. 10s.

HICKES'S TWO TREATISES ON THE CHRISTIAN PRIESTHOOD. 3 vols., 8vo., 15s.

JOHNSON'S (JOHN) THEOLOGICAL WORKS. 2 vols., 8vo., 10s.
——————— ENGLISH CANONS. 2 vols., 12s.

LAUD'S (ABP.) COMPLETE WORKS. 7 vols., (9 Parts,) 8vo., £2 17s.

L'ESTRANGE'S ALLIANCE OF DIVINE OFFICES. 8vo., 6s.

MARSHALL'S PENITENTIAL DISCIPLINE. (This volume cannot be sold separate from the complete set.)

NICHOLSON'S (BP.) EXPOSITION OF THE CATECHISM. (This volume cannot be sold separate from the complete set.)

OVERALL'S (BP.) CONVOCATION-BOOK OF 1606. 8vo., 5s.

PEARSON'S (BP.) VINDICIÆ EPISTOLARUM S. IGNATII.
2 vols. 8vo., 10s.

THORNDIKE'S (HERBERT) THEOLOGICAL WORKS COMPLETE. 6 vols., (10 Parts,) 8vo., £2 10s.

WILSON'S (BP.) WORKS COMPLETE. With LIFE, by Rev.
J. KEBLE. 7 vols., (8 Parts,) 8vo., £3 3s.

A complete set, £21.

THE AUTHORIZED EDITIONS OF
THE CHRISTIAN YEAR,

With the Author's latest Corrections and Additions.

NOTICE.—Messrs. PARKER are the sole Publishers of the Editions of the "Christian Year" issued with the sanction and under the direction of the Author's representatives. All Editions without their imprint are unauthorized.

SMALL 4to. EDITION.	**32mo. EDITION.**	
Handsomely printed on toned paper, with red border lines and initial letters. Cloth extra 10 6	Cloth boards, gilt edges . 1 6	
	Cloth, limp 1 0	
DEMY 8vo. EDITION.	**48mo. EDITION.**	
Cloth 6 0	Cloth, limp 0 6	
	Roan 1 6	
FOOLSCAP 8vo. EDITION.	**FACSIMILE OF THE 1ST EDITION**, with a list of the variations from the Original Text which the Author made in later Editions. 2 vols., 12mo., boards . 7 6	
Cloth 3 6		
24mo. EDITION.		
Cloth, red lines . . . 2 6		

The above Editions (except the Facsimile of the First Edition) are kept in a variety of bindings, which may be ordered through the Trade, or direct from the Publishers. The chief bindings are Morocco plain, Morocco Antique, Calf Antique, and Vellum, the prices varying according to the style.

By the same Author.

LYRA INNOCENTIUM. Thoughts in Verse on Christian Children. *Thirteenth Edition.* Fcap. 8vo., cloth, 5s.

———— 48mo. edition, limp cloth, 6d.; cloth boards, 1s.

MISCELLANEOUS POEMS BY THE REV. JOHN KEBLE, M.A., Vicar of Hursley. [With Preface by G. M.] *Third Edition.* Fcap., cloth, 6s.

THE PSALTER, OR PSALMS OF DAVID: In English Verse. *Fourth Edition.* Fcap., cloth, 6s.

———— 18mo., cloth, 1s.

The above may also be had in various bindings.

A CONCORDANCE TO THE "CHRISTIAN YEAR." Fcap. 8vo., toned paper, cloth, 4s.

MUSINGS ON THE "CHRISTIAN YEAR;" WITH GLEANINGS FROM THIRTY YEARS' INTERCOURSE WITH THE LATE Rev. J. KEBLE, by CHARLOTTE M. YONGE; to which are added Recollections of Hursley, by FRANCES M. WILBRAHAM. *Second Edition.* Fcap. 8vo., cloth, 7s. 6d.

MEMOIR OF THE REV. J. KEBLE, M.A. By Sir J. T. COLERIDGE. *Fourth and Cheaper Edition.* Post 8vo., cloth, 6s.

Church Poetry.

RE-ISSUE OF THE POETICAL WORKS OF THE LATE REV. ISAAC WILLIAMS.

THE CATHEDRAL; or, The Catholic and Apostolic Church in England. Fcap. 8vo., cloth, 5s.; 32mo., cloth, 2s. 6d.

THE BAPTISTERY; or, The Way of Eternal Life. With Plates by BOETIUS A BOLSWERT. Fcap. 8vo., cloth, 7s. 6d.; 32mo., cloth, 2s. 6d.

HYMNS FROM THE PARISIAN BREVIARY. 32mo., cloth, 2s. 6d.

THE CHRISTIAN SCHOLAR. Fcap. 8vo., cl., 5s.; 32mo., cl., 2s. 6d.

THOUGHTS IN PAST YEARS. 32mo., cloth, 2s. 6d.

THE SEVEN DAYS OF THE OLD AND NEW CREATION. Fcap. 8vo., cloth, 3s. 6d.

THE CHILD'S CHRISTIAN YEAR.

THE CHILD'S CHRISTIAN YEAR. Hymns for every Sunday and Holyday throughout the Year. *Cheap Edition*, 18mo., cloth, 1s.

BISHOP CLEVELAND COXE.

CHRISTIAN BALLADS AND POEMS. By ARTHUR CLEVELAND COXE, D.D., Bishop of Western New York. A New Edition. Fcap. 8vo. cloth, 3s. Also selected Poems in a packet, 32mo., 1s.

DR. FREDERICK G. LEE.

THE BELLS OF BOTTEVILLE TOWER; A Christmas Story in Verse: and other Poems. By FREDERICK G. LEE, Author of "The Martyrs of Vienne and Lyons," "Petronilla," &c. Fcap. 8vo., with Illustrations, cloth, 4s. 6d.

Parochial.

THE CONFIRMATION CLASS-BOOK: Notes for Lessons, with APPENDIX, containing Questions and Summaries for the Use of the Candidates. By E. M. HOLMES, LL.B., Rector of Marsh Gibbon, Bucks; Diocesan Inspector of Schools; Author of the "Catechist's Manual." Fcap. 8vo., limp cloth, 2s. 6d.

Also, in wrapper, THE QUESTIONS AND SUMMARIES separate, 4 sets of 128 pp. in packet, 1s. each.

THE CATECHIST'S MANUAL; with an Introduction by the late SAMUEL WILBERFORCE, D.D., Lord Bishop of Winchester. *Fifth Thousand.* Crown 8vo., limp cloth, 5s.

A MANUAL OF PASTORAL VISITATION, intended for the Use of the Clergy in their Visitation of the Sick and Afflicted. By a PARISH PRIEST. Dedicated, by permission, to His Grace the Archbishop of Dublin. Second Edition, Crown 8vo., limp cloth, 3s. 6d.; roan, 4s.

A SERIES OF WALL PICTURES illustrating the New Testament. The Set of 16 Pictures, size 22 inches by 19 inches, 12s.

COTTAGE PICTURES FROM THE OLD TESTAMENT. A Series of Twenty-eight large folio Engravings, brilliantly coloured by hand. The Set, 7s. 6d.

COTTAGE PICTURES FROM THE NEW TESTAMENT. A Series of Twenty-eight large folio Engravings, brilliantly coloured. The Set, 7s. 6d.

Upwards of 8,000 Sets of these Cottage Pictures have been sold.

TWELVE SACRED PRINTS FOR PAROCHIAL USE. Printed in Sepia, with Ornamental Borders. *The Set*, One Shilling; or *each*, One Penny.

Upwards of 100,000 of these Prints have already been sold.

MISCELLANEOUS.

THE ELEMENTS OF PSYCHOLOGY.

THE ELEMENTS OF PSYCHOLOGY, ON THE PRINCIPLES OF BENEKE, Stated and Illustrated in a Simple and Popular Manner by Dr. G. Raue, Professor in the Medical College, Philadelphia; Fourth Edition, considerably Altered, Improved, and Enlarged, by Johann Gottlieb Dressler, late Director of the Normal School at Bautzen. Translated from the German. Post 8vo., cloth, 6s.

REV. CANON GREGORY.

ARE WE BETTER THAN OUR FATHERS? or, A Comparative View of the Social Position of England at the Revolution of 1688, and at the Present Time. FOUR LECTURES delivered in St. Paul's Cathedral. By Robert Gregory, M.A., Canon of St. Paul's. Crown 8vo., 2s. 6d.

REV. CANON JENKINS.

THE AGE OF THE MARTYRS; or, the First Three Centuries of the Work of the Church of our Lord and Saviour Jesus Christ. By the late Rev. J. D. Jenkins, B.D., Canon of Pieter Maritzburg; Fellow of Jesus College, Oxford. Crown 8vo., cloth, 3s. 6d.

PROFESSOR GOLDWIN SMITH.

THE REORGANIZATION OF THE UNIVERSITY OF OXFORD. By Goldwin Smith. Post 8vo., limp cloth, 2s.

LECTURES ON THE STUDY OF HISTORY. Delivered in Oxford, 1859—61. *Second Edition.* Crown 8vo., limp cloth, 3s. 6d.

IRISH HISTORY AND IRISH CHARACTER. Cheap Edition, Fcap. 8vo., sewed, 1s. 6d.

THE EMPIRE. A Series of Letters published in "The Daily News," 1862, 1863. Post 8vo., cloth, price 6s.

MRS. ALGERNON KINGSFORD.

ROSAMUNDA THE PRINCESS: An Historical Romance of the Sixth Century; the Crocus, Water-reed, Rose and Marigold, Painter of Venice, Noble Love, Romance of a Ring, and other Tales. By Mrs. Algernon Kingsford. 8vo., cloth, with Twenty-four Illustrations, 6s.

THE EXILE FROM PARADISE.

THE EXILE FROM PARADISE, translated by the Author of the "Life of S. Teresa." Fcap., cloth, 1s. 6d.

H. A. MUNRO-BUTLER-JOHNSTONE, M.P.

THE FAIR OF NIJNI-NOVGOROD. With a Map and Twelve Illustrations. By H. A. Munro-Butler-Johnstone, M.P. Second Edition, Fcap. 8vo., cloth, 5s.

THE TURKS: their Character, Manners, and Institutions, as bearing on the Eastern Question. By H. A. Munro-Butler-Johnstone, M.P. 8vo., sewed, 1s.

VILHELM THOMSEN.

THE RELATIONS BETWEEN ANCIENT RUSSIA AND SCANDINAVIA, and the Origin of the Russian State. THREE LECTURES delivered at the Taylor Institution, Oxford, in May, 1876, by Dr. Vilhelm Thomsen, Professor at the University of Copenhagen. Small 8vo., cloth.
[*Just ready.*

C. A. VANSITTART CONYBEARE, B.A.

THE PLACE OF ICELAND IN THE HISTORY OF EUROPEAN INSTITUTIONS; being the Lothian Prize Essay, 1877. By C. A. Vansittart Conybeare, B.A., late Junior Student of Christ Church, Oxford, and Assistant Master of Manchester Grammar School. Crown 8vo., cloth, 4s. 6d.

THE PRAYER-BOOK CALENDAR.

THE CALENDAR OF THE PRAYER-BOOK ILLUSTRATED.
(Comprising the first portion of the "Calendar of the Anglican Church," with additional Illustrations, an Appendix on Emblems, &c.) With Two Hundred Engravings from Medieval Works of Art. *Sixth Thousand.* Fcap. 8vo., cl., 6s.

SIR G. G. SCOTT, F.S.A.

GLEANINGS FROM WESTMINSTER ABBEY. By SIR GEORGE GILBERT SCOTT, R.A., F.S.A. With Appendices supplying Further Particulars, and completing the History of the Abbey Buildings, by Several Writers. *Second Edition*, enlarged, containing many new Illustrations by O. Jewitt and others. Medium 8vo., 10s. 6d.

THE LATE CHARLES WINSTON.

AN INQUIRY INTO THE DIFFERENCE OF STYLE OBSERVABLE IN ANCIENT GLASS PAINTINGS, especially in England, with Hints on Glass Painting, by the late CHARLES WINSTON. With Corrections and Additions by the Author. 2 vols., Medium 8vo., cloth, £1 11s. 6d.

REV. SAMUEL LYSONS, F.S.A.

OUR BRITISH ANCESTORS: WHO AND WHAT WERE THEY? An Inquiry serving to elucidate the Traditional History of the Early Britons by means of recent Excavations, Etymology, Remnants of Religious Worship, Inscriptions, Craniology, and Fragmentary Collateral History. By the Rev. SAMUEL LYSONS, M.A., F.S.A., Rector of Rodmarton, and Perpetual Curate of St. Luke's, Gloucester. Post 8vo., cloth, 5s.

M. VIOLLET-LE-DUC.

ON MILITARY ARCHITECTURE; Translated from the French of M. VIOLLET-LE-DUC. By M. MACDERMOTT, Esq., Architect. With the 151 original French Engravings. Medium 8vo., cloth, 10s 6d.

JOHN HEWITT.

ANCIENT ARMOUR AND WEAPONS IN EUROPE. By JOHN HEWITT, Member of the Archæological Institute of Great Britain. Vols. II. and III., comprising the Period from the Fourteenth to the Seventeenth Century, completing the work, £1 12s. Also Vol. I., from the Iron Period of the Northern Nations to the end of the Thirteenth Century, 18s. The work complete, 3 vols., 8vo., £2 10s.

REV. PROFESSOR STUBBS.

THE TRACT "DE INVENTIONE SANCTÆ CRUCIS NOSTRÆ IN MONTE ACUTO ET DE DUCTIONE EJUSDEM APUD WALTHAM," now first printed from the Manuscript in the British Museum, with Introduction and Notes by WILLIAM STUBBS, M.A. Royal 8vo., 5s.; Demy 8vo., 3s. 6d.

NORTHERN ANTIQUITIES.

THE PRIMEVAL ANTIQUITIES of ENGLAND and DENMARK COMPARED. By J. J. A. WORSAAE. Translated and applied to the illustration of similar remains in England, by W. J. THOMS, F.S.A., &c. With numerous Illustrations. 8vo., cloth, 5s.

OUR ENGLISH HOME:
Its Early History and Progress. With Notes on the Introduction of Domestic Inventions. New Edition, Crown 8vo., cloth, 3s. 6d.

ARCHITECTURE AND ARCHÆOLOGY.

JOHN HENRY PARKER, C.B., F.S.A., HON. M.A. OXON.

AN INTRODUCTION TO THE STUDY OF GOTHIC ARCHITECTURE. *Fourth Edition,* Revised and Enlarged, with 189 Illustrations, with a Topographical and Glossarial Index. Fcap. 8vo., cloth, 5s.

A CONCISE GLOSSARY OF TERMS USED IN GRECIAN, ROMAN, ITALIAN, AND GOTHIC ARCHITECTURE. A New Edition, revised. Fcap. 8vo., with 470 Illustrations, in ornamental cloth, 7s. 6d.

AN ATTEMPT TO DISCRIMINATE THE STYLES OF ARCHITECTURE IN ENGLAND, from the Conquest to the Reformation; with a Sketch of the Grecian and Roman Orders. By the late THOMAS RICKMAN, F.S.A. *Seventh Edition,* with considerable Additions, chiefly Historical, by JOHN HENRY PARKER, C.B., F.S.A., &c. 8vo. [*Nearly ready.*

DOMESTIC ARCHITECTURE OF THE MIDDLE AGES, with numerous Engravings from Existing Remains, and Historical Illustrations from Contemporary Manuscripts. By the late T. HUDSON TURNER, Esq. From the Norman Conquest to the Thirteenth Century; interspersed with Remarks on Domestic Manners during the same Period. 8vo., cloth, £1 1s. *A Reprint.*

———————— FROM EDWARD I. TO RICHARD II. (the Edwardian Period, or the Decorated Style). By the Editor of "The Glossary of Architecture." 8vo., cloth, £1 1s.

Also,

———————— FROM RICHARD II. TO HENRY VIII. (or the Perpendicular Style). With numerous Illustrations of Existing Remains, from Original Drawings. In Two Vols., 8vo., £1 10s.

THE ARCHÆOLOGY OF ROME. By JOHN HENRY PARKER, C.B.

Part 7. **THE COLOSSEUM AT ROME** Compared with other Amphitheatres; with Thirty-six Plates. Medium 8vo., cloth, 10s. 6d.

Part 8. **THE AQUEDUCTS OF ROME,** Traced from their Sources to their Mouths, with Thirty-six Plates, Maps, and Plans. Medium 8vo., cloth, 15s.

Part 9. **THE TOMBS IN AND NEAR ROME,** with the Columbaria and the Painted Tombs on the Via Latina, with Twenty-four Plates in Photo-engraving.

Part 10. **MYTHOLOGY IN FUNEREAL SCULPTURE, AND EARLY CHRISTIAN SCULPTURE,** with Sixteen Plates. *These Two Parts in one Volume.* Medium 8vo., cloth, 15s.

Part 11. **CHURCH AND ALTAR DECORATIONS IN ROME,** including Mosaic Pictures and Cosmati Work. With 20 Plates and numerous Diagrams. Medium 8vo., cloth, 10s. 6d.

Part 12. **THE CATACOMBS,** or Ancient Cemeteries of Rome, with Twenty-four Plates and Plans. Medium 8vo., cloth, 15s.

SEPULCHRAL CROSSES.

A MANUAL for the STUDY of SEPULCHRAL SLABS and CROSSES of the MIDDLE AGES. By the Rev. EDWARD L. CUTTS, B.A. Illustrated by upwards of 300 Engravings. 8vo., cloth, 6s.

MEDIÆVAL BRASSES.

A MANUAL OF MONUMENTAL BRASSES. Comprising an Introduction to the Study of these Memorials, and a List of those remaining in the British Isles. With Two Hundred Illustrations. By the late Rev. HERBERT HAINES, M.A., of Exeter College, Oxford. 2 vols., 8vo., cloth, 12s.

ENGLISH COUNTRY HOUSES.

SIXTY-ONE VIEWS AND PLANS of recently erected Mansions, Private Residences, Parsonage-Houses, Farm-Houses, Lodges, and Cottages; with Sketches of Furniture and Fittings; and A Practical Treatise on House-Building. By WILLIAM WILKINSON, Architect, Oxford. Second Edition, Royal 8vo., ornamental cloth, £1 5s.

NEW AND STANDARD EDUCATIONAL WORKS. 13

THE ANNALS OF ENGLAND. An Epitome of English History. From Cotemporary Writers, the Rolls of Parliament, and other Public Records. A LIBRARY EDITION, revised and enlarged, with additional Woodcuts: with a Recommendatory Note by the Regius Professor of Modern History, Oxford. 8vo., half-bound, 12s.

A CONTINUATION of the above, from the Accession of George I. to the Present Time. [*In preparation.*

THE SCHOOL EDITION OF THE ANNALS OF ENGLAND. In Five Half-crown Parts. 1. Britons, Romans, Saxons, Normans. 2. The Plantagenets. 3. The Tudors. 4. The Stuarts. 5. The Restoration, to the Death of Queen Anne. Fcap. 8vo., cloth.

THE NEW SCHOOL - HISTORY OF ENGLAND, from Early Writers and the National Records. By the Author of "The Annals of England." *Sixth Thousand.* Crown 8vo., with Four Maps, limp cloth, 5s.; Coloured Maps, half roan, 6s.

A HISTORY OF THE ENGLISH CHURCH from its Foundation to the Reign of Queen Mary. By MARY CHARLOTTE STAPLEY. Third Edition, Revised, with a Recommendatory Notice by Dean Hook. Crown 8vo., cloth boards, 5s.

POETARUM SCENICORUM GRÆCORUM, Æschyli, Sophoclis, Euripidis, et Aristophanis, Fabulæ, Superstites, et Perditarum Fragmenta. Ex recognitione GUIL. DINDORFII. Editio Quinta. Royal 8vo., cloth, £1 1s.

THUCYDIDES, with Notes, chiefly Historical and Geographical. By the late T. ARNOLD, D.D. With Indices by the Rev. R. P. G. TIDDEMAN. *Eighth Edition.* 3 vols., 8vo., cloth lettered, £1 16s.

JELF'S GREEK GRAMMAR.—A Grammar of the Greek Language, chiefly from the text of Raphael Kühner. By WM. EDW. JELF, B.D., late Student and Censor of Ch. Ch. *Fourth Edition, with Additions and Corrections.* 2 vols. 8vo., £1 10s.

LAWS OF THE GREEK ACCENTS. By JOHN GRIFFITHS, D.D., Warden of Wadham College, Oxford. *Sixteenth Edition.* 16mo., price 6d.

RUDIMENTARY RULES, with Examples, for the Use of Beginners in Greek Prose Composition. By JOHN MITCHINSON, D.C.L., late Head Master of the King's School, Canterbury, (now Bishop of Barbadoes). 16mo., sewed, 1s.

TWELVE RUDIMENTARY RULES FOR LATIN PROSE COMPOSITION: with Examples and Exercises, for the use of Beginners. By the Rev. E. MOORE, D.D., Principal of St. Edmund Hall, Oxford. *Second Edit.* 16mo., 6d.

MADVIG'S LATIN GRAMMAR. A Latin Grammar for the Use of Schools. By Professor MADVIG, with additions by the Author. Translated by the Rev. G. WOODS, M.A. *New Edition, with an Index of Authors.* 8vo., cloth, 12s.

ERASMI COLLOQUIA SELECTA: Arranged for Translation and Re-translation; adapted for the Use of Boys who have begun the Latin Syntax. By EDWARD C. LOWE, D.D., Head Master of S. John's Middle School, Hurstpierpoint. Fcap. 8vo., strong binding, 3s.

PORTA LATINA: A Selection from Latin Authors, for Translation and Re-Translation; arranged in a Progressive Course, as an Introduction to the Latin Tongue. By EDWARD C. LOWE, D.D., Head Master of Hurstpierpoint School; Editor of Erasmus' "Colloquies," &c. Fcap. 8vo., strongly bound, 3s.

A GRAMMATICAL ANALYSIS OF THE HEBREW PSALTER; being an Explanatory Interpretation of Every Word contained in the Book of Psalms, intended chiefly for the Use of Beginners in the Study of Hebrew. By JOANA JULIA GRESWELL. Post 8vo., cloth, 6s.

SUNDAY - SCHOOL EXERCISES, Collected and Revised from Manuscripts of Burghclere School-children, under the teaching of the Rev. W. B. BARTER, late Rector of Highclere and Burghclere; Edited by his Son-in-law, the BISHOP OF ST. ANDREW'S. *Second Edition.* Crown 8vo., cloth, 5s.

A FIRST LOGIC BOOK, by D. P. CHASE, M.A., Principal of St. Mary Hall, Oxford. Small 4to., sewed, 3s.

A SERIES OF GREEK AND LATIN CLASSICS
FOR THE USE OF SCHOOLS.

GREEK POETS.

	Cloth. s. d.		Cloth. s. d.
Æschylus	3 0	Sophocles	3 0
Aristophanes. 2 vols.	6 0	Homeri Ilias	3 6
Euripides. 3 vols.	6 6	——— Odyssea	3 0
——— Tragœdiæ Sex	3 6		

GREEK PROSE WRITERS.

Aristotelis Ethica	2 0	Thucydides. 2 vols.	5 0
Demosthenes de Corona, et Æschines in Ctesiphontem	2 0	Xenophontis Memorabilia	1 4
		——— Anabasis	2 0
Herodotus. 2 vols.	6 0		

LATIN POETS.

Horatius	2 0	Lucretius	2 0
Juvenalis et Persius	1 6	Phædrus	1 4
Lucanus	2 6	Virgilius	2 6

LATIN PROSE WRITERS.

Cæsaris Commentarii, cum Supplementis Auli Hirtii et aliorum 2	6	Ciceronis Tusc. Disp. Lib. V.	2 0
		Ciceronis Orationes Selectæ	3 6
——— Commentarii de Bello Gallico	1 6	Cornelius Nepos	1 4
		Livius. 4 vols.	6 0
Cicero De Officiis, de Senectute, et de Amicitia	2 0	Sallustius	2 0
		Tacitus. 2 vols.	5 0

TEXTS WITH SHORT NOTES.
UNIFORM WITH THE SERIES OF "OXFORD POCKET CLASSICS."

GREEK WRITERS. TEXTS AND NOTES.

SOPHOCLES.

	s. d.		s. d.
AJAX (*Text and Notes*)	1 0	ANTIGONE (*Text and Notes*)	1 0
ELECTRA ,,	1 0	PHILOCTETES ,,	1 0
ŒDIPUS REX ,,	1 0	TRACHINIÆ ,,	1 0
ŒDIPUS COLONEUS ,,	1 0		

The Notes only, in one vol., cloth, 3s.

ÆSCHYLUS.

PERSÆ (*Text and Notes*)	1 0	CHOEPHORÆ (*Text and Notes*)	1 0
PROMETHEUS VINCTUS ,,	1 0	EUMENIDES ,,	1 0
SEPTEM CONTRA THEBAS ,,	1 0	SUPPLICES ,,	1 0
AGAMEMNON ,,	1 0		

The Notes only, in one vol., cloth, 3s. 6d.

ARISTOPHANES.

THE KNIGHTS (*Text and Notes*)	1 0	ACHARNIANS (*Text and Notes*)	1 0
THE BIRDS (*Text and Notes*)	1 0		

EURIPIDES.

	s. d.		s. d.
Hecuba (*Text and Notes*)	1 0	Phœnissæ (*Text and Notes*)	1 0
Medea „	1 0	Alcestis „	1 0
Orestes „	1 0	The above, Notes only, in one vol., cloth, 3s.	
Hippolytus „	1 0	Bacchæ „	1 0

DEMOSTHENES.

De Corona (*Text and Notes*) . 2 0 | Olynthiac Orations . . 1 0

HOMERUS.
XENOPHON.

Ilias, Lib. i.—vi. (*Text and Notes*) . . . . 2 0 | Memorabilia (*Text and Notes*) 2 6

ÆSCHINES.
ARISTOTLE.

In Ctesiphontem (*Text and Notes*) . . . . 2 0 | De Arte Poetica (*Text and Notes*) . cloth, 2s.; sewed 1 6
| De Re Publica „ 3s. „ 2 6

LATIN WRITERS. TEXTS AND NOTES.

VIRGILIUS.

Bucolica (*Text and Notes*)	1 0	Æneidos, Lib. i.—iii. (*Text and Notes*)	1 0
Georgica „	2 0		

HORATIUS.

Carmina, &c. (*Text and Notes*)	2 0	Epistolæ et Ars Poetica (*Text and Notes*)	1 0
Satiræ „	1 0		

The Notes only, in one vol., cloth, 2s.

SALLUSTIUS.

Jugurtha (*Text and Notes*) . 1 6 | Catilina (*Text and Notes*) . 1 0

M. T. CICERO.

In Q. Cæcilium—Divinatio (*Text and Notes*) . . 1 0	In Catilinam . . . 1 0
In Verrem Actio Prima . 1 0	Pro Plancio (*Text and Notes*) . 1 6
Pro Lege Manilia, et Pro Archia 1 0	Pro Milone 1 0
	Pro Roscio 1 0
	Orationes Philippicæ, I., II. 1 6

The above, Notes only, in one vol., cloth, 3s. 6d.

De Senectute et De Amicitia 1 0	Epistolæ Selectæ. Pars I. 1 6

CÆSAR.
CORNELIUS NEPOS.

De Bello Gallico, Lib. i.—iii. (*Text and Notes*) . . 1 0 | Lives (*Text and Notes*) . . 1 6

LIVIUS.
PHÆDRUS.

Fabulæ (*Text and Notes*) . . 1 0

Lib. xxi.—xxiv. (*Text and Notes*) sewed 4 0	
Ditto in cloth . . . 4 6	

TACITUS.

The Annals. Notes only, 2 vols., 16mo., cloth . . . 7 0

Portions of several other Authors are in preparation.

Uniform with the Oxford Pocket Classics.

THE LIVES OF THE MOST EMINENT ENGLISH POETS; WITH CRITICAL OBSERVATIONS ON THEIR WORKS. By Samuel Johnson. 3 vols., 24mo., cloth, 2s. 6d. each.

THE LIVES OF ADDISON, DRYDEN, AND POPE, with Critical Observations on their Works. By Samuel Johnson. With Analyses of the Lives. 24mo., cloth, 2s.

CHOICE EXTRACTS FROM MODERN FRENCH AUTHORS, for the use of Schools. 18mo., cloth, 3s.

BOOKS, &c., RELATING TO OXFORD.

A HANDBOOK FOR VISITORS TO OXFORD. Illustrated with Woodcuts by Jewitt, and Steel Plates by Le Keux. *A New Edition.* 8vo., cloth, 12s.

THE OXFORD UNIVERSITY CALENDAR for 1877. Corrected to the end of December, 1876. 12mo., cloth, 4s. 6d.

THE OXFORD TEN-YEAR BOOK: A Complete Register of University Honours and Distinctions, made up to the end of the Year 1870. Crown 8vo., roan, 7s. 6d.

PASS AND CLASS: An Oxford Guide-Book through the Courses of *Literæ Humaniores,* Mathematics, Natural Science, &c. By MONTAGU BURROWS, Chichele Professor of Modern History. *Third Edition.* Revised and Enlarged; with Appendices on the Indian Civil Service, the Diplomatic Service, and the Local Examinations. Fcap. 8vo., cloth, price 2s.

UNIVERSITY OF OXFORD LOCAL EXAMINATIONS. Examination Papers and Division Lists for the years 1860 and 1861. 8vo., *each* 3s. 6d.

————— Examination Papers for the years 1870, 1871, 1872, 1873, 1874, 1875, 1876, *each* 2s.

————— Division Lists for the years 1867, 1868, *each* 1s. 6d.

————————— for the years 1869, 1870, 1871, 1872, 1873, 1874, 1875, 1876, *each* 2s.

NEW VOLUME OF HISTORICAL TALES.

Fcap. 8vo., with Four Illustrations, cloth, 5s.

ENGLAND—THE MEDIÆVAL PERIOD. FOUR TALES by the Rev. H. C. ADAMS, Vicar of Dry Sandford; Author of "Wilton of Cuthbert's," "Schoolboy Honour," &c.

Contents—The Orphan of Evesham, or The Jews and the Mendicant Orders; Mark's Wedding, or Lollardy; The White Rose of Lynden, or The Monks and the Bible; The Prior's Ward, or The Broken Unity of the Church.

CHEAPER ISSUE OF TALES FOR YOUNG MEN AND WOMEN.

In Six Half-crown Vols., cloth.

Vol. I. contains F. E. PAGET's Mother and Son, Wanted a Wife, and Hobson's Choice.

Vol. II. F. E. PAGET's Windycote Hall, Squitch, Tenants at Tinkers' End.

Vol. III. W. E. HEYGATE's Two Cottages, The Sisters, and Old Jarvis's Will.

Vol. IV. W. E. HEYGATE's James Bright the Shopman, The Politician, Irrevocable.

Vol. V. R. KING's The Strike, and Jonas Clint; N. BROWN's Two to One, and False Honour.

Vol. VI. J. M. NEALE's Railway Accident; E. MONRO's The Recruit, Susan, Servants' Influence, Mary Thomas, or Dissent at Evenly; H. HAYMAN's Caroline Elton, or Vanity and Jealousy.

Each Volume is bound as a distinct and complete work, and sold separately for PRESENTS.

www.ingramcontent.com/pod-product-compliance
Lightning Source LLC
Chambersburg PA
CBHW020335240426
43673CB00039B/941